ASSESSING PERFORMANCE

ASSESSING PERFORMANCE

Designing, Scoring, and Validating Performance Tasks

Robert L. Johnson
James A. Penny   **Belita Gordon**

THE GUILFORD PRESS
New York   London

© 2009 The Guilford Press
A Division of Guilford Publications, Inc.
72 Spring Street, New York, NY 10012
www.guilford.com

Printed in the United States of America

This book is printed on acid-free paper.

Last digit is print number: 9   8   7   6   5   4   3   2   1

Library of Congress Cataloging-in-Publication Data

Johnson, Robert L.
   Assessing performance : designing, scoring, and validating performance tasks / by Robert L. Johnson, James A. Penny, Belita Gordon.
      p. cm.
   Includes bibliographical references and index.
   ISBN 978-1-59385-988-6 (pbk.)—ISBN 978-1-59385-989-3 (hardcover)
   1. Employees—Rating of.   2. Educational evaluation.   3. Performance—Evaluation.   I. Penny, James A.   II. Gordon, Belita, 1947–   III. Title.
   HF5549.5.R3J64 2009
   658.3'125—dc22
                                                                    2008022315

Preface

THE NEED FOR THIS BOOK

Performance assessments include writing assessments in state testing programs, clinical examinations in medical licensure, essays in bar examinations, singing performances in the arts, and portfolios in national certification for teachers. Research into this assessment methodology burgeoned in the late 1980s and continues today. The literature on performance assessment is found in journals and texts across disciplines, such as education, licensure, and program evaluation. In *Assessing Performance*, we bridge the literature across disciplines to provide a guide for assessment practitioners as they develop performance assessments.

OUR APPROACH

Assessing Performance synthesizes the literature to describe methods for developing performance assessments from initial design to validation. The text progresses from the design of a performance assessment to constructing an assessment, administering the performance assessment, developing scoring materials, training raters, conducting operational scoring, and completing item-level and test-level analyses. As an introductory text, *Assessing Performance* will help you to answer such questions as:

1. What are the elements of a performance assessment?

2. What can I do to reduce rater bias in scoring performance tasks?

3. Should I score with a checklist, analytic rubric, or holistic rubric?

4. Should I use a 4-point rating scale, a 6-point rating scale, or a scale with more points?

5. How do I investigate the reliability and validity associated with the performance assessment?

We have arranged the book in the sequence that assessment practitioners will complete in developing a performance assessment. We use examples to make concrete the concepts and strategies that we discuss. For the reader new to the performance assessment field, reading the book from front to back will provide an introduction to the language and critical issues in the field. For those who work with performance assessments, the text provides a point of comparison between your practices and those described in the literature.

Assessing Performance incorporates several pedagogical features to assist the reader. In the first chapter, we describe the assessments that are used throughout the book to illustrate the design and validation of performance tasks. Each chapter that describes the development of a performance assessment culminates with a checklist of activities to complete at that stage of development. In the checklist, the development activities are clustered to organize myriad details into manageable sets of related tasks. In addition, we offer chapter questions that allow the reader to reflect on the concepts and strategies developed in the text and identify further readings for those who want additional information. A glossary at the end of the book provides readers with a common understanding of the terminology used in the field. Additionally, an extensive reference list, with over 300 entries, provides readers with other resources related to performance assessments.

THE AUDIENCES

We wrote *Assessing Performance* for several audiences. Assessment practitioners are one intended audience for *Assessing Performance*. The text describes concepts and procedures relevant to staff in state testing programs, licensure and certification programs, program evaluations, and research studies. Doctoral students in educational research programs comprise another audience for the text. Doctoral students will benefit from the systematic, in-depth treatment of the design and validation of performance assessments. *Assessing Performance* can be used to supplement other texts on testing and measurement. It also can be used as the primary text for a class that focuses on performance assessment. In addition, the book can serve as a resource for doctoral students in other degree areas whose research involves performance assessment, such as scoring music improvisation, assessing writing, or interviewing standardized patients. And, as one reviewer told us, in an education agency the book can serve as a self-study for new content specialists who have limited background in assessment.

Speaking of the reviewers, we would like to thank Edward H. Haertel, Stanford University; J. Christine Harmes, James Madison University; John Hattie, University of Auckland; George Englehard, Jr., Emory University; and Barbara Plake, University of Nebraska–Lincoln. We also want to thank Vaishali Uchil for her help in preparing the graphics we used in our figures, Laura McFadden for the drawings of the rater in Chapter 7, and Vasanthi Rao for her feedback about the text. *Assessing Performance* would not be as rich without examples of performance assessments and scoring guides. For sharing these materials, we send our thanks to the American Board of Pediatric Dentistry, the Georgia Department of Education, Lincoln Public Schools, the South Carolina Department of Education, and the South Carolina Arts Assessment Program. And, we want to thank our editor at The Guilford Press, C. Deborah Laughton, for her guidance and patience in this process.

We hope that the implementation and documentation of the strategies described in *Assessing Performance* will assist readers to develop assessments that can support accurate decisions in education, licensure, certification, research, and program evaluation. As you will notice as you read, our synthesis describes methods developed and perfected by practitioners and writers in the field of performance assessment. We hope to hear from you about new methodologies that we should incorporate in future editions of *Assessing Performance*. We invite you to contact the senior author at:

ROBERT L. JOHNSON
College of Education
University of South Carolina
Columbia, SC 29208

We look forward to hearing from you!

Contents

CHAPTER 1

An Overview
of Performance Assessment

INTRODUCTION

Performance assessment permeates much of our world. Children encounter performance assessment as they move through school grades, in particular by the use of writing assessments, which now are often a part of final graduation requirements and college entry. In music, students audition for admission into a program. Prospective physicians are tested using standardized patients (i.e., actors portraying patients). Olympic competitors regularly face performance assessment. Pilots train in simulators, but the final test for licensure involves flying an airplane. The adolescent rite of passage to obtain a driver's license involves driving a car with a state examiner.

As we shall see shortly, assessing performance is not a recent phenomenon; examples of performance assessment are available from early Chinese culture. Much more recent, however, is the research into methods to improve the development and scoring of performance assessments. Our purpose in *Assessing Performance* is to share this research and to present a methodology for the design and scoring of such performances.

DEFINING PERFORMANCE
AND PERFORMANCE ASSESSMENT

Given that performance assessments can be as diverse as writing essays, singing in music auditions, and diagnosing standardized patients, we

1

first need to develop a common definition of the terms "performance" and "performance assessment."

Performance Defined

In writing about performance assessment, Fitzpatrick and Morrison (1971) state that "The performance is a sequence of responses aimed at modifying the environment in specified ways" (p. 239). For example, Olympic figure skaters use movement, costumes, and music to transform an ice rink from an expanse of frozen white to an energy-filled tapestry of motion and color. In the National Assessment of Educational Progress (NAEP), a nationally representative and continuing assessment of students in grades 4, 8, and 12 (see Table 1.1), students develop collages about a place of importance to them, such as a former home or a friend's house (Persky, Sandene, & Askew, 1998). In terms of modifying the environment, these students use markers, oil pastels, and colored paper to change a sheet of blank paper into a collage about their memories of a place of importance to them.

This "sequence of responses" includes the behaviors of an examinee—what an examinee says, does, or creates (Messick, 1994; Mislevy, Steinberg, & Almond, 2002; Mislevy, Wilson, Ercikan, & Chudowsky, 2003). Thus many authors define performance as how an examinee behaves or acts, an idea supported by Gitomer (1993), who succinctly defined performance as "simply the execution of an action" (p. 244).

Performance Assessment Defined

In a performance assessment, examinees demonstrate their knowledge and skills by engaging in a process or constructing a product. More broadly, a performance assessment is a system composed of (1) a purpose for the assessment, (2) tasks (or prompts) that elicit the performance, (3) a response demand that focuses the examinee's performance, and (4) systematic methods for rating performances (Ruiz-Primo & Shavelson, 1996; Shavelson, Solano-Flores, & Ruiz-Primo, 1998; Stiggins, 1987a).

This systems approach appears consistent with the performance assessments in the NAEP. An example of the elements of a 12th-grade performance task from the NAEP United States history assessment is shown in Figures 1.1 to 1.4. The assessment involves examinees in "explaining issues, identifying historical patterns, establishing cause-and-effect relationships" within the historical theme of *gathering of people, culture, and ideas* (National Center for Education Statistics

TABLE 1.1. Examples of Assessments and Their Purposes

Name of assessment	Examinee population	Purpose	Description	Use
Even Start Family Literacy Portfolio	Adult participants in a literacy and parenting skills program	Assess changes in parent and child interactions Improve program services	Portfolio developed by participant and program staff	Program evaluation
Georgia High School Writing Test (GHSWT)	Students in junior and senior years of high school	Determine examinees' qualification for graduation from high school[a]	Persuasive essay	Educational testing
Multistate Performance Test (MPT)	Law candidates	Determine examinees' competence to practice law[b]	Written performance tasks	Licensure
National Assessment of Educational Progress (NAEP)	Students in grades 4, 8, and 12	Provide descriptive information at the state and national level about examinees' achievement in reading, writing, mathematics, science, visual and performing arts, etc.	Multiple-choice, constructed-response, extended-response, and performance tasks	Educational testing
National Board for Professional Teaching Standards (NBPTS)	Classroom teachers	Determine if a teacher is accomplished and qualified for national certification	Portfolio entries reflecting various facets of teaching and content-based essay exercises	Certification
Objective Structured Video Exam (OSVE)	Medical students	Assess examinees' recognition and understanding of the consequences of various communication skills in a patient–doctor interaction	Video-based clinical examination	Educational testing

(continued)

3

TABLE 1.1. (continued)

Name of assessment	Examinee population	Purpose	Description	Use
Oral Clinical Examination (OCE)	Candidates seeking to become a Board-certified pediatric dentist	Evaluate the candidates' knowledge and ability to solve clinical cases in pediatric dentistry[c]	Case studies (i.e., clinical vignettes) in which a brief medical/dental history is followed by the showing of images on a flat-panel display; candidate discusses each case and examiners ask questions	Certification
QUASAR Cognitive Assessment Instrument	Middle school students	Assess student's ability to problem-solve, reason, and communicate mathematically	Constructed-response mathematical tasks	Program evaluation
SAT Writing	Applicants to colleges	Inform admissions decisions[d]	One analytic essay	Educational testing
South Carolina Arts Assessment Program (SCAAP)	Students in grade 4	Assess student's arts achievement in relation to arts curriculum standards	Multiple choice items and performance tasks in visual arts and music	Educational testing research
United States Medical Licensure Examination Step 2: Clinical Skills (USMLE Step 2 CS)	Medical students or graduates	Assess whether an examinee can demonstrate the fundamental clinical skills essential for safe patient care under supervision[e]	Clinical examinations	Licensure

[a]The GHSWT is one requirement for earning a high school diploma.
[b]The MPT is one of several tests that a board of bar examiners may use in determining competence to practice law.
[c]The Oral Clinical Examination is part of the examination for certification.
[d]The SAT Writing is one piece of information used in making admissions decisions.
[e]The USMLE Step 2 CS is one of a three-step examination for medical licensure.

4

CONTENT CLASSIFICATION

Historical Theme

Gathering of People, Cultures, and Ideas

Defining Questions:

- What racial, ethnic, religious, and national groups formed this nation? Why have people immigrated to the land that became the United States, and why has the country continued to attract so many immigrants? What have been the patterns and conditions of this immigration (e.g., voluntarily in search of economic opportunity, religious freedom, and political refuge; involuntarily in bondage as slaves; or under other conditions, such as indentured servants and contract laborers)? How has the racial, ethnic, and religious composition of the nation changed over time? What racial, ethnic, and religious tensions arose? What issues have been resolved? What issues remain? What were the patterns of settlement? How and why have these settlement patterns changed?

- What common and diverse cultural traditions did Americans develop? How did Native Americans and other racial, ethnic, religious, and national groups contribute to the creation of a common culture in the United States as well as to the development of distinct ethnic cultures? What individuals and defining events contributed to these developments? What roles have community and region played in these shared and distinct cultures? What primary documents and historical sources—such as original documents, speeches, cartoons, artifacts, photos, art, music, architecture, literature, drama, dance, popular culture, biographies, journals, folklore, historic sites, and oral histories—record the development of American culture?

- What have been the changing patterns of social organization in American society (e.g., class structure, social mobility, social discrimination, family structure, neighborhood, and community)? How have these patterns been reflected in the daily lives of Americans?

- What have been the roles of men and women in American society? How and why have these roles differed across racial, ethnic, regional, and class lines? How and why have gender roles changed?

Cognitive Level

Historical Analysis and Interpretation

Historical Analysis and Interpretation—explaining issues, identifying historical patterns, establishing cause-and-effect relationships, finding value statements, establishing significance, applying historical knowledge, weighing evidence to draw sound conclusions, making defensible generalizations, and rendering insightful accounts of the past.

FIGURE 1.1. Content that provides the focus of the NAEP history performance task. From the National Center for Education Statistics, U.S. Department of Education (2005).

[NCES], U.S. Department of Education, 2005, ¶ 5). Figure 1.2 shows the task and the response demand. Figure 1.3 shows a scoring guide, often referred to as a rubric, that frames the scoring process for the rater and systematizes the rating of performances. To operationalize the scoring levels described in the rubric, a student response at the "Appropriate" score level is paired with the scorer's commentary supporting the rating of "Appropriate" (see Figure 1.4). Other exemplars of student

---

History Question

Subject: History   **Grade:** 12   **Block:** 2001–12H3   **No.:** 3

Both parts of Question 3 are about the statement below.
"My logic teaches me that land cannot be sold. The Great Spirit gave the land to his children to live upon. . . . Nothing can be sold but such things as can be carried away."

—Black Hawk, Chief of the Sac and Fox

3. In the space below, list two ways in which the beliefs about land ownership held by many Native Americans (such as Black Hawk) differed from the beliefs about land ownership probably held by many White Americans. In your answer use both the quote above and your knowledge of history.

WAYS IN WHICH BELIEFS ABOUT
LAND OWNERSHIP DIFFERED

1. _____

_____

_____

2. _____

_____

_____

In the space below, explain how the differences in beliefs about land ownership you identified affected the relationship between White Americans and Native Americans.

_____

_____

_____

FIGURE 1.2. Performance task from the NAEP United States history examination. From the National Center for Education Statistics, U.S. Department of Education (2005).

Scoring Guide

Score and Description

Appropriate

The response is able to identify two differences in views of land ownership and to explain, with some specificity, the ways these affected the relationship between Native Americans and Europeans; for example, "White Americans wanted to own their own land for farming, and so they forced many Native Americans off their tribal lands. This led to many wars over land."

Essential

The response identifies two differences correctly, although one may be weaker than the other and provides no explanation or a very weak explanation. For example: "White Americans made the Native Americans angry because White Americans wanted more and more land."

OR

The response discusses one important difference and correctly explains how this difference affects the relationship between White Americans and Native Americans.

Partial

The response identifies one belief or one difference but goes no further, OR the response understands the problems in Native American–White American relations but cannot relate these problems to beliefs about land ownership.

Inappropriate

The response does not identify differences or relate these differences to Native American–White American problems.

FIGURE 1.3. Scoring guide for the history item. From the National Center for Education Statistics, U.S. Department of Education (2005).

responses similarly operationalize the performance levels of "Essential," "Partial," and "Inappropriate." Considered in combination—the purpose, the task, the scoring guide, and the exemplars—form a system for assessing examinee knowledge and skills.

The approach to performance assessment we will take in this text is consistent with the systems approach. We examine the process of assessing performance by establishing the purpose of the assessment, developing tasks that require examinees to respond in a certain manner, and the scoring of those responses.

Exemplar of Student Response

1. For the White Americans, land was equated with liberty and prosperity and life was generally materialistically friendly. The Native American people instead viewed nature and land as sacred things that were more powerful than themselves.

2. The Native Americans believed in coexisting with nature and in giving as well as receiving goods from it. Native Americans viewed land as a commodity and a resource to be used themselves.

In the space below, explain how the differences in beliefs about land ownership you identified affected the relationship between White Americans and Native Americans.

The general life-philosophies of the Native American peoples and those of White Americans viewed land as a material asset while Native Americans viewed land as a spiritual gift. Because of these basic differences, White Americans believed that they owned the land that had been sacred to the Native Americans for centuries before the Colonists arrived on the continent. These clashing philosophies on human rights to land caused land wars and many lost lives.

Scorer's Commentary

The student identifies two differences between the beliefs about land ownership held by many Native Americans and the beliefs about land ownership probably held by many White Americans. The response also provides an acceptable explanation of how those differences affected the relationship between Native Americans and White Americans.

FIGURE 1.4. Exemplar of an examinee response and scorer's commentary at the performance level of "Appropriate" for the NAEP history item. From the National Center for Education Statistics, U.S. Department of Education (2005).

TYPES OF PERFORMANCE ASSESSMENTS

We use the term "performance assessment" as shorthand for the type of assessment referred to as performance and product evaluation (Fitzpatrick & Morrison, 1971).[1] The categories of *product* and *performance* assessments offered by Fitzpatrick and Morrison (1971) encompass the

---

[1]Messick (1994) notes that performances and products are distinct; however, they are typically described under the general heading of performance assessment.

various types of performance assessments used in educational and credentialing testing, research, and program evaluations.

Products

One product form of performance assessment is the ubiquitous essay. Essays are a form of extended-response that require the examinee to write a description, analysis, or summary in one or more paragraphs (Feuer & Fulton, 1993). Other extended-response products include term papers, laboratory reports, drawings, and dance performances. Products also include short, constructed-response items that require an examinee to briefly answer questions about reading passages, solve a mathematics problem, or complete a graph or diagram.

Performances

Performances include both oral assessments and demonstrations. In these instances, the assessment focuses on process. An example of an oral assessment occurs when a teacher assesses a student's oral reading fluency and speaking skills (Stiggins, 1987a). In addition, state and national assessments of music gauge students' ability to sing (i.e., oral assessment) (Persky et al., 1998; Yap, Schneider, Johnson, Mazzie, & Porchea, 2003).

Another example of an oral assessment is the Oral Clinical Examination (OCE), used in the certification of pediatric dentists (American Board of Pediatric Dentistry, 2007). Pediatric dentists seeking diplomate status (a form of board certification) with the American Board of Pediatric Dentistry (ABPD) must pass an eligibility review and two examinations. The second of the two examinations is the OCE, in which examinees are presented with a series of clinical cases. The examinee listens to a verbal description of a clinical case and reviews slides. During this process, the examinee may ask the examiners to clarify the case; the examiners may also ask questions of the examinee. The intent is for the examinee to demonstrate sufficient knowledge to diagnose and formulate treatment for the dental condition presented. The examiners (i.e., judges) use a 4-point scoring rubric in three areas to independently rate the response of each examinee. Although the assessment is performed in real time, the performance is videotaped in the event that the performance requires follow-up review.

The use of demonstration as a performance assessment occurs in the National Interpreter Certification examination (Registry of Interpreters for the Deaf, 2006). In this examination, candidates for certification demonstrate their ability to sign for the Deaf. Another example of demonstration comes from the South Carolina Arts Assessment Program (SCAAP), in which students demonstrate their ability to improvise using rhythm sticks (Yap et al., 2003).

Performances and Products

In some instances, performance assessments involve a combination of performances and products. For example, experiments require students to engage in the scientific process by developing hypotheses, planning and executing experiments, and summarizing findings (Feuer & Fulton, 1993). The focus of the assessment can be the execution of the experiment (i.e., a demonstration), the laboratory report that describes the results (i.e., a product), or both. Similarly, a writing portfolio might be conceptualized as a product if the entries only reflect final products; however, including drafts that provide information about the writing process would change the focus of the portfolio to include process and product.

In the teacher certification for the National Board for Professional Teaching Standards (NBPTS), a portfolio component contains video recordings of a teacher's instructional activities (i.e., process) and the teacher's written reflection about the instruction (i.e., product) (NBPTS, 2004a). As a component of graduation requirements in higher education, doctoral candidates participate in an oral defense (i.e., an oral performance) of their dissertations (i.e., a product). Also, computer simulations offer the opportunity to review an examinee's final solution and to follow the procedures the examinee employed in arriving at the solution.

APPLICATIONS

In this section we take a closer look at the use of performance assessment in education, employment, research, and program evaluation.

Performance Assessment in Education

Many states assess writing competency in their annual testing program. The *Annual Survey of Student Assessment Programs, 2000/2001* (Council of Chief State School Officers, 2002) reports that 43 states included a writing assessment in their testing programs. In several states students' public school experience culminates with a writing proficiency test that is part of the criteria for receiving a high school diploma (National Education Goals Panel, 1996). For example, as shown in Table 1.1, the state of Georgia uses a writing test as one component of an assessment to determine an examinee's qualification for graduation from high school.

The use of writing assessments to make decisions about examinees continues into their entry into college, where students compose essays to determine their placement level in composition classes (e.g., Hayes, Hatch, & Silk, 2000; Willard-Traub, Decker, Reed, & Johnston, 2000). In addition, second-language (L2) writing assessments are used at some universities to make placement decisions about students for whom English is a second language (ESL) (Weigle, 1998, 1999).

At the end of the 20th century, performance assessments were a major component of the assessment system of the Kentucky State Department of Education (Gong & Reidy, 1996; Guskey, 1994). The Kentucky Instructional Results Information System (KIRIS) was used to reward schools that showed substantial improvements and to sanction schools that failed to improve. Guskey (1994) notes that performance assessment was used to "compel educators at all levels in the Commonwealth to focus instructional activities on the kinds of higher-level skills that will be essential for success in the 21st century" (p. 3). At its peak, the KIRIS assessment included constructed-response and extended-response items along with writing and mathematics portfolios.

To gauge educational progress, performance assessments have been included in both national and international testing programs. For example, the Trends in International Mathematics and Science Study (TIMSS) provides information about mathematics and science achievement of students in 46 countries (Gonzales et al., 2004). Performance assessments in TIMSS have required that examinees take their pulses and graph the data, interpret and draw conclusions from tables, determine which of a set of batteries are functional, and measure scale models of furniture and then convert the measures to actual sizes (Jakwerth, 1999).

In reading, an example of a performance assessment used in NAEP (see Table 1.1) required students to predict a fictional character's reaction to a hypothetical situation (Grigg, Daane, Jin, & Campbell, 2003). NAEP also used performance assessments in mathematics that required examinees to use a graph to support an argument (Braswell et al., 2001) and in science to categorize eight living things by an important physical characteristic (O'Sullivan, Lauko, Grigg, Qian, & Zhang, 2003).

In medical schools, one form of performance assessment is the objective structured clinical examination (OSCE). Schwartz, Donnelly,

Sloan, Johnson, and Stroedel (1995) describe an OSCE in which an intern obtains a directed history from an actual or simulated (i.e. role-playing) patient. A faculty instructor observes the intern's interaction with the patient and uses a checklist to record the intern's actions and questions. Examinees can also be required to perform physical examination techniques, such as palpating the abdomen, listening to heart or breath sounds, and/or checking reflexes. In another part of the assessment, a faculty member asks a series of questions with short answers and then evaluates the examinee's oral responses. The instructor completes a checklist in scoring the intern's responses.

Performance Assessment in Employment

Performance assessments have long been used in an employment context. For example, in the field of law, the licensure process in 30 states requires that applicants for admission to practice law complete the Multistate Performance Test (see Table 1.1). In the Multistate Performance Test, the examinees perform such tasks as reviewing documents to write a proposal for a settlement or construct closing arguments for a case (National Conference of Bar Examiners [NCBE] & American Bar Association [ABA], 2005). Sixteen states require that applicants to practice law take the Multistate Essay Examination. This performance assessment consists of a collection of essay questions in which applicants identify legal issues in a hypothetical scenario, separate relevant and irrelevant material presented in the scenario, present a reasoned analysis of the legal issues, and show an understanding of the legal principles relevant to the solution of the issues.

Performance tests of military personnel have included diverse tasks. Types of tasks have included directing a helicopter landing, performing CPR, assembling automatic weapons, and determining grid coordinates on a map (Shavelson, Mayberry, Li, & Webb, 1990).

Performance Assessment in Research and Program Evaluation

The use of performance assessment occurs frequently in literacy research (e.g., Baker & Wigfield, 1999; Ceprano & Garan, 1998). Such was the case when first-grade students exchanged letters with pen pals at a university (Ceprano & Garan, 1998). The researchers developed an assessment rubric to document the first-grade students' development of voice (e.g., word choice, sentence structure) in their writing as well as to examine the technical aspects (e.g., spelling, punctuation, sentence structure, self-initiated topics) of the students' letters.

Baker and Wigfield (1999) used student answers to open-response interpretive questions to study the relationships among motivation, student reading activity, and achievement. The authors also developed a scoring rubric to rate student responses. Note that the assessment system in both research studies contained the task and rubric components of a performance assessment system.

Another research example comes to us from the NAEP writing assessment. Many classroom teachers think of writing as a process and "employ a variety of strategies to encourage students to take time to think about their ideas, to plan ways they might express those ideas in writing, and to revise their writing to refine and better express their ideas" (Greenwald, Persky, Campbell, & Mazzeo, 1999, p. 92). To examine the role of preplanning in writing performance, the 1998 NAEP writing assessment included a space in their test booklets for students to plan their responses for each of two prompts (Greenwald et al., 1999). The authors report that students who engaged in planning (e.g., developed lists, webs, outlines) in the available space for both of the writing prompts had higher average scores than students who planned for only one essay. Similarly, those who planned for one of the writing prompts scored higher than those who did not plan for either of the writing tasks. In another research-based use of performance assessment, student drawings of their teachers at work in the classroom have been used to document reform efforts in schools(Haney, Russell, & Bebell, 2004).

Evaluations have used portfolios in reviews of programs in literacy, the humanities, and family literacy (Johnson, Willeke, Bergman, & Steiner, 1997; Lau & LeMahieu, 1997; LeMahieu, Gitomer, & Eresh, 1995; Popp, 1992; Thompson, Bosn, & Ruma, 1993; Valencia & Au, 1997). For example, the evaluation of a family literacy program in Lincoln, Nebraska, incorporated portfolios as a data collection method to document changes in the participants (Johnson, Fisher, Willeke, & McDaniel, 2003; Johnson, McDaniel, & Willeke, 2000; Johnson, Willeke, & Steiner, 1998). The staff of the family literacy program (i.e., Even Start) collaborated with the evaluators to design a portfolio system to document participants' development of parenting skills and literacy skills.

As we have seen, performance assessment is pervasive in education, employment, and research and evaluation. Yet one might ask, "Why use performance assessments in these testing programs? What unique qualities does the performance assessment bring to these examinations?"

WHY PERFORMANCE ASSESSMENT?

During much of the 20th century, testing programs used multiple-choice items in their assessments. However, as we will see in the section on the origins of performance assessment, prior to the 20th century assessment often involved demonstrations or development of a product.

Today testing programs in education and credentialing programs often use both multiple-choice and performance assessment. Incorporating both performance tasks and multiple-choice items into an assessment may be due in part to assessment practitioners' conceptualizing multiple-choice items and performance assessment as part of an item-format continuum (Fortune & Cromack, 1995; Gronlund, 2006; Johanson & Motlomelo, 1998; Messick, 1996; Snow, 1993). Figure 1.5 shows a continuum of item formats and examples of qualities to consider when determining the appropriate form of assessment for a given testing situation. For example, if authenticity and cognitive complexity are key qualities for an assessment that you are designing, then one of the performance assessment item formats will better address these qualities. If, however, breadth in coverage and costs are central to the assessment, then a selected-response format should be considered.

Performance Assessment Formats					Selected-Response Formats	
Work Samples	Simulations	Projects	Essays	Short Answer	Multiple Choice	True–False
More authentic	←————————————→				Less authentic	
More cognitively complex	←————————————→				Less cognitively complex	
More in-depth content coverage	←————————————→				More breadth in content coverage	
Examinee constructed response structure	←————————————→				Test developer response structure	
More expensive	←————————————→				Less expensive	

FIGURE 1.5. Example of an item-format continuum and qualities of the formats. Data from Fortune and Cromack (1995); Gronlund (2006); Johanson and Motlomelo (1998); Snow (1993).

Licensure examinations often use several hundred multiple-choice items to measure the breadth of examinee knowledge. However, to document the development of skills such as interacting with a patient, licensure programs also include some form of performance assessment. By combining performance assessment with multiple-choice items, testing programs benefit from the strengths of each form of assessment (Lane & Stone, 2006).

Qualities to consider in the use of performance assessment include (1) authenticity, (2) context, (3) cognitive complexity, (4) in-depth content coverage, (5) examinee-structured response, (6) credibility, (7) costs, and (8) reform (e.g., Lane & Stone, 2006; Linn, Baker, & Dunbar, 1991; Wiggins, 1992). A closer look at the previous examples of performance assessments provides insights into the qualities that they bring to a testing situation.

Authenticity

A key quality to consider in using performance assessment is authenticity, the degree to which the assessment reflects the knowledge and skills important to a field (Fitzpatrick & Morrison, 1971; Gitomer, 1993; Wiggins, 1992). Fortune and Cromack (1995) address the authenticity of tasks in discussing the "concept of fidelity" (p. 150), which relates to the degree to which a clinical examination in licensure requires the same knowledge and skills as the task requires on the job.

The quality of authenticity is evidenced in the OCSE, in which interns interact with patients to obtain a history. In this assessment the medical interns demonstrate skills they will use in the clinical setting. Authenticity was also evidenced in the research study that investigated 1st grade students' development of writing skills. Recall that the task involved the students in exchanges of letters with university students. Thus, first-grade students demonstrated their writing skills consistent with how the skill would be applied in life.

Context

Related to authenticity is the quality of context. In a performance assessment, context frames the design of tasks to assess complex skills within the real-world situations in which the skills will be applied. Resnick and Resnick (1992) criticize assessments that assume that a complex skill is fixed and will manifest in the same way, at any time, across contexts.

They argue that complex skills should be assessed in the same context in which they will be used. In education, Baron (1991) suggests that performance tasks be presented in real-world contexts so that students will learn that their skills and knowledge are valuable beyond the classroom. The context for a task in the Multistate Performance Test is established by using (1) a memorandum from a supervising attorney to describe the assignment and (2) documents that contain the facts of the case (NCBE, 2006). In the case of United States Medical Licensure Examination, the performance assessment is in a simulated clinical setting in which medical students and graduates demonstrate their ability "to gather information from patients, perform physical examinations, and communicate their findings to patients and colleagues" (Federation of State Medical Boards of the United States & National Board of Medical Examiners, 2008, p. 3).

Cognitive Complexity

Probably one of the most evident qualities of performance assessments is their cognitive complexity (Bachman, 2002; Eisner, 1999; Khattri & Sweet, 1996; Messick, 1996; Ryan, 2006). Performance assessments can be used to gauge examinees' use of higher-order cognitive strategies such as structuring a problem or assessment task, formulating a plan to address the problem, applying information, constructing responses, and explaining the process through which they develop their answers. In the applications of performance assessments we have examined thus far, higher-order cognition was evident when students in the science assessment for NAEP categorized (i.e., classified) organisms by a key physical characteristic. Similarly, the Multistate Performance Test engages examinees in the bar examination in analysis and synthesis when reviewing documents and constructing legal arguments.

In-Depth Coverage

Another quality of performance assessment is the in-depth content coverage of knowledge and skills (Messick, 1996). In the NBPTS portfolio component, teachers complete in-depth analyses of videotaped interactions with students; review samples of the students' work; and write commentaries describing, analyzing, and reflecting on the entries.

The in-depth coverage associated with performance assessment will dictate relatively few tasks being used as compared with assessments that use multiple-choice or a mix of multiple-choice and performance tasks. If an assessment is composed of a small number of tasks, such as essays for a bar examination, then scores may not generalize to a broader domain (Lane & Stone, 2006). Such may be the reason that credentialing programs that employ performance assessments also often have a multiple-choice component to extend the breadth of coverage.

Examinee-Structured Response

A hallmark of a performance assessment is that it requires examinees to construct a response rather than choose an answer from a set of options as in selected-response formats (Wiley & Haertel, 1996). This quality is evident in all of the examples we have presented. In the SCAAP examples, the students produce drawings for the visual arts assessment and sing for the music assessment. In the task from the NAEP history assessment students write about differences in beliefs about ownership between White Americans and Native Americans. In addition, in the Oral Clinical Examination, candidates for diplomate status in pediatric dentistry discuss the medical issues relevant to a case study and are questioned by examiners.

Credibility

Credibility contributes to the use of performance-based assessments in the certification process for the National Board for Professional Teaching Standards (NBPTS, 2006a). The certification process eschews use of any multiple-choice items because this response format lacked credibility with the governing board. Another example of the issue of credibility comes from state testing programs' replacement of multiple-choice measures of language expression with writing samples (Stiggins, 1987b). Stiggins notes that this change occurred because language arts educators considered writing samples to be the most valid method for assessing composition skills and their professional organization, the National Council of Teachers of English, demanded the most valid form of assessment.

Costs

Costs are another consideration in the use of performance assessments (Resnick & Resnick, 1992; Ryan, 2006) because the expenses involved in the administration and scoring of performance assessments can be considerable. Costs include both (1) the expense of hiring someone to observe an examinee's performance and/or to score an examinee's products and (2) the time required to assess using the performance assessment format. For example, the fee of the United States Medical Licensing Examination™ (USMLE), a three-part licensure test, for the performance-based test of Clinical Skills was approximately $1,000 in 2008, whereas the multiple-choice-based test of Clinical Knowledge was approximately $500 (National Board of Medical Examiners [NBME], 2008). In terms of the time required to assess the relevant skills, the Clinical Knowledge test in the USMLE contains 370 multiple-choice items completed in an 8-hour period. In contrast, in the Clinical Skills section of the test, examinees complete 12 tasks in an 8-hour period.

These costs are not unique to the USMLE. The fee for the NBPTS certification process in which a teacher develops a portfolio and writes essays was $2,500 in 2008 (NBPTS, 2008). Teachers spend up to a year preparing their portfolios and a day at an assessment center, where they demonstrate their content knowledge in response to six exercises with 30 minutes to respond to each. Thus performance tasks should be used for assessing the complex knowledge and skills required in a content area or professional field.

Reform

Performance assessment has also been used to drive reform. Resnick and Resnick (1992) summarize this aspect of assessment in stating,

> You get what you assess.
> You do not get what you do not assess.
> Build assessments toward which you want educators to teach. (p. 59)

In the instance of reform, performance assessments affected change when the Even Start portfolios brought more focus to program activities (Johnson et al., 1998). The portfolio focused staff attention on program goals and promoted closer alignment of their activities with the goals of Even Start.

These qualities offer a framework for assessment developers to consider when deciding whether to use performance assessments or a combination of performance assessment and multiple-choice. In the next section, we provide an overview of the long tradition of making decisions based on performance assessment.

ORIGINS OF PERFORMANCE ASSESSMENT

Performance assessment is not a new phenomenon. Madaus and O'Dwyer (1999) trace the origins of performance testing to China.[2] Beginning with the Han Dynasty in 210 B.C.E. until the first decade of the 1900s (Nitko, 1983), candidates for civil service completed performance assessments. During the Sung Dynasty (960–1279 C.E.), the performance tests addressed a number of disciplines: letters, law, history, rituals, and classical study (Franke, 1968; Kracke, 1953). The most esteemed assessment was associated with the field of letters. The letters examination was based on the canon of Confucian classics and included "completing passages from memory; summarizing the meanings of the classics; composing a discussion, a poetic description, and a piece of poetry; and, finally, demonstrating reasoning ability by discussing five (seeming) conflicts within the classics" (Madaus & O'Dwyer, 1999, p. 690).

Kracke (1953) recounts that as early as 1023 C.E. it was proposed that other fields (e.g., law, history, ritual, and classics) incorporate a section of problems for solution. However, not all government officials prized compositions that allowed candidates to demonstrate reasoning skills. Some officials raised the concern that the scoring of the questions would be too subjective and reverted instead to questions with rote answers. Here we see an early instance of the primary criticism of performance assessments—the subjectivity of scoring.

Candidates for the military completed an examination in which they demonstrated three skills: marksmanship, military talent, and scholarship (Miyazaki, 1976). This examination emphasized assessment through performance:

> Marksmanship, both on foot and on horseback, was assessed against fixed criteria. For example, examinees had to shoot three arrows from a horse at a man-shaped target 5¼ feet high. Three hits received an "excellent" score, two were deemed a "good" score, one hit was a "pass," and zero hits meant elimination. (Madaus & O'Dwyer, 1999, p. 690)

According to Madaus and O'Dwyer (1999), during the Middle Ages in Europe, performance assessments were used to certify guild members. To become a master in the guild system "it sufficed to have served an apprenticeship [and] to undergo an examination (the so-called masterpiece) which was then both simple and practical" (Boissonnade, 1927,

---

[2]Much of this section is based on the work of Madaus and O'Dwyer (1999).

p. 212). The apprentice bowl, produced by those completing their training at Waterford Crystal, provides a modern example of a masterpiece that an apprentice would create for promotion (Madaus & O'Dwyer, 1999).

In liberal arts examinations in 12th-century Europe, performance assessment took the form of theological oral disputations in Latin (Madaus & O'Dwyer, 1999). The exams required students to debate the concepts contained in a body of literature and to resolve any contradictions. In the examination, "The student had to show the ability to remember relevant and acceptable knowledge, the ability to present it in eloquent form, and a tacit conformity to orthodoxy, educational and social" (Hoskin, 1979, p. 138).

Disputations continued into the 17th century (Madaus & O'Dwyer, 1999). At Oxford the disputation opened with the examinee making a statement on his question; opponents would then dispute the examinee's response. In turn, the examinee would rebut each opponent's arguments. Evaluation consisted of the moderator's qualitative judgment about the examinees' and opponents' performances (Hoskin, 1979).

Although rare, written exams occurred in 14th-century Europe, and by the 16th century Jesuits used compositions in their examinations (Madaus & O'Dwyer, 1999). To be promoted, students in Jesuit schools had to pass a test consisting of two parts: a written composition in Latin and an oral examination on the grammar, syntax, and style of the text that the student had written. From 1747 to 1750 Cambridge University used an exam with oral and written components to test students (Webber, 1989). The written exam allowed better assessment of an examinee's attainment in mathematics. However, subjectivity and partiality were recognized as problems when candidates were ranked based on examiners' qualitative judgments of examinees' styles of performance across the oral and written portions of the examination.

The history of performance assessment in education in North America includes oral recitations and can be traced to the beginnings of college education in North America (Rudolph, 1990). Oral exams were used in Massachusetts as early as 1709 (Morris, 1961). Horace Mann replaced the oral exam in the Boston public schools with an essay exam in 1845.

Prior to the Civil War, testing requirements for candidates for accounting positions at the Treasury Department included writing a business letter (Hale, 1982). In the early 1900s, to assign military personnel to specialized tasks and rate officers for appointment and promotion, John B. Watson and other psychologists developed a series of tests based on oral questions (Hale, 1982). In these oral examinations, military personnel answered questions based on various trades, photographs, and sample tasks.

Early in the 20th century essay tests were challenged, in part due to studies that showed the unreliability of the scoring of essay exams (Starch & Elliot, 1912, 1913). Frederick Kelly's introduction of multiple-choice items in 1915 facilitated the development of standardized, norm-referenced tests, further challenging the use of essays (Madaus & O'Dwyer, 1999; Office of Technology Assessment, 1992). For instance, in 1926 the College Board first introduced the SAT with questions using multiple-choice answers (Resnick, 1982). The College Board discontinued essay examinations in 1947, but the Advanced Placement tests incorporated constructed-response answers and raters for scoring examinee responses in the 1950s (Resnick, 1982). Recently, the College Board has incorporated writing assessments in the SAT and the Graduate Record Examination.

In the early 1960s, Morris (1961) noted efforts to return to the more direct performance assessment. He wrote,

> Examiners for selection for the armed and civil services, for the church, for teacher training and even secondary education, have attempted to construct artificial situations similar to those in which candidates would actually find themselves if successful. The examiners observe and assess the candidates' behaviour in these situations and their response to appropriate set tasks. These experiments, however, are in their infancy and it is too soon to comment on their usefulness or to predict whether the days of indirect testing are numbered. (p. 43)

A decade later, Fitzpatrick and Morrison (1971) argued that

> it is often desirable to increase the "realism" of the test to a degree that permits evaluation of the capability of the student to perform correctly in some class of *criterion situations*. The criterion situations are those in which the learning is to be applied. There are often vocational in nature but may be related to avocations, consumer skills, citizenship behaviors, or any other type of performance that is considered important enough to be taught. (p. 237)

The 1980s and 1990s saw a resurgence in the use of performance assessment in education. For example, in the 1980s, state testing programs replaced multiple-choice measures of language usage, grammar, and mechanics with writing samples (Stiggins, 1987b). Continuing the trend in the early 1990s, state departments of education and school districts incorporated mathematics and writing portfolios into their testing programs (Gong & Reidy, 1996; Koretz, Stecher, Klein, & McCaffrey, 1994; LeMahieu et al., 1995).

In licensure, the 1980s marked a decline in performance testing due to the expense and the high correlation between scores on performance and written tests (Knapp & Knapp, 1995). However, return to the use of performance assessment in the form of clinical examinations occurred due to "a mistrust of paper-and-pencil or multiple-choice tests, a need to see a candidate work with people, and a need to see the candidate perform in a work setting integrating the physical and cognitive skill areas" (Fortune & Cromack, 1995, p. 155).

Today performance assessment plays an important role in examinees' lives from their entry into public school, through their matriculation into a university, and into their professional lives. Given the importance of the decisions made at these critical junctures, assessment developers seek to create high-quality assessments, and the key to quality is validity and reliability.

ISSUES OF RELIABILITY AND VALIDITY IN PERFORMANCE ASSESSMENT

One goal of practitioners who use performance assessments is to report a reliable score that accurately reflects an examinee's proficiency in the domain of interest, such as writing. In this section, we develop the concepts of reliability and validity. Throughout the remainder of this book, we revisit these issues as they apply to designing the assessment, constructing performance tasks, administering the assessment, developing scoring materials, training raters, scoring and reporting, and analyzing scores.

Reliability

By reliability, we mean the consistency of examinees' scores across such facets as occasions, tasks, and raters. In other words, reliability addresses whether an examinee's score would be the same if she were to take the exam on a different occasion, complete different tasks, or be scored by different raters. Intuitively we understand that an examinee might be presented with an essay question that focuses on an area in which she has little knowledge; however, if a different essay question had been selected for the examination, then the content might be familiar to the examinee and she would perform differently. To remediate such circumstances, we include multiple prompts in an examination and use multiple raters in scoring the tasks. Also, examinees for high stakes assessments, such as high school exit examinations or licensure examinations, are allowed to retake the examination on subsequent occasions.

Validity

Validity addresses the accuracy of our inferences (e.g., decisions) based on our interpretation of the performance assessment scores. That is, based on the scores from the assessment, are we likely to make accurate (i.e., valid) decisions about an examinee? Will our decisions about licensing a candidate in nursing be valid? Will we make valid decisions about students' ability to write based on our writing assessment?

Two sources that contribute error to our inferences are construct underrepresentation and construct-irrelevant variance (Messick, 1996). In the instance of performance assessment and construct underrepresentation, we might ask whether an assessment is too narrow and fails to include important content, dimensions, or facets related to the construct that is the focus of the assessment. An example would be a credentialing examination that omitted tasks crucial to safe practice. Scores from the examination might indicate that the examinee has the required skills for safe practice; however, the credentialing decision might result in admission into a profession someone who has not mastered critical knowledge and skills.

Messick (1996) indicates that in the case of construct-irrelevant variance "the assessment is too broad, containing excess reliable variance that is irrelevant to the interpreted construct" (p. 5). Such would be the case if a stringent rater consistently scored papers low. The low scores of the rater would lead us to inappropriate decisions about examinees' understanding.

Improvements Supporting the Reliability and Validity of Performance Assessments

Training raters has improved the reliability of scores from performance assessments. Training involves raters learning to score according to a rubric (see Figure 1.3) that describes the levels of performance and is illustrated by anchor responses (see Figure 1.4) that provide concrete examples of each performance level (Cherry & Meyer, 1993; Coffman,

1971a; Hieronymous, Hoover, Cantor, & Oberley, 1987; Mullis, 1984). Moreover, score reliability has been improved by studies to determine the optimal number of raters needed to score a response and the optimal number of tasks to include in an assessment (e.g., Dunbar, Koretz, & Hoover, 1991; Godshalk, Swineford, & Coffman, 1966; Lane, Liu, Ankenmann, & Stone, 1996; Shavelson, Baxter, & Gao, 1993).

Improvements in operational scoring include methods of quality control, such as the intermixing (i.e., seeding) of previously scored responses in the group of unscored responses. When raters score the seeded responses, their scores are compared to the previously established scores to detect raters who might be assigning scores no longer based on the criteria of the rubric. In addition, quality control involves the monitoring of rater scores by highly experienced readers who serve as table or team leaders (Cherry & Meyer, 1993; Coffman, 1971a; Hieronymous et al., 1987; Mullis, 1984; Weigle, 1998, 1999, 2002). Moreover, the use of FACETS, a Rasch-based program, has advanced the diagnosis of rater severity and leniency in the scoring of essays (e.g., Engelhard, 1994; Myford & Wolfe, 2002; Weigle, 1998, 1999).

In the following chapters of *Assessing Performance*, we present these and other methods for improving the reliability and validity associated with performance tasks. In our discussions we will revisit the issues of reliability and validity to illustrate the effect of each on the consistency of scores and accuracy of decisions based on those scores.

Why is such a rigorous treatment of these qualities necessary? The procedures outlined in *Assessing Performance* are potential sources of validity evidence. Developers of performance assessments should both follow such rigorous procedures and document them. In the following discussions, we blend the literature on performance assessment with actual applications of the procedures based on our experiences as assessment practitioners in education, licensure and certification, program evaluation, and research.

FURTHER READINGS

Lane, S., & Stone, C. (2006). Performance assessment. In R. Brennan (Ed.), *Educational measurement* (4th ed., pp. 387–431). Westport, CT: American Council on Education and Praeger.

Provides a synthesis of the literature on the design and use of performance assessments in large-scale educational testing. Topics include a description of performance assessment, the uses of performance assessments, their design and scoring, the review of the validity of performance assessments, and applications of generalizability theory and item response theory in performance assessment.

Madaus, G., & O'Dwyer, L. (1999). A short history of performance assessment. *Phi Delta Kappan, 80*(9), 688–695.

Provides an overview of the history of performance assessment. The timeline dates back to the origins of performance assessment in China.

Chapter Questions

1. Other than the examples provided in this chapter, what are instances of performance assessments that are used to make decisions about examinees?

2. The Board of Law Examiners in many states administers the multiple-choice Multistate Bar Examination and an essay examination. In terms of assessing examinee knowledge of the practice of law, what is gained by adding an essay component to the multiple-choice test?

3. Is the Multistate Performance Test a performance-based or product-based examination? Explain your reasoning for the decision you make.

4. Feuer and Fulton (1993) indicate that the continuum of formats of performance ranges from simple examinee-constructed responses to comprehensive demonstrations or samples of work produced over time. List some examples of simple constructed responses and comprehensive samples of work.

5. If the NAEP visual arts assessment did not include a task in which the students draw a picture, would this omission be an issue of construct underrepresentation or construct-irrelevant variance? Explain your reasoning.

CHAPTER 2

Designing the Assessment

INTRODUCTION

A primary issue faced by the developers of an assessment is to determine what it will look like. An assessment might be composed of a mix of multiple-choice items, essays, and performance tasks. An example comes to us from the certification of orthotists and prosthetists, professionals who develop devices for patients with disabling conditions of the limbs and spine. In their credentialing examination, orthotists and prosthetists complete three types of certification examinations: (1) a multiple-choice examination that assesses such topics as anatomy, kinesiology, material science, and practice management; (2) a written simulation examination that gauges examinees' clinical decision-making skills in situations they might encounter in daily clinical practice; and (3) a clinical examination that requires examinees to demonstrate their practical abilities, such as patient evaluation, prescription criteria, measurement techniques, fitting, alignment, and appropriate handling of patients in a clinical environment (American Board for Certification in Orthotics, Prosthetics, and Pedorthics, n.d.). Thus, in the design of the orthotics and prosthetics examination, the test developers considered the fit of performance tasks within the overall design of an assessment. To gauge examinees' understanding and skill, the certification board developed an assessment composed of multiple-choice items and performance tasks.

In this chapter, we present the development of test specifications, which is a detailed description for an examination (American Educational Research Association [AERA], American Psychological Association [APA], & National Council on Measurement in Education [NCME], 1999, p. 183), as a systematic way to delineate the myriad details that

26

must be considered in the design of an assessment for education, credentialing, research, or program evaluation. Prior to our discussion, we
want to define some key terms used in the literature. Because a performance task can be one component of a comprehensive assessment, we
use the term "test" to refer to an assessment that might be an amalgam
of performance tasks, essays, and multiple-choice items. We use the term
"item" to refer to a specific task, whether the response format is multiple
choice, constructed response (e.g., short performance task), or extended
response (e.g., essay).

Consideration of an assessment's purpose, its content, and the task
formats informs the development of test specifications that, in turn, guide
the design of items and tasks for the assessment and serve as a quality control when the development of educational tests and credentialing examinations is contracted to test companies. The test specifications
guide the test developers in the production of an assessment consistent
with the important content as identified by professionals in education or
the knowledge, skills, and abilities (KSAs) as identified by subject-matter
experts (SMEs) in a profession. In the instance of an assessment developed in-house for a research study or program evaluation, the development of test specifications reminds the researcher or evaluator of the
various tasks to complete in the design of an assessment prior to its use.

We want to stress that the development of test specifications is completed before any tasks are developed. Writing the test specifications will
provide direction in task development and help you to avoid having to
backtrack when you discover that critical aspects of the assessment were
overlooked in the rush to task construction. Thus in this chapter we
review the design of the test specifications. The actual development of
individual performance tasks for an assessment is the topic of Chapters
3 and 4.

Prior to describing the process of specifying the design, we provide
one additional clarification related to the language used in the literature
to describe the design process. The terms "test framework," "test specifications," and "specifications table" are critical terms used to describe
various aspects of the design process. To promote clarity in the following
discussion, we provide the following definitions.

A test framework provides a description of how the construct or
domain will be represented and "delineates the aspects (e.g., content,
skills, processes, diagnostic features) of the construct or domain to be
measured" (AERA, APA, & NCME, 1999, p. 37). For example, a framework in mathematics would describe the current conceptualization of the
subject area in terms of the traditional topics of numbers and operations,

algebra, geometry, measurement, and data analysis and probability, but the test framework would also include the current expectation that students be able to communicate mathematical ideas orally and in written form (National Council of Teachers of Mathematics [NCTM], 2000). Thus the phrase "test framework" refers to a section of the test design that describes the construct or domain that is the focus of the assessment.

We adopt the Standards (AERA, APA, & NCME, 1999) definition of test specifications:

> A detailed description for a test . . . that specifies the number or proportion of items that assess each content and process/skill area; the format of items, responses, and scoring rubrics and procedures; and the desired psychometric properties of the items and test such as the distribution of item difficulty and discrimination indices. (p. 183)

The *test specifications*, then, provide a description of the test's characteristics and components.

A *table of specifications* lists the test content and specifies the number or percentage of test items that cover each content area. Often the list is a two-way table with content specified as row headers and process skills as column headers (Crocker & Algina, 1986). The table of specifications is but one component of the test specifications.

These terms will assist us as we examine the various aspects of an assessment that should be specified in the design of a test. First steps in the development of an assessment are:

1. Establishing its purpose.

2. Defining a framework that delineates the construct or domain that is the focus of the assessment.

3. Writing specifications for the test content or KSAs and the response formats.

PURPOSE OF THE ASSESSMENT

Design begins with a statement of the test purpose and the delineation of the construct or content domain to be assessed (AERA, APA, & NCME, 1999; Lane & Stone, 2006). For example, assessing students' arts achievement in relation to arts curriculum standards is the purpose of the music and visual arts assessments in the South Carolina Arts Assessment Program (SCAAP) (Yap, Moore, & Peng, 2005). A review of Table 1.1 in Chapter 1 shows some of the varied purposes of tests: improving program services, determining an examinee's qualification for high school graduation, informing admissions decisions at universities, and deciding whether an examinee can demonstrate the fundamental clinical skills essential for safe practice.

Defining the purpose and specifying the nature of the inferences are critical in the development of an assessment (Millman & Greene, 1993). The purpose of the test provides an operational definition of the proposed assessment and guides decisions related to design activities (Downing, 2006). Stemming from test purpose are content definition, methods used to define the content domain, and the hypothesized construct. The test purposes and the intended inferences (e.g., decisions, judgments, predictions) to be made from the test results (i.e., scores) then guide the design of the assessment (AERA, APA, & NCME, 1999).

Credentialing examinations illustrate the purpose of the test guiding its design. The general purpose of credentialing examinations is to assure the public that individuals in a field are qualified to practice in a profession (Raymond, 2001, 2005; Raymond & Neustel, 2006; Wang, Schnipke, & Witt, 2005). For example, in describing the United States Medical Licensing Examination Step 2 Clinical Skills (CS), the Federation of State Medical Boards of the United States and National Board of Medical Examiners (FSMBUS & NBME, 2008) indicate that the patient cases in this clinical examination (i.e., performance assessment) are designed to elicit a process of history taking and physical examination that demonstrates the examinee's ability to list and pursue various plausible diagnoses. The agencies also indicate that the exam assesses whether examinees "can demonstrate the fundamental clinical skills essential for safe and effective patient care under supervision" (p. 10). To gauge whether examinees have the essential skills for safe practice, the design of USMLE Step 2 CS is based on cases in which a medical student interacts with standardized patients. However, first the KSAs essential for safe practice had to be identified and cases developed based on them—a topic discussed later in this chapter.

Writing about the use of essays in licensure examinations in the field of law, Lenel (1990b) emphasizes the importance of establishing the test purpose. She notes that "On bar examinations, the examiner ultimately is concerned about what a score tells about the examinee's competence to practice" (Lenel, 1990a, pp. 19–20). In considering the purpose of the exam and test content, she states, "the bar examiner must consider the kinds of knowledge and skills necessary for the competent practice of law and the level of knowledge or skill that is necessary to protect the public (i.e., what is meant by 'minimal degree of competency')" (Lenel, 1990b, p. 41). In explaining the purpose of licensure examinations in the field of law, Lenel reminds us that the essential knowledge and skills should be delineated and advanced skills should be avoided in a test of minimal competency.

In education, tests are often used to make inferences about the student's (1) mastery of content in curriculum domains, (2) abilities in cognitive domains, and (3) potential in a future criterion setting (Millman & Greene, 1993). Lane (1993) provides an illustration from the curricular domain in her description of a mathematics performance assessment that her team developed to measure program outcomes in QUASAR (Quantitative Understanding: Amplifying Student Achievement and Reasoning). The QUASAR project emphasized higher-level thinking and reasoning in mathematics in a middle school setting. To assess students' development of mathematics competence during their participation in the program, Lane and colleagues developed the QUASAR Cognitive Assessment Instrument (QCAI). Examples of performance tasks included (1) writing a story about a day in a character's life based on a bar graph that depicted the number of hours spent in various activities (e.g., school, sleep, television); (2) describing a pattern and drawing the next iteration; and (3) recommending whether a character should buy a weekly or daily bus pass given a set of conditions. The purpose of these performance tasks was to provide a measure of program outcomes by gauging student gains in higher-level thinking and reasoning in mathematics. The purpose then guided the development of mathematics performance tasks that tap into student reasoning and problem solving.

An example of an educational assessment with a purpose targeted in the cognitive domain is Project STAR (Student Task Assessments and Rubrics). The assessment is a series of performance tasks developed to identify gifted students in underrepresented populations or students not identified by traditional assessments (VanTassel-Baska, Jonson, & Avery, 2002). Students' verbal and nonverbal skills are assessed using an open-ended format. The verbal section includes problem solving, persuasive writing, analogies, verbal relationships, letter puzzles, and verbal reasoning. The nonverbal section includes arithmetic problem solving, number concepts, logic, proportional reasoning, patterns, number theory, spatial reasoning/visualization, spatial patterning, geometry, and transformations. Thus the tasks focus on skills typically associated with the cognitive domain.

Two writing assessments provide an illustration of the use of performance assessments to predict potential in a future criterion setting. The SAT writing section predicts a student's academic performance during the first year in college (Norris, Oppler, Kuang, Day, & Adams, 2006). Also, as part of the GRE, examinees write two analytical essays that can be used in admissions decisions to predict success in program completion (Educational Testing Service, 2002).

To identify the purpose of an assessment, you should ask yourself whether the purpose is examinees' understanding of subject-area content in curriculum domains, their abilities in cognitive domains, or their potential in a future criterion setting. If the assessment is to make decisions about learning outcomes, then what subject areas should be included? Is the purpose of the assessment to gauge minimal competency of examinees to enter a profession? If so, what tasks will inform a decision about an examinee's competence to engage in safe practice? In asking what decisions you intend to make based on the scores, you will identify the test purpose.

As we have seen, in both education and licensure, establishing the purpose of the assessment is a critical first step in the test design. With the purpose established, a next step is to develop a test framework to delineate the construct or domain that is to be assessed.

FRAMEWORK

The purpose of the assessment informs the development of a framework that "delineates the aspects (e.g., content, skills, processes, and diagnostic features) of the construct or domain to be measured" (AERA, APA, & NCME, 1999, p. 37). The description of the domain or construct should clearly establish the dimensions of knowledge, skills, processes, and so on, included in the assessment and the dimensions that are excluded. For example, the NAEP reading assessment framework delineates the construct of reading along two dimensions: context for reading (e.g., reading for literary experience, for information, to perform a task) and aspects of reading (i.e., methods by which readers develop an understanding of text) (Grigg et al., 2003). Understanding of text focuses on examinees' comprehension strategies of forming a general understanding, developing interpretations, making reader–text connections, and examining content and structure. These reading strategies, then, are aspects of the construct of reading.

TABLE 2.1. Content and Cognitive Dimensions of the NAEP Science Assessment

Knowing and doing	Fields of science		
	Earth (30%)	Physical (30%)	Life (40%)
Conceptual understanding (45%)	13.5%	13.5%	18%
Scientific investigation (30%)	9%	9%	12%
Practical reasoning (25%)	7.5%	7.5%	10%

Nature of science (e.g., history of science and technology, the habits of mind, and methods of inquiry and problem solving)

Themes (e.g., systems, models, patterns of change)

Note. Adapted from the National Assessment Governing Board (2004c).

The NAEP science assessment framework conceptualizes understanding of science along content and cognitive dimensions (O'Sullivan et al., 2003). As shown in Table 2.1, the content dimension is represented by three fields of science: earth, physical, and life. The cognitive dimension focuses on three elements of knowing and doing science: conceptual understanding, scientific investigation, and practical reasoning. Also crucial to the NAEP science framework are the overarching domains of the nature of science and themes, which guide development of items that integrate the three fields of science. Thus the development of items and tasks for the science assessment is framed by consideration of (1) the fields of science, (2) the elements of knowing and doing science, (3) the nature of science, and (4) the themes of science.

A clearly articulated theory of learning in the content area should provide the basis for selection of test content and activities (AERA, APA, & NCME, 1999; Webb, 2006). Webb (2006) notes that a behaviorist approach might emphasize specific skills, concepts, and principles, whereas a cognitive approach might emphasize the relationships among skills, concepts, and principles. Thus in developing test specifications, you might consider explicating a theory of learning in the test framework.

Where does one begin to develop a framework? The NAEP assessments and QCAI use the current thinking in the field to identify the dimensions of the constructs of interest. In the design of the framework for the NAEP mathematics assessment, for example, committee members included mathematics educators, mathematicians, curriculum supervisors, university professors, and testing specialists (National Assessment Governing Board [NAGB], 2004a). In developing the QCAI mathematics performance assessment, Lane (1993) describes using the literature in the field and the content standards established by the National Council of Teachers of Mathematics.

An example of a framework from program evaluation is provided by the Even Start program of Lincoln, Nebraska (see Table 1.1). Even Start is a program to help adult participants to develop literacy and parenting skills. Staff and an evaluation specialist used program goals and related literature to frame the portfolio assessment used to evaluate changes in parent and child interactions. Subsequently, staff used this information to improve program services (Johnson, Fisher, et al., 2003).

A final example of a framework is provided by the Oral Clinical Examination administered by the American Board of Pediatric Dentistry (ABPD, 2007). The ABPD uses a performance examination as the capstone event in the board certification of pediatric dentists. The framework for the examination has three dimensions: (1) Data Gathering/Diagnosis, (2) Management/Treatment Planning, and (3) Treatment Variations/Complications. Clinical cases from these three areas are administered by examiners, who use a 4-point analytic rubric to assess responses to cases presented to each candidate for board certification (Penny, 2006).

TEST SPECIFICATIONS

Test specifications are the foundation of the test design process. They describe the characteristics of an appropriate assessment for a content area or domain and include such elements as the content and processes to be assessed, the format of test items, and the number and types of questions to be included (Lane & Stone, 2006; Lenel, 1990b; Raymond, 2001; Roeber, 1996). In essence, specification of the assessment content and processes operationalizes the construct and helps ensure the congruence between intended and actual test-score inferences (Dwyer, 1998; Millman & Greene, 1993), which is an issue of validity.

In writing about performance assessment, Wiley and Haertel (1996) state, "A task specification sets the conditions under which a test performance can take place. It allows a task to be defined in such a way that it can be performed more than one time by more than one person or group" (p. 75). Consistent with such a description is the information provided to examinees about the United States Medical Licensing Examination: Step 2 Clinical Skills. Test developers inform examinees that the cases in Step 2 Clinical Skills are based on an examination blueprint (Federation of State Medical Boards of the United States & National Board of Medical Examiners, 2008). The test developers note that

> an examination blueprint [specifications] defines the requirements for each examination, regardless of where and when it is administered. The sample of cases selected for each examination reflects a balance of cases that is fair and equitable across all examinees. On any examination day, the set of cases will differ from the combination presented the day before or the following day, but each set of cases has a comparable degree of difficulty. (p. 4)

Note that both Wiley and Haertel (1996) and the developers of the United States Medical Licensing Examination: Step 2 Clinical Skills present the task specifications in terms of consistency of testing across conditions. Such a role for test specifications is consistent with the Standards statement that the specifications guide the development of parallel tests (i.e., interchangeable forms of a test) and short forms of a test (AERA, APA, & NCME, 1999) in that the specifications define a task in such a manner that it can be performed across comparable conditions, such as across parallel forms.

Test specifications are critical in the design of performance assessments due to their more heterogeneous format than selected-response questions (Haertel & Linn, 1996). Haertel and Linn note that "more detailed specifications are called for because there is more to specify. Timing, materials, specific administration instructions and conditions, and other aspects of performance exercises are more variable than for multiple-choice questions" (p. 72).

Various benefits accrue from the development of test specifications. Test specifications guide item writers, frame the review and classification of items by SMEs, and assist test personnel in maintaining continuity in test content and difficulty over time and parallel forms (Raymond, 2001; Raymond & Neustel, 2006). If made public (e.g., posted on a website or printed in test registration materials), test specifications inform educators and examinees of test content. Also, specifications in the development of performance assessments ensure that the tasks systematically represent the dimensions of interest (AERA, APA, & NCME, 1999). The specifications assure more comprehensive coverage of the domain, provide logical and empirical evidence of the degree to which the task and scoring criteria reflect the skills and processes specified by the domain definition, and contribute validity evidence.

Elements of Test Specifications

The elements of test specifications will be as diverse as the types of assessments used in education, credentialing, program evaluation, and research. However, a heuristic for generating the elements for the test specifications for any given assessment is to consider the stages in the development of an assessment: defining content/KSAs for a given examinee population, developing items and tasks, administering the examination, scoring and reporting, and reviewing the psychometric properties of the instrument. We use this structure to discuss the various elements to consider in developing test specifications.

Table 2.2 presents an outline of many of the elements that should be considered in developing a test specification. The table could be converted to a checklist to guide the design of an assessment. However, the list should not be considered exhaustive; it would likely require additional specifications for preparation to develop a large-scale test. Also, in the case of a program evaluation or research study, the list likely overspecifies the aspects of an assessment and any irrelevant aspects would be trimmed.

Defining Content/KSAs and the Examinee Population

As shown in Table 2.2, test specifications include a list of the subject-area content or KSAs that are the focus of the assessment (AERA, APA, & NCME, 1999; Downing, 2006; Lenel, 1990b; Millman & Greene, 1993; Raymond, 2001). We elaborate on issues to consider in specifying content and KSAs.

Examinee Characteristics. Because the purpose of a test is typically to determine the understanding of a particular group of examinees, part of the identification of subject-area content and KSAs is the description of the examinee population. The content of a science examination for students in second grade will differ from the content of a science examination for students in eighth grade. Similarly, the KSAs that guide the

TABLE 2.2. Elements of Test Specifications Organized by the Stages in Test Development

<hr>

Defining content/KSAs

- Characteristics of the examinees (e.g., grade level, profession, primary language spoken)
- Subject matter (content)
- Skills (process)
- Distribution of items by subject and/or skills in a table of specifications
- Requirement of parallel forms

Developing tasks

- Number of items/tasks
- Time allotment for each task
- Parallel forms
- Response format (e.g., essay, work sample, portfolio)
- Stimulus materials (e.g., reading passages, facsimiles of historical documents, bar graphs, standardized patients)
- Contexts (i.e., "real-world" settings for tasks)
- Equipment (e.g., levers and pulleys for science, stethoscopes for clinical examinations)
- Physical environment (computer-based or Internet test; mock ambulatory clinic)
- Reading level of tasks
- Test-format accommodations (e.g., Braille, large print, tapes)
- Task shells
- Format of the assessment (e.g., test booklet, portfolio packaging)
- Sample materials and scoring criteria for examinees

Administering the test

- Manuals for test administrator and examiners
- Training materials for standardized patients
- General test directions for the examinees (e.g., allowable resources, such as calculators; time per section; scheduled breaks)
- Test dates
- Number of sessions and testing time
- Administrative accommodations (e.g., length of testing session, private room, transcriber)
- Technological support (e.g., computers, video cameras)

Scoring and reporting

- Training and scoring facilities—on site or remote
- Rater qualifications (e.g., education level, subject-matter expertise, score on a raters' qualifying test)
- Criteria for evaluating examinee performance
- Types of scoring guides (i.e., checklist, analytic rubric, holistic rubric)
- Weighting of items/tasks
- Type of score interpretation—normative or criterion-referenced
- Type of scores (composite, scale, performance levels)
- Interpretive guides for test users (e.g., examinees, credentialing board members, teachers)
- Timeline for reporting scores

(continued)

TABLE 2.2. *(continued)*

Reviewing psychometric properties
- Item/task properties (e.g., difficulty and discrimination)
- Interrater reliability
- Score reliability
- Equating
- Validity

Note. Summarized from AERA, APA, and NCME (1999); Downing (2006); Haertel & Linn (1996); International Test Commission (2006); Lane (1993); Lane and Stone (2006); Lenel (1990b); Millman and Greene (1993); MPR Associates (1997); Reckase (1997); and Stecher et al. (2000).

development of a licensure examination for registered nurses will differ from the KSAs that frame the development of an examination for licensed practical nurses. Given that item writers use test specifications for developing items and tasks appropriate for a specific examinee population, describing the examinees is important.

Also important for test developers to consider are examinee characteristics unrelated to the identified test purpose and content but that might affect examinees' performance on the test (Millman & Greene, 1993). One example is the short attention span of young children because such an examinee characteristic requires developers to attend to the test length. By describing the examinee population in the specifications, test developers can attend to the appropriateness of the content and other test characteristics for the particular examinee population. Because the procedure for identifying the important content or KSAs differs for education and credentialing examinations, we discuss them separately in the following two sections.

Content Specifications for Educational Assessments. When developing items for an educational assessment, testing programs at state departments of education use the content standards identified for a given subject area. Content standards are statements of what students should know and be able to do (International Reading Association [IRA] & National Council of Teachers of English [NCTE], 1996; Roeber, 1996; Webb, 2006). For example, a standard related to writing is:

Students apply knowledge of language structure, language conventions (e.g., spelling and punctuation), media techniques, figurative language, and genre to create, critique, and discuss print and nonprint texts. (IRA & NCTE, 1996, p. 3)

Identification of key content is accomplished by convening committees that include teachers in the content area, curriculum specialists, politicians, and educational policymakers (IRA & NCTE, 1996; Jaeger, Mullis, Bourque, & Shakrani, 1996; National Council of Teachers of Mathematics [NCTM], 2000). In the instance of the English language arts standards, the IRA and the NCTE included in this process the staff from both organizations; members of both organizations, including teachers, administrators, and university professors; chairs of the Black and Latino organizational caucuses; representatives and reading specialists at state departments of education; representatives of literacy organizations; and staff from testing companies, such as the Educational Testing Service and American College Testing Program.

The work of national organizations, such as the NCTE and NCTM, inform the development of the content standards for state curriculum and assessment, as well as the identification of content for assessments developed for research and program evaluation. As an example from research and evaluation, in the development of the QCAI to gauge student competence in mathematics, Lane (1993) and her colleagues used the following NCTM content standards: "making connections, understanding concepts and procedures, becoming a mathematical problem solver, learning to reason mathematically, and learning to communicate mathematical ideas" (p. 17). The performance tasks that they developed required students to problem-solve, reason, and communicate mathematically.

At the state level teachers, administrators, subject-area coordinators, and professors elaborate on the national standards to develop content standards that are approved by the state legislature (Webb, 2006). An example is the following from the English language arts standards in South Carolina. The expectation is that students in high school English will

> E1-1.3 Interpret devices of figurative language (including extended metaphor, oxymoron, and paradox). (South Carolina Department of Education, 2007, p. 77)

Thus, as in the national standards, high school students in South Carolina are expected to be able to evaluate an author's use of figurative language. Examples of content standards in art, history, mathematics, science, and writing from other states are shown in Table 3.1 and Figures 3.2 and 4.1. Additional examples of content standards can be found on websites of state departments of education.

KSA Specifications for Credentialing Examinations. In licensure testing, advisory committees of SMEs in a professional field collaborate with testing specialists to identify the tasks and define the KSAs needed for safe, effective practice (AERA, APA, & NCME, 1999, p. 156). Practice (i.e., job) analyses provide the basis for the identification of tasks important to a field and these tasks are reviewed for the KSAs required for competent performance. The KSAs subsequently become the basis for the test specifications for a licensure or certification examination, whether written examinations, simulations, or performance assessments (Kane, 1997; Raymond, 2005).

The purpose of the practice analysis is to provide an overall description of patterns of professional practice and describe the patterns across diverse clients, work settings, and activities within those settings. Wang and colleagues (2005) provide the following common core of procedures in practice analyses:

1. Ask subject matter experts (SMEs) to identify a list of job tasks or activities performed at work and to define the test content domain of the profession. The tasks/activities may also be grouped in terms of the test content areas.

2. Develop a survey questionnaire using the list of tasks/activities.

3. Select a representative sample of practitioners in the profession to respond to the survey.

4. Have the survey respondents rate each task in terms of separate aspects of the task, such as frequency of performance, criticality to public protection, difficulty of learning, and necessity at time of initial licensure/certification.

5. Analyze the survey data and determine the relative importance of these tasks.

6. Use the resulting quantitative measures of task importance to develop test specifications delineating the content [KSAs] to be assessed and the relative weight each content area should receive. (pp. 15–16)

In this manner, linkage is established between the KSAs in the test specifications and the tasks that professionals identify in the practice analysis as being important for competent practice. Such linkage provides support for the validity of credentialing decisions based on the examination scores.

Kane (1997) describes a model-based practice analysis to inform the development of the KSAs for the test specifications. Building on the work of LaDuca (1994), Kane (1997) proposes the use of an a priori practice model to structure the data collection and analysis required to identify the KSAs for a profession. Development of the practice model begins with SMEs generating a working hypothesis of patterns of practice based on prior research and experts' experiences; this step appears consistent with step 1 above. A model can be developed that describes practitioners' responsibilities through identification of (1) the work setting, (2) activities within the work setting, and (3) the KSAs (i.e., competency categories) required to perform the activities. The dimensions of the contextual effects of work setting and activities within those settings are important because professional duties are likely to be specific within a setting (LaDuca, 2006; Raymond, 2002; Wang, Witt, & Schnipke, 2006). For example, the responsibilities of a registered nurse are likely to vary across the settings of a doctor's office, a hospital ward, and a clinic. Indicating the need to consider context in the development of practice analysis, a study of contextual effects in a practice analysis for physician assistants revealed that the importance of knowledge and skills varied according to patient acuity (e.g., acute limited, chronic progressive, life-threatening emergency) (De Champlain & LaDuca, 2007).

These categories of setting, activities, and KSAs provide a framework for a survey, as described in step 2 above, to obtain information about the KSAs required to competently perform the activities in work-related settings. In the survey each competency category is accompanied by a scale that might address frequency (i.e., task performed not at all, monthly, weekly, daily), criticality (i.e., inappropriate performance of task will result in little or no harm, moderate harm, serious harm), and importance (i.e., overall the task is not at all important, of slight importance, moderately important, absolutely essential) (Raymond, 2001, 2002; Raymond & Neustel, 2006). These scales allow the developers to gauge the importance of each competence and weight them accordingly when developing the test specifications.

Raymond and Neustel (2006) provide an example of a task statement from a practice analysis in radiography quality management. The task statement, Determine optimal temperature for film processor, is accompanied by three scales: (1) Not Responsible for This Task, (2) Frequency (Yearly, Monthly, Weekly, Daily), and (3) Importance (Low, Moderate, High). In the instance of a task for which a practitioner was not responsible, he would fill in the bubble in the Not Responsible column and move to the next task statement. If the task were a responsibility of a practitioner, then she would also mark the appropriate column under the Frequency and Importance scales.

A practice analysis (e.g., survey of practitioners) is completed, as described in steps 3 and 4 above, and the data confirm or disconfirm aspects of the model (Kane, 1997). Based on the data, the practice model is refined and the final model is used to translate the practice analysis results and the competency categories into test specifications (see steps 4 and 5).

Table of Specifications. In educational and credentialing examinations, a table of specifications is used to organize the content or KSAs into categories. The table indicates the number or percentage of items to be allocated to each content area or KSA area and the number or percentage of items to assess process skills (Crocker & Algina, 1986; Downing, 2006). The distribution of items should be congruent with the conceptualization of the domain or construct (Millman & Greene, 1993). An example of translating content standards into a table of specifications is provided by the NAEP science assessment. As shown in the table of specifications in Table 2.1, the science assessment specifies both a content dimension (Fields of Science) and cognitive dimension (Knowing and Doing) (National Assessment Governing Board, 2004c). The types of items and tasks to be written are defined by the juncture of the two dimensions.

The target time was also specified for the components of these two dimensions. For example, with conceptual understanding allocated 45% of the testing time and life sciences allocated 40%, then the time allocation for items relating to conceptual understanding in the life sciences would be 18% (i.e., 45% × 40% = 18%).

Integration of the fields of science was addressed by the incorporation of the nature of science and the themes of science into the specifications table. These aspects of science then guided the writing of items and tasks. Figure 2.1 provides an example of a task that NAEP classified as assessing examinees' practical reasoning in the physical sciences. Practical reasoning requires examinees to use and apply science understanding in new, real-world applications (O'Sullivan et al., 2003).

Parallel Forms. Requirements for parallel forms of the assessment should also be stipulated. Parallel forms of an assessment are constructed with the same specifications table; thus the tasks within the assessments address the same content and processes. However, the items and tasks in the parallel forms will be variations of the problems. For example, in one form of a social studies performance assessment, students might be asked to describe the factors that contributed to a conflict in Korea, the

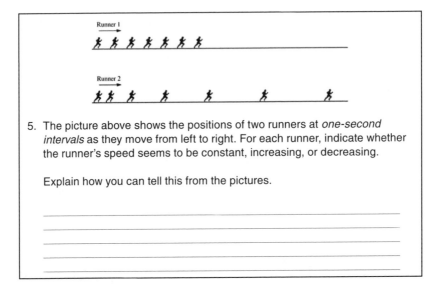

5. The picture above shows the positions of two runners at *one-second intervals* as they move from left to right. For each runner, indicate whether the runner's speed seems to be constant, increasing, or decreasing.

   Explain how you can tell this from the pictures.

FIGURE 2.1. NAEP science item classified as physical science and practical reasoning. From the National Center for Education Statistics (2005).

Persian Gulf, or Vietnam. In a parallel form of the assessment, the task might offer the students the option of writing about causes of a conflict in China, Cuba, or Rwanda. Thus the assessment focuses on similar content and process skills, but uses variations on the problems.

Parallel forms, then, are useful in pre- and posttest situations in research studies and program evaluations. Administration of parallel forms reduces the possibility that any change in scores is attributable to examinee familiarity with the test. Parallel forms also serve a security purpose in credentialing examinations and other high-stakes tests in that no one test is readministered every time, making it more difficult for examinees to learn the exact items on the test. If parallel forms are required, this affects other aspects of the specifications, such as the number of tasks to be developed and the need for equating scores across test forms, so specifying the development of parallel forms should be an early consideration.

Developing Tasks

The specifications also describe the types of tasks that are appropriate to assess the content and KSAs relevant to a field (Downing, 2006; Millman

& Greene, 1993). Aspects of tasks to specify include the response formats, such as performance tasks, portfolios, multiple-choice, or some combination of formats (AERA, APA, & NCME, 1999). Ask yourself, "To assess the cognitive skills and content, will multiple-choice alone suffice? Will examinees only respond by essay or will they need to demonstrate the execution of a skill? Should the assessment be a mix of multiple-choice and performances? How many items will be required?" The NAEP reading assessment, for example, included multiple-choice, short constructed-response, and extended constructed-response items (Grigg et al., 2003).

Figure 2.2 provides an example of the specification of content, number of items, and item format. To gauge student understanding in the visual arts, the South Carolina Arts Assessment Program (SCAAP)

Table of Specifications for Visual Arts Content Standards

Content Standard	Percentages
1. Understanding and Applying Media, Techniques, and Processes	15%
2. Using Knowledge of Structures and Functions	25%
3. Choosing and Evaluating a Range of Subject Matter, Symbols, and Ideas	15%
4. Understanding the Visual Arts in Relation to History and Cultures	15%
5. Reflecting upon and Assessing the Merits of Their Work and the Work of Others	20%
6. Making Connections between Visual Arts and Other Disciplines	10%

Visual Arts Assessment Test Specifications

Item Type	Number of Items	Points per Item	Total Points per Item Type
Multiple choice	45	1	45
Performance Task	2	3 for Task 1 3 for Task 2a 3 for Task 2b	9

FIGURE 2.2. Specifications for the SCAAP Visual Arts Assessment. From Yap, Moore, and Peng (2005). Reproduced with permission from the South Carolina Arts Assessment Program.

administers both multiple-choice and performance tasks: 45 Web-based, multiple-choice items and two performance tasks (Yap et al., 2005). The specifications table in Figure 2.2 provides the targeted percentages of items for each content standard. At the bottom of Figure 2.2 is the allocation of items according to response formats.

The South Carolina visual arts standards adopt the national standards (Music Educators National Conference, 1994) and elaborate on them. This is consistent with our earlier observation that state standards often build on the work of national organizations. Notice that the SCAAP table of specifications has a column labeled Content Standard but does not designate a process dimension (e.g., analyze, apply). This is because the South Carolina standards incorporate the cognitive process into the standards. For example, in the visual arts, the high school standard Using Knowledge of Structures and Functions indicates that students will

> Identify and describe the interrelationships among the elements and principles of design that communicate a variety of artistic perspectives and purposes.
>
> A. Create artworks that use appropriate structures and functions to solve specific visual arts problems.
> B. Evaluate the effectiveness of artworks in terms of structure and function. (South Carolina Department of Education [SCDE], 2003, p. 137)

Thus the standards integrate content with process skills, such as "create" and "evaluate," and a separate dimension is not required in the specifications table.

In considering the number of tasks to specify for an assessment, a body of research into task score variance indicates that an examinee's performance is task specific—that is, an examinee's score will not closely predict his or her score on another task. In other words, an examinee's score is likely to vary from one task to another (e.g., Brennan & Johnson, 1995; Dunbar et al., 1991; Gao, Shavelson, & Baxter, 1994; Linn & Burton, 1994; Shavelson et al., 1993; Webb, Schlackman, & Sugre, 2000). This poses a problem because we generally are interested in making decisions about examinees' likely performance across similar tasks, not on any one specific task. For example, when an English faculty member uses a writing sample to place a student in an entry-level writing class, the faulty member considers the sample to be reflective of the student's general writing ability. However, as we noted above, making a decision on one specific task (e.g., a writing sample) is risky because another writing sample might differ in quality and the decision for placement would be different. For this reason, when additional writing assessments appear to show greater competence, then changing a student's placement to a more advanced class (Smith, 1993) appears to be a reasonable option.

To address the specificity problem, if an assessment uses only performance tasks, then multiple tasks are required for score reliability. For example, in the field of credentialing, Wolfe and Gitomer (2001) report that the 10 exercises associated with the NBPTS Early Childhood/Generalist assessment produced reasonably reliable examinee scores. In education, in a study of performance-based science tasks for the California Assessment Program, nine tasks scored by one rater produced reliable scores (Brennan & Johnson, 1995). Thus in an assessment composed only of performance tasks, 9–10 tasks may be required for examinees' scores to be reliable.

Due to the considerable variability of performance of an examinee across tasks, Dunbar and colleagues (1991) stress the importance of traditional content specifications for performance assessments because in order to make an inference to a domain, the sampling of tasks must take into consideration task specificity. That is, if only one task is used to assess examinee performance, the score probably reflects an examinee's skills on that particular task. However if several tasks are used, or the assessment is a combination of multiple-choice, constructed-response, and performance tasks, then the examinee's score is likely to generalize to the construct or domain. Messick (1994), for example, indicates that domain coverage in performance assessment can be improved by combining briefer, structured exercises with extended performance tasks.

Specifications can provide guidance for task development by including item shells. An item shell is a hollow item that provides a framework for generating similar items (Haladyna & Shindoll, 1989; Solano-Flores, Jovanovic, Shavelson, & Bachman, 1999). Originally developed as a systematic method for writing multiple-choice items (Haladyna, 2004), shells have been applied in the development of science performance tasks (Solano-Flores et al., 1999; Stecher et al., 2000).

Figure 2.3 provides an example of a shell for developing persuasive writing prompts. The directions will be the same across prompts. The elements that will change are the *Writing Situation* and the *Directions for Writing*. An example of a potential *Writing Situation* and the *Directions for Writing* for a prompt are shown in Figure 2.4.

ITEM SHELL

Persuasive Writing Topic

Writing Situation

Four to six sentences that present an issue in a recognizable, meaningful context and that provide both sides of the issue.

The final sentence presents an audience and cues the writer to begin thinking about the issue and taking a side.

Directions for Writing

Two to three sentences that remind the writer of the issue and audience and to provide support for the position the writer takes on the issue. A format (letter, speech, essay) is suggested.

Student Writing Checklist for Persuasive Writing

Prepare Yourself to Write

☐ Read the Writing Situation and Directions for Writing carefully.

☐ Brainstorm for ideas.

☐ Consider how to address your audience.

☐ Decide what ideas to include and how to organize them.

☐ Write only in English.

Make Your Paper Meaningful

☐ Use your knowledge and/or personal experiences that are related to the topic.

☐ Express a clear point of view.

☐ Fully support your argument with specific details, examples, and convincing reasons.

☐ Include an appeal to logic and/or emotions.

☐ Present your ideas in a clear and logical order.

☐ Stay on topic.

Make Your Paper Interesting to Read

☐ Use examples and details that would be convincing to your audience.

☐ Use appropriate voice that shows your interest in the topic.

☐ Use precise, descriptive, vivid words.

☐ Vary the type, structure, and length of your sentences.

☐ Use effective transitions.

(continued)

FIGURE 2.3. An example of a task shell for a persuasive writing prompt.

> **Edit and Revise Your Paper**
>
> ☐ Consider rearranging your ideas and changing words to make your paper more effective.
>
> ☐ Add information or details to make your paper complete.
>
> ☐ Proofread your paper for usage, punctuation, capitalization, and spelling.

FIGURE 2.3. *(continued)*

In order to include task shells in the specifications, the shells must first be developed. In the case of multiple-choice items, Haladyna (2004) recommends basing the shell on a previously developed item that performed appropriately. He suggests underlining the keywords or phrases that represent the content of the item. Next, variations for each keyword or phrase is identified. Such a process is applied in Figure 2.5 to two seventh-grade performance tasks previously field-tested for the South Carolina Palmetto Achievement Challenge Test (Creighton, 2006). The science item was developed to assess the following content standards:

a. design a scientific investigation

b. select appropriate tools to perform tests

> **PERSUASIVE WRITING TOPIC**
>
> **Writing Situation**
> The issue of censoring or banning books has received much national attention. Recently, however, the controversy became a local issue when parents in your community objected to a book that their teenager had obtained from the high school library. The parents' campaign to have the book removed permanently from the library has aroused mixed reactions from students, teachers, and other parents. Decide how you feel about the issue of banning books.
>
> **Directions for Writing**
> Write a letter to the editor of the school newspaper in which you either defend a parent's right to have a book banned or oppose such a ban. Clearly state your position. Try to convince readers of the paper to agree with you by providing well-developed supporting arguments.

FIGURE 2.4. An example of a *Writing Situation* and *Directions for Writing* for a persuasive writing prompt. Reproduced from permission from the Georgia Department of Education (2001).

Science Items	
A student wants to demonstrate the process of condensation. Describe a demonstration that could be performed. Be sure to include:	A student wants to demonstrate the effect of temperature on the rate of dissolving. Describe a demonstration that could be performed. Be sure to include:
• the materials to be used to perform the demonstration,	• the materials to be used to perform the demonstration,
• the hypothesis, and	• the hypothesis, and
• the steps to follow during the demonstration.	• the steps to follow during the demonstration.
Materials: _____	Materials: _____
Hypothesis: _____	Hypothesis: _____
Steps: _____	Steps: _____

Social Studies Items	
Each of the following world regions was a "hot spot" in the 1900s.	Each of the following world regions was a "hot spot" in the 1900s.
• Israel	• China
• The Korean Peninsula	• Cuba
• Vietnam	• Japan
• The Persian Gulf	• Rwanda
Select one world region from the list and answer the following three questions about conflict in that area.	Select one world region from the list and answer the following three questions about conflict in that area.
a. Identify the area you selected and summarize the conflict that occurred.	a. Identify the area you selected and summarize tthe conflict that occurred.
b. In your summary, identify the major participants in the conflict.	b. In your summary, identify the major participants in the conflict.
c. Explain the historical reasons for the conflict.	c. Explain the historical reasons for the conflict.
d. Explain why the conflict has had a major effect on the rest of the world.	d. Explain why the conflict has had a major effect on the rest of the world.

FIGURE 2.5. Examples of task shells for generating similar items. Adapted by permission from the South Carolina Department of Education.

c. state hypotheses in ways that include the independent and dependent variables

d. use written expression to communicate scientific procedures. (SCDE, 2000a, pp. 42–43)

Rather than have students demonstrate their understanding of the scientific process by writing the method for demonstrating the process of condensation, students could be asked to write about demonstrating the effect of temperature on the rate of dissolving. Other possibilities include writing about the scientific method for demonstrating the process of evaporation or studying the effect of magnetism on motion.

The social studies item was developed to assess the following standard, "The learner will demonstrate an understanding of the politics and social developments of world regions. The student should be able to analyze the causes and consequences of world conflicts" (SCDE, 2000b, p. 45). Changing the names of the countries allows the test developer to sample students' understanding of politics and social development in a different set of world regions.

Other considerations in developing tasks include the types of stimulus materials (e.g., authentic reading passages [MPR Associates, 1997]); the reading level of the tasks (Stecher et al., 2000); time allotments for each task; the packaging of the assessment (e.g., test booklet, portfolio container); the equipment required to complete each task (e.g., audiotapes); and the physical environment (e.g., ambulatory clinic setting, testing centers with computers). Development of sample tasks must be specified if testing agencies plan to give examinees sample materials to familiarize themselves with the assessment, as recommended in the Standards (AERA, APA, & NCME, 1999). Also, the legal requirements of the Americans with Disabilities Act (ADA), passed by Congress in 1990 to prohibit discrimination against persons with disabilities (Duhl & Duhl, 2004), require that specifications address accommodations in the test format, such as Braille, large print, or audiotapes.

Administration

In developing the test specifications, you should also delineate the various components in the administration of the assessment (see Table 2.2). The specifications should establish test dates, the number of sessions, and testing time. General directions for examinees about completing the test, such as the time allocated for a section or the use of calculators, must be specified and developed. The preceding information will then be incorporated into the administration manuals for test administrators and examiners. Administrative accommodations to meet ADA requirements, such as use of extended test sessions or transcribers, also should be addressed. Finally, the types of technological assistance for computers and other equipment must be established for computer-based tests and clinical examinations.

Scoring and Reporting

Test specifications also address the scoring of the assessment and reporting of scores (Downing, 2006; Webb, 2006). Whether training and scoring will be conducted on-site or via the Internet must be specified. Also, the qualifications of the raters should be specified. Must raters be college graduates or is a high school degree acceptable? Do you require raters to be SMEs?

The criteria to be used in the scoring guides to evaluate examinee performance must be specified and be consistent with the test framework (AERA, APA, & NCME 1999; Millman & Greene, 1993). The types of scoring guides (e.g., checklist, analytic rubric, holistic rubric) and number of performance levels require specification. The guide used by NAEP to score the physical science item is shown in Figure 2.6. Notice that only four levels of performance were described. The number of performance levels used in analytic and holistic scoring guides is typically 4 or 6 and must be specified.

As an example of the relation between test purpose and specification of scoring method, recall the portfolio assessment for the Even Start family literacy program (see Table 1.1). In deciding the scoring method, program staff discussed that a holistic rubric, which requires that raters consider all aspects of literacy simultaneously and award one overall score, fit philosophically with their integrated view of family literacy (Johnson, Fisher, et al., 2003). They also considered that one purpose of the portfolio assessment was for program improvement. Program improvement, however, required an analytic rubric to provide detailed information about program strengths and weaknesses. The program staff reached consensus on the use of both rubrics, resulting in the two-stage scoring system in which raters first determined a proficiency level for each goal on the analytic rubric. In the second stage, raters reviewed the descriptions of the four proficiency levels (described on the holistic rubric) and then assigned a holistic score to the portfolio.

The specification of the types of scores is required. Here test developers should consider any weighting of items or tasks, the type of score

---

Scoring Guide

Score and Description

Complete
Student correctly indicates that Runner 1 has a constant speed (or moves at a steady pace) because equal distances are covered each second, and that Runner 2's speed is increasing because increasing distances are covered in each successive second (spacing increases).

Essential
Student correctly indicates the speed of Runner 1 (constant or moves at a steady pace) and Runner 2 (increasing), and gives a correct explanation for one of the runners.

Partial
Student correctly indicates the speed of Runner 1 (constant or moves at a steady pace), and Runner 2 (increasing) but gives no explanation.
OR
Student response correctly indicates speed of one runner with explanation.

Unsatisfactory/Incorrect
Student indicates no or only one correct speed.

FIGURE 2.6. Scoring guide used in rating the physical science item reasoning. From the National Center for Education Statistics, U.S. Department of Education (2005).

interpretation (i.e., normative or criterion referenced), and types of scores (e.g., composite, scale, proficiency). For example, the Georgia High School Writing Test weights the domain of Ideas 40% and the domains of Conventions, Style, and Organization each 20% in calculating a final score (Georgia Department of Education, 2007). Also, the specifications should establish a timeline for scoring and reporting the test results.

Reviewing Psychometric Properties

The psychometric properties of the assessment also require specification (AERA, APA, & NCME, 1999; Millman & Greene, 1993; Reckase, 1997; Webb, 2006). Properties to specify at the item or task level include the difficulty and discrimination levels, differential item functioning levels, and interrater reliability. At the test level, properties to specify include score reliability, equating methods, and types of validity evidence. These topics will be discussed in detail in Chapters 9 and 10.

ADVISORY COMMITTEES

Interwoven throughout all the discussions about the design of an assessment is the role of advisory committees. Preparations for the development of an assessment should begin with the selection of members of advisory committees. More than one committee is required because committee members will provide different kinds of expertise and will serve various constituencies in the test development process. An advisory committee will identify important content and skills for inclusion in the assessment. A committee of measurement specialists will provide technical advice about the components of the assessment. Yet another committee might serve to review the tasks for alignment with the test purpose, their technical quality (e.g., clarity of instruction, lack of ambiguity, absence of irrelevance), and absence of bias in tasks and scoring rubrics (Lane, 1993). For example, in licensure, SMEs identify relevant tasks or KSAs to include on a survey for a practice analysis. When survey results are tabulated, SMEs interpret the information and make decisions about the critical KSAs to include in the test specifications (Wang et al., 2005).

In educational testing, advisory members have included teachers, curriculum specialists, state supervisors, administrators, parents, cognitive psychologists, and university faculty (MPR Associates, 1997; Millman & Greene, 1993; National Assessment Governing Board, 2004a, 2004b). Other advisory members included representatives of subject-area associations, business and industry, government, and unions. Also included were members of the public and private education sectors.

Using external experts to review the specifications serves to assure content quality and representativeness (AERA, APA, & NCME, 1999). Such a review provides evidence that the test items and scoring criteria represent the defined domain and test specifications. Panels may be used to classify items and scoring criteria according to categories on the test specifications. In addition, the work of advisory committees can be informed by a technical advisory group with expertise in measurement (MPR Associates, 1997).

The inclusion of individuals from defined populations with a stake in the assessment is critical in the recruitment and selection of committee members (AERA, APA, & NCME, 1999; Bond, Moss, & Carr,

1996). Bond and colleagues (1996) indicate that diversity of committee members is crucial throughout test design: specification of the content framework, development and review of tasks, and construction of valid and reliable scoring methods. They advise that committee members represent different cultures, ethnic groups, and social backgrounds. Diversity is critical in the development of specifications for a performance assessment because the specification process is the first source for bias in an assessment. Bond and colleagues (1996) note that in the development of an arts assessment, "individuals of different racial, ethnic, or gender groups will probably vary substantially in their opinions about what range of content should be included for an arts assessment; what performance tasks should be included; and how the scoring should be developed and applied" (p. 120).

DOCUMENTATION

The specifications for the design of a test provide documentation to support the validity of the assessment. The *Standards* note that in licensure examination,

> when the validation rests in part on the appropriateness of test content, the procedures followed in specifying and generating test content should be described and justified in reference to the construct the test is intended to measure or the domain it is intended to represent. If the definition of the content sampled incorporates criteria, such as importance, frequency, or criticality, these criteria should also be clearly explained and justified. (AERA , APA, & NCME, 1999, p. 18)

Downing (2006) reminds us of the need for test design to be systematic when he writes, "All of these details must be well executed to produce a test that estimates examinee achievement or ability fairly and consistently in the content domain purported to be measured by the test and *to provide documented evidence in support of test score inferences*" (p. 3; emphasis added).

The procedures described in this chapter will help you design an assessment plan that will serve as one form of validity evidence for score interpretation. Checklist 2.1 provides a summary of procedures that, if completed, will contribute to an assessment that supports valid inferences about examinees.

FURTHER READINGS

International Test Commission. (2006). International guidelines on computer-based and internet-delivered testing. *International Journal of Testing, 6*(2), 143–171.

Provides guidelines for the design and delivery of computer-based and Internet tests. Guidelines are targeted to test developers, test publishers, and test users. The guidelines can be downloaded at *www.intestcom.org/guidelines/.*

Raymond, M. (2005). An NCME module on developing and administering practice analysis questionnaires. *Educational Measurement: Issues and Practice, 24*(2), 29–41.

Outlines the procedures involved in developing and administering practice analysis surveys. Also discusses data analysis methods that are useful for practice analyses.

Chapter Questions

1. Review Table 2.2. If an arts assessment required analysis of paintings, in which section would you indicate that permissions to use paintings are required?

2. Figure 2.7 is from the technical documents for the South Carolina Arts Assessment Program.

   a. Is this an example of a test framework, test specifications, or table of specifications?

   b. Which area requires the fewest items to be developed?

   c. Which area requires the most items to be developed?

3. Many states have been developing alternative assessments for students with disabilities for whom the usual state assessment is not appropriate. Who should be included on the advisory committees?

Content Standard	Percentages for Multiple-Choice Items
1. Singing: Singing, alone and with others, a varied repertoire of music	Performance Task
2. Playing Instruments: Playing instruments alone and with others	0% (not included)
3. Improvisation: Improvising melodies, variations, and accompaniments	Performance Task
4. Composition: Composing and arranging music within specified guidelines	10%
5. Reading and Notating: Reading and notating music	30%
6. Analysis: Listening to, analyzing, and describing music	25%
7. Evaluation: Evaluating music and music performances	15%
8. Connections: Understanding relationships between music, the other arts, and disciplines outside the arts	5%
9. History and Culture: Understanding music in relation to history and culture	15%

FIGURE 2.7. Document from the SCAAP Music Assessment. From *Technical Documentation for the South Carolina Arts Assessment Program (SCAAP) Year 3: 4th-grade music and visual arts assessments* (2005). Adapted with permission from the South Carolina Arts Assessment Program.

CHECKLIST 2.1

Completed	To-Do List for Designing an Assessment
✓	Identify the purpose of the assessment (e.g., specify the decisions that will be made with the assessment). pp. 28–31
	Develop a framework that describes the construct or domain of interest. pp. 31–33
	Test Specifications
	Content and Knowledge, Skills, and Abilities
	Describe examinee characteristics (e.g., age, education level). pp. 35–37
	Work with expert committees to establish the important content standards or KSAs that are the focus of the assessment. pp. 37–41
	Develop a table of specifications that indicates the distribution of items by content and processes. p. 41
	Indicate requirement for parallel forms. pp. 41–42
	Task Features
	Describe the types of tasks (e.g., performance tasks, portfolios, multiple-choice items) that are appropriate for assessing the content standards or KSAs. pp. 42–44
	Describe task features (e.g., stimulus materials, reading level, equipment, time allotment, ADA accommodations). p. 49
	Determine the number of items to be developed. pp. 44–45
	Develop task shells to provide frameworks to guide item writers in the construction of performance tasks. pp. 45–49
	Administration
	Specify manuals for test administrators, examiners, proctors, and other test staff. pp. 49–50
	Specify development of general test directions (e.g., time per section, allowable resources, such as calculators) for the examinees. p. 49
	Establish test dates, testing time, and number of sessions. p. 49
	Describe technological support. p. 50
	Specify ADA administrative accommodations (e.g., extended testing session, private room). p. 50

(continued)

		Scoring and Reporting
		Describe any weighting of items in the determination of the overall test score. p. 50
		State the types of scores (e.g., composite, scale) and score interpretation. pp. 50–51
		Establish the timeline for scoring and reporting. p. 51
		Describe rater qualifications (e.g., education level, subject-matter expertise). p. 50
		Specify criteria for evaluating performance and types of scoring guides. p. 50
		Psychometric Properties
		State requirements for item-level properties (e.g., difficulty, discrimination, interrater reliability, differential item functioning levels). pp. 51–52
		Specify test-level properties (e.g., score reliability, equating, validity). pp. 51–52
		Advisory Committee
		Review the draft of the specifications with an expert committee to determine if any essential specifications should be added or if any design specifications can be eliminated. pp. 52–53
		Documentation
		Document in reports the design process to support validity. p. 53

CHAPTER 3

Construction of a Performance Task

INTRODUCTION

So you want to build a performance examination to replace or perhaps augment the multiple-choice examination you have been using. You know your multiple-choice examination has been found reliable in many studies. You know the content coverage of the multiple-choice examination is well documented and appropriate for your purpose. However, you want more from the assessment than you feel the multiple-choice examination can provide.

If you are developing a credentialing examination, perhaps you want to know how well a candidate can test for mold in the crawlspace of a house. You know you can write many items to determine how well the candidate knows the material involved in this task, but how do you write a multiple-choice question to determine whether the candidate has developed the manual dexterity to use the equipment effectively?

Whether in education or credentialing, the challenge before you is to develop tasks for use in the new assessment that will ensure that the quality of the assessment is at least comparable with that of the previous assessment. To achieve comparable quality you need several things. You need the content coverage to be equivalent. You need the scores to be reliable. You need to know that you will make accurate inferences about what the examinee can do. You need the tasks to be doable by the examinees in a reasonable amount of time and at a reasonable cost. You need the tasks by which examinees can produce observable outcomes that your judges can evaluate. You need your new examination to withstand scrutiny from many perspectives.

How do you build quality into a performance assessment, one task at a time? This chapter presents the process by which you develop the

58

tasks from which you can construct your performance assessment to meet these many needs.

ELEMENTS OF A PERFORMANCE ASSESSMENT TASK

Six elements of task construction, along with the decisions required for each element, are described below. In the following sections, we describe the elements of task construction and examine the applications of those elements in assessments used in education, credentialing, program evaluation, and research. We culminate each of these sections by examining the application of the element in the design of the Oral Clinical Examination (OCE), developed by the American Board of Pediatric Dentistry (ABPD) (see Table 1.1).

The six key elements of developing a performance task are the item writers, content, process skills, context, audience, and task structure. Although they are presented separately, the aspects of performance assessment interact with and influence one another. For example, a task to measure a student's knowledge of turtles (the content), could require comparison and contrast of land and sea turtles or ask the student to "invent" a turtle that would thrive in a water or land habitat (the cognitive process skills). Furthermore, the task could provide examinees the option of responding with a written explanation and/or labeled illustrations (the response format stipulated in the task structure).

Item Writers

A first step in the development of a performance task is to identify the item writers, who will incorporate the qualities of performance tasks into the exercises. For the task to have credibility, the writers should be SMEs or practitioners in the field (Downing, 2006; Hertz & Chinn, 2000). The expertise of the item writers contributes to the construct and content validity associated with the assessment. That is, item writers with expertise in an area should be familiar with the content and able to translate the subject matter into items that represent the construct or content domains.

In education, the item writers for state- and district-level tests are often practicing or former teachers in the content area (Welch, 2006). In a program evaluation the program staff works with an evaluation specialist to develop the assessment (Johnson et al., 1998). In the instance of credentialing examinations, task developers have included (1) teachers for the advanced certification of the NBPTS, (2) lawyers for state boards of bar examiners, and (3) medical educators and clinicians for the United States Medical Licensing Examination (FSMBUS & NBME, 2008; NBPTS, 2006b; Walljasper, 1999).

When a performance assessment is developed for a research study, members of the research team either adopt a current assessment or develop the task. For example, to study the validity of certification decisions for the National Board for Professional Teaching Standards (NBPTS), Bond, Smith, Baker, and Hattie (2000) completed a review of the research literature to identify dimensions of quality teacher performance. They used these dimensions to develop rubrics to score casebooks that contained (1) teachers' instructional objectives and lesson plans, (2) coded observational protocols of teacher and student activities and interactions, and (3) transcripts of scripted interviews with teachers and their students. In a later study, Smith, Gordon, Colby, and Wang (2005) examined NBPTS teachers' instruction for depth of learning and students' work exhibiting different depths of learning. To do so the authors developed a depth-of-knowledge rubric to score the teacher files.

Bond and colleagues (1996) also note the importance of diversity in the experts who will select or develop the performance tasks. They remind us that in choosing or developing tasks for an arts assessment, experts from different cultures, social backgrounds, and ethnic or gender groups "will probably vary substantially in their opinions about . . . what performance tasks should be included" (p. 120). Diversity also serves to assure that the wording and context of performance tasks are relevant to all examinee groups in the interest of fairness and equity. For example, a portfolio assessment of family literacy skills (e.g., parent and child interactions, parent modeling reading/storytelling skills for child) that allowed only entries of a parent reading to his or her child would fail to capture the singing to a child, or the storytelling that occurs in families with English as a second language (Johnson, Fisher, et al., 2003).

The OCE uses tasks developed from the practice of the dentists who are members of the examination development committee. Given that children are the focus of the tasks, parents grant permission to use photographs of their children in clinical cases, and the ABPD takes steps to protect the confidentiality of the children involved in the cases. However, the use of documented clinical cases for the construction of tasks to be used in the OCE clearly creates a context that stakeholders can recognize immediately as being appropriate for the assessment. In addition, the examination development committee selects the clinical cases and prepares the examination tasks such that the diversity seen in practice is represented in the examination.

Content

Texts on test development advise guiding the writing of items (i.e., multiple-choice and performance tasks) based on a set of test specifications. The development of the test specifications was described in Chapter 2. Here we revisit the aspects of the test specifications that will guide the writing of performance tasks.

In education, a table of specifications provides a list of the learning outcomes to be tested using the two dimensions of content and cognitive processes (Crocker & Algina, 1986; Thorndike, 2005). Baron (1991) contends that the content of performance tasks is primary and that to be effective they "must incorporate the big ideas and essential concepts, principles, and processes in a discipline" (p. 308). In education, much of the work of identifying the "big picture" has been led by national organizations such as the National Council of Teachers of Mathematics, the National Council of Teachers of English, the American Association for the Advancement of Science, and the New Standards Project. Each of these organizations has identified the concepts and processes critical to a field and published content standards to guide educators in instruction. States have followed the lead of national organizations as they revise their own curriculum or performance standards.

Table 3.1 provides examples of content standards from history, mathematics, visual arts, English language arts, and science. Beside each content standard is a task kernel that is the rudiment of a performance task that could be used in assessing student knowledge. More examples of content standards are available on the websites of the state departments of education.

In an evaluation, the program goals and objectives will inform the content addressed in the assessment. For example, the staff of the Even Start family literacy program in Lincoln, Nebraska, reviewed their mission statement and program documents to identify the literacy goals to be evaluated through use of the family literacy portfolio (Johnson, Fisher, et al., 2003; Johnson, McDaniel, et al., 2000; Johnson et al., 1998). After review of the program documents, the family educators and program coordinator developed six program goals to describe the family literacy skills that parents should know and practice (Figure 3.1). These goals specified the family literacy areas for program services and

TABLE 3.1. Examples of Content Standards and Tasks

		Standard	Task kernel
State *Subject* *Grade/* *course*	**Virginia** **History** **United States** **History: 1877** **to the Present**	USII.1 The student will demonstrate skills for historical and geographical analysis, including the ability to h) interpret patriotic slogans and excerpts from notable speeches and documents. (Virginia Department of Education, 2001, p. 1)	The Declaration of Independence states, "We hold these truths to be self-evident, that all men are created equal, that they are endowed by their Creator with certain unalienable Rights, that among these are Life, Liberty and the Pursuit of Happiness." Explain the significance of this statement to current or historical civil rights movements. Provide examples of civil rights movements. Relate the examples to the quote.
State *Subject* *Grade/* *course*	Florida Mathematics 6–8	Standard 3: The student uses statistical methods to make inferences and valid arguments about real-world situations. (MA.E.3.3) 1. Formulates hypotheses, designs experiments, collects and interprets data, and evaluates hypotheses by making inferences and drawing conclusions based on statistics (range, mean, median, and mode) and tables, graphs, and charts. (Florida Department of Education, 2005, p. 3)	The students in our schools are diverse. The school board has asked that each school make sure that the diversity is also reflected in the books that we have in our media centers. The principal at your school has asked for you to design a study to collect data to show the diversity of our student body is reflected in the library books. Describe the following: The research question How you will collect data The statistics you will use to answer the research question
State *Subject* *Grade/* *course*	South Carolina Arts 3–5	II. Using knowledge of structures and functions such as elements and principles of design. Aesthetic Perception/Creative Expression—Students will demonstrate a knowledge of the elements and principles of design and show an aesthetic awareness of the visual	Happy. Excited. Sad. Anxious. These are some of the feelings that we experience each day. Artists use elements and principles of design to create feelings in the viewers of their drawings. Use the color pencils to draw a self-portrait which shows you as happy, sad, calm, or some other emotion.

(continued)

TABLE 3.1. *(continued)*

		Standard	Task kernel
		and tactile qualities in the environment that are found in works of art. a. Describe, both orally and in writing, how the various elements and principles of design function to evoke different responses in the viewer of an artwork. (South Carolina Department of Education, 2003, p. 141)	Then write a paragraph that tells how the elements and principles of design that you used in your drawing will cause a viewer of your art to respond.
State *Subject* *Grade/* *course*	California Language Arts 9–10	2.1. Write biographical or autobiographical narratives or short stories: a. Relate a sequence of events and communicate the significance of the events to the audience. (California State Board of Education, 2005, p. 60)	Describe an important event in your life. Describe the sequence of events and communicate the significance of the event to the reader.
State *Subject* *Grade/* *course*	Massachusetts Science 6–8	Energy and Living Things 14. Explain the roles and relationships among producers, consumers, and decomposers in the process of energy transfer in a food web. (Massachusetts Department of Education, 2001)	Draw a picture to show the relationships among the organisms in the following list. Write a paragraph that explains the roles and relationships. • Wolves • Grass • Bacteria • Rabbits

for which the portfolio would be used to review the program. Goal 1 in Figure 3.1, for example, indicates that the portfolio should contain evidence of a parent beginning to model reading, storytelling, and writing as part of his interactions with his child.

In licensure testing, the content areas to be assessed are the KSAs critical for an examinee to demonstrate in order to assure competent practice and protection of the public (Stoker & Impara, 1995). For example, in medicine the critical skills in the conduct of the examination a newborn might include a review of the baby's general appearance, such as "1. Posturing (flexed, limp, etc), 2. Color (cyanosis, mottling, etc.), 3. Degree of distress if any" (University of Utah Department of

- Goal 1: Parent models reading/storytelling, writing, and math skills for her/his child.
- Goal 2: Parent models for his/her child goal-setting and planning of activities.
- Goal 3: Parent promotes self-esteem in child by providing, for example, physical contact and/or positive verbal comments.
- Goal 4: Parent functions as her/his child's teacher.
- Goal 5: Parent and child interact in child-centered activities selected by the child.
- Goal 6: Parent creates an environment that contributes to the physical, social, and emotional well-being of her/his child.

FIGURE 3.1. Goals defining family literacy knowledge and skills. Reproduced with permission from Lincoln Public Schools, Lincoln, Nebraska.

Pediatrics, n.d.). In Chapter 2, we outlined the process for conducting a practice analysis to identify the KSAs appropriate for a credentialing examination.

The importance of appropriately identifying crucial KSAs is reflected in the statement in the *Standards for Educational and Psychological Testing* that "validation of credentialing tests depends mainly on content-related evidence, often in the form of judgments that the test adequately represents the content domain of the occupation or specialty being considered" (AERA, APA, & NCME, 1999, p. 157). Lenel (1990a) states, "the case for the validity of a licensure examination can be made much more easily if the tasks on that examination resemble actual job requirements" (p. 19).

Fortune and Cromack (1995) note that clinical examinations, which are one form of performance assessment, require that the examinee complete tasks that the practice analysis identified as critical in the performance of professional duties. The authors state, "First comes the task, then critical elements of the task are identified and defined as criteria to be scored, hence items" (p. 151).

A different strategy for the identification of content is described by van der Vleuten and Swanson (1990), who state, "The first step in developing SP-based [standardized-patient] tests is identification of the skills to be assessed. The tasks to be used at individual stations follow naturally, and these tasks constrain decisions regarding station format and length" (p. 66). (A "station" is the area at which the examinee performs the task required in the assessment. For example, a station could be prepared with a standardized patient complaining of chest pains and the examinee is expected to respond to the complaint.)

The description offered by van der Vleuten and Swanson (1990) appears to be more in line with the typical development of a test or performance task in which the key skills and knowledge are outlined and then the items and tasks developed (see Chapter 2), such that a sampling of items and tasks can be selected for use in an examination. Why do we use sampling? Because it is rarely possible to ask an examinee to answer every conceivable question or to perform every conceivable activity. Fitzpatrick and Morrison (1971) note that all of the relevant, important subject matter cannot be covered in a single test or a few tasks; thus test developers must employ a sampling procedure to select a limited number of tasks that cover what is most important.

Content sampling for the OCE follows a four-part outline (e.g., preventative and restorative dentistry, growth, and development) to guide all exam development activities sponsored by the ABPD. Each part of the outline requires clinical cases for the examinee to process according to an established algorithm used in clinical practice (e.g., taking history precedes diagnosis, and diagnosis precedes treatment planning). In addition, each clinical situation is prepared such that a balance in difficulty is maintained across the steps from gathering history to follow-up assessment.

Ancillary Knowledge and Skills

Developers of an assessment also should consider ancillary requirements for a task (Haertel & Linn, 1996). Ancillary requirements for a task include "construct-irrelevant knowledge, skills, or dispositions required for task success" (Haertel & Linn, 1996, p. 65). Construct irrelevance may be introduced by reading demands, writing requirements, and the task context (Lane, 1993). These ancillary skills may influence examinee scores, thus clouding the validity of decisions associated with a task. An illustration of ancillary demands is when tasks require examinees to read directions; write a paragraph-length constructed response or an essay-length extended response; or present their findings orally. In the case of a language arts assessment or medical board examination, communication skills might fall within the targeted knowledge and skills of the assessment. However, in the instance of a science assessment or prosthetics licensure examination, such skills might be considered ancillary requirements. Also, the familiarity of the context of a performance task must be considered for examinees of differing cultural or ethnic backgrounds (Lane, 1993).

The issue here is to reduce the effect of ancillary requirements on examinee scores. Reading requirements generally are addressed by controlling the readability level of vocabulary used in directions and stimulus materials. Selection of the appropriate response format can help control for writing or communication skills.

A science performance assessment provides an example of ancillary knowledge. Stecher and colleagues (2000) studied varying readability levels in science performance tasks developed for eighth-grade students. Using reading formulas available in Microsoft Word Version 6.0™, they estimated reading grade level using Flesh–Kincaid, Coleman–Liau, and Bormuth (Microsoft, 1993/1994, p. 101). These formulas use word length, sentence length, and structural elements of the text to estimate the grade level at which a typical student could read the material with comprehension. Stecher and colleagues averaged the three readability estimates for each performance task. Averages for the readability of the tasks ranged from 6.2 to 7.3, indicating that the typical eighth-grade student should be able to read both tasks. However, the authors remind us, "Students who were reading well below grade level might have had difficulty reading the open-response tasks" (p. 152).

The effect of ancillary skills is managed in the OCE in a different manner than described in the preceding paragraphs. In particular, the OCE is an oral examination somewhat similar in design to a structured interview, and it is reasonable to expect that some examinees would be more comfortable, if not better able, with one element of the assessment than with another. For example, an examinee more skilled at extemporaneous speaking might receive a better score than a less well-spoken examinee by virtue of oral communication skills instead of requisite knowledge. To reduce the effects of such ancillary skills on OCE results, the board provides sample tests online for candidates to review, where the intent is to educate the examinees on exactly what they will be expected to do during the examination. The first year in which the sample tests were available, the quality of candidate responses, as indicated by candidate scores and pass rate, increased substantially.

Cognitive Process Skills

In this section, we examine the use of process skills in constructing performance tasks. In education, process skills generally refer to the cognitive processes an examinee uses to complete a task such as remembering or understanding, whereas in licensure, process skills refer to the practice-related behaviors that are part of the professional responsibilities or job duties expected of the examinee (Raymond, 2002). To avoid confusion, we use the more specific phrase *cognitive process skills* to describe the cognitive dimensions of tasks that should be considered in task development.

Bloom's initial taxonomy (Bloom, 1956) and the subsequent revision (Anderson & Krathwohl, 2001) guide the development and classification of multiple-choice items and performance tasks in education and in some credentialing examinations. In Bloom's original taxonomy, the cognitive domains identify processes related to recall or recognition of knowledge, thinking, problem solving, and creating. More specifically, as seen in the top row of Table 3.2, the taxonomy classifies learning outcomes (i.e., objectives) in terms of whether the outcomes, for example, focus on students' development of skills to:

1. Recall factual knowledge.
2. Comprehend new materials.
3. Apply rules and principles to new problems or contexts.
4. Analyze material to understand the relationships between the parts.
5. Synthesize elements or ideas to create a new whole.
6. Evaluate ideas based on derived criteria.

The taxonomy is hierarchical in nature, moving from the simple recall of knowledge to the complex development of criteria to evaluate ideas and products. The taxonomy provides a system for classification of examinee behaviors in terms of the manner in which examinees should act or think as the result of an educational experience.

In the bottom row of Table 3.2 are assessment activities that guide the development of items that gauge examinees' understanding at that cognitive level. For example, to assess examinees' understanding of the sonata, you might ask them to define the musical form (knowledge), to compose a sonata (synthesis), or critique a sonata (evaluation). Notice that at the synthesis and evaluation levels of the taxonomy a performance task will most likely be the appropriate form of assessment. Multiple-choice items can often gauge examinee understanding at the lower levels of knowledge, comprehension, application, and analysis.

TABLE 3.2. Bloom's Cognitive Categories and Assessment Activities

	Knowledge	Comprehension	Application	Analysis	Synthesis	Evaluation
Cognitive categories	Knowledge—the recall of specifics, universals, methods, processes, patterns, structures, or settings	Comprehension—the understanding of the meaning and intent of material	Application—the use of abstractions, such as rules, in particular situations	Analysis—the separation of material into its elements or constituent parts such that the relationships between the parts is made evident	Synthesis—the combining of elements to form a pattern or structure that was not evident previously	Evaluation—the judgment of the degree that materials satisfy criteria
Assessment activities	Define, identify, label, list, locate, match, name, recall, recognize, remember, repeat, select, state, tell, underline	Change, conclude, convert, draw, dramatize, explain, extend, infer, interpret, paraphrase, predict, rephrase, restate, retell, summarize, translate, transform	Complete, compute, generalize, operate, organize, solve, use	Associate, categorize, classify, compare, contrast, debate, diagram, differentiate, distinguish, group, outline, relate, separate, subdivide	Assemble, categorize, compose, construct, create, design, formulate, hypothesize, plan, produce, propose, write	Appraise, argue, assess, critique, judge, justify, revise, support, validate

Note. Summarized from Bloom (1956), Gronlund (2003), and Metfessel, Michael, and Kirsner (1969).

The Bloom's taxonomy originally was developed to build a system for classifying educational objectives. The relevance of the taxonomy to the development of licensure and certification examinations may be seen when Bloom writes, "Objectives may also be inferred from the tasks, problems, and observations used to test or evaluate the presence of these behaviors" (1956, p. 12). Assessment practitioners in education and credentialing, evaluators, and researchers use tasks, problems, and observations to document examinees' performance levels. The knowledge and skills may require simple recall of the function of an organ or require synthesis of information to formulate an argument as might be the case in a bar examination. A cognitive taxonomy offers a systematic method to develop items that gauge an examinee's ability to use his or her knowledge and skills to perform a task. Use of a taxonomy offers assurance of the representativeness of the cognitive skills included in an examination and supports the validity of the decisions made about examinees' cognitive skills and strategies.

An example of Bloom's taxonomy is seen in licensure in the test plan for the National Council Licensure Examination for Licensed Practical/Vocational Nurses (National Council of State Boards of Nursing [NCSBN], 2004). The NCSBN informs examinees that most of the items are written at the application or higher levels of cognition.

The ABPD requires a passing score on a multiple-choice examination (Qualifying Examination, or QE) before an examinee may take the OCE. As such, the QE comprises items easily classified to the first four levels of Bloom's taxonomy. In contrast, the OCE tasks are targeted directly and uniquely to the upper three levels of Bloom's taxonomy. This commonly found model of testing permits an organization to assess directly both what an examinee knows and what an examinee can do.

A revised Bloom's taxonomy was developed by Anderson and Krathwohl (2001). As shown in Figure 3.2, the revised taxonomy classifies objectives along two dimensions: knowledge and cognitive process. The cognitive process dimension is similar to the original taxonomy. One change is the expression of the cognitive categories in terms of verbs (e.g., remember, apply, analyze). This change emphasizes what the examinee is expected to do.

New to the revised Bloom's taxonomy is the knowledge dimension, which is delineated by four types of knowledge: factual, conceptual, procedural, and metacognitive. The intersection of the cognitive and knowledge dimensions is where the learning outcomes can be classified. For example, the dimensions of *Create* and *Procedural Knowledge* describe the learning objective of "formulates hypotheses, designs experiments, collects and interprets data, and evaluates hypotheses by making infer-ences and drawing conclusions based on statistics (range, mean, median, and mode) and tables, graphs, and charts" (Florida Department of Edu-cation, 2005, p. 3). A performance assessment that requires examinees to complete such a task would gauge their skills in creating an experi-ment and completing the procedures to test a hypothesis. In preparation of an examination, specification of item development along these two dimensions guides the development of items across the range of cognitive and knowledge dimensions.

Another resource is Marzano's (2001) New Taxonomy, which is well suited for the development of performance assessments. Mar-zano's taxonomy builds on Bloom's original taxonomy as it presents a new framework. Marzano suggests that by viewing knowledge as "that which is acted upon by various mental processes," his taxonomy avoids the confusion in Bloom's system of types of knowledge and mental oper-ations (p. 28). Marzano identifies three domains of knowledge: informa-tion, mental procedures, and psychomotor procedures. Mental proce-dures differ in both form and function from informational knowledge. Informational knowledge is the "what" of human knowledge, whereas procedural knowledge is the "how-to."

The domain of information is hierarchical. It includes organizing ideas (i.e., principles and generalizations) at the top and details, with vocabulary, at the bottom (see Figure 3.3). Mental procedures can be also organized into a simple hierarchy. At the top of the hierarchy are macroprocedures. Marzano (2001) describes these as robust procedures that result in a variety of possible products or outcomes and involve execution of many interrelated subprocedures. Macroprocedures require controlled execution. An example of a macroprocedure is writing. The process of writing results in diverse forms of expression and requires attention to such subprocedures as content, organization, style, sentence formation, and conventions.

In the middle of the hierarchy are tactics and algorithms (Marzano, 2001). Tactics are general rules that neither generate a variety of prod-ucts nor incorporate a variety of subcomponents. In addition, tactics do not consist of a set of steps that must be executed in a specific order. An example of a tactic is reading a histogram, which requires attention to the title, labels and units for the x and y axis, and determining the rela-tionship of the information in the two axes.

In contrast to tactics, algorithms have very specific steps with spe-cific outcomes that do not vary in application. An example is the execu-tion of the steps in taking a patient's blood pressure. At the bottom of

The Knowledge Dimension	The Cognitive Process Dimension					
	Remember—retrieve knowledge from memory	Understand—construct meaning from communications	Apply—implement a procedure in a given situation	Analyze—break material into its parts and determine how parts relate to one another and an overall structure	Evaluate—make judgments based on criteria	Create—bring elements together to form a new pattern or structure
A. Factual Knowledge—of basic elements associated with a discipline						
B. Conceptual Knowledge—of interrelationships among the basic elements within more complex structures				Explain the roles and relationships among producers, consumers, and decomposers in the process of energy[1]		Describe orally and in written form how the various uses of elements and principles of design [in the visual arts] cause different responses in the viewer[2]
C. Procedural Knowledge—of how to do something, skills, methods, techniques used to do something, and criteria for when to use such						Formulates hypotheses, designs experiments, collects and interprets data, and evaluates hypotheses by making inferences and drawing conclusions based on statistics (range, mean, median, and mode) and tables, graphs, and charts[3]
D. Metacognitive Knowledge—of cognition and self awareness of one's own cognition						

FIGURE 3.2. Dimensions in *A Taxonomy for Learning, Teaching, and Assessing* with examples of classification of content standards. From Anderson, L. W., Krathwohl, D. R., Airasian, P. W., Cruikshank, K. A., Mayer, R. E., Pintrich, P. R., Raths, J., & Wittrock, M. C. *A taxonomy for learning, teaching, and assessing: A revision of Bloom's taxonomy of educational objectives*, Abridged edition, 1st edition. ©2001. Reprinted by permission of Pearson Education, Inc., Upper Saddle River, NJ. Copyright 2001 by Pearson Education, Inc. Reprinted by permission. [1]Massachusetts Department of Education (2001), [2]South Carolina Department of Education (2003), [3]Florida Department of Education (2005).

the hierarchy is a single rule or small set of rules with no accompanying steps. Beginning sentences with capitals provides an example of a rule. Figure 3.3 presents the hierarchical components of the informational and procedural domains of knowledge.

According to Marzano (2001), procedural knowledge is learned in three stages. In the initial cognitive stage the learner can verbalize and perform crude approximations and may rehearse the information required to execute the skill. This stage is similar to informational knowledge because the person "knows it" but cannot "do it." In the associative phase, performance is smoothed out and errors are detected and deleted. In the autonomous phase, the procedure is refined, automated, and takes very little space in working memory. An example of procedural knowledge from the medical field includes communication skills used in a doctor–patient encounter, such as use of open and closed questions, clarification, summarizing, and closing (Humphris & Kaney, 200).

The new taxonomy is a planning tool for performance assessments, helping item writers think about what an examinee *does* with what she *knows*. Thus the taxonomy can serve as a heuristic for item writers in developing assessments used in education, licensure, program evaluation, and educational research.

An example of the difference in the depth of examinee understanding, illustrated by generalizations versus details in the domain of information, provides insight into the development of writing tasks and scoring rubrics. A generalization is a statement for which examples can

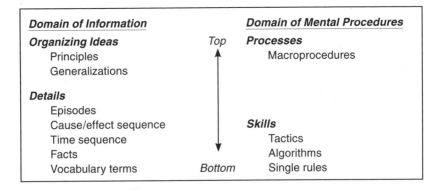

FIGURE 3.3. Knowledge: The domain of information and the domain of mental procedures. Summarized from Marzano (2001).

be provided. A fact (a type of detail), however, is specific and does not transfer to other contexts. In a writing sample a generalization would be the writer's controlling idea, the focus of the student composition, or the theme or message. For a reader to understand the writer's generalization, the writer has to support it with "exemplifying and illustrative" details. Writers who produce unsupported generalizations fail to develop their topic. Writers who produce an abundance of details without a unifying generalization produce lists rather than essays or coherent wholes. The new taxonomy provides an important perspective for getting at an examinee's *depth* of knowledge of the subject or concept. It can also provide an indication of the cognitive complexity of performance tasks.

Context

Context refers not so much to the setting in which examinees complete a performance task but rather how that context frames the design of the tasks themselves. Resnick and Resnick (1992) criticize standardized assessments for assuming that a complex skill is fixed and will manifest in the same way, at any time, across contexts. They argue that complex skills should be assessed in the same context in which they are used. They offer as an example the mismatch between editing someone else's work and the ability to edit one's own. Students who can spot and correct someone else's errors are not necessarily able to recognize and fix their own, which is what they must be able to do to be considered writers.

In education, Baron (1991) suggests that performance tasks be presented in real-world contexts so that students are engaged and so that they learn that their skills and knowledge are valuable beyond the classroom. In medicine, the context for a clinical examination might be a parent seeking advice about a special diet for his child (Humphris & Kaney, 200). In clinical examinations, the idea is for examinees to interact with standardized patients as if they were interviewing or examining an actual patient (van der Vleuten & Swanson, 1990). Pediatric dentistry uses clinical cases directly from dental practice to create tasks for the OCE. In terms of the physical setting, clinical examinations in medicine are conducted in settings similar to an ambulatory clinic (De Champlain, Macmillan, King, Klass, & Margolis, 1999). In the development of a medical licensure examination, based on the practice model and job analysis, content experts indicated that a majority of test items should be placed in the context of continued care (LaDuca, Downing, & Henzel, 1995).

Developers of performance tasks must also ensure that the context is new to the examinee. If the context is not new (i.e., examinees have previous exposure to the task in the same context), then the cognitive skills required for completion of the task may require only memory and not analysis and synthesis of the task information. For example, asking student examinees to write about the overused topic *person whom you most admire* might produce responses that do not reflect the students' ability. A competent writer, bored with the topic, might resort to formulaic writing just to complete the task. A less skilled writer might reproduce a polished piece, memorized complete with the teacher edits.

In licensure tests for law, Lenel (1990b) suggests that actual court cases should not be the basis for questions "unless the intent is to assess examinees' familiarity with that case. If the intent is to measure reasoning ability rather than knowledge of substantive law, all necessary facts should be given" (p. 43).

Audience

When creating a performance task the item writer needs to consider three types of audiences: (1) the examinees who will complete the task, (2) the audience addressed in the task, and (3) the individuals who will use the results.

Examinees as the Audience

In terms of who will complete the task, examinee characteristics influence the language demands, the length of time to complete a single task or set of tasks, and the resources or materials that can be utilized. As discussed earlier in the section on ancillary knowledge, the language demands of a task should be reviewed to determine that the reading level will not interfere in examinees' understanding of the demands of the task.

Consideration of examinees' age level and attention span led the designers of the proposed National Voluntary Test[1] in reading to propose two 45-minute sessions for fourth-grade students (MPR Associates, 1997). In contrast, the testing time for licensure and certification examinations typically is 1 to 3 days (e.g., FSMBUS & NBME, 2008; National Conference of Bar Examiners, 2004).

---

[1]Due to lack of support, the National Voluntary Test was never developed and implemented.

In terms of the resources or materials that can be used, developers must consider that task directions for young examinees require larger print and, in some cases, the teacher should read the directions. In a performance task in history, middle school students might be able to handle supplementary materials such as facsimiles of historical documents; however, materials for elementary students would need to be integrated into the task booklet.

In licensure testing, the idea of the examinee as an audience is illustrated in law board examinations. In consideration that the licensure examination is for *minimal* competence, Lenel (1990b) states, "Consider the intended audience when writing a question. The bar examination is intended to discriminate between those who are competent to practice and those who are not. The intent is not to identify the most capable examinees" (p. 43). Similarly, the ABPD goes to considerable lengths to specify the minimal expectations required to pass the OCE and to achieve the diplomate designation.

Addressees as the Audience

The audience addressed in the task is an explicit component in medical clinical examinations that include the interpersonal aspect of the doctor–patient encounter as one of the skills to be assessed. For the examinee (e.g., a medical student or physician about to begin supervised practice), the audience is the actor playing the role of a patient. During the encounter, tasks might require examinees to take a brief patient history or counsel a patient (De Champlain, Macmillan, King, et al., 1999; De Champlain, Macmillan, Margolis, et al., 1999; Macmillan, De Champlain, & Klass, 1999; van der Vleuten & Swanson, 1990). At the conclusion of the encounter, the standardized patient completes a rating scale to assess the examinee's interpersonal skills. Thus, the patient plays a critical role as the audience for this performance assessment (De Champlain, Macmillan, King, et al., 1999; De Champlain, Macmillan, Margolis, et al., 1999; Macmillan et al., 1999).

Test Users as the Audience

The user audience must be able to understand (and often apply) the scoring criteria. The tasks need to generate easily understood and useful data about examinee mastery, strength, and weaknesses. For example licensing agencies require data from the performance tasks in order to make decisions about admitting an examinee to the profession. Thus this audience requires the task to be easily scored and transformed into a pass or fail score.

The user audience also has to consider the assessment and the data it produces as credible. For example, the NBPTS includes in its requirements for an assessment that it is professionally credible and publicly acceptable (NBPTS, 2006a). Thus because of the national focus on performance assessment during the development period of the NBPTS assessment system, the certification process uses performance-based assessments, which include a teaching portfolio with student work samples, video excerpts of instruction, and analyses of the candidate's teaching and the students' learning. The certification process also requires that candidates respond to written exercises that probe the depth of the teacher's subject-matter knowledge, as well as his or her understanding of how to teach those subjects (NBPTS, 2007). The process eschews multiple-choice items because this response form lacked credibility with the governing board.

Task Structure

One of the most important considerations in developing an assessment is task structure. Khattri, Reeve, and Kane (1998) offer the following framework for task structure: (1) task/topic, (2) the time to complete, (3) the nature of the products, (4) the resources to be used, and (5) the degree of control the examinee has over the preceding four elements. We use their framework to describe the issues that assessment practitioners will want to consider in structuring a task.

Task/Topic

The task may tap (1) cognitive skills, (2) metacognitive abilities if the examinee is to demonstrate awareness of his/her own thinking, or (3) social skills if the task is completed by a group. As discussed earlier in this chapter, the selection of topic will be informed by the content standards, practice analysis, program goals and objectives, or research focus.

Time

Time can range from a specified and enforced time limit to "whenever" the examinee considers the task complete. A portfolio might be developed over the course of a year (Johnson et al., 1998; Mills, 1996). In contrast, medical clinical examinations often allow 15 minutes for an examinee to complete a task associated with a session, with multiple sessions composing the assessment (Clauser et al., 1993; De Champlain, Macmillan, Margolis, et al., 1999; Macmillan et al., 1999).

If time restrictions are part of a performance assessment, then enough time should be allocated that speed is not an issue because decisions about examinees' knowledge and skills become confounded with examinees' ability to work quickly (Chambers, Boulet, & Gary, 2000; van der Vleuten & Swanson, 1990). Lenel (1990b) states, "Keep the time limits in mind when writing a question. If the examiner is looking for a well-organized, well-reasoned answer, examinees must be given enough time to think about and prepare their response" (p. 43).

In an investigation about whether a 15-minute time allocation was adequate for encounters in medical clinical examinations, Chambers and colleagues (2000) reported that examinees on average used slightly less than 15 minutes. Examinees did vary the time examining the patient by case complexity; however, examinees did not differ in time according to either examinee or standardized patient gender.

Examinees complete the OCE in two 1-hour sessions, both on the same day. Each session presents four clinical cases, which the Board calls vignettes. The 1-hour time limit is applied to the session, not the vignette. The time an examinee spends in the discussion of a vignette is generally determined by the examinee, although the examiners can terminate the discussion if the candidate has too little or too much to say. The time spent in the discussion of a vignette has no direct bearing on the scores assigned to the discussion by the examiners.

Response Format

We prefer the phrase "response format" here to modify "the nature of the products" used by Khattri and colleagues (1998) to acknowledge the role of product and *process* in performance assessment. The format of the response selected for an assessment is affected by whether it is important and possible to look at the product, the process that leads to the product, or both (Fortune & Cromack, 1995; Stiggins, 1987a; Wiley & Haertel, 1996). The experts in a field collaborate with a test developer to determine whether product or performance will be scored, based on how the score is to be interpreted and the results are to be used. It is more efficient to score the product, but if improvement feedback is to be provided, observing and evaluating the process becomes important (Clauser, 2000).

In medicine, clinical tasks may require an examinee to develop an end *product*, such as a prosthetic device, whereas other tasks require examinees to engage in a *process*, such as an intubation (i.e., the introduction of a tube into the trachea in preparation for administering anesthesia). Still other examinations require both process and product. In the certification examination for the NBPTS, candidates produce videotapes of their teaching (process) and write analyses (product) about the videotapes (NBPTS, 2005).

In the Objective Structured Video Exam (OSVE), examinees watch a videotape of a patient and doctor interaction. On a single sheet of paper (i.e., front and back), examinees complete three tasks:

Task 1: Identify Communication Skills with brief description to help locate wherein the intervention you noticed the skill (one skill per box)—maximum 16 marks,

Task 2: Discuss the Consequences of each Skill—maximum 16 marks, and

Task 3: Suggest Alternative Communication Skills and give reason for preference—up to three marks per box, i.e., maximum 18 marks. (Humphris & Kaney, 200, pp. 940–941)

Note the degree of structure of the response. In Task 1, the examinees are instructed to list one communication skill (e.g., greeting, eye contact) per box and they receive up to 16 points per box.

In a standardized-patient assessment, examinees complete a post-encounter note (PEN) for each case (De Champlain, Macmillan, King, et al., 1999; De Champlain, Macmillan, Margolis, et al., 1999; Macmillan et al., 1999). In the PEN the examinee presents the main clinical findings.

Examinees taking the OCE discuss the clinical cases presented in the sessions. Examinees ask questions, review images, and respond to open-ended questions from the examiners. Examinee responses are expected to include citations to current literature and evidence-based practice, even for clinical cases with which the examinee might have no direct experience. At the end of the examinee's discussion of a given clinical situation, the examiners record scores according to a predetermined scoring rubric. The examiners do not discuss the scoring with the examinees, nor do they seek consensus on scores.

To this end, the response form of the OCE is discussion. However, all discussions are videotaped. The primary purpose of the taping is for use in the event that an examinee appeals a scoring decision. The tapes are also used for examiner training and task development.

Resources

In developing a performance task, consideration must also be given to the stimulus and supplementary materials that will be provided with the assessment (Roeber, 1996). The task may contain all the data or the examinee may supply it (e.g., creating a graph based on numbers supplied vs. conducting interviews to collect the numbers that are then graphed and would vary across examinees). The materials required for a performance assessment might be as simple as paper and pencil for the essay section of a high school exit exam, or as complex as a simulation of an ambulatory clinic for a medical licensure examination.

In education, science performance assessments have included the equipment to conduct a hands-on experiment to investigate the two topics of inclines and friction (Solano-Flores et al., 1999). Materials for the inclines task included a model truck, marbles, a flat board, a model-size ladder, a bucket, and washers. In a music assessment, the material requirements for one task included rhythm sticks for students to create an improvisation after listening to a beginning beat (Yap et al., 2003). Additional test materials in the music assessment included (1) a CD player to play the prerecorded instructions and stimulus music and (2) a cassette recorder with tapes to record each student's identification information and his or her performance.

The medical field provides an example of a performance assessment with complex material requirements. In clinical examinations in medicine, the examinees rotate through stations and complete tasks relating to history taking, physical examination, and communication. Each station simulates an encounter between a doctor (the examinee) and a patient. In a chest pain case, the task might require examinees to take a history, read an electrocardiogram, provide a diagnosis, and initiate treatment (van der Vleuten & Swanson, 1990). Stimulus materials include the patient, who is an actor trained to portray a medical condition in a consistent manner across encounters. These actors, referred to as standardized patients, are generally non-physicians trained to play the role of a patient. The standardized patient might be asymptomatic; present stable abnormal findings, such as heart murmurs or joint abnormalities; or simulate physical findings, such as abnormal reflexes or diminished breath sounds (van der Vleuten & Swanson, 1990). Training the standardized patients for one study required 15 hours (De Champlain,

Macmillan, King, et al., 1999). Other material requirements included a physical space for the clinical encounter; the medical equipment; and a form for completing a post-encounter note to report main clinical findings (De Champlain, Macmillan, King, et al., 1999; De Champlain, Macmillan, Margolis, et al., 1999; Macmillan et al., 1999).

Stimulus materials also might include videotape or computer-based simulations, such as a tape of patient and clinician interactions. Humphris and Kaney (200) developed the OSVE to assess "the number of alternative skills that the student believes will be of assistance in improving the patient–doctor interaction" (p. 939). The selection of the videotape, in contrast to interaction with a standardized patient, allowed the administration of the OSVE to large groups of medical students.

The National Conference of Bar Examiners developed the Multistate Performance Test (NCBE, 2001) as one of the licensing examinations it provides to state bar admission boards. Examples of performance tasks in the Multistate Performance Test include writing a letter to a client, a persuasive memorandum or brief, a will, a proposal for settlement or agreement, or a closing argument. Materials used in completing the task include a memorandum, a file, and a library. The memorandum, written by a supervising attorney, details the specific assignment that the examinee is to complete. The file contains the source documents that provide all the case-related facts. Materials included in the file are interview transcripts, depositions, hearings or trials, pleadings, correspondence, client documents, police reports, and lawyer's notes. Contributing to the authenticity of the task, file materials contain relevant and irrelevant facts. The library includes cases, statutes, regulations, and rules that are a mix of relevant and irrelevant materials. The library materials provide sufficient substantive information for the examinee to extract the legal principles required to analyze the problem and perform the task.

Substantial resources are required to develop and administer the OCE. The examination is given in a secure building that was specifically designed to accommodate the needs of oral examinations. Separate entrances and exits are provided to keep the examiners separate from the examinees at all times except during testing. (The two groups even stay in separate hotels.) The test delivery rooms are equipped with computer networking to provide the examination graphics from a single secure server. These rooms also have closed-circuit TV networking to provide additional security as well as to permit the examination to be videotaped. However, no resource is provided to examinees beyond the single sheet of paper on which they may write notes during the examination. These papers are collected and destroyed after each examination session.

Degree of Control

Degree of control ranges from very tight to loose, influencing the form of the response. Time can range from a specified and enforced time limit to "whenever" the examinee considers the task complete. Products can be left entirely up to the examinee to determine in nature and number or tightly prescribed (15 or fewer pages, 1-inch margins, double-spaced, Times New Roman in a 12-point font). As described earlier, a task may contain all the data or the examinee may supply it (creating a graph based on numbers supplied versus conducting interviews to collect the numbers that are then graphed and that would vary across examinees). The ranges illustrate the extremes of examinee control from little or none to extensive.

The degree of control can be illustrated with the portfolio used in the aforementioned Even Start literacy program (Johnson et al., 1998; Johnson, McDaniel, et al., 200; Johnson, Fisher, et al., 2003). To guide the selection of artifacts, the staff developed a portfolio log based on the program goals. In other words, the portfolio goals functioned as selection criteria for inclusion of artifacts in the portfolio. As shown in Table 3.3, the six literacy goals were listed as column headers in the log. In the left-hand column, the program staff member who worked with the family listed each artifact entered into the portfolio. The staff member then placed a check under each goal for which the artifact was relevant. Although the selection of artifacts was structured, the portfolio contents varied. Program activities were tailored to issues relevant to each family; thus the products of these activities (i.e., artifacts) differed across families, and the specific content of the portfolios varied. At the end of each year, portfolios included such artifacts as crafts, videotapes, audiotapes, pictures, essays, and checklists.

The examinee is permitted some degree of control during the OCE. Upon entering the examination room, the examinee may request different examiners if the examinee feels that one or both of the current examiners cannot render a fair assessment. For example, an examinee might feel that a previous personal encounter with an examiner has left the examiner with a predisposition that would lower the examinee's score.

In addition, the examinee is permitted to ask questions regarding the clinical cases (vignette); however, the examiners are not permitted to answer all questions. The examinee may also ask to see a previous slide again. The examinee may make brief notes regarding the slides.

Finally, the examinee controls the time spent on each vignette up to the time limit imposed on the session, although examiners can direct the

TABLE 3.3. Portfolio Log Used to Link Artifacts and Family Literacy Goals

Item/artifact	Date	Age of child	Parent models literacy skills	Parent models goal setting and planning	Parent promotes self-esteem	Parent functions as teacher	Parent–child interact in child-selected activities	Environment contributes to well-being of child
Videotape of father reading to child	11/11/98	4 years	✓			✓	✓	

Note. Reproduced with permission from Lincoln Public Schools, Lincoln, Nebraska.

examinee if too much time is being spent in one area. Previous studies by the ABPD have indicated that the time limit placed on each session of four vignettes does not effect the quality of examinee responses.

QUALITIES TO REVIEW

In the previous sections we described key considerations that item writers should attend to when constructing a performance task. As part of the development process, you will want to ensure the quality of the tasks by reviewing the drafts. In preparing to review tasks, you should convene a committee composed of SMEs and those who will use the test. In your selection of committee members you should attend to diversity, selecting members who represent the various constituencies involved with the assessment (Bond et al., 1996). The following section describes criteria that the review committee can use to examine the quality of the tasks. To be considered are (1) alignment with content standards or KSAs, (2) clarity and language demands, (3) meaningfulness, (4) transparency, (5) sensitivity and fairness, and (6) practicality and consequences.

Alignment with the Content Standards or KSAs

Alignment with content standards or knowledge, skills, and abilities begins with the review of an assessment to determine the congruence of the standards or KSAs with the performance task and the scoring criteria. If the assessment is high stakes, professionals in the field who did not develop the actual tasks (and would therefore be unlikely to have preconceived ideas about what they think the task measures) should complete a formal content validation. A validation review might require members of the committee to identify the standards or KSAs being measured by a task and their lists matched against those of the item writers.

The United States Medical Licensing Examination™ is a three-step examination that uses multiple-choice items in two tests and clinical examinations in one test. The medical cases in the clinical examination "represent the kinds of patients and problems normally encountered during medical practice in the United States" (FSMBUS & NBME, 2008, p. 4). Prior to use in the United States Medical Licensing Examination: Step 2 Clinical Skills, cases are reviewed by examination committees composed of medical educators and clinicians representing the teaching, practicing, and licensing communities across the United States (FSM-

BUS & NBME, 2007). At least two committees critically review each test item or case, revising or discarding any questionable materials.

To serve the fairness and to minimize bias of an assessment, Bond and colleagues (1996) also emphasize the importance of assuring diversity among the committee members who will review the tasks to be selected for examinees to complete. Considering our earlier discussion about the considerable variability of examinees across tasks, that is, the tendency for an examinee's score to differ across various tasks, then the wording and context of those tasks has implications for fairness and equity. Issues of wording or context being preferential to subgroups might be addressed by attending to diversity in the committees reviewing the content or KSAs associated with performance tasks.

The content selection of the OCE is guided first by the four content areas, each of which is represented equally to the others. Each content area is further broken down into four subareas. On the QE these subareas are equally weighted with minor exceptions. (There are 400 multiple-choice items on the QE, and balancing the 16 subareas is easily done.) The subareas are not equally weighted on the OCE because of the limited number of vignettes that can be presented in the two 1-hour sessions. Second, vignettes are selected by topic area such as comprehensive care, behavior management, and trauma. However, the distribution by topic area is not yet mandated.

Clarity of the Task and Language Demands

This criterion refers simply to the likelihood that examinees will produce what you want them to produce (van der Vleuten & Swanson, 1990). Unfortunately, examinees might not interpret the task directions as intended. Their perceptions about the task demands are best determined in tryouts, before the task counts. One method is to interview examinees in the field test to learn about their reasons for their responses (Ruth & Murphy, 1988; van der Vleuten & Swanson, 1990). Ambiguous questions can lead to ambiguous responses and difficulty in scoring those responses. To avoid such a situation, in developing essay questions for a bar examination, Lenel (1990a) advises that "questions should be focused and well-structured" (p. 20). She also states, "Make sure questions are carefully focused, that the purpose and limits of the question are clear. . . . On longer essays, it is often helpful to break down the call of the question into a series of questions" (Lenel, 1990b, p. 43).

Clarity is directly related to the language demands of the task. Language demands apply to the difficulty of the vocabulary and sentence structure and the concept density of reading material for both first- and second-language learners. Abedi (2003) presents a method of "linguistic modification of test items" that goes far beyond traditional editing. The CRESST Linguistic Modification Rubric begins with identifying the specific language demands of the particular discipline and content being assessed. Low-frequency vocabulary that is not connected, and therefore not essential to the content being assessed, is avoided. Modifications address length, unfamiliar lexicon (including idioms and words from other contexts), levels of abstraction, passive voice, and unnecessary text. Combined with the readability review offered in Microsoft Word as described earlier, such a rubric will help to control the ancillary skills of reading.

Because the OCE involves little or no direct reading materials, aside from charts such as histograms, readability reviews are not necessary. However, the examination development committee spends a substantial amount of time reviewing each vignette to determine that the materials presented are sufficiently clear for the examinee to interpret them in the intended manner. Are the graphics sufficiently focused? Is the intent of the graphic clear, or does extraneous imagery make the intent difficult to perceive? Are the questions developed for use by the examiners sufficiently leading without giving away the intent of the vignette?

Meaningfulness

Educators (e.g., Arter, 1992; Baron, 1991; Simmons & Resnick, 1993) recommend that tasks be important to examinees and that they be set in authentic, real-world contexts in order to be meaningful and to engage examinees. As discussed earlier in this chapter, context frames the design of tasks in such a manner as to assess complex skills within the real-world contexts in which the skills will be used. Meaningfulness can also be viewed from the perspective of the complexity of cognitive processes, with the expectation that performance tasks will involve greater complexity than selected response items (Wiley & Haertel, 1991).

In a discussion of the item formats used in licensure testing, LaDuca and colleagues (1995) state that a strength of constructed-response items is that they "appear to pose more authentic real-life problem-solving assessments, because real-life problems rarely come with a ready-made set of possible answers" (p. 126). In considering the assessments in licensure tests, Fortune and Cromack (1995) address the authenticity of tasks in discussing the "concept of fidelity" (p. 150), which relates to the degree to which a clinical examination requires the same knowledge and skills as the actual task requires on the job. They indicate task fidelity ranges on a continuum from multiple choice to essay, oral tests, simulations, and actual performance of the task. Fortune and Cromack (1995) state that a clinical examination that is to gauge complex coordination of knowledge and skills requires the examinee to perform in a real or near-real situation.

The tasks developed for the OCE are derived directly from clinical practice. As such, they each represent real world situations that a pediatric dentist might encounter. Even if the examinee has not personally been exposed to a given clinical situation, he is expected to have studied sufficiently to recognize the situation and develop a reasonable treatment plan. Who knows? Next week in the dentist's office, a child could present a set of symptoms well documented in practice but not yet witnessed by the attending dentist.

Transparency

Transparency refers to clarity both in terms of what the examinee is to do and how the performance (product, process, or both) will be evaluated (Baron, 1991). For example scoring criteria (i.e., the operationalization of standards into scoring rubrics) are more useful if provided to examinees prior to an assessment. Students, for example, require repeated practice with the scoring criteria to evaluate their own work in order for expectations to be clear. The portfolio assessment in the state assessment of Kentucky provides an example of transparency (Gong & Reidy, 1996). For their portfolios, each student examinee selects examples of work that reflect the student's achievement of the state standards. Transparency in expectations was promoted by availability of a scoring rubric and annotated student work that illustrates important features of the performance levels in the rubric.

Sharing scoring criteria is also advised in standardized patient assessments (van der Vleuten & Swanson, 1990). To avoid a mismatch of examinee perceptions about task demands and those of the test designer, the authors advise that examinees receive information about the purpose and format of the test in advance. They indicate that examinees are likely to better understand the intent of the test if they receive practice tests, sample checklists, rating forms, and videotapes of previous examinations.

Examinees taking the OCE are given complete descriptions of what they will be expected to know and what they will be expected to do during the examination. Model responses are available that permit the examinees to see explicitly what the examiners are expecting. The scoring criteria and examination content specifications are publically available on the Internet, and examinees are explicitly directed to these materials when they register for the OCE. There can be little doubt regarding the purpose, format, and content of the OCE.

Sensitivity and Fairness

Sensitivity is most commonly thought of in terms of the bias reviews that address concerns of the relation of demographic characteristics (e.g., gender, ethnicity, socioeconomic status) with examinee performance or elements of a test that create emotional interference. These concerns are illustrated in Figure 3.4. Sensitivity requires familiarity with diverse examinee populations. Fair assessments provide all examinees with the opportunity to demonstrate what they know and have had the opportunity to learn (McMillan, 2001). Smith, Smith, and De Lisi (2001) encourage test developers to broaden the frame of reference to include classes of examinees not usually included in formal bias reviews. These might be examinees who are shy or otherwise uncomfortable "perform-

---

- What are the characteristics of the examinee population? What are the subgroups? What are the historical differences in achievement for the subgroups? What data sources have identified the achievement differences? What do the differences suggest about bias?
- Does the task require knowledge that can reasonably be assumed to be "common knowledge," or does that task cover knowledge or skills that examinees had the opportunity to learn? For all examinees? If no, does the task supply the information that would enable examinees to demonstrate their knowledge, skills, and/or abilities?
- Can a sufficient and/or adequate response to the task be generated based on experience, acquired knowledge, or both sources? Does the source match the standard?
- Does the task require experiences (either firsthand or secondhand) that can reasonably be assumed to be in the experiential base of a diverse body of examinees?
- Will the task elicit negative emotional responses that could prevent the examinees from producing an effective response? Is this interference more likely to occur for a particular subgroup of examinees? If so, which examinees?

FIGURE 3.4. Examples of guiding questions for sensitivity and bias review.

ing" in front of others, who lack access to the Internet, or who do not have parental assistance with school work.

In education, some tasks have required students to respond to controversial reading materials or to share experiences that many families would consider private (Baker, 1997). Such tasks introduce error in scores if they shift the focus of the assessment from the content to the examinee's emotional reaction to the material. That is, an examinee's score might reflect his emotional response, which is not the focus of the assessment, and any score reflecting the examinee's understanding, which is the focus of the assessment, might be underestimated or overestimated. In addition, when educators are required to defend their selection of materials, they must shift their time and attention from teaching and assessing important learning.

Sensitivity and bias review in certification and licensure is quite similar to what we find in education. It is the intent of examination developers to assess the knowledge, skills, and abilities of examinees, and to this end, tasks that are likely to elicit strong emotional responses from examinee are avoided. For example in 2004 a committee met to develop additional tasks for a performance examination. (We cannot disclose identifying information because of nondisclosure agreements that were in effect at the time of this writing.) One of the task developers wrote a scenario in which the examinee was working with a first-time mother who had at that moment learned that her baby had died. After some debate, the committee discarded the task because the consensus was that the task was too much at risk to elicit strong emotional responses in some examinees and thus interfere with the assessment of their knowledge and skills.

Practicality and Consequences

In his text on classroom assessment, McMillan (2001) identifies two elements of task construction with implications for review criteria: the practicality of the assessment and its consequences for examinees and decision makers. He asks us, "Is the information obtained worth the resources and time required to obtain it?" (p. 73). The question includes time to administer and score and how easily the results can be interpreted.

Positive consequences for examinees include motivation, learning important concepts, problem solving, and the application of what is learned. Policymakers such as credentialing boards and department of education officials benefit when the assessment provides the information they need to make decisions about examinees.

The consequence of an assessment can be illustrated in the incorporation of direct writing assessments into state testing programs in the 1980s. As a classroom teacher during this period, the first author experienced the consequences of the state writing assessment in North Carolina. Simply put, the assessment changed classroom practices. Prior to the addition of the writing assessment, language arts activities in classrooms often consisted of the completion of chapter exercises on the conventions of written language (e.g., capitalization, punctuation, grammar). Teachers infrequently engaged students in the writing process. With the advent of the state writing assessment, teachers expanded language arts activities to include writing. In addition, teachers began to seek professional development in the teaching of writing. This is an example the principle of Resnick and Resnick (1992) that "You get what you assess" (p. 59)—one of the consequential considerations in assessment. Thus Resnick and Resnick (1992) acknowledge the power that a testing program has in shaping the curriculum and propose using this phenomenon to reform classroom practices by creating assessments that test students' critical thinking skills.

As another example of consequences, Newble and Jaeger (1983) report that faculty at a medical school were not satisfied with the medical students' participation on the ward. The students, instead, focused their time on lectures and their texts, which were the basis for their multiple-choice final examinations. The addition of a standardized patient component of a practical exam resulted in medical students increasing their time on clinical work and ward-related learning activities and decreasing time spent preparing for written tests. Again, you get what you assess.

Many hospitals now predicate hospital privileges for dentists on the dentists having achieved diplomate status. For this reason, more attention has been placed on the OCE. Each year, program directors at teaching institutions receive reports of the composite performance of program graduates for reviewing the efficacy of the current curriculum. To this end the OCE influences what is taught in the nation's dental schools, which in turn motivates the periodic review of examination content to ensure that it reflects current practice. Moreover, the reports to program directors have grown from a simple reporting of pass–fail ratios and now include a sophisticated diagnostic report of content areas along with the necessary caveats regarding interpretations when the sampling of examinees is small.

Reviewing the quality of tasks assists in ensuring that the tasks focus on important skills and that examinees understand the expectations set forth by the task. In Chapter 4, the construction of essay prompts for the Georgia Writing Assessments provides an example of a task development.

FURTHER READINGS

Anderson, L., & Krathwohl, D. (Eds.). (2001). *A taxonomy for learning, teaching, and assessing: A revision of Bloom's taxonomy of educational objectives* (abr. ed.). New York: Longman.

Updates the original Bloom's taxonomy. Revision includes adding a knowledge dimension and expressing the cognitive processes in the form of verbs. Provides numerous examples.

Raymond, M. (2002). A practical guide to practice analysis for credentialing examinations. *Educational Measurement: Issues and Practice, 21*(3), 25–37.

Provides an overview of the issues involved in conducting a practice analysis. Discusses practice analysis methods, types of rating scales, test plans, multivariate data analysis procedures, weights, and additional resources.

Chapter Questions

1. Classify the following reading standard using Bloom's taxonomy and the revised Bloom's taxonomy:

   A student will organize the main idea and details to form a summary. (Virginia Department of Education, 2003)

2. The NCBE states that the Multistate Performance Test assesses six fundamental skills that are required for the performance of many tasks in the law profession. One skill that the NCBE lists is legal analysis and reasoning, which requires the applicant to demonstrate the ability to analyze and apply legal rules and principles. Legal analysis and reasoning includes the ability to do the following:

   a. Identify and formulate legal issues.

   b. Identify relevant legal rules within a given set of legal materials.

   c. Formulate relevant legal theories.

d. Elaborate legal theories.

e. Evaluate legal theories.

f. Criticize and synthesize legal argumentation. (ABA, 1992; NCBE, 2001)

Use the taxonomies of Bloom, Anderson and Krathwol, and Marzano to classify the abilities by cognitive processes.

American Bar Association (ABA). (1992). *Legal education and professional development: An educational continuum.* Retrieved August 5, 2006, from *www.abanet.org/legaled/publications/onlinepubs/maccrate.html#Chapter%20 Five.*

National Council of Bar Examiners (NCBE). (2001). Multistate tests: The Multistate Performance Tests. Retrieved August 5, 2006, from *www.ncbex.org/tests. htm*

3. Review the task kernels in Table 3.1. Which of the kernels may raise questions in a sensitivity review? (Hint: See the last bullet in Figure 3.4.)

   a. Should the item(s) be removed? If so, explain why.

   b. Could the item(s) be revised to be made acceptable? If so, what revisions would you suggest?

4. For the task kernel of the science standard in Table 3.1, what ancillary skills will the student examinee use in completing the task?

   a. Describe how these ancillary skills influence the validity of the examination.

5. What ancillary knowledge and skills are required for the certification assessment from the NBPTS?

   a. Describe how these ancillary skills influence the validity of the examination.

6. What procedures described in Chapter 3 support the validity associated with an assessment?

7. In Table 3.1, the task kernel for language arts does not stipulate a specific audience for which the examinee should write. Considering that performance assessments should be in a real-life context, what possible audiences for the examinee's response can you identify?

   a. How might the validity of the assessment be different for the different audiences that you identify?

CHECKLIST 3.1

Completed	To-Do List for Constructing Performance Tasks
✓	Identify item writers, for example members of a research team, SMEs, program staff, practitioners in a profession. Attend to the diversity of the item writers. pp. 59–61
	Writing the Task
	Review the table of specifications with the content and process skills identified in the design of the assessment. Determine which content standards or KSAs might be best assessed by a performance task. pp. 61–65, 66–73
	Identify ancillary knowledge and skills (e.g., writing in a social studies assessment) to reduce their effects on examinee scores. pp. 65–66
	Consider framing the task in the context in which it will be used (e.g., writing a letter to the editor, taking patients' medical histories in a simulated ambulatory clinic, writing a closing argument for a trial). pp. 73–74
	Consider audience in terms of the examinees who will perform the task. Consider the appropriateness of the language demands, length of tasks, and resources that can be used. pp. 74–75
	Specify the audience to be addressed in the task (e.g., general public in a letter to the editor, jury members in a closing argument, patients in a clinical examination). p. 75
	Consider audience in terms of those who will use the results (e.g., credentialing boards, state departments of education). User audience issues might include the credibility of the response format, speed in scoring, and easy translation of scores into pass–fail decisions. pp. 75–76
	Structure the task by specifying the topic as it relates to content standards or KSAs. p. 76
	Consider the time frame for the examinee to complete the task. pp. 76–77
	Decide whether the content or skills are best assessed by a product (e.g., essay, post-encounter note, portfolio) or performance (e.g., interviewing a patient, teaching a lesson). pp. 77–79
	Determine the resources (i.e., stimulus and supplementary materials) that are part of the task. pp. 79–80

(continued)

CHECKLIST 3.1 *(page 2 of 2)*

Completed	To-Do List for Constructing Performance Tasks
	Determine the degree of control that the examinee has in the completion of the task. Consider the degree of control that the examinee has in determining the topic of the task, the timeline for its completion, the response format, and the resources. pp. 81–83
	Reviewing the Tasks
	Convene a committee of SMEs or practitioners in a profession to review the tasks. Attend to the diversity of committee members in forming the committee. p. 83
	Confirm the alignment between the task and its intended content standards or KSAs. pp. 83–84
	Check the clarity of the task and its language demands by reviewing the language demands and field testing items. pp. 84–85
	Gauge the meaningfulness of a task (e.g., presented within a specific, real-life context; requires the same content or KSAs as in real-world contexts). pp. 85–86
	Examine the level of transparency of the assessment (e.g., publishing scoring rubrics, providing practice items). pp. 86–87
	Review the tasks for sensitivity and fairness. pp. 87–88
	Consider the practicality of the task (i.e., time demands and financial resources) and likely consequences from its use (e.g., shift classroom instruction and assessment to more complex content and process skills; focus program activities on skills associated with the task). pp. 88–89

CHAPTER 4

An Example of Constructing a Performance Assessment

INTRODUCTION

Statewide writing assessments, in place since the 1980s, illustrate large-scale performance assessments that often have high stakes, such as graduation or promotion, attached to the outcome. Both the stakes and the size of the constituency impose a degree of rigor in task construction especially relevant to large-scale testing programs, whether for state education departments or national credentialing agencies. These steps also are informative in the development of performance assessments for program evaluation and research studies.

In education, development of a writing assessment includes:

1. A review of language arts content standards to identify the standards to be assessed

2. Alignment of the writing prompts, scoring rubrics, and administration conditions with the standards

3. Design features and review criteria for prompt development

4. Design features for scoring rubrics

5. Field testing tryouts

6. Benchmarking/range finding

7. Scoring/rater training and monitoring

8. Sensitivity and bias review

9. Standard setting

10. Staff development for teachers

Like the writing process, the phases of test development are recursive. For example, the rubric is developed early in the process; however, it is refined as it is applied to papers in the initial selection of student essays that will serve as examples for each score level of the rubric, a process referred to as range finding or benchmarking. These phases vary somewhat depending on whether a new test is being developed or an existing one revised. In new development, all steps apply. Revision of an existing program may be limited to prompt development and tryouts of new prompts because the ones in the item bank have been used or the curriculum standards have changed. In the latter case, scoring rubrics would be developed and standard setting conducted in addition to prompt development.

The scope of this book precludes detailed discussion of all the phases listed above in order to fully describe prompt task construction, which addresses the review of the standards; alignment of the assessment with the standards; prompt design and review; field testing; and sensitivity and bias review. Rubric design and review, rater training, scoring, and standard setting are addressed in subsequent chapters in this text. The topics of equating and staff development are left to other texts.

REVIEW OF LANGUAGE ARTS CONTENT STANDARDS

Writing assessment on a large scale begins with a review of the language arts content standards and the identification of the standards to be assessed. Advisory committees consisting of classroom teachers, language arts supervisors, and teacher-educators conduct this review, typically led by assessment and curriculum experts from state departments of education. Committee members are selected to ensure content knowledge and pedagogical expertise and to fully reflect the demographic characteristics of the examinee population. It is helpful to have members who are knowledgeable about special needs populations and students who typically perform poorly on writing tests so that their concerns can be raised and addressed before substantive problems are discovered in the prompt and bias review process.

Including teachers who represent the grade levels on either side of the grade being assessed provides a reality check of what students know and can do and the knowledge and skills they will need to succeed at the next level. Teachers also provide ideas about how to use the assessment as a tool for improving instruction and learning and play an important role in creating the staff development component of the assessment package.

The language arts content or curriculum standards include some writing skills that cannot appropriately or feasibly be assessed in a standardized context. The standards also vary in importance to the language arts community. Writing standards typically include (1) genres or types of writing and the distinguishing characteristics of each; (2) writing for a variety of purposes and audiences; (3) conventions—the rules of written, edited English; (4) the writing process; and (5) use of resources and tools (e.g., the Internet, word processors, dictionaries). Standards to be tested are selected based on their value for instruction; their appropriateness for coverage in a performance-based, standardized context; and the constraints imposed by budget, scoring requirements, and time.

Advisory committees debate how they can use the reality of testing to promote sound instruction (recall our conversation about consequences). Although the conventions of written language are included in the standards, on-demand writing assessments are rough drafts typically produced without access to the tools that writers use to check the rules. To create writing tasks and scoring rubrics that value conventions over the development and organization of ideas could lead teachers to emphasize grammar worksheets—you get what you assess (Resnick & Resnick, 1992). Furthermore, conventions can be efficiently assessed in selected-response tests, so it may not be necessary or desirable to emphasize them in a writing test. In contrast, testing student capabilities to incorporate stylistic elements of multiple types of writing or genres can have positive instructional impact (i.e., consequences).

Genre offers an illustration of one of the issues considered by an advisory committee. Personal experience narratives, long considered the "easiest" genre, are not easy for students who, for reasons of culture or gender, are reluctant to share their realities. Imaginative narratives challenge those students who by temperament are inclined to "stick to the facts" or who are linear thinkers. More important, the nonfiction narrative, the form of narrative found outside of literature and language arts classrooms, is rarely taught or tested. If the writing test includes a range of genres, such as exposition and persuasion, those writers who find narrative more difficult can be taught general skills about development (e.g., how much detail is enough, what is relevant) and organization (e.g., the purpose of the parts of a text—introduction, body, and conclusion—or the logical relationships of comparison–contrast or cause–effect) in the context of informational writing. Then teachers can guide students to transfer these skills to the study of other types of writing.

ALIGNMENT OF WRITING PROMPTS, SCORING RUBRICS, AND ADMINISTRATION CONDITIONS WITH THE STANDARDS

The standards serve as background for constructing all aspects of the testing materials, not just the writing prompts. Figure 4.1 shows the alignment of a prompt with the Georgia English language arts standards by connecting wording cues in the prompt to elements in the standard. At the bottom of the figure the persuasive writing topic is linked to the eighth-grade standards (i.e., ELA8W2-b,[1] ELA8W2-d, ELA8W2-f, and ELA8W2-g) that are assessed by the prompt elements "Decide how you would change your school's dress code" and "Write an essay to convince your principal to change your school's dress code." Thus in responding to the prompt, students will state a clear position or perspective in support of a proposition or proposal (ELA8W2-b). Other standards are of course assessed, but not contained in this example. This particular standard on persuasive writing is introduced and taught at several grades before it is tested, providing students with the opportunity to learn.

If the test is to be used to encourage instruction in the writing process, administration conditions and test materials can approximate the phases in writing, providing the students with cues to plan, draft, edit, and revise. In addition to the scannable response booklet, test materials can include forms for prewriting and drafting and a writing checklist that guides students through these phases of composing. Directions to students can include familiar process-writing terms.

Figure 4.2 shows the alignment of this same standard to a section of the analytic rubric. The Georgia writing rubric for eighth-grade contains four domains: Ideas, Organization, Style, and Conventions. In the current version of the rubric, each domain is scored on a 5-point scale. In Figure 4.2, the top performance level (i.e., a 5) is shown for each domain. A more complete version of the rubric is shown in Chapter 6 in Figure 6.2.

As shown in the top center section of Figure 4.2, the domain of Ideas includes a consistent focus on the assigned topic and purpose

---

[1] English language arts, grade 8, writing standard 2, element b.

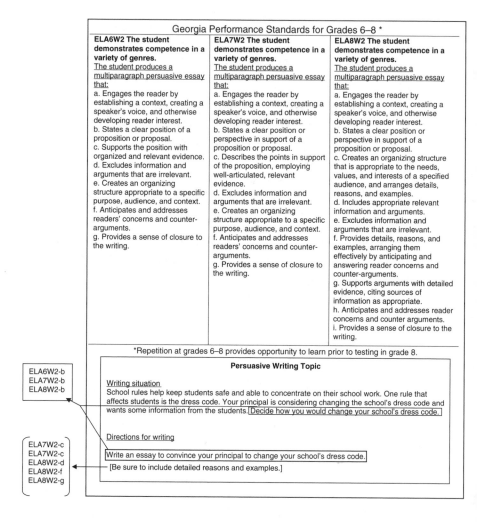

Georgia Performance Standards for Grades 6–8 *		
ELA6W2 The student demonstrates competence in a variety of genres. <u>The student produces a multiparagraph persuasive essay that:</u>	**ELA7W2 The student demonstrates competence in a variety of genres.** <u>The student produces a multiparagraph persuasive essay that:</u>	**ELA8W2 The student demonstrates competence in a variety of genres.** <u>The student produces a multiparagraph persuasive essay that:</u>
a. Engages the reader by establishing a context, creating a speaker's voice, and otherwise developing reader interest.	a. Engages the reader by establishing a context, creating a speaker's voice, and otherwise developing reader interest.	a. Engages the reader by establishing a context, creating a speaker's voice, and otherwise developing reader interest.
b. States a clear position of a proposition or proposal.	b. States a clear position or perspective in support of a proposition or proposal.	b. States a clear position or perspective in support of a proposition or proposal.
c. Supports the position with organized and relevant evidence.	c. Describes the points in support of the proposition, employing well-articulated, relevant evidence.	c. Creates an organizing structure that is appropriate to the needs, values, and interests of a specified audience, and arranges details, reasons, and examples.
d. Excludes information and arguments that are irrelevant.	d. Excludes information and arguments that are irrelevant.	d. Includes appropriate relevant information and arguments.
e. Creates an organizing structure appropriate to a specific purpose, audience, and context.	e. Creates an organizing structure appropriate to a specific purpose, audience, and context.	e. Excludes information and arguments that are irrelevant.
f. Anticipates and addresses readers' concerns and counter-arguments.	f. Anticipates and addresses readers' concerns and counter-arguments.	f. Provides details, reasons, and examples, arranging them effectively by anticipating and answering reader concerns and counter-arguments.
g. Provides a sense of closure to the writing.	g. Provides a sense of closure to the writing.	g. Supports arguments with detailed evidence, citing sources of information as appropriate.
		h. Anticipates and addresses reader concerns and counter arguments.
		i. Provides a sense of closure to the writing.

*Repetition at grades 6–8 provides opportunity to learn prior to testing in grade 8.

ELA6W2-b
ELA7W2-b
ELA8W2-b

Persuasive Writing Topic

<u>Writing situation</u>
School rules help keep students safe and able to concentrate on their school work. One rule that affects students is the dress code. Your principal is considering changing the school's dress code and wants some information from the students. [Decide how you would change your school's dress code.]

ELA7W2-c
ELA7W2-c
ELA8W2-d
ELA8W2-f
ELA8W2-g

<u>Directions for writing</u>

[Write an essay to convince your principal to change your school's dress code.]
[Be sure to include detailed reasons and examples.]

FIGURE 4.1. A sample of alignment of a writing prompt with language arts standards for Georgia's Grade 8 Writing Test. Reproduced with permission from the Georgia Department of Education (*www.georgiastandards.org*).

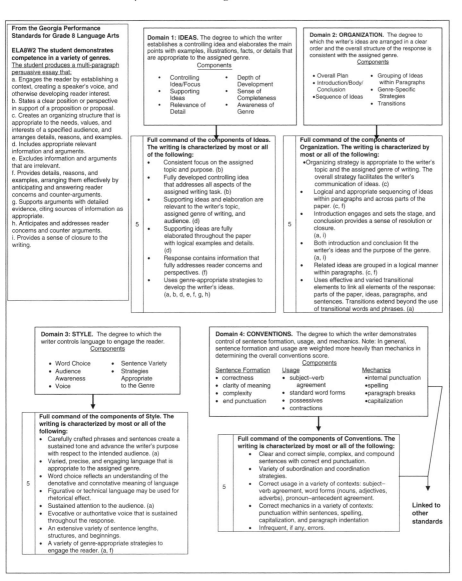

FIGURE 4.2. A sample of alignment of a section of Georgia's Grade 8 Writing Test scoring rubrics with the Georgia Performance Standards. Reproduced with permission of the Georgia Department of Education (*www.georgiastandards. org*).

(ELA8W2-b), fully developed controlling idea that addresses all aspects of the assigned writing task (ELA8W2-b), supporting ideas and elaboration are relevant to the writer's topic, assigned genre of writing, and audience (ELA8W2-d). Similarly, the domains of *Organization*, *Style*, and *Conventions* are linked to the ELA standards, thus supporting the content validity (and construct representativeness) of the writing assessment.

DESIGN FEATURES AND REVIEW CRITERIA FOR PROMPT DEVELOPMENT

Although Ruth and Murphy (1988) have identified the characteristics of prompts consistent with rhetorical demands, prompt task construction for large-scale assessment is more complex than considerations of topic, purpose, and audience (Weigle, 2002). State assessment tasks are created in a political climate with competing constituencies. Writing teachers and experts firmly believe that students do their best writing when they choose and are engaged in their topic. Allowing students to do so, however, can penalize those who are accustomed to teacher-assigned topics or it can result in sensitive, even inappropriate, subjects. Furthermore, difficulties in the consistent application of scoring rubrics can result from too broad a range of responses. High-stakes writing assessment tasks are constructed to maximize the examinee's content or topic familiarity and to minimize emotional interference. Prompt construction often begins with the identification of "prompt kernels" or lists of familiar and appropriate subjects. The process also includes identifying and eliminating overused topics, which requires a review of adopted commercial materials or knowledgeable teachers, serving as prompt writers, who recognize and delete overused topics.

Writing Prompt Development Considerations

In preparing to develop a prompt, potential topics are compiled for advisory committee review. Sources include current secure test banks; widely used textbooks and other instructional materials; and public item banks from commercial materials, state testing websites, and online prompt banks. At this stage, the topics are screened for grade-level appropriateness, required background knowledge familiarity, and avoidance of controversy. Sensitive or overused topics are flagged for prompt-writer training, to demonstrate what *not* to do. Topic kernels are evaluated by the committee to determine whether they are within the realm of student experiences—either experiential or academic—whichever source of knowledge is consistent with the standards being assessed.

Once potential topics have been compiled into a list of topic kernels that are appropriate for the target population, decisions about genre and the use of prompt specifications are applied. If genre-specific standards are to be assessed, they are kept in mind as the prompt is drafted. A topic that lends itself to the particular genre of writing must be selected. If persuasive writing is the target, the topic must be an issue with differing and defensible viewpoints. If examinees are expected to respond to audience concerns about the issue or to produce a counterargument, they must be familiar with both the issue and the audience.

A topic for expository writing must be "common knowledge," one that students know in-depth, or the test materials themselves must include documents or text providing sufficient background information for writers to complete the writing task. Recall the earlier example of the legal materials provided for examinees for the Multistate Performance Test (National Conference of Bar Examiners, 2001). A document-based test increases the testing time but reflects what is expected of students in school settings. Narrative topics need to lend themselves to storytelling rather than plot summaries or retellings or lists of everything the writer did in a specified time period. Figure 4.3 presents topic concerns that are addressed before full-length prompts are drafted.

Although a formal sensitivity review takes place once student impact data are available from field testing, topics that fail to meet sensitivity and bias baseline requirements are eliminated from the topic pool prior to field testing. Modifications or suggested ways to approach the topic can expand the topic pool at this point. For example, while "appearance" could be problematic for overweight teens, it could be developed as a prompt about what teens can do to be healthy. "Allowances" or "money" could be problematic for students from low-income families but could evolve into a prompt about school fund-raising. Screening criteria vary across testing programs but generally include considerations of appropriateness, diversity, values, and privacy.

It is helpful to work from specifications that contain the agreed-upon elements (Weigle, 2002). A consistent prompt format presented to students in their writing classroom prior to formal testing reduces what the examinees have to think about at the actual time of testing so that they can concentrate on the writing process. Prompt-writing rules should be

Compile List of Potential Topic Kernels

- What topics are available for this grade level from a variety of sources?
- Which topics are inappropriate? Why?
- Which topics are overused?

Review Topics for Familiarity to Examinee Population

- Can students at this grade level write an effective response based on knowledge of the topic that they have acquired through first- or secondhand experience? Or, can students at this grade level who have prior knowledge of an academic nature write an effective response that is either primarily academic or a blend of personal experience and academic knowledge?
- Are students who typically perform poorly on writing tests familiar with the topic?
- What, if any, are the key concepts that need to be defined or clarified through examples in the full-length prompt?
- What, if any, are keywords that would be used if this topic is turned into a full-length prompt? Is this vocabulary familiar to the students? Can it be simplified or clarified?
- Is the topic better suited to a different age level?

Review Topics for Sensitivity and Bias Concerns

- Is the writing task appropriate with respect to gender, ethnicity/race, age of students, disability, geographical region, socioeconomic status, and English as a second language?
- Can students who differ with respect to experience based on gender, ethnic group, socioeconomic status, and geographical region respond to the topic?
- Is the topic of a sensitive nature or likely to be interpreted as such? Does it address or would it elicit large numbers of responses focusing on sex, drugs, violence, death, body image, or religion? Will it lead to the revelation of private values, family matters, or confessions of unreported crimes?
- If the topic itself has sensitivity problems, can it be modified or developed in an appropriate way? How?
- If inappropriate for the target examinee population, is the topic appropriate for use with a different grade level? What grade?

FIGURE 4.3. Topic selection questions.

created to determine the types of information (such as audience and form of the response) and cues that will be provided either in the general test directions to the students or in writing–revising checklists. The prompt itself may contain all the necessary directions and cues. Figure 4.4 lists the design features that an item writer should consider when developing writing prompts. The features appropriate for particular standards and age groups can be selected and turned into prompt specifications so that prompt writers include all the necessary elements.

Prompt-Writing Steps

Directions for prompt writing are presented below. They assume prompt writers have been trained in the process. Training includes an overview of the relevant performance standards, explanation of the prompt specifications with examples of well-written prompts, and reminders about language demands and bias issues. One of the most beneficial training activities requires the prompt writers to edit and improve prompts that contain typical flaws.

The following steps guide the development of a prompt:

1. Select one of the appropriate topic kernels.

2. Follow the prompt template, item specification, or sample prompt format.

3. Brainstorm about 10 different ways students at this grade level could develop a response to the topic in the required genre. Make sure that students of high, middle, and low writing ability can generate a variety of responses. Make sure that most approaches could be developed into multiparagraph responses (unless the standard calls for a shorter writing sample).

4. Identify key terms and/or vocabulary and decide how to define or clarify them with examples, synonyms, or paraphrases. Use examples that let the lower-ability writer quickly know he/she does understand the topic. Avoid examples that prescribe the response or that elicit formulaic writing.

5. Decide on an audience that is appropriate for the topic and genre and that is known to the writers. Consider the impact of that audience on the level of language, primary supporting points, and elaboration students would have to include to score within the effective range.

The Topic or General Subject	Format of the Writer's Response
• Is familiar to all examinees • Satisfies sensitivity and bias concerns • Allows student to develop a response from either an experiential or academic knowledge base • Elicits diverse responses	• Fits the writer's purpose • Conforms to scoring criteria

The Topic or General Subject
- Is familiar to all examinees
- Satisfies sensitivity and bias concerns
- Allows student to develop a response from either an experiential or academic knowledge base
- Elicits diverse responses

A Context or Setup to Help the Writer Understand the Topic
- Introduces the topic
- Leads in to the writer's task

The Writer's Purpose
- Matches the required type of writing (exposition, narration, persuasion)
- Fits the topic

The Reader Audience
- Is consistent with writer's purpose
- Is familiar to all examinees

Genre/Mode
- Identifies genre or mode
- Cues expected method of development
- Cues appropriate forms of support or reasoning

Format of the Writer's Response
- Fits the writer's purpose
- Conforms to scoring criteria

Format of the Prompt Itself
- Is consistent across prompts
- Cues the writer

Hints or Cues
- Confirms that the writer understands the topic
- Guides the writer about what to include
- Guides the writer about how to structure the response
- Indicates how the response will be evaluated

Writing Checklist
- Reinforces the use of the writing process in the test context
- Conveys the scoring criteria to the writer
- Assumes prior and repeated use in instructional setting prior to test administration
- May be genre-specific

Content and/or Performance Standards
- To ensure alignment with the curriculum, appropriate portions of the prompt are linked to specific standards (Figure 4.1)

FIGURE 4.4. Design features of writing prompts for large-scale assessment.

6. Provide a clear purpose for the writer that is appropriate for the genre and topic. Make sure the audience and the purpose fit together.

7. Determine if genre cues are needed and what they will be.

8. Think of a way to begin the prompt (opening sentence[s] or stimulus material) that quickly presents the topic, engages the writer's interest, and sets the topic in a meaningful context.

9. Include concise directions to the writer about what to write and for whom. These directions will contain cues about genre and methods of development. If the prompt is lengthy, remind the writer of the topic.

10. Once the entire prompt is drafted, repeat step 3 for eliciting a variety of responses.

Review of On-Demand Writing Prompts for Large-Scale Assessment

Figure 4.5 presents a checklist used to review writing prompts for the Georgia Writing Test. Although the categories in the review checklist overlap to some degree, focusing on them individually can guide the review and selection of prompts for field testing. In addition to questions, explanations are provided in training to assist the reviewer's understanding of the concern addressed by each question.

Figures 4.6 and 4.7 illustrate the results of the review process as it might be applied to two prompts. Figure 4.6 illustrates the need to attend to clarity—that is, the prompt developer should use language (e.g., "convince") that indicates the examinee should be persuasive. Also, issues of familiarity and bias are illustrated in that the concept of a "welcoming committee" might be unfamiliar to students from small, stable communities and the concept might be unappealing to males. In addition, Figure 4.6 provides an illustration of two potential audiences: a welcoming committee and the principal.

Figure 4.7 shows that the topic of heroes might miscue examinees into writing a persuasive essay and requires language to cue expository writing. In this case, the phrase "compare and contrast" serves to cue the examinee to the genre of writing. Changes to the prompt also include making the task more familiar by stating "Think of two people whom you believe are heroes. . . ."

Consistency with the Content and/or Performance Standards

Accept
as is   Revise

☐   ☐   List your expectations of an effective or proficient response. Does the prompt make these expectations clear to the writer?

☐   ☐   Does the prompt cue the writer to compose a writing sample that is consistent with the criteria in the scoring rubrics? If the writing sample is to be scored analytically, can the student text be evaluated in all the traits?

☐   ☐   Does the prompt contain so much information it will lead to copying rather than composing?

☐   ☐   Will the hints to the students about "what to include" result in discrete responses to parts of the prompt rather than a coherent whole? (For example, "what I did, when I did it, how it happened, and how I felt about it.")

☐   ☐   Will the examples constrain rather than expand the writer's own ideas?

☐   ☐   Will the prompt generate lists rather than compositions?

☐   ☐   Is the prompt consistent with the standards to be assessed?

Clarity and Completeness

Accept
as is   Revise

☐   ☐   Is the prompt clear and complete "enough" given that examinees cannot ask questions in a testing context?

☐   ☐   Does the prompt contain multiple messages about the expected response or does it contain multiple audiences?

☐   ☐   Does the prompt contain an audience and meaningful purpose? If format (such as letter or editorial) is to be evaluated, is this requirement clear to the writer? If the format is simply part of the authentic context—hence not a requirement—is this clear to the writer?

Appropriateness

Accept
as is   Revise

☐   ☐   Is the prompt a familiar, widely practiced topic? If so, the practice effect may render the topic inappropriate for large-scale assessment. Students who have practiced the actual topic may appear to write better than they are capable of doing independently, or they may write poorly, thinking they have already "done" this assignment.

☐   ☐   Is the vocabulary appropriate for the examinees?

☐   ☐   Is the sentence structure (length, complexity) appropriate for the reading ability of the examinees?

☐   ☐   Does the task require prewriting or other instructional activities that cannot be built into the testing context?

(continued)

FIGURE 4.5. Prompt review questions.

Interest

Accept
as is Revise

☐   ☐   Does the topic allow for a wide range of responses, satisfying both writer and reader needs for engagement?

☐   ☐   Is the topic of intrinsic interest to the student writers? How do you know?

☐   ☐   Does the prompt lead to formulaic responses? Does the prompt oversuggest an organizational plan, supporting points, or position on an issue?

☐   ☐   Does the topic and/or prompt language lead to clichéd, overly polite, or otherwise shallow responses?

☐   ☐   Will the prompt lead to repetition ("I would . . . I would . . . I would")?

☐   ☐   Will the prompt lead to lists rather than coherent, cohesive texts?

Sensitivity and Bias

Accept
as is Revise

☐   ☐   Does the topic create biasing elements that advantage or disadvantage a subgroup of the test population? Can students who differ in terms of gender, ethnic group, socioeconomic status, and geographic region respond to the topic?

☐   ☐   Does the topic create emotional interference? Is it likely to elicit problematic responses?

☐   ☐   Is the topic itself of a sensitive nature such as religion, sex, body image, drugs, violence, or death? Is it likely to lead to a sensitive response such as the sharing of personal, family-related, or private matters or the confession of an unreported crime?

FIGURE 4.5. *(continued)*

Initial Draft	*Critique*
Writing Situation The United States is a mobile population. When families move, schools are affected. Every year students from different states or countries transfer from one school to another. Your school has a student-run welcome committee, and it is taking suggestions for helping new students learn about your school. Directions for Writing In a letter to the welcome committee, suggest how the committee can help new students learn about your school. Explain why these suggestions would be helpful.	***Clarity and Appropriateness/Topic Familiarity:*** *The nature of the issue is unclear. The opening sentences, which put the issue in a larger, adult context, are likely to intimidate the writers rather than help them understand the issue. They also delay getting to the point—that is, the actual topic. Students from small, stable communities could be unfamiliar with the problem new students experience and/or with the concept of a "welcome committee."* ***Recommendations*** 1. Frame the topic as a teen issue. 2. Make the issue clear, with different positions possible, so that writers understand the need to be persuasive. 3. Provide a familiar audience.
Revised Prompt Writing Situation Change is part of life but it is not always easy. When families move, students have to change schools. They must make new friends and learn from new teachers. They may even have to find different sports or clubs to join. Your school has been getting students from other states and even from other countries. How could you help them be successful and happy in your school? The principal wants students like you to design a "welcome to our school" program. Directions for Writing Write a letter to the principal. Convince the principal that your ideas will help new students succeed and be happy in your school.	***Appropriateness/Topic Familiarity:*** *The issue is framed in a more recognizable way by linking it to "changing schools" and by providing a series of examples. The principal as the audience suits the task.* ***Bias:*** *The concept itself, welcoming new students to a school, may reflect gender bias. This potential may be minimized by the examples of academics, sports, and clubs, in addition to friendship.*

FIGURE 4.6. Revision of a middle grades persuasive writing topic using the review checklist.

Initial Draft	Critique
Writing Situation You have studied heroes in literature and in your social studies classes. You may read about heroes in the newspaper or watch them on TV. All heroes are people we look up to.	***Consistency with Content Standards:*** *The topic of "hero" is likely to elicit persuasive writing. If the goal is to measure expository writing, the cues and the writing task have to make the "explanatory" purposes clear to the writer.*
Directions for Writing Write a report that explains what a hero is.	***Appropriateness/Topic Familiarity:*** *The initial draft of the writing task leads the student to write about an abstraction, making the task more difficult than it needs to be.* ***Recommendations*** 1. Make the expository purpose clear. 2. Make the writing task more concrete.
Revised Prompt **Writing Situation** You know about heroes from literature and history. You also know about them from current events and your own life. Heroes can be famous or everyday people. They can be alive now or in the past. Think of two people whom you believe are heroes and what makes them heroes.	***Appropriateness/Topic Familiarity and Interest:*** *The revised prompt cues the writer to think about a broader range of heroes, increasing the likelihood the writer will be able to select two heroes the writer knows well.* ***Consistency with Content Standards:*** *The writing task specifies a type of expository writing, comparison–contrast.*
Directions for Writing Write an essay in which you compare and contrast your two heroes. Your essay should explain why these two people are heroes and the ways in which they are alike and different.	***Appropriateness/Topic Familiarity:*** *Finally, the revised prompt enables the writer to reason and write from the known—two actual heroes—to the more difficult abstraction—what is a hero. Students without a depth of knowledge of literary or historical figures can respond to the topic.*

FIGURE 4.7. Revision of a middle grades expository writing topic using the review checklist.

SENSITIVITY AND BIAS REVIEW

Sensitivity and bias concerns are addressed throughout the task construction of writing prompts to minimize the chances of field testing inappropriate prompts. This would, of course, be unfair to students and damaging to the testing program. A formal review of the prompts is conducted once performance data are analyzed. Bias reviewers are selected to represent the entire examinee population, with special consideration given to participation of teachers who work with minorities, special education populations, and second-language learners. The review process begins with instruction in the nature of item bias in a writing test context so that the reviewers apply a common lens and set of criteria. Figure 4.8 presents a sample overview.

The overview is followed by an independent reading of the prompts to answer a set of questions addressing bias as related to prior knowledge, experience, and emotional responses of the examinees. These questions are:

1. Does the writing prompt require knowledge that can be reasonably assumed to be common for all students taking the writing assessment? As you answer the question, consider groups based on gender, race and ethnicity, religion, socioeconomic status (SES), religion, and geographic region.

2. Does the prompt require experiences (first- or secondhand) that can be reasonably assumed to be available to all students taking the writing assessment?

3. Will the prompt elicit emotional responses that would interfere with producing an effective response? Is the interference more likely to occur for a particular group?

Initially, the reviewers respond in writing to the prompt. The independent written review is important so that dominant personalities are not allowed to overwhelm quieter ones in the subsequent group discussion. Facilitators call upon all participants to share what they have written. The review also focuses the reviewers' attention on the task of making decisions about evidence of potential bias. Limiting the task to bias review is particularly important with English language arts teachers, as their first inclination is to revise the tasks, not review. The group discussion quickly narrows to an examination of the small number of prompts the reviewers have independently identified as potentially biased. This

---

Questions to be Answered by the Bias Review

- Is the writing prompt relevant to a diverse population? Can students who differ in terms of gender, ethnic group, geographic region, socioeconomic status, and religion respond to the prompt in a manner that reflects their writing ability without interference from subgroup membership?
- Is the writing prompt free of biasing elements for the different groups of the examinee population? Does the prompt advantage or disadvantage any group?

Definition of Prompt Bias

- The extent to which a prompt unfairly penalizes or rewards a group of examinees on the basis of personal characteristics such as gender, ethnicity, or socioeconomic status.
- Prompt bias occurs when a prompt measures factors related to an examinee's group membership rather than the writing skills the test intends to measure.
- Prompt bias occurs when one group of examinees does not perform as well as another group of examinees but both groups are at the same achievement level with respect to writing skills.
- A biasing element is any aspect of the writing prompt that might reasonably be assumed to interfere with the measurement of an examinee's writing skills.

Types of Bias

1. Lack of relevant prior knowledge or experience.
   - The false assumption that information needed to respond to a prompt is "common knowledge" for the student-examinee population.
2. Insensitivity.
   - The presence of offensive words or ideas in the prompt that may distract an examinee's attention from the writing task.
3. Unfamiliar language.
   - The use of unfamiliar vocabulary or the unusual usage of words or terms.

FIGURE 4.8. Sensitivity and bias overview.

discussion begins the consensus-building process. A reviewer who identifies a prompt as problematic for her population may be told by a peer who has the same student population that it would not be difficult or that the difficulty is for reasons other than bias.

In field testing the prompts, decision rules about the minimum number of participants for subgroups are applied to identify other student populations to include in the bias review. If special populations like second-language learners and special education students are to be included in sensitivity and bias review, they must have participated in the field test; their participation requires the cooperation of local school systems that know testing is a challenge for these students. Demographic data must be captured at the time of field testing to identify students' group membership according to race/ethnicity, gender, geographic region, special education status, and English proficiency. Participation in the school lunch program is often the only indicator of SES, and these data are often available at the school, not the student level.

Presenting score data in graphic form for each group, such as gender, makes it easier to identify prompt differences based on subgroup membership. Although difference alone is not evidence of bias, it does provide important initial information about which prompts are functioning differently. Performance data are used to identify prompts that merit an additional look; sometimes these same prompts have been identified in the initial expert, independent review, but this is not always the case.

In the final step after field testing, reviewers read the prompts again independently, indicating in writing whether the prompt is free of potential bias and therefore suitable for a statewide bank, or biased and therefore rejected. If a reviewer rejects a prompt, written reasons are required, and these reasons must be based on the guidelines established at the beginning of the meeting. State departments of education establish a threshold of acceptance (what percentage of the reviewers must accept a prompt) before the bias review. We recommend that this threshold includes decision rules about what to do with ratings from a clear outlier (i.e., a reviewer who rejects most of the prompts or rejects them for idiosyncratic reasons).

FIELD-TESTING WRITING PROMPTS

No matter how many times teachers or others review the prompts, no matter how familiar they are with the examinee population, a writing prompt is not ready for high-stakes testing until it has been tried by a sample of student writers. Ideally, the development process is a leisurely one, allowing for small-scale tryouts when a test is initially being developed. The number of topics would have to be kept small so that the bank is not compromised, but a small tryout in committee members' schools can provide information about students' ability to read lengthier, more complex topics or to respond to new genres. These topics and sample student papers serve a dual purpose because they can become assessment guides that inform teachers about a new test. Information from the initial tryouts also can direct the revision process or development of a larger number of prompts and confirm students have sufficient time to complete the writing samples. However, preliminary tryouts are not always an option, and the test developers must then create a sufficient number of prompts to be able to drop those that do not meet the psychometric property of equivalent difficulty with other prompts.

Whether the tryouts are informal, or a rigorous statewide field test with comparable or matched groups, or all prompts spiraled within each classroom, student responses always reveal the unanticipated. Identifying and understanding "problem prompts" requires more than looking at prompt means and score distributions. It requires knowledgeable readers—those who keep a mental tally of miscues or other types of prompt problems. For example, students asked to write about an "invention" might write about an "invitation" or "convention." The frequency of such miscues and knowledge of the demographic characteristics could lead to revision of the prompt (and subsequent retesting) to provide easily recognized examples in close approximation to the keyword so that less able readers would know the topic. Another type of prompt problem that shows up in student responses more clearly than in scores are prompts that generate more off-genre responses (narratives instead of expository) when students are triggered by mixed cues in the prompt such as "write about an interesting place . . . *a trip you took* . . . explain what makes the place interesting." Prompts that elicit high rates of clichéd responses, or the same repetitive supporting points from thousands of students ("It is my favorite holiday because of food, folks, and fun"), reveal that they do not know enough about a topic to develop it.

A field test allows you to investigate whether a performance task is ready to administer to examinees. At the time the item is placed before examinees, it becomes the responsibility of those who administer the examination to ensure that the manner in which the examination administration occurs is appropriate and consistent for all test takers. This matter, then, becomes the focus of the next chapter.

FURTHER READING

Johnson, R., Willeke, M., & Steiner, D. (1998). Stakeholder collaboration in the design and implementation of a family literacy portfolio assessment. *American Journal of Evaluation, 19*(3), 339–353.

Describes the development of a portfolio system for use in a program evaluation. Addresses the establishment of purpose of the portfolio, its structure, and the scoring methods.

Chapter Questions

1. We state that when the domains of Organization, Style, and Conventions are linked to the ELA standards, this linkage supports content validity. Thinking of validity in terms of the validity of inferences (e.g., decisions, predictions) we will make based on the writing scores, how does the linkage of the domains support validity?

2. Apply the six criteria listed in Chapter 3 in the "Qualities to Review" section (p. 83) to a review of the revised writing prompt in Figure 4.7.

   a. Identify the strengths of the prompt.

   b. Identify the limitations of the prompt.

   c. What changes, if any, would you make to the prompt?

   d. Explain how the changes you suggest improve the prompt.

CHAPTER 5

Administration

INTRODUCTION

After the development of the performance tasks is completed, the assessment is ready for administering to examinees. Key to a successful administration is the preparation of instructions and the training of staff. This is true whether the performance assessment will be used for licensure of hundreds of examinees, a multisite evaluation of an educational program, or the conduct of a small-scale research study.

Guiding the administration of any assessment is the need for comparability of test scores across testing conditions, such as time, essay items, tasks, equipment, and test administration sites (Cohen & Wollack, 2006; Dwyer, 1993; Haertel & Linn, 1996; Messick, 1993). Those who administer an assessment often want to look at differences in examinees' scores across time. A law school, for example, might want to know whether changes in course offerings are associated with more examinees passing the tasks in the Multistate Performance Test (National Conference of Bar Examiners [NCBE], 2005). However if the difficulty of the tasks used in the bar examination varies across years, then the faculty will not know whether a spike in scores was due to recent changes in course offerings or due to the tasks in the Multistate Performance Test focusing on less demanding topics than before. Only if the context of the test is similar across administrations will scores be comparable and test users able to ascertain that changes in scores are likely due to changes in examinee proficiency. In the case of the law examination, only if the tasks are of equal difficulty will the faculty know that any differences in examinee scores are not related to the unique demands of the tasks from one test form to another, and thus, any increase (or decrease) in examinee performance is more likely due to the changes in the course offerings.

STANDARDIZATION

Comparability of scores across contexts is strengthened by the standardization of the test administration. Fortune and Cromack (1995) state, "Standardization involves creating the conditions that assure uniformity of the tests with regard to administration, difficulty, clarity in scoring, and establishing psychometric evidence of the quality of the test" (p. 159). Consider, for example, an evaluator who includes a writing assessment to gauge outcomes of a literacy program. If the pre- and posttests are completed using the same administration instructions, then variation in examinee scores is likely due to the program rather than to changes in instructions for test administration. "When directions to examinees, testing conditions, and scoring procedures follow the same detailed procedures, the test is said to be standardized" (AERA, APA, & NCME, 1999, p. 61). It is such standardization that supports the comparability of the pre- and posttest scores.

Standardization also is considered a fairness issue (Fortune & Cromack, 1995). "For tests designed to assess the examinee's knowledge, skills, or abilities, standardization helps to ensure that all examinees have the same opportunity to demonstrate their competencies" (AERA, APA, & NCME, 1999, p. 61). According to Dwyer (1993), the goal of standardization is to provide "identical conditions of test administration, or the 'level playing field' notion that inferences about the comparability of individuals or groups can only be drawn when comparable tasks, under comparable conditions, have been undertaken" (pp. 270–271). In essence, the goal of standardization is to "provide accurate and comparable measurement for everyone, and unfair advantage to no one" (AERA, APA, & NCME, 1999, p. 61).

The United States Medical Licensing Examination (FSMBUS & NBME, 2004) acknowledges this role of standardization in stating to examinees, "… you will have the same opportunity as all other examinees to demonstrate your clinical skills proficiency. The examination is standardized, so that all examinees receive the same information when they ask standardized patients the same or similar questions" (p. 4). This idea of comparability and fairness will be important later when we discuss the topics of test accommodations and test security.

Clemans (1971) states that standardization "implies rigid control over the conditions of administration. It is, in fact, this control that permits the instrument to be termed standardized" (p. 190). However, the degree to which an assessment is standardized varies (AERA, APA, & NCME, 1999, p. 61). For example, some credentialing agencies use equivalent test forms (i.e., tests developed based on the same test specifications) across administrations rather than the same form (Lamb, 2001). Haertel and Linn (1996) provide an example of a continuum of standardization by contrasting a highly structured assessment which meets Clemans's description of standardization with a more fluid assessment that illustrates the statement of AERA/APA/NCME. At one end of the continuum each student in a class

> works alone, silently attending to his or her own paper. If space permits, students may be seated at every other desk. All have received identical instructions, read from a script provided for the test administrator. They work from identical sets of printed questions, recording their responses on identical answer sheets. Rules about what student questions the teacher may answer (and how they are to be answered), whether calculators may be used, and similar matters are clearly specified. The test is accurately timed. (Haertel & Linn, 1996, pp. 60–61)

Haertel and Linn (1996) then offer the contrast of a more fluid administration of a performance assessment:

> Students might be working in groups; might be using nontext equipment or manipulables; might be free to consult whatever reference materials happened to be available in the classroom; might be free to ask the teacher questions the task designers never anticipated. (p. 61)

According to Haertel and Linn (1996), portfolios further complicate standardization. They state:

> The portfolio usually consists of some required and some optional entries representing the student's best work, culled from up to a year or more of classroom instruction. In this context, rules about appropriate versus inappropriate collaboration or coaching are hard to specify and harder to enforce. A major determinant of the quality of portfolios from a given classroom is likely to be the amount of time and effort the teacher devotes to portfolio-relevant assignments. In addition, the conditions under which students create their portfolios may vary substantially from one classroom to another. Research papers written by students with access to well-stocked school libraries versus an incomplete set of encyclopedias are clearly not

comparable unless the conditions under which they were created can somehow be taken into account—a problem for which there is as yet no solution. (p. 61)

Although it appears that standardization, and thus score comparability, is unachievable for performance assessment, standardization *can*
be incorporated into the design of the assessment. For example, contributing to standardized conditions in portfolios is the specification of (1)
the conditions of choice for entries and (2) guidelines about the limits
of collaboration (AERA, APA, & NCME, 1999, p. 61). An illustration
of this point is provided by the process completed by teachers seeking
certification by the National Board of Professional Teaching Standards
(NBPTS). As part of the certification process, teachers develop portfolios in which they reflect on student work samples (NBPTS, 2004b). For
one component of the portfolio used in English language arts certification, teachers select two students' responses to two texts and two writing prompts. The student responses, the texts, and the writing prompts
are teacher selected. However, every portfolio must contain these forms
of student writing and the teacher's written commentary in which he
analyzes the students' work and reflects on his teaching.

Before proceeding we should clarify a common misconception about
standardization. By the examples that have been given, it should be clear
that standardization is *not* a synonym for multiple-choice, norm-referenced tests (Cohen & Wollack, 2006). In a discussion on performance
assessment, Messick (1993a) notes that standardization serves the purpose of supporting the comparability of scores for both norm-referenced
score interpretation and criterion-referenced interpretations (p. 69). Given
that scores from multiple-choice tests and performance assessments can
be used for norm-referenced or criterion-referenced interpretations, the
process of standardization supports the comparability of scores for multiple choice tests across test administrations and the comparability of
scores from performance assessments across administrations.

The question might be asked whether standardization is only an
issue for large-scale testing. In other words, is standardization an issue
for an assessment conducted as part of a small research study or program evaluation? Often research studies want to gauge whether examinees' scores from one administration are different in another administration; that is, they want to apply the familiar pre- and posttest research
design. Recall the law school faculty who wanted to examine whether
differences in scores over time were due to changes in the course offerings. Without standardization of the administration instructions and

task prompts, a positive change might be due to (1) changes in the course offerings, (2) improved test administration instructions, (3) less demanding tasks, or (4) some combination of the preceding.

A similar dilemma could occur in a research study on the benefits of an experimental instructional strategy in the teaching of writing. If the administration of the assessment allows the use of word processing programs for the students associated with the experimental condition, and no such equipment is allowed in the testing of the student instructed using conventional instructional strategies, then any differences might be due to (1) the benefits of the experimental instructional strategy, (2) the availability of word processing programs, or (3) both. Without standardization of test administration, validity is of concern because of the uncertainty of decisions about the reasons for changes in examinee performances. So, uniformity (i.e., standardization) of the test context supports valid comparisons of examinees' scores across time or types of interventions—whether in large-scale assessment programs or single-site program evaluations.

How do you achieve standardization? Standardization requires developing directions for the examinees, preparing administration instructions for the staff (e.g., test administrator, examiners, and proctors), planning accommodations for examinees with disabilities, and establishing measures to secure test materials. In the following sections we present methods for standardizing the administration of an assessment. Much of the literature we draw on addresses the administration of multiple-choice tests or tests that use both multiple-choice items and performance assessments. We blend the relevant ideas from these sources to describe issues in the administration of an assessment that may be focused on performance assessment only or a combination of multiple-choice and performance assessment.

In addition, the literature variously refers to the staff administering an assessment as test administrators, examiners, proctors, and monitors. The roles and responsibilities associated with these descriptors differ depending on the source. In our discussion the test administrator manages the staff, arranges schedules and rooms, and oversees the distribution of materials. The test examiners distribute the tests and read the test instructions to the examinees. Proctors assist the test examiners in distributing materials and monitoring the room for possible inappropriate examinee behaviors. Finally, to illustrate the process of administering a test, throughout the narrative we intersperse the story of Scott, a vice president for operations at a company that develops and delivers examinations for use in certification and licensure.

Need for Directions

Standardized directions, those for examinees, proctors, examiners, and test administrators, support the uniform administration of the test (Fortune & Cromack, 1995). Uniformity of administration reduces extraneous influences on examinees' scores. As Clemans (1971) states, "Score variations should be due to differences in ability, not to different examination conditions" (p. 190). Said another way, the development of test instructions is meant to "minimize the score variance that results from factors external to the examinees" (Clemans, 1971, p. 189). The concern about score variation reflects the likelihood that "items developed under one set of conditions may yield very different results when administered under another set" (Clemans, 1971, p. 189).

For instance, consider the likely effect on writing scores of the following two sets of directions:

Directions: Write your essay on the following two pages. You have one hour to write your essay.

Directions: Write your response on the Final Writing pages in your test booklet.

- You may make a graphic organizer (such as a web, list, or outline) and write a rough draft on scratch paper.
- After you write the rough draft, you must write the final draft on the Final Writing pages in your test booklet.
- You may use a dictionary or thesaurus.
- You must write only one final draft on the pages in your test booklet.
- You should read over your final draft and make neat changes in your test booklet. (South Carolina Department of Education [SCDE], 2005a, p. 57)

These two disparate sets of directions would produce scores that are not comparable. Why is this so? From *The NAEP 1998 Writing Report Card for the Nation and the States* (Greenwald et al., 1999), we know that students who plan their response to a writing prompt have higher average writing scores than students who do not. Thus if the first set of directions were used for a pretest and the second set of instructions for a posttest, the researcher or program evaluator would not know whether any increase in scores was due to (1) a writing program, (2) examinees being instructed to plan their response for the posttest, or (3) both.

However, in a standardized administration the test examiners would have a script with the same set of directions that were to be read for the pre- and posttest. The uniform directions, then, would serve to produce examinee scores that are comparable across administrations.

Developing Directions

In writing directions for the administration of an assessment, some issues are relevant to all involved: examinees, test administrators, examiners, proctors, and actors (e.g., standardized patients). Some considerations are role specific, for example, the responsibilities of a proctor in an administration. In this section, we first consider general issues in writing administration directions that are relevant to all involved in the test process. Subsequently we consider the relevant details for writing administration directions for examinees and the test staff.

General Considerations in Writing Administration Directions

The development of the administration directions perhaps does not share the creativity and excitement of constructing a performance task, so the temptation is to write the administration directions only when absolutely necessary. However, the development of the test administration directions should not be left until the last minute. Instead, the development of the directions for test administration should parallel the development of the test (Clemans, 1971; Siegel, 1986). Clemans (1971) notes that because the directions for administration are integral to the assessment, the administration directions should be in *final* form before the test is operational. As part of the test development, then, he notes that when tasks are piloted that are novel in format or content, it is desirable also to pilot the directions to make sure they are understood. As part of this development, he suggests that "a critique by administrators or examinees may be helpful in suggesting changes that will improve communications between [test] author, examiner, and examinee and that will serve to eliminate requirements specified by the author that prove unrealistic in an operational setting" (p. 190).

In preparing directions, the target is for them to have the same meaning for the examinee, examiner, and administrator (Clemans, 1971). This requires that directions be clear and simple. In writing the directions, it might help to assume that the examiner and examinee do not know anything about the task. A delicate balance, however, must be achieved so that the directions are not condescending.

In formatting the instructions, Clemans (1971) states, "It is the author's task to find those elements or characteristics of format that will be the most effective in causing examiners and examinees to follow directions accurately" (p. 191). Visual factors to consider include boldface, italics, underlining, enlargement, contrasting colors, circling key phrases or passages, or using bullets to highlight key points. Examples of visual factors are presented in the following sections.

Examinee Directions

In a manner of thinking, directions to examinees begin long before the examination day. Often examinees first engage the examination process through their registration, although many are automatically registered by virtue of their standing (e.g., students in school and an end-of-course examination). Once registered, examinees receive information regarding the date, time, and location of the examination. In addition to the logistical information, examinees might also receive information regarding appropriate dress (e.g., layers to accommodate personal preference if the room is found to be too warm or cool), suggestions for not bringing personal items into the examination room (NBME, 2003), and perhaps even getting a good night's sleep the evening before the examination.

Also to prepare examinees for the assessment, a descriptive handbook might be provided in advance of testing (Clemans, 1971). Such descriptions can be seen in review of the websites for the analytical writing test for the Graduate Record Examination (Education Testing Service [ETS], 2005); the Multistate Essay Exam and Multistate Performance Test (NCBE, 2005); and Step 2 Clinical Skills of the United States Medical License Examination (FSMBUS & NMBE, 2005). These sites provide information about the tests as well as examples of the tasks.

Examinees should also be told which types of materials and equipment that they can use or will be available for their use. In one state, examinees may use a dictionary or thesaurus in one section of the high school exit examination (SCDE, 2005b). In the writing assessment of the National Assessment of Educational Progress (NAEP), students received a brochure with suggestions about planning, editing, and revising their writing (Persky et al., 2003). Additional materials that may be allowed in the assessments include pencils, scratch paper, and calculators for the mathematics section.

In terms of the directions for the assessment, Siegel (1986) indicates that the development of a work sample (i.e., a performance task) should include the preparation of examiner and examinee directions, as well as an administrator manual. He recommends that examinee directions be developed for each task. In some instances examinee directions might be administered from a CD or tape (Yap et al., 2005). Important to include in the examinees' directions are:

1. A statement of the task
2. Required test materials
3. General directions
4. How to make responses
5. Time limitations
6. How to correct inadvertent responses
7. What type of assistance examinees may receive if they do not understand the task (AERA, APA, & NCME, 1999; Clemans, 1971; Cohen & Wollack, 2006; Siegel, 1986)

Directions should also orient examinees to test materials such as a computer, calculators, or numeric grids that may be used with math performance items. Examinees should have cues where to GO ON and to STOP in a section of a test (Clemans, 1971). In addition, they should be told whether they may return to earlier sections of the test.

Practice exercises can help with the orientation of examinees to the assessment. This would especially be true for practice on equipment used in the assessment, unless the use of the equipment is part of the assessment. For example, some achievement tests include a practice test to familiarize students with test formats.

In preparing examinee directions for performance assessments, we do well to remember the advice of Bond and colleagues (1996), who state, "The objective of assessment should be not so much the standardization of *instructions,* as ensuring that examinees have a common understanding of the tasks involved" (p. 121). The importance of the test staff in achieving this end is reflected in their statement that "Because performance assessment is, or can be, richly interactive, it is vitally important that administrators not only understand the constructs being assessed, but it is essential that they know how to discern when an examinee does not understand what is being asked and what kinds of additional explanation is needed" (Bond et al., pp. 121–122). Thus, we turn to the topic of administration directions for the test staff.

Administration Directions for Staff

Administration manuals should also be developed for each staff member involved in the test. Although each testing organization establishes policy and procedures that test staff follow, a common set of expectations guide the training of examination proctors and test site administrators. In this section, we present a description of relevant topics for inclusion in the administration manuals for staff.

Test Administrator Directions. Table 5.1 presents an outline that can guide the development of a test administration manual. Major topics include a description of the assessment, the roles and responsibilities of staff, the handling of test materials, the establishment of an appropriate test environment, examinee instructions, administration procedures, and preparation of test materials for return to the testing agency. Another method to organize an administration manual is to cover the topics according to the test timeline: Before the Examination, During the Examination, and After the Examination (NBME, 2003; SCDE, 2005a). Whichever method you use to organize the manual, in planning for the test administration, Clemans (1971) indicates it is useful to consider:

1. For whom is the test developed?
2. When will it be used?
3. Where will it be administered?
4. Who will give the examination?
5. Will alternate forms be essential?
6. Will it be administered to individuals or groups and, if to groups, of what size?
7. What response format will be most appropriate?
8. Will any special preparation of the examinee be necessary? (p. 189)

Answers to these questions will guide you in the development of the manuals.

Critical in a test administrator manual is an outline of the responsibilities of the administrator and staff. A review of the list of administrator responsibilities in Table 5.2 shows the myriad duties that the administrator completes in preparation for the testing. Test administrators plan the various schedules required for the test, make arrangements for the facilities required for the test, attend to the equipment needed for the administration, and select and train the test staff.

TABLE 5.1. Outline of Potential Topics for a Test Administration Manual

  I. Description of the assessment
    A. Purpose of the assessment
    B. Assessment structure and time allotments
    C. Schedule for test administration
    D. Discussion of the importance of a uniform administration and comparability of scores
    E. Test security
    F. Test accommodations
    G. Ethical test practices
  II. Staff (administrator, examiners, proctors, and actors)
    A. Qualifications for selection
    B. Responsibilities
    C. Training
  III. Test materials
    A. Receipt and secure storage
    B. Supplementary materials required (e.g., clock, calculators, dictionaries)
  IV. Test Environment
    A. Facility availability
    B. Room arrangement
    C. Seating arrangement
    D. Equipment for testing rooms and centers
  V. Examinees
    A. Eligibility
    B. Notification about test
    C. Materials allowed/not allowed to bring to the test site
    D. Admissions procedures for examinees
  VI. Administration
    A. Procedures for distribution of materials
    B. Directions for completion of examinee identification information
    C. Instructions (i.e., script) to be read to examinees
    D. Timing the examination sessions
    E. Instructions for the examiner and proctor about assistance that they may provide
    F. Review of equipment used in the test
    G. Completion of practice items
    H. Instructions for completing each item type (e.g., multiple choice, constructed response, essay)
    I. Guidelines for examinees who finish prior to the allotted time
    J. Collection of materials at end of administration
  VII. Preparation of test materials for return to test agency
    A. Irregularity reports
    B. Count of test materials
    C. Packaging of materials

Note. Summarized from Clemans (1971); Fitzpatrick and Morrison (1971); Massachusetts Department of Education (2005); National Board of Medical Examiners (2003); and South Carolina Department of Education (2005a).

TABLE 5.2. Typical Responsibilities of Test Administrators

Prior to the test

- Review the administration directions, test booklets, and answer sheets.
- Develop and distribute testing schedules: weeks to administer the test, daily schedule, length of testing sessions, breaks.
- Provide examinees with the time and location for the test, the materials needed (pencil), the name of the examiner, and the make-up date.
- Develop checklists for the steps completed in administration of tests, packaging of completed tests.
- Establish testing stations and rotation schedules.
- Plan for the distribution of materials on the examination day.
- Select staff (e.g., examiners, proctors, and actors).
- Tell examiners and proctors their duties during each stage of the test administration.
- Provide each examiner with a copy of the manual and the test (if security permits).
- Train actors in simulations in their roles and to follow the script closely.
- Train the observers of performances/simulations to understand the criteria and scoring rules.
- Check the functioning of equipment used in completion of performance tasks.
- Rehearse administration with new examiners.
- Determine that the correct number of tests are available.
- Review the examination rooms to make the physical environment as optimal as possible.
- Ensure that those who are not being tested do not disturb the testing environment.

During the test

- Make sure that all needed materials are available.
- Sign out only the secure materials needed for that day of testing.
- Ensure that all personnel involved in the test administration adhere to test security guidelines. Report any breach of test security.
- Monitor the test administration by briefly visiting each testing room.
- Be available to answer questions that may arise.
- Return and sign in all secure test materials at the end of testing each day.

After the test

- Ensure that all examination materials are collected after testing.
- Label tests on which an examinee lost considerable time because of sickness or emergency.
- Record any testing irregularities, such as individual examinee sudden illness, writing careless answers, or group being interrupted or distracted.
- Return all test materials and equipment to a secure location.

Note. Summarized from Clemans (1971); Fitzpatrick and Morrison (1971); Massachusetts Department of Education (2005); Roeber (1996); and South Carolina Department of Education (2005a).

Another important role of the test administrator is ensuring the security of the test materials (AERA, APA, & NCME, 1999). Generally, a test site administrator is expected to confirm the contents of the packages arriving from the testing agency (NBME, 2003; SCDE, 2005a). If the contents of the shipment do not match the inventory, the test site administrator will alert the testing agency of the discrepancy. In addition, the test site administrator will also ensure that sufficient materials are available for the number of examinees scheduled for the examination. Some testing agencies permit "walk-on" examinees and ship more materials than needed for the registered examinees. Testing agencies generally expect that test site administrators will keep test materials in a secure location until the time of the examination (NBME, 2003; SCDE, 2005a). At the end of the examination, the test administrator collects the materials for return to the appropriate department or agency. Test materials should be stored in a secure place to prevent theft and protect the confidentiality of examinees.

An administrator manual includes information required for the training of examiners and proctors and descriptions of the test situations. Topics for the manual include:

1. The logic for the testing program

2. The organizational structure

3. Roles and responsibilities of staff members

4. Training materials, directions for administering each task

5. A list of test materials and equipment

6. Procedures for ensuring standardization

7. The handling of special problems, test security

8. Forms for keeping records (SCDE, 2001; Siegel, 1986)

The checklist of administrative activities in Figure 5.1 shows one type of form included in an administrators' manual for a state testing program (SCDE, 2005b).

Examiner Directions. Duties of the examiners include distributing the test, reading the script during the examination, monitoring examinees, and collecting the completed tasks (see Table 5.3). Examiners generally receive examination materials from the test site administrator shortly before the examination begins, and these materials are kept in a

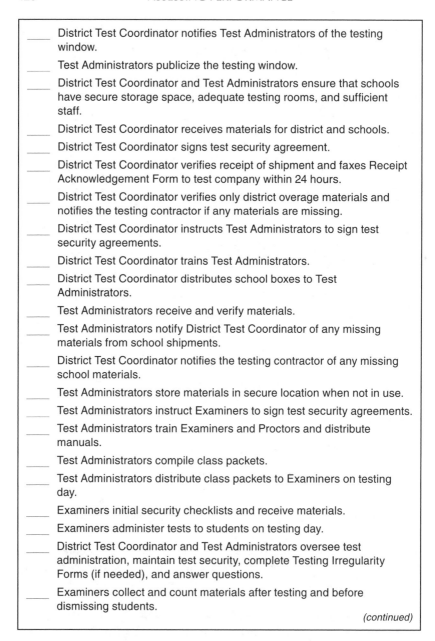

____ District Test Coordinator notifies Test Administrators of the testing window.

____ Test Administrators publicize the testing window.

____ District Test Coordinator and Test Administrators ensure that schools have secure storage space, adequate testing rooms, and sufficient staff.

____ District Test Coordinator receives materials for district and schools.

____ District Test Coordinator signs test security agreement.

____ District Test Coordinator verifies receipt of shipment and faxes Receipt Acknowledgement Form to test company within 24 hours.

____ District Test Coordinator verifies only district overage materials and notifies the testing contractor if any materials are missing.

____ District Test Coordinator instructs Test Administrators to sign test security agreements.

____ District Test Coordinator trains Test Administrators.

____ District Test Coordinator distributes school boxes to Test Administrators.

____ Test Administrators receive and verify materials.

____ Test Administrators notify District Test Coordinator of any missing materials from school shipments.

____ District Test Coordinator notifies the testing contractor of any missing school materials.

____ Test Administrators store materials in secure location when not in use.

____ Test Administrators instruct Examiners to sign test security agreements.

____ Test Administrators train Examiners and Proctors and distribute manuals.

____ Test Administrators compile class packets.

____ Test Administrators distribute class packets to Examiners on testing day.

____ Examiners initial security checklists and receive materials.

____ Examiners administer tests to students on testing day.

____ District Test Coordinator and Test Administrators oversee test administration, maintain test security, complete Testing Irregularity Forms (if needed), and answer questions.

____ Examiners collect and count materials after testing and before dismissing students.

(continued)

FIGURE 5.1. Example of a checklist of test administrative activities in a state assessment administered in schools. Adapted with permission from the South Carolina Department of Education (2005b).

____	Examiners return materials and make-up rosters to Test Administrators immediately after testing.
____	Examiners initial security checklists for return of materials.
____	Test Administrators collect and account for all materials.
____	Examiners give make-up tests, receive materials, and initial the security checklists on testing day.
____	Examiners administer make-up tests.
____	Examiners collect and count all make-up materials after testing and before dismissing students.
____	Test Administrators return scorable materials to District Test Coordinator.
____	District Test Coordinator schedules return of scorable materials to the testing contractor.
____	Test Administrators return nonscorable materials to District Test Coordinator.
____	District Test Coordinator takes inventory of all school shipments and returns nonscorable materials to the testing contractor.

FIGURE 5.1. *(continued)*

safe location under the supervision of the examiner until all examinees are admitted to the testing room. With the admission process complete, the test examiner will distribute the examination materials as protocols require, recording which examinee received which materials.

The examiners' manual should include a list of materials and equipment. Types of materials listed include examinee information sheets; a do-not-disturb testing sign; test books; readers, dictionaries, and thesauruses for language arts tests; protractors, rulers, and calculators for mathematics tests; the examiner's manual; pencils; and a clock or stopwatch (Clemans, 1971; SCDE, 2005a). A checklist in the examiner's manual can summarize the materials.

A key component of the examiners' manual is a script that guides the process of the testing. The instructional script read by the examiner to the examinees is designed to ensure that all examinees, regardless of administration or examiner, receive the same, or at least a highly similar, examination experience. Personal differences in the examiner and physical differences in examination sites should be minor and contribute nothing substantial to the performance of one examinee over another. Deviations from the script without compelling reason (e.g.,

TABLE 5.3. Typical Responsibilities of Examiners

Prior to the test

- Review the testing schedule, administration directions, test booklet, and answer sheet.
- Tell proctors their duties.
- Learn permissible answers to examinees' inquiries.
- Learn her role if she serves as an actor in a simulation.
- Learn the scoring criteria if he is an observer in a simulation.
- Rehearse administering the test.
- Collect and count the materials required for the testing.
- Make arrangements so there will be no disturbances.

During the test

- Administer pretest if appropriate.
- Read instructions slowly, clearly, and loud enough to be heard by all examinees.
- Use exact wording of the directions to standardize testing conditions for all examinees.
- Time the examination.
- Monitor whether examinees' responses are written in correct section.
- Prevent talking or sharing answers.
- Provide assistance only in the mechanics of the test.
- Avoid coaching examinees.
- Monitor that examinees use only the allowable supplemental materials specified in the administrative manual.
- Announce when a half-hour remains for tests of more than an hour.
- Inform the administrator if any problem occurs.
- Help maintain test security by moving about the room and monitoring unusual examinee behaviors.

After the test

- Label tests for which examinees lost considerable time due to sickness or emergency.
- Record any testing irregularities, such as an individual examinee's sudden illness, an individual writing careless answers, or the group of examinees being interrupted or distracted.
- Have proctors collect test materials, count the materials, arrange the stack in serial order number or alphabetically, and check against a list.

Note. Summarized from Clemans (1971); Fitzpatrick and Morrison (1971); and South Carolina Department of Education (2005a).

ADA compliance) are discouraged. Adherence to the script limits the potential that one examinee will experience testing conditions that could have an unintended and unanticipated influence on the examination outcomes.

In some scripts the directions that are to be read to the examinees are highlighted by using a different font format, such as bold (SCDE, 2005a, 2005b). Also, as seen in Figure 5.2, examiners' manuals use graphics and shading to highlight the information that should be read to examinees (SCDE, 2005a, 2005b). Directions meant only for the examiner should use a plain font. Included in these directions would be instructions about where to pause and the speed with which the examiner should read (Clemans, 1971).

In testing examinees, at the beginning of the test session the examiner should announce the test, its purpose, and, in the case of young students, the importance of examinees applying themselves (Clemans, 1971). To ensure that everyone has an understanding of the directions, the test examiner should read the directions aloud as the examinees read

DIRECTIONS
This test is divided into two sessions: 1 and 2. You will take Session 1 today and Session 2 tomorrow. Today's session contains one extended-response question asking you to write a composition, followed by reading selections with multiple-choice questions.

Write your composition and mark your answers to the multiple-choice questions directly in your test booklet. Use only a number two pencil to write your composition and mark your answer choices.

WRITING PROMPT
- Read the prompt carefully before you begin to write.
- Use a dictionary and thesaurus to write your composition.
- Be sure your composition addresses all parts of the prompt.
- Refer to the checklist below the prompt with the features of good writing.
  Do your prewriting on the separate, lined scratch paper provided—your prewriting WILL NOT be scored.
- Allow enough time to write your FINAL composition in the test booklet on the three lined pages marked "Writing" at the top.

FIGURE 5.2. An example of the type of formatting used to highlight instructions that are to be read to the examinees (South Carolina Department of Education, 2005b).

silently. When a change in item type occurs, a new set of directions should occur and the directions should be read aloud. The inclusion of sample questions can help clarify instructions.

Directions to examiners should also specify what they can and cannot do. For example, are examiners allowed to help student examinees pronounce words in a set of science task directions? Instructions should also clarify for examinees the focus of the task. An example would be for an examiner to instruct examinees who are completing a writing assessment that it is important to make sure their essay has a clear message and that mistakes in spelling and punctuation do not interfere with their message.

If the test is timed, a place to record the beginning and ending time should be included in the examiner's manual. The examiner's directions should be to tell the examinee the amount of time for a particular section of a test. For sections of an examination that last more than an hour, the directions to the examiner should indicate that she announce when a half-hour remains (Clemans, 1971). Other intervals may be used as long as the timing of the announcements is part of the examiner directions.

Test examiners are trained to begin an examination on time. Deviations from the starting time occasionally arise when problems occur with admitting candidates into the examination room. In addition, late-arriving examinees can disturb the concentration of the other examinees. For this reason some testing agencies do not permit examinees to enter the examination room after the official beginning of the test session, although some agencies do permit a grace period (e.g., 30 minutes) to accommodate examinees who have experienced minor trouble (e.g., traffic) reaching the examination site. Generally, late-arriving examinees who are permitted to enter the examination room are not permitted additional time to complete the examination (NBME, 2003).

It is the responsibility of the test examiner to make sure that all materials are returned, counted, and filed (NBME, 2003). When the examination is finished the examinees are usually permitted to turn in all materials and leave the testing room. In some instances examinees leave the room as a group, and it is the test examiner's responsibility to ensure that all materials are collected and secure before releasing the examinees. When the inventory of test materials indicates missing components, some testing agencies do not permit examiners to release the examinees until the testing agency itself grants the examiners permission to release the examinees (NBME, 2003). In such an instance, examinees leaving the room without the permission of the examiners expose themselves to consequences ranging from nullified examination results to suspicion of theft.

Test examiners generally return examination materials to the test administrator immediately after the examination. Both examiner and test site administrator complete an inventory of the materials and agree on the counts to ensure that all materials are still secure (NBME, 2003). Shortly after the examination, the test administrator returns the materials to the testing agency. Representatives at the testing agency review and inventory the materials returned, contacting the test administrator in the event of a discrepancy.

Proctor/Monitor Directions. Table 5.4 lists the responsibilities of proctors or monitors. Proctors assist the examiner in distributing test materials and equipment, monitoring examinees during the test, and collecting materials after the test. A key role for the proctor is to monitor examinee behavior to forestall any attempts at cheating or copying the content of the test (Dows, 2005; Newton, 2005). One proctor can monitor 15–25 examinees (e.g., SCDE, 2005a).

Other than the instructions in the script, during the examination, proctors' responses to examinees are generally limited to requests to be excused from the examination room to visit the bathroom, although other personal circumstances can arise. Testing agencies rarely authorize the proctors to answer direct questions from examinees regarding the examination. Examinees with questions regarding examination content are usually encouraged to write such questions on a comment form that is returned to the testing agency with the other examination materials. To permit proctors to discuss examination content with individual examinees could compromise the standardization of the examination administration.

Actor and Observer Directions. In some simulations and performance assessments, the examinee interacts with actors who play a role in the task. For instance, the United States Medical License Examination includes a performance task in which the examinees interact with a standardized patient (FSMBUS & NCBE, 2008). The actor who plays the patient must understand her role and follow the instructions closely (Fitzpatrick & Morrison, 1971). Also, in some performances, an observer scores the performance as it occurs. Just as it is crucial for the actor to follow her script, the observer must understand the scoring criteria and rules. The scoring of performances will be addressed in subsequent chapters.

TABLE 5.4. Typical Responsibilities of Proctors/Monitors

Prior to the test

- Learn the testing schedule.
- Read the administration directions.
- Help prepare the room.
- Fill out student information sheets.
- Retrieve additional test materials from the test administrator if needed prior to or during testing.
- Make sure each examinee has the test booklet with his/her identification information.

During the test

- Monitor whether responses are written in correct place.
- Discourage talking or sharing answers.
- Provide assistance only in the mechanics of the test.
- Avoid coaching examinees.
- Monitor that examinees use only the allowable supplemental materials specified in the administrative manual.
- Inform the administrator if any problem occurs.
- Help maintain test security by monitoring unusual behaviors, such as an examinee being unusually nervous, sitting in unusual positions, finishing the examination very quickly, or spending an inordinate amount of time on a few questions.
- Check restrooms before allowing examinees to enter to make sure the area is free of reference materials (e.g., books, notes).
- Serve as a messenger during testing if an emergency occurs.

After the test

- Label tests for which examinees lost considerable time due to sickness or emergency.
- Record any testing irregularities, such as individual examinee's sudden illness, an individual writing careless answers, or the group of examinees being interrupted or distracted.
- Help collect tests at the end of testing.
- Collect equipment (e.g., rulers, protractors) used in the assessment.

Note. Summarized from Cohen and Wollack (2006) and South Carolina Department of Education (2005a).

Training of Staff

The development of staff administration manuals and examinee directions is for naught if staff is not trained in the use of the materials. Handing a staff member a manual and expecting him or her to self-train is unreasonable. The importance of trained staff is reflected in the statement of Bond and colleagues (1996) that "the selection and training of administrators and scorers are critical features of the overall validity of the assessment" and "attention must be paid to administrators and scorers, and their biases" (p. 121). Staff training should provide explanations of all procedures and practice in the administration of the training and testing situations (Siegel, 1986).

Test administrators must conduct training sessions for all examiners, including possible substitute examiners and proctors (SCDE, 2005b). Training should also include examiners responsible for customized administrations, such as accommodations that require individual administration of the test. Topics for the training of examiners include the logistics of administering the test, the directions for completing any examinee information, the script for administration, security of the test material, distribution and collection of test material, irregular behavior, questions from examinees, restroom break policy, emergency situations, specific duties for each proctor, and staff biases (Bond et al., 1996; NBME, 2003; SCDE, 2005b). Training sessions also should stress the need to account for all materials before, during, and after testing.

Training should also address the uses of any manipulatives and equipment required for any performance task. In some instances the examiner may also serve as the actor who plays a role in the simulation and the observer who records the performance (Fitzpatrick & Morrison, 1971). If the examiners are also observers or actors in the task, then their training will address the recording and scoring of responses (Roeber, 1996). Those with acceptable scoring levels of accuracy will be certified as examiners, whereas others must receive additional training or be dismissed from the assessment project. We present additional scoring guidelines in the following chapters.

Testing Environment

Standardization requires a testing environment that provides reasonable comfort and that avoids noise, disruption during testing, inadequate lighting, limited work space, and poorly reproduced materials (AERA, APA, & NCME, 1999). Also, to keep the environment conducive for testing, some testing agencies prohibit intrusive equipment, such as cell phones, pagers, beepers, calculators that "talk," radios, and food (NBME, 2003; SCDE, 2005b).

In terms of performance assessment in elementary or secondary schools, Haertel and Linn (1996) note that challenges to comparability include the accuracy of timing due to variation in equipment setup and cleanup; the number of students in a class; the size of the room and configuration of facilities (e.g., desks, sink, electrical outlets); and the demands made on the test administrator to maintain order and provide

BOX 5.1. ADMINISTERING A LICENSURE EXAMINATION

Scott is the vice president for operations at a company that develops and delivers examinations for use in certification and licensure. He manages the delivery for very small and moderately large testing organizations, where "very small" might mean as few as a dozen examinations per year, whereas "moderately large" might mean more than 10,000 examinations per year. We present his story in chronological order, beginning with the signed contract that specifies a date and location (and probably more than one location) of an examination, ending with the return of testing materials and scoring of examinee results.

Several Months before the Examination

When Scott receives notice that an examination is scheduled, his first action is to contract with an organization (e.g., hotel, college) in the city where the test is to be given, after determining that the available space meets the requirements of the examination. Many exams occur in multiple cities on the same day. Some exams require little more than tables and chairs with sufficient space (e.g., 3 to 4 feet) between to ensure privacy of the examinee. Other exams require an extensive setup for materials used during the testing. (Scott tells the story of one organization that rented an entire hotel in downtown Chicago to provide sufficient space for the examination while maintaining adequate security of test materials and separation of the examinees.)

In addition to securing a site suitable for the administration of the examination, Scott identifies test site administrators from a list he maintains of people trained and available for this work. The test site administrators, in turn, identify test examiners. Because Scott manages the administration of exams around the world, his list of supervisors is extensive. In all cases, the people on the contact list have passed training in the protocols of test site administration as defined by Scott's company.

Ten Weeks before the Exam

Because Scott manages the delivery of nearly 150 exam titles each year, the preparation for a given administration is heavily scripted, and project management is an important skill for Scott to have and use. Even if the exam preparation involves little more than the copying of printed materials, that printing begins 10 weeks before the delivery of the examination. If the examination involves the use of other materials, Scott must identify the vendors for those materials and make the appropriate arrangements. Such arrangements could be as mundane as the purchase of 1,000 four-function calculators (solar powered, not battery). However, those arrangements could be more complex, such as the instance where an examination required the procurement of 43 severed horse heads.

In addition to ordering the materials for the examination, Scott also wraps up the loose ends regarding the test sites and the test site administrators at the "10 week prior" window. Occasionally, letters are lost in the mail and the contracts for examination sites need to be re-sent. Other times, test site administrators need a nudge to return agreements for the examination and confirmations of adequate numbers of test examiners. Regardless, these matters must be resolved well in advance of the examination.

Six Weeks before the Examination

Six weeks before the examination, Scott reviews the information regarding each site. This information includes the space and facilities available, the shipping information for each site, and the recent performance of the test site administrators and examiners. If he finds that a site has become unavailable, he still has time, but not much, to find a new one. He also has time to adjust space rentals and administrator contracts to reflect changes in the scale (e.g., number of examinees) of the examination.

In addition, he knows at this point what types of materials he will be shipping to the sites, and although the convergence of shipping and sites can seem somewhat pragmatic, there are times when the consideration of what is going where is important. For example in one instance he received a surprise call the day before an examination from a test site administrator indicating that no materials had arrived, and the follow-up investigation determined that the shipment was being held in Chinese customs.

Because there is very little that Scott can do to expedite the passage of several boxes of printed materials across the Chinese border, in this instance he decided to break with security protocols and fax a copy of the exam and answer sheets to the site administrator, who in turn made the necessary copies. (Materials such as the severed horse heads would most likely be procured locally for a foreign administration.)

logistical support. To the degree possible, such factors require standardization. As an example, the United States Medical License Examination includes a standardized patient performance assessment referred to as Step 2 Clinical Skills. In order to standardize the assessment, the examinee must take the examination at one of five Clinical Skills Evaluation Centers scattered throughout the United States (FSMBUS & NBME, 2004). In this assessment the examinees ask the standardized patient questions and perform a physical examination to gather information to develop a preliminary diagnosis and a diagnostic work-up plan. The developers of this complex assessment have introduced uniformity to the assessment by training actors to portray a patient with a clinical problem. The actors (i.e., standardized patients) are trained so that all examinees receive the same information when they ask the standard-

ized patient the same or similar questions. The environment is standardized by providing each examinee with a simulated medical examination
room in which the same equipment is available in all rooms (FSMBUS
& NBME, 2005). In addition, proctors are responsible for attending to
malfunctioning equipment.

Test Sites for Computer-Based and Internet-Delivered Examinations

As pencil-and-paper examinations change to a degree when moved to
electronic form, so do the test sites. Test environments now have computers on the desks, and those computers have some form of network
access appropriate for the application. In addition, those computers have
software available for use with the examination. If the examination
includes the use of a printer, then a printer will be appropriately available. Earphones must be available with each computer if the examination makes use of audio and microphones for recording voice (SCAAP,
2006). Test staff must have instructions about the use of the equipment
and software. This special equipment requires staff to understand the
appropriate procedures to follow. As shown in Figure 5.3, SCAAP
(2006) uses the screen capture utility in Windows® to write directions
that guide staff through the administration and recording of the music
performance tasks.

Other aspects of the test site are unchanged. The examinees must
be sufficiently separated to preclude interference and to maintain exami-

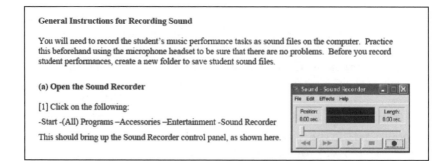

FIGURE 5.3. An example of the use of graphics to guide test examiners through
the steps in the recording of an examinees' music performance in a computer-
based assessment.

nation security (SCAAP, 2006). The room must have adequate lighting and ventilation. The room must be quiet with reasonable accessibility to water and restrooms. At least one proctor must be in the room, although the number of proctors required depends on factors such as room size, examination complexity, and the age and number of examinees.

Accommodations

Testing accommodations are required when standardized forms "of presenting information or of responding may not be suitable for specific individuals, such as persons with some kinds of disability, or persons with limited proficiency in the language of the test, so that accommodations may be needed" (AERA, APA, & NCME, 1999, p. 61). Accommodations in testing is a result of the Americans with Disabilities Act (ADA) passed by Congress in 1990 to prohibit discrimination against persons with disabilities (Duhl & Duhl, 2004; Sireci, 2005). The ADA protects examinees with physical and mental disabilities, who are otherwise qualified (i.e., the examinee "meets the essential eligibility requirements for the receipt of services or the participation in programs or activities provided by a public entity" [ADA, 1990, Section 201]) by extending reasonable accommodations to level the playing field relative to nondisabled examinees, without giving an unfair advantage to those with disabilities.

Recall that earlier we said the goal of standardizing test administration is to "provide accurate and comparable measurement for everyone, and unfair advantage to no one" (AERA, APA, & NCME, 1999, p. 61). Standardization requires that everyone receives the same examination (or a reasonably parallel form). Everyone receives the same time, materials, instruction, and environment. The idea is that the only factor contributing to the performance of an examinee on the examination is his or her standing on the knowledge and skills (i.e., construct) that the examination measures; all other factors are equivalent for all examinees.

It may appear that accommodation by its very nature compromises, if not negates, the standardization of the examination. Why? Every instance of accommodation represents an exception permitted to one examinee that was not made available to all examinees. However, legal opinion holds that accommodations made to standardized conditions only create the conditions under which examinees with disabilities, but who are otherwise qualified, can compete fairly with examinees without disabilities (Duhl & Duhl, 2004).

AERA, APA, and NCME (1999) recommend that examinees should be informed prior to testing about procedures for requesting and receiving accommodations. Such a procedure is followed for the sponsoring organizations for the Graduate Record Examination (ETS, 2005) and the United States Medical Licensing Examination (FSMBUS & NBME, 2007), which have information about test accommodations available on their websites.

In education, the appropriateness of providing test accommodations is determined by state policy (e.g., SCDE, 2005a). Accommodations are appropriate when specified in a student's individualized education plan (IEP). The IEP is a document that stipulates the instructional goals and objectives for a student with special needs, in addition to the appropriate forms of testing. A state policy might also stipulate accommodations for examinees with limited English proficiency.

In licensure, testing agencies generally evaluate particular requests for accommodations on a case-by-case basis (Duhl & Duhl, 2004). Any request for accommodation should be supported by medical opinion (Duhl & Duhl, 2004). If an agency plans to decline an accommodation request, then it should have a medical expert review the case. Legal challenges to requests denied will require the agency to show the request is unreasonable based on efficiency, cost, feasibility, and test validity. Duhl and Duhl (2004) indicate that to this point courts have neither required agencies to provide accommodations that threaten test security for licensure examinations nor required the lowering of pass scores or waiving of the licensure examination—in this instance, in the bar examination.

What are common accommodations? They include large print, magnifying devices, Braille, audiotapes, word processing devices, readers, transcribers, voice recognition devices, increased rest periods between examination segments, and private rooms to take the examination while removed from the distractions produced by a room full of other examinees (Cohen & Wollack, 2006; Duhl & Duhl, 2004; Massachusetts Department of Education, 2005; Sireci, 2005). Accommodations also include increased time limits for testing—generally allowing 1.5 or 2 times the standard time (Cohen & Wollack, 2006). Additional accommodations used for students in the National Assessment of Educational Progress have included one-on-one testing, bilingual dictionaries, and small-group testing (O'Sullivan et al., 2003; Persky et al., 2003).

Appropriate accommodations should be provided for computer-based and Internet-delivered examinations (International Test Commission, 2006). The International Guidelines on Computer-Based and Internet Delivered Testing provide guidance for addressing accommodations in the design and development of these tests.

In the past, many testing agencies have flagged examination results achieved under accommodations, most often by placing a mark (e.g., an asterisk) by the examinee's score on the test report. Although such practice is congruent with the standards described in the *Standards for Educational and Psychological Testing* (AERA, APA, & NCME, 1999), it is considered discriminatory by many people. To avoid the legal consequences of reporting examination results in a manner that many perceive as discriminatory, many testing agencies have stopped flagging such scores (Sireci, 2005).

BOX 5.2. ADMINISTERING A LICENSURE EXAMINATION
(continued)

Four Weeks before the Exam

One month before administration of the examination, Scott calls each test site administrator to confirm the room reservations and the recruitment of proctors. If changes must be made, there is still time to do so, depending on the magnitude of the change. In addition, Scott confirms the accuracy of the addresses he has for the shipments of materials to the test site administrators and the site directions he will send to the examinees.

It is now, 1 month out from the examination, when Scott receives official notification of ADA requirements that he must accommodate. These accommodations can take many forms. Sometimes Scott must arrange for printed materials to be larger. Most often, he has to arrange for a longer examination period, usually time and a half or double time. Occasionally he will need to arrange a separate testing environment for examinees needing to take the examination without having other candidates in the vicinity.

Three Weeks before the Exam

At 3 weeks before the examination, Scott has made the necessary arrangements for the requests for ADA accommodations that he received. Examinations with larger type are being produced. A reader has been approved in response to an examinee's request for such an accommodation. A special room and separate proctor will be available for another examinee. The reservation for a test site and contract with a proctor has been extended to permit a longer administration.

Scott has informed the examinees of the exam location and provided suggestions about preparations for taking the examination. These suggestions include dressing in layers to accommodate personal taste in room temperature, bringing earplugs if ambient noises present a distraction, and other suggestions designed to make the test-taking experience a little less difficult.

He also sends final registration information to the test site administrators, who in turn might have to arrange additional space at some locations because of ADA accommodations or increased attendance. Finally he sends notice to his shipping department that they can expect to ship materials for the examination the following week. (He might send this notice earlier if international shipments were included.)

Two Weeks before the Exam

Two weeks before the examination administration, Scott checks that all materials have been shipped to the correct places. He checks with each test site administrator to confirm reservations, proctors, and ADA accommodations. Each site is rechecked for conditions such as adequate space, tables, chairs, and clocks. He also confirms that the facility will open early enough for the exam and that the examination space is sufficiently removed from other large activities (e.g., wedding receptions, cheerleader practice) that might interfere with the examination.

One Week before the Exam

Seven days before the examination, Scott sends the final updates to the test rosters to the test site administrators. The administrators confirm that the conditions of the examination sites remain adequate. Occasionally, local construction, weather, and unexpected events necessitate rapid communication with the examinees and sometimes the selection of a replacement examination site. (More than once, Scott has had to arrange alternative examination sites because of inclement weather on very short notice. Once, "short notice" involved 12 hours and a Boston snowstorm.)

In the communication with the test site administrators, Scott reminds each that all examination materials must be returned within 24 hours of the exam. He goes over special considerations appropriate for both the examination and the examinees. Some examinations permit "walk-on" examinees; others do not. Some examinations require the distribution of materials at particular times. One of the examinations that Scott delivers arrives at the examination site in an armored truck under armed guard, and Scott makes certain that the test site administrators know how to receive and return examination materials from those guards.

Security

Test security is a final factor in test administration that supports comparability of scores (Haertel & Linn, 1996). Test security helps to assure that no examinees have an unfair advantage (AERA, APA, & NCME, 1999). Historically, the issue of unfairness did not stop examinees from attempting to have an advantage in the civil service examinations in China more than 1,000 years ago (Cizek, 2001a). To prepare for the civil service examination, some examinees wrote on the fabric of an under-garment some 722 responses to potential examination questions. Today, as we shall see, methods for cheating have proliferated and become more sophisticated.

Examination security during administration, much as other secure activities, involves many details that are generally not visible to the public. In addition, the security of the examination begins long before the examinees reach the room and continues long after they depart. Trusted personnel reproduce test booklets in secure areas and gather ancillary materials (e.g., calculators) that are in turn numbered and stored in a secure area. Generally, information regarding the numbers and types of materials that are gathered for an examination are considered as secure as the examination itself because a clever examinee with some infor-mation regarding the equipment and materials likely to appear in the examination could use that information to build an unfair advantage over the other examinees.

The loss of an examination can involve a great deal more than the recovery of the exam or regeneration of analogous content (Lamb, 2001). Many examinations are linked from one version to the next by the use of a subset of items common to both versions. These common items are used to equate statistically the scores across examination versions to ensure that all examinees are held to the same passing standard (i.e., the minimum score required to pass an examination), regardless of the difficulty of a particular examination version.

If the content of an examination that contains common items is made public, then the testing agency responsible for replacing the lost content is also responsible for creating a new passing standard. Although care can be taken when creating a new passing standard, the new standard will at best only be comparable to the old; it will not be equivalent. To this end, subsequent examinees will be held to a new passing standard that only approximates the old standard. Granted, all passing standards undergo review from time to time, but that activity is better undertaken as a part of the formal assessment process rather than as a response to a compromised examination.

One challenge in the use of performance assessments is the exam-inees' ability to remember the items and discuss them with others. Con-tributing to this is the novelty of the tasks, the use of a smaller number of such tasks, requirements for special equipment, and greater exam-inee interest and involvement (Haertel & Linn, 1996). Haertel and Linn (1996) suggest limiting the exposure of tasks by administering a task to different, randomly equivalent groups of examinees in successive years. Such a method would be feasible if the focus is on overall trends as opposed to measurement of individuals. However, in licensure and certification decisions it is the examinee who is of interest.

Preexamination Security

During the development of the test, breaches of security may occur. The Pennsylvania Board of Law Examiners implemented procedures to maintain security of test materials for their bar examination (Dows, 2005). The agency prints, packages, and stores essay materials in-house and stores the Multistate Bar Examination (MBE; NCBE, 2006) at the site. To protect these materials, the Board office in Pennsylvania uses key-card access and digital cameras to electronically monitor entrances and record visitors (Dows, 2005). In addition, visitors must be accompanied by staff.

Another threat to security occurs in the drafting and review of essays (Dows, 2005). Drafts of essay questions for the Pennsylvania bar examination are developed by Board members and stored on out-of-house computer networks. Although the files were password protected, they were vulnerable to hackers. Also, possible exposure of files stored on disks, paper, or memory sticks posed a problem. The remedy was to buy a laptop for each examiner and train them to use encryption and passwords when electronically transferring files for review.

To protect test security, some agencies have agreement forms that must be signed by those who come in contact with items during development or the test during administration. The form shown in Figure 5.4 is signed by anyone who has access to secure testing materials. The form describes their responsibility to follow the security procedures outlined in the agreement and take the necessary precautions to ensure test security at all times (SCDE, 2005b).

The loss of a test poses security threats. Although materials are counted and shipped with tracking, they are recounted upon receipt to ensure (1) that an examinee's materials have not been lost, and (2) that no secure materials turn up in public. Nonetheless, testing is a human process, and materials are occasionally lost despite best practices.

When the loss is a matter of a tracked package lost in transit, it will usually reappear at some point. Occasionally, the package is gone forever, and at that point the testing officials are faced with the decision of declaring the examination "compromised." If the package was lost in transit to the examination site and there is no replacement examination,

STATE OF SOUTH CAROLINA
DEPARTMENT OF EDUCATION
Office of Assessment
Agreement to Maintain Test Security and Confidentiality
For District Test Coordinators, School Test Coordinators,
and Test Administrators

Test security is essential to obtain reliable and valid scores for accountability purposes. Accordingly, the Department of Education must take every step to assure the security and confidentiality of the state test materials. It is the responsibility of those individuals who serve as test coordinators, test administrators, and monitors; those who handle test materials; and/or those who use the results to follow test security laws, regulations, and procedures. The test administration manual for each test provides detailed test security information and administration guidelines. District Test Coordinators (DTCs), School Test Coordinators (STCs), and Test Administrators (TAs) are expected to read and follow the instructions provided in these manuals.

To help all personnel involved in testing have a common understanding of test security and appropriate testing practices, District and School Test Coordinators must provide appropriate training for these individuals. Test administrators, monitors, and/or other individuals who assist in the distribution and packing of test materials must be familiar with test security laws, regulations, and procedures, as well as with their responsibilities for each test. Test administration manuals and/ or other appropriate materials should be distributed to these personnel at least one week prior to the testing window. DTCs and STCs must review test security policies and procedures with them and must encourage them to read all appropriate materials.

I acknowledge that I will have access to one or more of the following tests that are a part of the South Carolina statewide testing program: BSAP, End-of-Course Examination Program (EOCEP), High School Assessment Program (HSAP), HSAP-Alt, PACT, or PACT-Alt. I acknowledge that I have or will provide appropriate training for all individuals involved in administering or monitoring the tests and/or handling test materials.

(continued)

FIGURE 5.4. Example of a test security agreement for staff who handle test materials. Reprinted with permission from the South Carolina Department of Education.

I understand the tests are secure, confidential, and proprietary documents owned by the Department of Education. I hereby agree that I will not discuss, disseminate, describe, or otherwise reveal the contents of the tests to anyone. I will not keep, copy, reproduce, or use in any manner inconsistent with the instructions provided by or through the State Department of Education any test, test question, or specific test content. I will not keep, copy, or reproduce in any manner inconsistent with the instructions provided by or through the State Department of Education any portion of examinee responses to any item or any section of a secure test, secure administration manual, oral administration script, or any other secure test materials. I will return all test materials on time to the appropriate person or place (i.e., to the District Test Coordinator for School Test Coordinators; to the testing contractor for District Test Coordinators). I will follow all of the state laws and regulations regarding testing ethics and test security.

I understand that failure to follow these laws, regulations, or procedures could result in action being taken against my certificate and/or criminal prosecution.

Signature   Print name

District and School   Date

1429 SENATE STREET COLUMBIA, SOUTH CAROLINA 29201
(803) 734-8492 FAX (803) 734-8624
HTTP://ED.SC.GOV/

FIGURE 5.4. *(continued)*

the testing officials find themselves in the position of having to cancel the administration, or at least postponing it until a replacement examination is available.

It is of interest to note here that the insurance provided by most common carriers applies only to the physical contents of the package. That is to say, the insurance will pay to replace the paper in the box, not the writing on the paper. Replacement of the content of the examination falls to the testing organization or its assigned vendor.

To ensure the appropriate person takes the examination, security should require identification (AERA, APA, & NCME, 1999). An admission letter and proper photo identification are generally required to enter the examination room. Examples of acceptable photo identification are usually a current driver's license, a current passport, or another current government-issued identification that includes a picture (e.g., military I.D.) (FSMBUS & NBME, 2008). Examples of unacceptable identification often seen at examination sites are expired forms of acceptable identification, gym membership cards, club membership cards, and other cards with a signature only (i.e., no identifying photograph). The examiner or proctor will compare the card picture to the face of the person in addition to comparing the card signature to the check-in signature of the person before assigning a seat or position to the examinee. Additional security measures used by test agencies include an admissions ticket, fingerprinting, identification badges, video cameras, and metal detectors (Dows, 2005).

Examination Security

Security during the examination includes limiting the items that are permitted into the examination room. Test booklets, answer sheets, simulation materials, pencils, erasers, and admission letters are generally allowed. The personal effects of the examinees are not permitted, although there is some discretion available to proctors and test site administrators. Calculators, especially those without alphabetic keyboards, might be permitted with some examinations. Generally not permitted are cell phones, pagers, cameras, and reference materials (e.g., books, notes, papers). Food and beverage are typically not permitted, although some exceptions are permitted if an examinee has sufficient reason (e.g., diabetic) to request an exception.

Other types of equipment not allowed include electronic imaging or photographic devices, personal digital assistants (e.g. Palm Pilots), headphones, some forms of calculators, digital watches, paging devices, recording/filming devices, electronic translators, briefcases, coats, or brimmed hats (Dows, 2005; NBME, 2003; SCDE, 2005b). Threats to security also include the visual and audio capture of test material through digital cameras disguised as lighters and working pens (Newton, 2005).

To reduce cheating and protect the integrity of test scores, seating charts and space between seats are recommended (AERA, APA, & NCME, 1999; NBME, 2003). Also, monitoring by the test examiner and proctor during the examination reduces the likelihood of cheating (AERA, APA, & NCME, 1999; Newton, 2005). The examiner and proctor should monitor examinees for being unusually nervous, sitting in unusual positions, finishing the examination very quickly, spending an inordinate amount of time on a few questions, or leaving the seat frequently to sharpen a pencil or to go to the bathroom (Cohen & Wollack, 2006).

Materials are generally tracked during the examination to ensure that they remain in the possession of the examinee or in the custody of the test examiner. Test materials are generally not shared between examinees because the use of such materials by one examinee can leave hints for the next (e.g., pencil marks left on tables of trigonometric values). In addition, examinees are generally not allowed to take materials from the view of the test examiner. In the event that an examinee must leave the examination room, the test examiner is usually responsible for gathering and retaining such materials until the examinee returns, say, from the bathroom (NBME, 2003). At the end of the examination the examinee surrenders all materials to the test examiner.

High-tech devices for cheating possibly provide information for the examinee during testing (Newton, 2005). During testing, wireless-fidelity equipment can be used to communicate with outside sources. Possible sources of information would be websites or text messaging with someone outside the room. Access to sources also occurs through cell phones, personal digital assistants, and wristwatches. Also, information stored on MP3 players and accessed through headphones or ear buds could be used during the examination. Devices can be bought either to detect or disrupt electronic devices; however, security can best be supported by proctors attending to examinee behavior and use of the equipment.

Best practice dictates that at least one test examiner remain in the examination room at all times (NBME, 2003), although the number of test examiners required is driven by the number of examinees and the policy of the testing organization (e.g., one test examiner for every 20 or 30 examinees). The policy of the testing organization will also dictate the degree of security found in the areas surrounding the testing room. Some organizations will post security personnel in the halls leading to the testing rooms and at the doors to the bathrooms; others will post security personnel in the bathrooms. Some organizations also place security at the building exits and the surrounding grounds to preclude the unauthorized transfer of information both to and from examinees.

ADA accommodations also present challenges to test security during administration in that test materials are forgotten and left in rooms (Lamb, 2001). Also, staggered start and stop times allow possible exchange of information about test content. In the bar examination for Pennsylvania, examinees with accommodations complete an affidavit indicating they did not discuss the exam with other examinees (Dows, 2005). Extra staff monitor the activities and assist with any specialized equipment.

Postexamination Security

After the test is over the usual protocol is for the examinee to give all materials to the test examiner, sign out on the test registry, and then leave the room quietly. Most testing organizations provide notice of copyright on the test materials and then remind examinees not to discuss the assessment with others. However, it is unlikely that any reasonable testing organization is going to engage secret police to monitor the postexamination discussions of examinees; the intent is to prevent examinees from making examination content available in public forums such as Internet posting and other publications. In fact, some organizations make use of Web crawlers for the very purpose of identifying sources of secure examination content on the Internet. Other organizations use statistical procedures to monitor item and examination performance in different populations to identify examination content that might no longer be secure.

Another potential problem is the loss of confidentiality if an examinee's completed examination is viewed by anyone other than test staff or scoring agency members with the appropriate authorization. In addition, protection of examination materials is required during scoring (Dows, 2005).

Prior to a cheating incident, a policy that defines cheating should be established in order for an agency to pursue and prosecute an alleged cheater (Dows, 2005). An agency should have due-process procedures established. Penalties also should be established, such as sanctions or criminal prosecution. On the report of a cheating incident an immediate investigation should be conducted. In gathering evidence, potential sources about cheating include examinees, as well as staff members and proctors who observed the behavior. Members of licensure boards can be interviewed if the breach is in the development or scoring stage. In the instance of the Multistate Bar Examination, a security director flies to the location of the security breach and interviews staff and examinees (Lamb, 2001).

Test Security during Computer Administration

The general elements of security do not change when the form changes from "classical" delivery to delivery by computer, assuming the examination is appropriate for electronic delivery. However, special considerations for computerized delivery exist that do not arise in classical delivery, or at least they arise in a different form.

Forms of Computerized Delivery. Two forms of networked computerized delivery are often used in testing. The difference between the two involves the manner in which the examination reaches the computer. The up-and-coming manner of delivery makes use of the Internet to move an examination from a server to a computer and an examinee. An example is the South Carolina Arts Assessment Program (SCAAP), in which students complete a Web-based assessment with both multiple-choice items and performance tasks. In the performance assessment component of SCAAP, a software program is used to record students' voices as they perform a familiar song (Yap et al., 2005). After testing is completed, each student's performance is downloaded and is ready for electronic scoring. Because the Internet is publicly accessible, steps must be taken to ensure that the content of the examination is not compromised as it travels between the server and the computer.

An alternative to the Internet is a private intranet that moves information between the examinee's computer and the testing agency's server. Intranets can be made as secure as necessary, but they must be built and maintained independently, which means that intranets are typically more expensive than Internet connections. For this reason few, if any, testing agencies are now building remote test sites that connect to an intranet. Instead, those organizations are making use of secure Internet connections.

The previous administration guidelines apply to on-demand assessments that occur on a specific date, at a specific time, and at a specific location. In the case of some performance assessments, such as portfolios, some of the administrative procedures will not be relevant. For example, the portfolio used in the certification of teachers by the NBPTS is constructed by the teacher in her school setting. The process typically takes about a year to complete. Thus security issues as they were described in this chapter play less of a role in a portfolio assessment. However, the NBPTS does provide teachers with directions about completing the portfolio, so the guidelines provided in this chapter about developing test directions will inform the development of the portfolio directions.

With the administration of an assessment completed, the scoring of examinees' performance begins. However, first the scoring tools must be developed and the raters trained. Chapter 6 describes the process of developing the tools required to train raters in the scoring of performance tasks.

BOX 5.3. SCOTT'S WORST NIGHTMARE

If you ask Scott about his worst nightmare, he will describe something from his reality, as he has already lived his worst nightmare: the lost exam. After the safety of examinees during the examination, Scott's greatest concern is the safety of the examination materials. Some examinations can cost as much as $1,000,000 to create. This is why Scott maintains close control over the chain of custody for examination materials. This is also why he insists on tight security from the printer to the loading dock, to the examination room, and back to his warehouse. He tracks the location of every examination by a serial number from the time of its creation until the test materials are placed in secure storage or destroyed.

Scott describes the proctor as the single most important component of examination security. Without a vigilant proctor, the unscrupulous examinee could take secure content from the examination room, either by directly stealing materials or perhaps by photographing materials with high-tech cameras.

During the Exam

Scott has little direct control over what happens during the administration of the examination; he must rely of the efficiency and effectiveness of his test site administrators and the proctors. Fortunately, experience has taught him on whom he can rely and on whom he cannot.

After the Examination

Within 10 days after the examination, Scott has received all the materials associated with the examination. These materials are counted and processed to be sure that everything that left was returned. Scott reviews the irregularity reports written by the proctors and decides which reports require follow-up action. One such report, which required no follow-up action, indicated that the proctor fell and rolled down the steps of the lecture hall after having distributed the examinations. The proctor was uninjured, and he reported that no examinee had been injured in the "drop and roll" demonstration. He also reported extending the examination administration time by exactly two minutes to "make up" for the unintentional distraction.

In addition to auditing the returned materials, Scott collects the comments written by the examinees, and then he passes those comments to the project manager after copying those that pertain to the administration. When all materials are returned and counted, when all answer sheets are graded, and when all irregularities are documented, Scott files the paperwork describing the administration and begins a new cycle (if he does not have one already underway).

FURTHER READING

Cohen, A., & Wollack, J. (2006). Test administration, security, scoring, and reporting. In R. Brennan (Ed.), *Educational measurement* (4th ed., pp. 355–386). Westport, CT: American Council on Education and Praeger.
Synthesizes the literature related to test administration.

Chapter Questions

1. If the developers of the NAEP visual and performing arts assessment wanted to include a performance task to assess student acting proficiency, what challenges to comparability must the developers address? In other words, what aspects of the performance task would you require to be standardized?

2. Consider a state that allows use of calculators on an examination, but does not provide calculators or specify the types of calculators allowed.

   a. How does this lack of standardization threaten comparability of scores and affect the interpretation of scores?

   b. How does this lack of standardization threaten the security of the examination?

   c. How does this lack of standardization influence the validity of the assessment?

   d. How could this lack of standardization be used to undermine the examination?

3. Review the *Outline of Potential Topics for a Test Administration Manual* (Table 5.1)and consider the administration of a set of reading and writing tasks for the evaluation of an adult literacy project. The project is only at one site and has 25 program participants.

   a. Which administration topics are most relevant in this case?

   b. What test administration staff will be required?

4. Consider a science achievement test and a test of reading comprehension for which a student requests an ADA accommodation for a reader. Why would a reader be considered an appropriate accommodation for the science test but not for the reading comprehension test?

CHECKLIST 5.1

Completed	To-Do List for Planning the Administration of Performance Tasks
✓	Parallel the development of test directions with the construction of the performance tasks. p. 121
	Draft directions to be simple and clear and have the same meaning for examinees, examiners, and administrators. p. 121
	Review a draft of the directions with test administrators, examiners, examinees, etc. p. 121
	Use text and page formats (e.g., boldface, enlargement, colors, spacing) to guide examinees and test staff to accurately follow directions. p. 122
	Pilot the test directions and finalize changes prior to operational testing. p. 121
	Examinee Directions
	Develop examinee handbook (or website page) with registration directions (e.g., date, time, location of examination; identification requirements for check-in; appropriate dress; personal effects and equipment allowed in examination room; requests for ADA accommodations; policies about cheating) and descriptive information about the test (e.g., content, KSAs, sample items). p. 122
	Write directions for examinees that state (1) the task, (2) required test materials, (3) general directions, (4) how to make responses (5) time limitations, (6) how to correct inadvertent responses, (7) what type of assistance they may receive if they do not understand the task, and (8) whether they may return to earlier sections of the test. p. 123
	Include in the directions an orientation to the test materials, such as computer software and equipment, numeric grids, or headphones. p. 123
	Use graphics in the test booklet to indicate whether examinees should GO ON or STOP. p. 123
	Administration Directions
	Develop manual that describes (1) the assessment, (2) the responsibilities of staff, (3) handling of test materials, (4) test environment (e.g., facilities, room arrangement), (5) examinees (e.g., eligibility, notification about test, admission to the examination site), (6) administration (e.g., distribution of materials, scripts, collection of materials at end of session), and (7) preparation of test materials for return to test agency. pp. 124–125

(continued)

	Delineate in the manual the responsibilities of the staff (e.g., test administrator, examiner, and proctor) and accompany the information with a checklist. pp. 124, 126–134
	Conduct staff training to explain the procedures and to provide practice in the administration of the test. pp. 134–135
	Testing Environment
	Arrange for a testing environment that provides reasonable comfort and that avoids noise, disruption in the testing, inadequate lighting, limited work space, and poorly reproduced materials. p. 135
	Standardize the performance environment to the extent possible by providing comparable equipment and logistics (e.g., number of examinees, size of room, availability of assistance). pp. 135, 137–138
	Standardize the software, equipment, and assistance available for computers. Provide instructions to staff about the use of the equipment and software. pp. 138–139
	Accommodations
	Establish timeline for requesting accommodations and publicize with examinee registration materials. pp. 139–140
	Review requests for accommodations, obtain expert opinion for accommodations requests that will be declined, and notify examinees of decisions. p. 140
	Security
	Formulate and publish policies about cheating and penalties. p. 149
	Establish procedures (e.g., limited access to facilities, encryption of files, test security, and confidentiality agreement) for the secure development of items and prompts. pp. 144–146
	Count materials to confirm numbers in tracking documents and store in location only accessible by test staff. p. 144
	Require photo identification and admissions letter for entry to the test site. p. 146
	Limit personal effects (e.g., briefcases, brimmed hats, palm pilots, digital watches, cell phones, pagers) and other equipment (e.g., MP3 players, cameras) allowed in the room. p. 147
	Arrange seating with space between examinees and prepare seating chart. p. 147
	Have at least one test staff member in the examination room at all times. p. 148

CHAPTER 6
Developing Tools for Scoring

SCENARIO

Examinee X and Examinee Y submit a complex set of performances that, given a careful look, appear qualitatively indistinguishable. However, Examinee X's materials are more artfully packaged because her school district provides teachers with state-of-the-art equipment and frequent staff development conducted by faculty from a nearby university.

The portfolios are scored at two separate sites so that enough raters with the necessary content expertise can be hired and trained, results can be returned efficiently, and the scoring contractor can meet deadlines. The first site has experienced raters and staff. Many of the raters at the first scoring site have also participated in the university's staff development program. Raters at the second site are to be trained and supervised by a staff working on this project for the first time. This second site has been added to meet the unanticipated volume of candidates.

The portfolio of Examinee X is scored at the first site, whereas the portfolio of Examinee Y is scored at the second site. Examinee X passes the exam, whereas Examinee Y does not. Although it is impossible to tease out all the variables and explain why Examinee X got a higher score than Examinee Y, and whether these results are accurate, we provide this scenario to illustrate some of the factors that might affect scores and decisions about examinees.

Is this what really happens around the edges of performance scoring centers? Rarely, but it does describe the mythology and misgivings that surround performance assessments. For examinees and test developers who are comfortable with the longevity of selected-response assessments, the rating of performance assessments raises questions. Scoring can go awry, but more typically the rating of examinee responses is effective due to the implementation of procedures described in this chapter (Huot, 1990; Kobrin & Kimmel, 2006, Lenel, 1990c; Stiggins, 1987a; Welch, 2006; Wolcott, 1998).

Although arbitrary situations and capricious rater judgments are the exception, anyone involved in performance assessment needs to accept that human judgment is error prone. Training and scoring need to incorporate procedures to detect, minimize, and correct human error. Variability, or lack of consistency in the raters' application of scoring criteria, is a major concern. Neither the raters who evaluate the performances nor the conditions under which the scoring takes place should affect the ratings. The quality of an examinee's performance alone should determine the final score. The goal of the scoring process is to ensure an estimate of an examinee's performance invariant across raters, assessment tasks, assessment sites, and other conditions.

To avoid arbitrary judgments, assessment practitioners have implemented methods to improve score accuracy. These methods include (1) the development of scoring guides, (2) the identification of benchmark responses that provide concrete examples of each proficiency level, (3) the design and the implementation of rater training, (4) the seeding of previously scored examinee performances into the group of unscored responses to detect those raters who might be drifting from the narrative of the scoring guide, and (5) the monitoring of rater scores by expert staff (Cherry & Meyer, 1993; Coffman, 1971a, 1971b; Hieronymous et al., 1987; Mullis, 1984; Weigle, 1998, 1999, 2002). In this chapter we describe the development of tools such as rubrics and benchmarks to guide raters in scoring. In Chapter 7, we examine the training of raters, and in Chapter 8 we discuss methods for monitoring raters during operational scoring.

DEVELOPMENT OF SCORING GUIDES

One of the most important steps in ensuring consistent application of the scoring criteria is the development of scoring guides (e.g., checklists and rubrics) that are clear, complete, and illustrated with benchmark performances (Camara, 2003; Stiggins, 1987a; Welch, 2006; Wolcott, 1998). Welch (2006) writes that "with well-articulated scoring rubrics and well-defined and monitored scoring processes, acceptable levels of reliability of the scoring process can be obtained for all types of inferences" (p. 312).

A scoring guide is designed to cover the essential features of a product or performance, (i.e., those features that content experts agree are important; Clauser, 2000). A scoring guide operationalizes or articulates the different possible performance levels of the content standards or KSAs. The development of a sound checklist or rubric thus begins by aligning it with the standards established for the particular domain, skills, or abilities. If the performance descriptions are separated into parts—also referred to as aspects, evaluative criteria, dimensions, domains, features, or traits—then the scoring guide is an analytic rubric (AERA, APA, & NCME, 1999; Daro, 1996; Mullis, 1984; Spandel, 2001; Quellmalz, 1986), whereas if a single rating is assigned, the rubric is holistic (AERA, APA, & NCME, 1999; Welch, 2006).

Holistic Rubrics

The basis for holistic scoring is that the performance, whether writing or a portfolio, is greater than any of its parts (Camara, 2003; Kobrin & Kimmel, 2006; Mullis, 1984; Quellmalz, 1986). In holistic scoring, the focus is on the prominent features of a performance. In the early years of large-scale writing assessment, holistic rubrics were valued for their focus on the "whole" essay, which writing experts believed would promote sound instruction in the interrelationship of the parts rather than separating writing instruction into editing exercises or worksheets (White, 1994).

Holistic rubrics often follow a paragraph or block format as shown in the National Association of Educational Progress (NAEP) rubric in Figure 6.1. Notice that the rubric describes six performance levels. Within each level are the evaluative criteria that the rater should consider when assigning a score. The criteria in this rubric address important elements in narrative writing, such as story development, descriptive details, connected events, varied sentence structure, specific word choices, sentence boundaries, grammar, spelling, and mechanics. Also note that the criteria are described across the six performance levels. For instance, in terms of connected events, the description moves from "Exhibits no control over organization" at the Unsatisfactory performance level to "Events are well connected and ties the stories together with transitions across the response" at the Excellent performance level. Between the two levels of Unsatisfactory and Excellent, the "connected events" criterion describes a continuum of performance.

Most important to the large-scale assessment of any content area, holistic rubrics make scoring efficient and economical—a major advan-

Score and Description

6 Excellent Response
- Tells a well-developed story with relevant descriptive details across the response.
- Events are well connected and tie the story together with transitions across the response.
- Sustains varied sentence structure and exhibits specific word choices.
- Exhibits control over sentence boundaries; errors in grammar, spelling, and mechanics do not interfere with understanding.

5 Skillful Response
- Tells a clear story with some development, including some relevant descriptive details.
- Events are connected in much of the response; may lack some transitions.
- Exhibits some variety in sentence structure and exhibits some specific word choices.
- Generally exhibits control over sentence boundaries; errors in grammar, spelling, and mechanics are minor and do not interfere with understanding.

4 Sufficient Response
- Tells a clear story with little development; has few details.
- Events are generally related; may contain brief digressions or inconsistencies.
- Generally has simple sentences and simple word choice; may exhibit uneven control over sentence boundaries.
- Has sentences that consist mostly of complete, clear, distinct thoughts; errors in grammar, spelling, and mechanics generally do not interfere with understanding.

3 Uneven Response (May be characterized by one or more of the following)
- Attempts to tell a story but tells only part of a story, gives a plan for a story, or is list-like.
- Lacks a clear progression of events; elements may not fit together or be in sequence.
- Exhibits uneven control over sentence boundaries and may have some inaccurate word choices.
- Errors in grammar, spelling, and mechanics sometimes interfere with understanding.

2 Insufficient Response (May be characterized by one or more of the following)
- Attempts a response, but is no more than a fragment or the beginning of a story OR is very repetitive.
- Very disorganized or too brief to detect organization.
- Exhibits little control over sentence boundaries and sentence formation; word choice is inaccurate in much of the response.
- Characterized by misspellings, missing words, incorrect word order; errors in grammar, spelling, and mechanics are severe enough to make understanding very difficult in much of the response.

1 Unsatisfactory Response (May be characterized by one or more of the following)
- Attempts a response, but may only paraphrase the prompt or be extremely brief.
- Exhibits no control over organization.
- Exhibits no control over sentence formation; word choice is inaccurate across the response.
- Characterized by misspellings, missing words, incorrect word order; errors in grammar, spelling, and mechanics severely impede understanding across the response.

FIGURE 6.1. Holistic rubric used in scoring narrative prompts in NAEP. From Persky, Daane, and Jin (2003, p. 86).

tage of this form of rubric (Quellmalz, 1986; Wolcott, 1998). Training and scoring are simplified because raters only need to learn to make a single kind of judgment. However, some find that the holistic rating task is more difficult because so much must be considered when making a decision about the appropriate score to assign.

From a diagnostic feedback perspective, holistic rubrics provide limited information to examinees—a key disadvantage of this form of scoring guide (Mullis, 1984). For example, in the score report that an examinee receives, only one overall score is reported. Thus, a writer's skills in developing a topic are not differentiated from his or her grammar skills. To continue the example, a holistic score would inform an examinee that she received a rating of 3 on a 4-point rubric, but the examinee would not know if her topic development prevented her from receiving a 4, or whether grammar skills were the reason.

Analytic Rubrics and Checklists

In contrast to holistic rubrics, analytic rubrics and checklists separate the whole into parts. In other words, a rater makes a judgment about each of the various elements of the performance. The more detailed analytic rubrics often contain bullet statements or format conventions that indicate the sections and types of information, as illustrated by the analytic writing rubrics used in Georgia (see Figure 6.2). Note that the Georgia analytic rubric allows for scoring across four domains: *Ideas, Organization, Style,* and *Conventions.* Thus, a rater will assign four scores to a student's writing sample.

In contrast to a holistic rubric, with an analytic scale raters can assign scores to some of the criteria and then focus on the remaining ones, rather than having to synthesize and balance all the strengths and weaknesses. Once raters gain experience, even though multiple decisions have to be made, raters can make analytic decisions about as quickly as a single holistic judgment.

Analytic training is more complex and time consuming than holistic scoring (Mullis, 1984), and more time is required up front to develop the training materials. Scoring sessions are more costly and longer—a disadvantage to this form. However, a key advantage is that those who use scores from an assessment to make decisions, such as teachers and project staff, consider the analytic feedback most useful (Johnson, Fisher, et al., 2003; Quellmalz, 1986). Another form of analytic scoring uses a

(Text continues on page 168)

Georgia Grade 8 Writing Assessment: Scoring Rubric
Domain 1: Ideas

Domain 1: IDEAS. The degree to which the writer establishes a controlling idea and elaborates the main points with examples, illustrations, facts, or details that are appropriate to the assigned genre.

Components

- Controlling Idea/Focus
- Supporting Ideas
- Relevance of Detail
- Depth of Development
- Sense of Completeness
- Awareness of Genre

1. Lack of control of the components of Ideas. The writing is characterized by the following:	2. Minimal control of the components of Ideas. The writing is characterized by most or all of the following:	3. Sufficient control of the components of Ideas. The writing is characterized by most or all of the following:	4. Consistent control of the components of Ideas. The writing is characterized by most or all of the following:	5. Full command of the components of Ideas. The writing is characterized by most or all of the following:
Lack of focus on the assigned topic and purpose	Limited focus on the assigned topic and purpose	Generally consistent focus on the assigned topic and purpose	Consistent focus on the assigned topic and purpose	Consistent focus on the assigned topic and purpose
Lack of a controlling idea	Minimally developed controlling idea that addresses some aspect of the assigned writing task	Developed controlling idea that addresses the assigned writing task	Well developed controlling idea that addresses the assigned writing task	Fully developed controlling idea that addresses all aspects of the assigned writing task
Absence of supporting ideas or unclear supporting ideas	Supporting ideas are vague, general, and/or undeveloped or some ideas may be partially developed,	Most supporting ideas and elaboration are relevant to the writer's topic and assigned genre of writing	Supporting ideas and elaboration are relevant to the writer's topic and assigned genre of writing	Supporting ideas and elaboration are relevant to the writer's topic, assigned genre of writing, and

audience				while others are simply listed without development
Supporting ideas are fully elaborated throughout the paper with logical examples and details	Supporting ideas are developed with specific examples and details	Supporting ideas are developed with some examples and details; some parts of the paper are well developed, but other parts of the paper are only partially developed	Response lacks sufficient information (due to brevity and/or repetition) to provide a sense of completeness and address reader concerns	Development is lacking due to brevity of the response and/or repetition of ideas
Response contains information that fully addresses reader concerns and perspectives	Response contains information that addresses reader concerns and perspectives	Response contains sufficient information to address the topic and some reader concerns and perspectives	Some points and details may be irrelevant or inappropriate for the writer's assigned topic, audience, and assigned genre of writing	Lacks a sense of completeness and fails to address reader concerns Majority of details are irrelevant
Uses genre-appropriate strategies to develop the writer's ideas	Response is appropriate to the assigned genre	Response is generally appropriate to the assigned genre	Response does not demonstrate genre awareness	Response is inappropriate to the assigned genre Insufficient student writing (due to brevity or copying the prompt) to determine competence in Ideas

(continued)

FIGURE 6.2. Analytic rubric for the Georgia Writing Assessment. Reproduced with permission from the Georgia Department of Education.

Georgia Grade 8 Writing Assessment: Scoring Rubric
Domain 2: Organization

Domain 2: ORGANIZATION. The degree to which the writer's ideas are arranged in a clear order and the overall structure of the response is consistent with the assigned genre.

Components

- Overall Plan
- Introduction/Body/Conclusion
- Sequence of Ideas
- Grouping of Ideas within Paragraphs
- Genre-Specific Strategies
- Transitions

1. Lack of control of the components of Organization. The writing is characterized by the following:	2. Minimal control of the components of Organization. The writing is characterized by most or all of the following:	3. Sufficient control of the components of Organization. The writing is characterized by most or all of the following:	4. Consistent control of the components of Organization. The writing is characterized by most or all of the following:	5. Full command of the components of Organization. The writing is characterized by most or all of the following:
No evidence of an organizing strategy	Organizing strategy is formulaic and/or inappropriate to the assigned genre	Organizational strategy is generally appropriate to the writer's ideas and purpose of the genre	Overall organizational strategy or structure is appropriate to the writer's ideas and purpose of the genre. Structure guides the reader through the text	Organizing strategy is appropriate to the writer's topic and the assigned genre of writing. The overall strategy facilitates the writer's communication of ideas
Unclear sequence of ideas	Minimal evidence of sequencing	Generally clear sequence of ideas	Logical sequencing of ideas across parts of the paper	Logical and appropriate sequencing of ideas within paragraphs and across parts of the paper
Lacks an introduction and/ or conclusion	May lack an introduction or a conclusion or include an	Introduction is clear and a conclusion provides closure	Introduction sets the stage, and conclusion ends the	Introduction engages and sets the stage, and

(continued)

	ineffective introduction or conclusion		piece of writing without repetition	conclusion provides a sense of resolution or closure Both introduction and conclusion fit the writer's ideas and the purpose of the genre
Unrelated ideas included within paragraphs	Ideas within paragraphs are not arranged in a meaningful order	Related ideas generally grouped together within paragraphs	Logical grouping of ideas within paragraphs	Related ideas are grouped in a logical manner within paragraphs
Lack of transitions or inappropriate transitions	Limited use of transitions (transitions may be formulaic, ineffective or overused)	Transitions link parts of the paper	Varied transitions link parts of the paper and link ideas within paragraphs	Uses effective and varied transitional elements to link all elements of the response: parts of the paper, ideas, paragraphs, and sentences. Transitions extend beyond the use of transitional words and phrases
Insufficient writing (due to brevity or copying the prompt) to determine competence in Organization	Demonstration of competence limited by the brevity of the response			

FIGURE 6.2. (continued)

Georgia Grade 8 Writing Assessment: Scoring Rubric
Domain 3: Style

Domain 3: STYLE. The degree to which the writer controls language to engage the reader.

Components

- Word Choice
- Audience Awareness
- Voice
- Sentence Variety
- Strategies Appropriate to the Genre

1. Lack of control of the components of Style. The writing is characterized by the following:	2. Minimal control of the components of Style. The writing is characterized by most or all of the following:	3. Sufficient control on the components of Style. The writing is characterized by most or all of the following:	4. Consistent control of the components of Style. The writing is characterized by most or all of the following:	5. Full command of the components of Style. The writing is characterized by most or all of the following:
Language and tone are flat and/or inappropriate to the task and reader	Language and tone are uneven (appropriate in some parts of the response, but flat throughout most of the response)	Language and tone are generally consistent with the writer's purpose and appropriate to the assigned genre	Language and tone are consistent with the writer's purpose and appropriate to the assigned genre	Carefully crafted phrases and sentences create a sustained tone and advance the writer's purpose with respect to the intended audience
Word choice is inaccurate, imprecise, and/or confusing	Word choice is simple, ordinary and/or repetitive	Word choice is generally engaging with occasional lapses into simple and ordinary language	Word choice is precise and engaging	Varied, precise, and engaging language that is appropriate to the assigned genre

Word choice reflects an understanding of the denotative and connotative meaning of language |

164

Little or no attention to audience	Limited awareness of audience	Awareness of audience may be limited to introduction and/or conclusion	Attention to audience in introduction, body, and conclusion	Figurative or technical language may be used for rhetorical effect
				Sustained attention to the audience
Writer's voice is not apparent	Minimal, inconsistent or indistinct voice	Writer's voice is clear and appropriate	Consistent and distinctive voice	Evocative or authoritative voice that is sustained throughout the response
Lack of sentence variety	Little variation in sentence length and structure	Some variation in sentence length and structure	Sentences vary in length and structure	An extensive variety of sentence lengths, structures, and beginnings
Insufficient student writing (due to brevity or copying the prompt) to determine competence in Style	Demonstration of competence limited by the brevity of the response	May include some genre-appropriate strategies	Some genre-appropriate strategies to engage the reader	A variety of genre-appropriate strategies to engage the reader

FIGURE 6.2. *(continued)*

(continued)

165

Georgia Grade 8 Writing Assessment: Scoring Rubric
Domain 4: Conventions

Domain 4: CONVENTIONS. The degree to which the writer demonstrates control of sentence formation, usage, and mechanics. *Note: In general, sentence formation and usage are weighted more heavily than mechanics in determining the overall conventions score.*

Components		
Sentence Formation	Usage	Mechanics
• correctness • clarity of meaning • complexity • end punctuation	• subject-verb agreement • standard word forms • possessives • contractions	• internal punctuation • spelling • paragraph breaks • capitalization
1. Lack of control of the components of Conventions. The writing is characterized by the following: Frequent sentence fragments, run-ons, and incorrect sentences End punctuation incorrect or lacking		
2. Minimal control of the components of Conventions. The writing is characterized by most or all of the following: Simple sentences formed correctly, but other sentences may be incomplete or overloaded Sentence structure is awkward and/or end punctuation may be missing or incorrect		
3. Sufficient control of the components of Conventions. The writing is characterized by most or all of the following: Sentences are generally correct with generally correct end punctuation Some errors in complex and compound sentences, and occasional sentence fragments, run-ons, or awkward sentences. Few errors with simple sentences		
4. Consistent control of the components of Conventions. The writing is characterized by most or all of the following: Correct simple, complex, and compound sentences with correct end punctuation and few errors		
5. Full command of the components of Conventions. The writing is characterized by most or all of the following: Clear and correct simple, complex, and compound sentences with correct end punctuation Variety of subordination and coordination strategies		

May contain frequent and severe errors in both usage and mechanics	May have frequent errors in usage and/or mechanics	Generally correct usage, but may contain some errors in subject-verb agreement, word forms, pronoun-antecedent agreement, verb tense, and commonly confused homonyms	Correct usage with few errors	Correct usage in a variety of contexts: subject-verb agreement, word forms (nouns, adjectives, adverbs), pronoun-antecedent agreement
	Minimal control in the three components of Conventions or one component may be strong while the other two are weak	Generally correct mechanics, but may contain some errors in spelling, capitalization, paragraph indentation, and punctuation within sentences	Correct mechanics with few errors	Correct mechanics in a variety of contexts: punctuation within sentences, spelling, capitalization, and paragraph indentation
Errors may interfere with or obscure meaning	Some errors may interfere with meaning	Few errors interfere with meaning	Errors are generally minor and do not interfere with meaning	Infrequent, if any, errors
Insufficient student writing (due to brevity or copying the prompt) to determine competence in Conventions	Demonstration of competence limited by the brevity of the response			

FIGURE 6.2. (continued)

Includes all the boards	
Provides a number of washers on the hook for every board	
The number of washers increases as surface roughness increases	
Makes more than one observation for each board with the same block	

FIGURE 6.3. Checklist for a science performance task on friction. Reproduced with permission from Solano-Flores, Jovanovic, Shavelson, and Bachman (1999). Copyright 1999 by Taylor & Francis Group, LLC.

checklist to dichotomously score each process step or criterion point in a task (Fortune & Cromack, 1995). Checklists appear to be integral to many licensure examinations. Gross (1993) states that in the development of a checklist for a licensure examination each skill is divided into component items, and each item is scored as "Yes" if the procedure is completed satisfactorily or "No" if performed incorrectly. A major disadvantage to this form of scoring guide is that the dichotomy (i.e., yes, no) does not provide information about the degree to which the examinee addressed the skill.

In the medical field, checklists have been used in standardized patient examinations to assess the examinee's ability in history taking, physical examination, and communication skills (De Champlain, Macmillan, King, et al., 1999; Macmillan et al., 1999). Checklists in these instances were case-specific and contained up to 25 dichotomously scored items.

In developing a checklist for law examinations, Lenel (1990c) recommends the preparation of a model answer and distillation of the model response into the elements of a good response. These elements can then be listed in a checklist. A similar approach was used in a science assessment in education to develop checklists for scoring tasks related to inclines and friction (Solano-Flores et al., 1999). As shown in Figure 6.3, the checklists contain a column with the process steps that the student examinees should complete and a column to indicate the presence or absence of the procedure.

DEVELOPMENT OF A SCORING GUIDE FRAMEWORK

Developing a scoring guide requires attention to identifying and operationalizing the relevant criteria; determining whether the form of the guide should be a holistic rubric, analytic rubric, or a checklist; deciding the length of the scale; and developing descriptors for each scale point. These elements of scoring rubrics are reviewed in the following sections.

Operationalization of Criteria

As discussed in Chapter 3, national educational organizations have established either content or performance standards for disciplines including language arts, mathematics, and the sciences. States also have their own sets of content standards. In addition, professional credentialing boards have identified critical knowledge, skills, and abilities important to qualify for practice in their field. By drafting scoring guides at the time of task development, the test developers can ensure that the rubrics or checklists are aligned with the content standards or KSAs that are the focus of the tasks (Welch, 2006), thus supporting the scorability of tasks and ensuring that the results make sense to the test users.

The performance standards for the Georgia Writing Assessment were introduced in Chapter 3 (see Figure 3.5). To operationalize the criteria for the writing assessment, as shown in Figure 6.2, the rubric contains a title identifying the domain, a definition of that domain, and a list of the dimensions or components of that domain.[1] For example, the first section of the Georgia analytic rubric in Figure 6.2 shows the domain title of Ideas at the top of the page and then the box contains the definition and the components. The definition is "The degree to which the writer establishes a controlling idea and elaborates the main points with examples, illustrations, facts, or details that are appropriate to the assigned genre."

The list of components in this domain includes controlling idea, supporting ideas, relevance of detail, and so on. The components identify the features of an essay that the rater would evaluate when scoring this particular domain; thus the components are different for the different domains. The components and the definition match the language in the performance standards. Each score point begins with a summary statement at the top of the column and then the description of skills for each component within the *Ideas* domain.

The highest score of 5 is described as writing characterized by consistent focus on the assigned topic and purpose; fully developed controlling idea that addresses all aspects of the assigned writing task;

---

[1]The rubrics have been reformatted for this text to highlight portions and design of the analytic rubrics.

and supporting ideas and elaboration are relevant to the writer's topic, assigned genre of writing, and audience. A score of 3, the midrange, was worded to be consistent with the expectations of student performance for seventh- and eighth-grade students as expressed in the Georgia Performance Standards. The summary statements and individual bulleted descriptions of the components show a continuum of increasing skill from left to right, 1 to 5.

Scoring Guides: Advantages and Disadvantages

Which type of scoring guide is preferable? The interrater reliability coefficient is a key criterion in deciding which form of scoring guide is best. Possible values for the interrater reliability coefficient range from 0 to 1. As the coefficient increases to 1.0, the raters' scores are in greater agreement. Scoring guides that support greater interrater reliability, coefficients of .80 or .90 for example, would be preferable. However, studies of interrater reliability offer conflicting findings for the use of holistic rubrics, analytic rubrics, and checklists. These conflicted findings are often the result of the rating scale in use.

In an overview of research in the field of writing assessment, Huot (1990) reports that the levels of interrater reliability achieved with holistic rubrics were generally lower than that achieved with analytic rubrics. For example, in a study of the scoring of writing samples, Veal and Hudson (1983) report interrater reliability of .90 for analytic ratings and a range of .69 to .76 for holistic ratings. In another overview of research in the direct assessment of writing samples, Breland (1983) reports that higher levels of interrater reliability were associated with analytic scoring, followed by holistic scoring. In the scoring of portfolios, Johnson, McDaniel, and colleagues (2000) report interrater reliability of .86 for summed analytic scores and .78 for holistic scores.

In a study of scoring science and social studies tasks, Creighton (2006) reports inconsistent results for type of scoring guide and interrater reliability levels. For a history item interrater reliability, as estimated with generalizability theory, was higher for an analytic rubric (.66) than for a holistic rubric (.51). However, for a geography/economics task, the raters applying the holistic rubric achieved a higher phi coefficient (.70) than did raters applying the analytic rubric (.56). In a science task related to ecology, raters applying the analytic rubric (.74) tended to have more consistent scores than raters using the holistic scoring guide (.63). In no instance were scores based on a checklist associated with the highest interrater reliability.

In another study of science performance tasks, Klein and colleagues (1998) report higher interrater reliability estimates using analytic scoring guides to assess the tasks. In contrast, Waltman, Kahn, and Koency (1998) report that a holistic rubric yielded more consistent estimates of interrater reliability in the scoring of science tasks than an analytic rubric.

It appears that no type of scoring guide is consistently associated with the highest levels of interrater reliability. Considering this lack of a relation between interrater reliability and the type of scoring guide, we suggest selecting the type of scoring guide based on the uses of the information and the availability of funds for scoring. For example, Arter and McTighe (2001) recommend holistic rubrics for evaluating simple performances or products since these do not really assess more than one important trait. The rubric for the "runner task" used in an NAEP assessment (Figure 2.1) focuses on one trait: whether students understand the meaning of the intervals between runners. Arter and McTighe (2001) also suggest holistic rubrics are suited for large-scale assessments, such as the NAEP, that report a "snapshot" of overall achievement.

Analytic rubrics are recommended for complex performances with multiple important elements and for providing feedback to stakeholders such as students, teachers, and parents. The scores assigned to the analytic criteria provide diagnostic information within the constraints imposed by a limited sampling of products (AERA, APA, & NCME, 1999; Lenel, 1990c; Mullis, 1984; Welch, 2006). In high-stakes assessments with the opportunity for retesting to meet the standards, analytic feedback can provide useful information for examinees. For example, candidates who must retake a licensure examination benefit from diagnostic feedback. In education, instruction in writing, for example, benefits from the identification of the important features of responses, typically the development of ideas, organization, personal expression and style, and conventions.

Another possibility would be to score holistically for a summary score *and* analytically for diagnostic purposes (Mullis, 1984). An instance of using both types of scoring guides is provided by the scoring of the Even Start portfolio (Johnson, Fisher, et al., 2003). In a two-stage scoring system, raters first review the artifacts in a portfolio to determine a proficiency level for each goal on an analytic rubric. In the second stage, raters review the descriptions of the four proficiency levels described on the holistic rubric, reflect on the evidence reviewed for the analytic score, and then assign a holistic score to the portfolio. Scoring both holistically and analytically is expensive, however. An alternative is

to score examinee performances in a holistic fashion and apply an analytic scale to those performances that fail to meet the standard.

Length of Scale

What should be the length of the scale(s) in the rubric? Lane and Stone
(2006) and Lenel (1990c) provide the sage advice that the scale should
have enough rating categories for differentiation between performance
levels and few enough that the distinction between the categories is not
blurred.

For a checklist, the answer for scale length is simple: one only needs
a place to indicate 0 or 1, no or yes. For analytic and holistic rubrics, the
literature provides us with guidance about the number of scale points
that are required for reasonable levels of interrater reliability. In early
studies that examined the scoring of essays, Godshalk and colleagues
(1966) report raters achieved a higher level of interrater reliability with
4-point scales than with a 3-point scale. However, McColly and Remstad (1965) note no differences between the interrater reliability estimates for scores based on a 4- and a 6-point scale.

Other studies on performance tasks reveal that high levels of interrater reliability can be achieved up to scales with 15 points. Longford
(1994) reports interrater reliability coefficients ranging from .79 to .96
on Advanced Placement (AP) examinations using a 10-point scale. Gosling (1966) reports high levels of interrater reliability for a 15-point scale
in which raters assigned grades from A+ to E–. To determine the differences in interrater reliability based on a 15-point scale as compared
to a 5-point scale, Coffman (1971a) conducted a simulation in which
he estimated reliability using the Pearson product–moment correlation
coefficient. He reports that a higher interrater reliability can be achieved
with a 15-point scale, but warns of the necessity of clearly defined labels
for each of the 15 points.

Also using simulations, Shumate, Surles, Johnson, and Penny
(2007) report that the number of scale points associated with a rubric
substantially affects generalizability estimates. As the number of scale
points increases, the generalizability coefficient estimate increases up
to a 12-point scale. Generalizability coefficient estimates based on
12-point, 14-point, 16-point, and continuous scales were virtually the
same, decreasing only about a .01 with each 2-point decrease in scale
points. Thus assessment practitioners will obtain virtually the same estimation of reliability with scales of greater length as they will with the

12-point scale. However, scoring projects often use 4- to 6-point scales, which can result in underestimated generalizability coefficients.

The use of score augmentation (Bond, 1998; Educational Testing Service [ETS], 1999; Penny, Johnson, & Gordon, 2000a, 2000b) with 4- and 6-point scales, a process described in Chapter 7 in the section "The Scoring Process," might counter the bias in generalizability estimates. With augmentation, by allowing raters to add a plus or minus to a rating, a 4-point scale approximates a 12-point scale, whereas a 6-point scale approximates an 18-point scale.

Another issue to consider is the range of the scale that is actually used by raters. Although interrater agreement rates generally are high, if one looks more closely the agreement levels reported in many technical reports and journal articles might be overestimates, as there are few points in the score scale. For example, in writing assessment programs with a long history, the lowest level of performance (e.g., 1 on a 4-point scale) has almost disappeared as performance has improved. The scale is further compressed at the upper end, as qualitatively different products are assigned the same rating (e.g., 4 on a 4-point scale). Some testing programs avoid scale compression by expanding from 4-point rubrics to 5- or 6-point rubrics. Georgia, for example, now uses a 5-point rating scale with each criterion instead of its previous 4-point scale.

Descriptors for Proficiency Levels

Once the number of score points has been determined, each dimension needs to be described along a continuum of proficiency. Note that for each score point on the Georgia rubric, an initial summary statement of the level of performance (e.g., full command of the components of Organization) is followed by a series of qualitative descriptions (e.g., organizational strategy, logical sequencing, introduction and conclusion) of each dimension. For each component within the domain, a description of the skill levels covers a continuum along the score range. For example, for the skill of "sequencing" the continuum is "Unclear sequence of ideas," to "Minimal evidence of sequencing," to "Generally clear sequence of ideas," to "Logical sequencing of ideas across parts of the papers," to "Logical and appropriate sequencing of ideas within paragraphs and across parts of the paper."

In preparing to write the descriptors, it helps for the developers of the rubric to ask and answer the question "What separates the examinees into two groups—those who are proficient and those who are not?"

This discussion is followed by the initial formulation of broad descriptions at three performance levels: the high, mid, and low range.

Writing the middle score point description(s) first allows you simply to remove skills for the lower end and add on expectations for the upper end. For example, in describing a writer's skill at developing a topic, the continuum might read:

Low	Mid	High
Absence of or unclear supporting ideas	Supporting ideas developed but uneven	Supporting ideas fully developed

The ranges can be further divided into two score points. For example, at the low end, score point 1 might be "absence of supporting ideas" while score point 2 would be "unclear supporting ideas."

If the assessment includes a standard-setting component (e.g., a passing score), instead of low, mid, and high, these ranges would be *exceeds, meets,* and *does not meet the standard.* This activity helps the test developers make decisions about how much will be required and whether some aspects of the performance are to be more highly valued than others. The levels might read something like the descriptions below, followed by domain-related language:

Upper range: consistent and strong evidence of all dimensions of the standards assessed

Midrange: clear evidence of all dimensions of the standards assessed, with evidence of some dimensions less compelling than others

Low range: significant limitations in the evidence of the standards assessed

Additional guidelines for writing the descriptors for scoring rubrics include:

1. Begin each score point with a summary description of the quality of the performance level. Avoid simple value judgment labels (such as *inadequate, adequate, very good*), as these can lead raters to overlook the actual domain and dimensions.

2. Be explicit about the extent of what must be demonstrated (*most, all*).

3. Sequence the components in the descriptors in the same order for each score point.

4. Write the description of solid performances at each score point.

5. If there are alternative ways of achieving the same score, include them.

6. Indicate whether the score can be achieved by compensation (i.e., some strengths compensating for some weaknesses or a weakness in a more highly weighted aspect of a performance overriding strengths).

7. Avoid counting words and absolutes (unless they apply to all responses to a task).

8. Make a glossary (terms used within the rubric) to include in training.

Once the descriptions are drafted, they must be applied to large numbers of examinee responses to serve as a reality check. This check leads to the discovery and corrections of ambiguity and missing guidelines.

AN EXAMPLE OF RUBRIC DEVELOPMENT

The rubrics used in scoring the portfolios for the Even Start evaluation provide an illustration of the decisions made in the development of a scoring guide. As shown in Figure 6.4, the Even Start analytic rubric was composed of six rating scales. The scales describe levels of proficiency for each of the Even Start goals that the staff members identified as being important in the development of family literacy skills (see Figure 3.1). The goals in the rubric are analogous to the analytic domains scored in writing assessments (Georgia Department of Education, 2006; SCDE, 1999) and the dimensions used to review literacy portfolios (LeMahieu et al., 1995; Valencia & Au, 1997). Thus just as a writing sample is scored along several domains (e.g. *Organization*, *Style* and *Conventions*), the contents of a portfolio were reviewed for the six family literacy goals.

Accompanying each goal were 5-point rating scales with descriptors at each extreme and the midpoint (Figure 6.4). Such a format is used in writing assessment in the Six-Trait Analytic Scoring Guide (Spandel, 2001). The Six-Trait guide also provides descriptors for scale points 1, 3, and 5 on a 5-point scale.

To develop the holistic rubric (see Figure 6.5), the six literacy goals were combined to form narratives that describe four levels of family lit-

(Text continues on page 180)

FAMILY LITERACY PORTFOLIO—ANALYTIC SCORING RUBRIC

Case No.: _____

Rater: _____

Date: _____

Directions: For each goal, select a rating for the portfolio. Indicate your rating by circling one number on each scale, or by checking "no evidence."

Parent models reading/storytelling, writing, math skills for her/his child.

1	2	3	4	5
Content reflects parent modeling few reading, math, writing skills		Content reflects parent modeling some reading, math, writing skills		Content reflects parent modeling many reading, math, writing skills

_____ No evidence of work on this goal is included in the portfolio.

Parent models for his/her child goal setting and planning of activities.

1	2	3	4	5
Content reflects little modeling of goal setting and planning of activities.		Content reflects some modeling of goal setting and planning of activities.		Content reflects a high level of modeling of goal setting and planning of activities.

_____ No evidence of work on this goal is included in the portfolio.

Parent promotes self-esteem in child by providing, for example, physical contact and/or positive verbal comments.

1	2	3	4	5
Content reflects little attention to development of positive self-esteem in child.		Content reflects some attention to development of positive self-esteem in child.		Content reflects a high level of attention to development of positive self-esteem in child.

_____ No evidence of work on this goal is included in the portfolio.

(continued)

FIGURE 6.4. The analytic rubric used to score the Even Start prortfolios.

Parent functions as her/his child's teacher.

1	2	3	4	5
Content shows few activities with parent teaching child.		Content shows some activities with parent teaching child.		Content shows parent typically functions as child's teacher.

_____ No evidence of work on this goal is included in the portfolio.

Parent and child interact in child-centered activities selected by the child.

1	2	3	4	5
Content shows little parent and child interaction in activities selected by the child.		Content shows some parent and child interaction in activities selected by the child.		Content shows much parent and child interaction in activities selected by the child.

_____ No evidence of work on this goal is included in the portfolio.

Parent creates an environment which contributes to the physical, social, and emotional well-being of her/his child.

1	2	3	4	5
Content reflects an environment that contributes little to the physical, social, and emotional well-being of child.		Content reflects an environment that contributes somewhat to the physical, social, or emotional well-being of child.		Content reflects an environment that contributes to the physical, social, and emotional well-being of child.

Directions: Read the Holistic Scoring Rubric. Based on your review of the portfolio, select one of the levels listed below.

Level of Portfolio: _____ Proficient   _____ Not Scorable

_____ Developing

_____ Emerging

_____ Not Yet

FIGURE 6.4. *(continued)*

Proficient

This portfolio provides a holistic picture of a family that demonstrates a *high level* of family literacy skills. Portfolio entries demonstrate that the parent models many literacy skills in reading, writing, and math. Also, the parent models goal-setting and planning of activities for her/his child. The content of the portfolio reflects a high level of attention to the development of positive self-esteem in the child.

Entries in the portfolio reflect many parenting practices that are developmentally appropriate for the child. There are examples of the parent functioning as the child's teacher. The content of the portfolio shows a high level of parent and child engaging in child-centered activities selected by the child. The entries in the portfolio characterize a parent who creates an environment that contributes to the physical, social, and emotional needs of the child.

Developing

This portfolio provides a holistic picture of a family that is developing *some* family literacy skills. The predominant characteristic that distinguishes a *Developing* level from a *Proficient* level in family literacy is evidence of some of the skills, but not all—or most—of the skills. The *Developing* level may also reflect a high level of attention to some aspects of family literacy, while other skills are not demonstrated in the portfolio.

Entries in the portfolio demonstrate that the parent models some literacy skills in reading, writing, and math. Also, the parent may model goal-setting and planning of activities for her/his child. The content of the portfolio reflects some attention to the development of positive self-esteem in the child.

Entries in the portfolio reflect some parenting practices that are developmentally appropriate for the child. There are some examples of the parent functioning as his/her child's teacher. The content of the portfolio may show parent and child engaging in child-centered activities selected by the child. The entries in the portfolio may characterize a parent who creates an environment that contributes to the physical, social, and emotional needs of the child.

Emerging

This portfolio provides a holistic picture of a family in which a *few* family literacy skills are present. The predominant characteristic that distinguishes an *Emerging* level from a *Developing* level in family literacy is evidence of only a few of the skills. Development of many of the family literacy skills are not demonstrated in the portfolio.

Entries in the portfolio may demonstrate that the parent is beginning to model a few literacy skills in reading, writing, and math. The parent may be beginning to model goal-setting and planning of activities for her/his child. The content of the portfolio reflects limited attention to the development of positive self-esteem in the child.

(continued)

FIGURE 6.5. The holistic scoring rubric used to score the Even Start family literacy portfolio.

The entries in the portfolio reflect attempts at a limited number of parenting practices that are developmentally appropriate for the child. There may be examples of the parent beginning to function as her/his child's teacher. The content of the portfolio may show parent and child beginning to engage in child-centered activities selected by the child. Entries may characterize a parent who has started to create an environment that contributes to the physical, social, and emotional needs of the child.

Not Yet

This portfolio provides a holistic picture of a family that has *not yet developed* family literacy skills. The predominant characteristic that distinguishes a *Not Yet* level from an *Emerging* level in family literacy is that the entries within the portfolio lack overall evidence of development of essential skills. The portfolio *may* demonstrate an area in such great need of development that, while the parent demonstrates some family literacy skills, the area in need of development is of greater consequence.

Entries in the portfolio demonstrate that the parent does not model literacy skills in reading, writing, or math. The parent does not model goal setting or planning of activities for the child. The content of the portfolio also reflects no attention to the development of positive self-esteem in the child.

Entries reflect parenting practices that may not be developmentally appropriate for the child. There is no evidence that the parent functions as her/his child's teacher. The content shows parent and child typically not interacting or primarily engaging in adult-centered activities selected by the parent. The entries in the portfolio characterize a parent who has not created an environment that contributes to the physical, social, and emotional needs of the child.

Not Scorable

The portfolio is not scorable if it *lacks entries that provide evidence of family literacy.* It is possible that there are few entries of any type contained within the portfolio. It is also possible that entries contained within the portfolio do not provide sufficient information to tell whether a family is at the *Not Yet, Emerging, Developing,* or the *Proficient Level;* thus the portfolio could not be scored.

Note: The portfolio will not be scored if the family has been in the family literacy program for *less than 3 months.*

FIGURE 6.5. *(continued)*

eracy: Proficient (presence of most of the family literacy skills), Developing (development of some, but not all, of those skills), Emerging (development of a few family literacy skills), and Not Yet (no evidence of development of such skills) (Johnson, Fisher, et al., 2003). Note that the descriptors take the block paragraph form discussed at the beginning of this chapter. Also note the parallel structure of the descriptions across the proficiency levels.

To distinguish between the proficiency levels, the staff added statements of the degree to which skills were evidenced. For instance, one statement read, "The predominant characteristic that distinguishes a *Developing Level* from a *Proficient Level* in family literacy is evidence of some of the skills, but not all—or most—of the skills."

During the development of the rubrics, Even Start staff decided to use both analytic and holistic scoring. Some team members indicated that the holistic rubric fit philosophically with their integrated view of family literacy, whereas others indicated that the analytic rubric provided detailed information that could be used for program improvement. The use of both rubrics resulted in a two-stage scoring system in which raters first reviewed the artifacts in a portfolio to determine a proficiency level for each goal on the analytic rubric. In the second stage, raters reviewed the descriptions of the four proficiency levels described on the holistic rubric, reflected on the evidence reviewed for the analytic score, and then assigned a holistic score to the portfolio (Johnson, Fisher, et al., 2003).

At this point you have a rubric that will guide raters in scoring performance tasks. However, in complex performances—those with numerous ways to respond "correctly"—even the best scoring rubrics are abstractions. The rubric only "tells" what a performance looks like. The rubric does not actually show raters examples of, for instance, what a performance at a score of 3 looks like. Discussed in the next section are exemplars that provide raters with concrete examples to define terms such as "sufficient," "varied instances," and "sustained control."

RANGEFINDING AND SELECTION OF EXEMPLAR RESPONSES

In addition to rubrics, the training of raters uses exemplars of performances to operationalize the evaluative criteria. In this section, we first describe the types of exemplars used in the training of raters, and then we describe the process used to select the exemplars.

Exemplar Responses

Examples of examinees' responses serve as benchmarks of each proficiency level, provide practice in rating, function as items for a qualifying examination for raters, and allow monitoring of raters' scores during operational scoring.

Benchmarks

Benchmarks, also referred to as anchors (Mullis, 1984; NCES, 2000), are actual performances used to anchor raters to the score scale. For example, the benchmarks for a visual arts task would consist of a sample of student drawings that ranged in proficiency from "Drawing does not address assigned topic, or drawing does not attempt to fill the space, or drawings are unrecognizable" to "Drawings include the assigned topic that fills the space. Drawings include many details, texture, or patterns on the creature and the background/foreground" (Yap et al., 2005, p. 20).

Another example of a benchmark is provided by the NAEP history item in Chapter 1 (Figure 1.4). In this instance, the student's response provides a benchmark for the performance level of "Appropriate." Such examples of performances at each score level serve to operationalize the criteria (AERA, APA, & NCME, 1999).

Benchmarks show a variety and range of responses across the scale (Daro, 1996); however, benchmarks are not the best or the worst at a score point. Wolcott (1998) describes benchmarks as responses that "represent the typical, midrange score of each point, thereby leaving room for other papers to receive similar scores" (p. 66). That is, benchmarks are typically solid, easily recognizable examples of score points, used to anchor raters to the scale and help them internalize each score point (what makes a 3 a 3) and distinguish between scores (the difference between a 3 and a 4). Depending on the various ways to achieve a single score point, there may be as few as two benchmarks per score point or as many as five. In some educational settings, student responses anchor a scoring guide to a grade level by using grade specific student responses for each score point (Claggett, 1999).

Practice Sets

Practice sets are examples of examinee responses that provide raters with performances to score during training. The number of example performances in practice sets will vary depending on the number of tasks to be scored; in scoring centers, the number of examinee responses in a practice set typically includes 10–20 solid performances (National Center for Education Statistics [NCES], 2000). Scoring practice sets move the rater to an understanding of the highs and lows within each score point.

Qualifying Sets

Qualifying sets are examples of performances that are used to determine whether a rater qualifies for scoring. Thus, after being introduced to the rubric, reviewing benchmarks for each performance level in the rubric, and scoring practice sets of performances, raters complete the qualifying set to see if they pass and are qualified for operational scoring. Between 10 and 20 qualifying responses are selected for a set to cover the range of the scale (Cohen & Wollack, 2006). Qualifying sets oversample the score points that raters will have to apply most often. These score points are known historically, in an ongoing program, or from rangefinding.

Monitoring Sets

Monitoring sets serve the same function as qualifying tests; however, monitoring sets are used during operational scoring. That is, raters score a new set of examinee responses that were prescored by the validation committee. Results from the monitoring sets determine whether a rater may continue scoring or needs additional training. Seeded responses, which are previously scored performances mixed in with live responses (Wolcott, 1998), are another form of monitoring. The seeded responses allow comparison of a rater's scores with the validation committee scores. Monitoring also includes attention to individual and group needs and correction of scoring irregularities, such as a trend toward loss of one end of the scale. Methods for addressing these scoring issues are described in Chapter 8.

Rangefinding

The identification and selection of exemplar performances for benchmarks, practice sets, qualifying sets, and monitoring sets is a process known as rangefinding. Rangefinding accomplishes a number of purposes. It addresses not only the range of the score scale but also the variety of responses that raters must be trained to score consistently and accurately. For a new assessment it answers the question of whether a task works well enough to proceed with scoring. For both new and ongoing assessments, it provides the scoring personnel with the overview of examinee responses that they need to determine what kind of exemplars the raters will need to see. And finally, for an ongoing assessment, it provides consistency of scoring from one administration to the next. To accomplish all these goals, personnel from the scoring agency and the grant agency work with content experts to find concrete examples of all score points (NCES, 2000; Welch, 2006).

Rangefinding begins with a review of existing scoring rubrics and exemplars for similar tasks, if these exist, to anchor all participants and set the stage for generalizing from previous tasks to the current one. If the assessment is new, rangefinding will include fine tuning of the newly developed scoring rubric.

The rangefinding committee, sometimes referred to as a validation committee (Yap et al., 2005), reviews large numbers of responses—from 150 to 300 student responses in the case of NAEP (NCES, 2000)—that have been preselected to represent the full range of examinee performances. If the assessment is high stakes, it is advisable to overselect responses from groups within the population who would be expected to fall below the standard. This provides additional examples for fine-tuning raters' scoring.

The committee identifies patterns of responses, typical responses, and scoring issues. For example, if the wording of a particular task has misled examinees, the committee will discuss about how to apply the rubric in such a case. An example is an expository writing prompt about *an interesting place* that elicits narrative responses ("the time we went there") instead of the intended genre. The responses would be selected to train raters to distinguish between pure narratives, responses that embed substantial exposition with a narrative framework, responses that only begin as a narrative but are primarily expository, and responses that are purely informational. Experienced scoring agencies, provided lead time, review enough responses to identify the issues that need to be addressed by the expert rangefinding committee.

The validation committee, as we have said, includes content experts and can include a small number of individuals who developed the actual tasks. Continuity, if possible, is desirable, with continuing committee members available to explain how a previous group applied the rubric for a different but similar task.

Ground rules for establishing the scores should be set ahead of time. Some tasks and responses are clear cut enough for unanimity, but consensus, or 80% exact agreement, is the norm. We recommend that rangefinding ratings be independent so that some members do not feel pressured to follow the group. For example, in educational settings we have observed that teachers lose confidence in their own judgment and follow the lead of "big name," published, or otherwise "expert" rangefinding participants. Skill is required to ensure that all committee members are heard and encouraged to speak. Another reason for independence of judgments is that some rangefinding committees include members who simply do not grasp the scoring system and yet others who for political reasons are determined to sabotage the process. For these reasons and others, there must be rules for handling outliers.

Following rangefinding, a large pool of exemplar performances will be available for use in training and monitoring. In large-scale assessment projects, the scoring center staff and client work together to select responses for benchmark, practice, qualifying, and monitoring purposes (NCES, 2000). For research studies and program evaluations, the primary investigator or evaluator might bear the sole responsibility for selecting the benchmark, practice, qualifying, and monitoring sets, or the process might be completed in collaboration with program staff (Johnson, Penny, Fisher, & Kuhs, 2003).

ADDITIONAL RATING TOOLS

Additional tools used in training raters include annotations, look-fors, and portfolio logs. In this section we describe each type of tool and its use in the training of raters.

Annotations

Often each response selected as a benchmark is accompanied by an annotation for the assigned score. These verbal justifications of the assigned score are also referred to as comments, written rationales, or commentaries (North Carolina Department of Instruction, 1999; Yap et al., 2005). An example of such an annotation is shown in the scorer's commentary in Figure 1.4. Notice that the rater justifies the score of Appropriate by referring to elements of the response that address the criteria in the rubric. Often the notes made during the discussion of the range-finding committee are incorporated into the annotations. Typically, benchmark annotations are provided to the raters, whereas annotations for the other responses used in training (i.e., practice and qualifying) serve as references for trainers so that information is delivered consistently to the raters.

Annotations serve several other important purposes. They provide a check on the score. If the score cannot be justified using the language of the rubric, the score is not accurate. Annotations also provide a historical record that is important from year to year as personnel change. In addition, they allow a new scoring agency or new supervisor (client) to "hear" their predecessor's thinking and generalize from it.

Look-Fors

Another tool for scoring of performance assessment is a list of "look-fors" (see Table 6.1). Johnson, McDaniel, and colleagues (2000) report that to improve interrater reliability for the Even Start portfolio, the staff and evaluators collaborated to develop a list of artifacts that provide evidence about the levels of family literacy. For each literacy goal a list of indicators was developed based on staff members' prior experiences in rating sessions. In addition, the indicators were derived from the staff's written comments on their scoring documents about which artifacts they used to arrive at a final score for each portfolio. These indicators provide a list of the types of artifacts that raters should look for when making decisions about the knowledge and skills expressed in the examinees' responses.

Portfolio Logs

In Chapter 3, we discussed the inclusion of a portfolio log in each Even Start portfolio (see Table 3.3). The goals (i.e., criteria) that are the focus of the portfolio assessment form the column headers of a table (Johnson et al., 1998; Johnson, Fisher, et al., 2003; Johnson, McDaniel, et al.,

TABLE 6.1. A List of "Look-Fors" Used in the Scoring of Goal 1 in the Even Start Portfolio

Parent models reading/storytelling, writing, math skills for her/his child.

- Journals, thank-you notes, a "reflection" attached to an artifact that was written by the parent (not necessarily done in front of the child)
- Attendance at adult education classes or programs (e.g., ESL or adult basic education classes, trade school, college, or university)
- Reading log
- Tape of parent singing or telling a story to the child
- Cooking experiences
- Family Literacy Checklist *(reads to child)*

Note. Reproduced with permission from the Lincoln Public Schools, Lincoln, Nebraska.

2000). Along the left-hand column are the artifacts that provide evidence about the family literacy goals. The Even Start participant simply writes the name of the artifact in the left-hand column and places a check mark or an X underneath the appropriate goal(s). When the portfolio is scored, the log provides information to the rater about which artifact(s) should be reviewed for each goal.

DECISION RULES AND NONSCORABLE RESPONSES

The reality of large-scale performance assessment is that not all the examinee responses "fit" the rubric guidelines. Some of the responses can be addressed by modifications to the rubric, such as adding a description about the insufficient length of the response to the lowest score. Other issues, such as responses that are incomprehensible, blank, a refusal to participate, offensive, copied, or not written in English (e.g., North Carolina Department of Instruction, 1999; Penny, 2003), are typically assigned a code corresponding to the reason (see Table 6.2).

Decision rules arise in response to particular tasks or when assessments are initially being developed. An example is when writing experts are faced with making decisions about the impact of factual accuracy on topic development. If the student writes about Benjamin Franklin, Harriet Tubman, or any other well-known hero, the quality of the facts would likely be known to the rater. If, however, the writer chooses a family member or otherwise unknown individual, the veracity of the information would not be known by the rater. Fairness requires a consistent decision rule: If the example or detail supported the point the writer was trying make, it was to be considered topic development (even if the information was known to be historically inaccurate).

The necessity for some decision rules is created by groups of examinees, often the most skilled. A task and rubric may have been written to require an explicit response while the more talented students replied with metaphor or analogy or in some other implicit manner. The rubric cannot be changed, but such responses can be included in training once the rangefinding experts decide how to handle such responses.

The tools described in this chapter frame the process of scoring performance tasks. The scoring tools help raters to attend to the important elements in an examinee's response. When raters consistently apply the criteria expressed in a scoring guide, they will increase the reliability of scores. However, raters must be trained in the application of these tools in the scoring of performances. Training is the focus of the next chapter.

TABLE 6.2. Sample of Nonscorable Codes for an Essay Test

Code	Exception	Explanation
		Assign this code to any response that …
A	Alert	May indicate a need for confidential review by a counselor or other professional within the school system. Examples include a student expressing suicidal thoughts or relating an account of possible child abuse.
B	Blank	Contains no student writing. Look through the entire folder before assigning this code; some responses may not begin on the first page.
C	Copied	Contains no original student writing, or includes an isolated original sentence (e.g., to introduce or conclude the paper). Examples include copying from test packet directions or documents.
I	Incomplete	Was not finished by the student.
IL	Illegible	Has handwriting that cannot be read. Before assigning this code, make a reasonable attempt to recognize enough words to use them as a basis for determining what the other words are.
IN	Incomprehensible	Contains few recognizable words, or it may contain recognizable words arranged in such a way that no meaning is conveyed. Read the paper thoroughly before assigning this code. Do not confuse spelling errors with incomprehensibility.
L	Text too Limited to Score	Is less than a coherent paragraph (a group of logically related sentences "working together").
NE	Non English	Is written in a foreign language.
NP	Non-prose	Is composed solely of doodling, song lyrics, and other nonprose responses.
NR	Refusal	Consists of a direct or indirect refusal to take the test.
OT	Off Topic	Does not address the writing task at any point in the response. Familiarize yourself with the assigned test form(s). (The scoring director will determine whether the response may be scored.)
P	Practice paper/ released items	Is based on practice papers or released prompts.
TA	Off Task	Does not fall within the parameters set forth by the writing task.
X	Offensive	Contains offensive language.

Note. Summarized from Georgia Department of Education (2001); Mead, Smith, and Melby (2003); New Jersey Department of Education (2005); North Carolina Department of Instruction (1999); Penny (2003); South Carolina Department of Education (2000c); West Virginia Department of Education (2007); and Weigle (2002).

FURTHER READINGS

Huot, B. (1990). The literature of direct writing assessment: Major concerns and prevailing trends. *Review of Educational Research, 60*(2), 237–263.

Addresses topic development, task selection, the relation between textual features and ratings, and influences on raters' judgments.

Wolcott, W., with Legg, S. (1998). *An overview of writing assessment: Theory, research, and practice.* Urbana, IL: National Council of Teachers of English.

Discusses the design of writing assessments, including portfolio assessment. Other topics include training, methods of scoring (e.g., holistic, analytic), and reliability and validity.

Chapter Questions

1. Which form of scoring guide (i.e., a checklist, holistic rubric, or analytic rubric) would provide the most useful feedback to an examinee who failed the writing component of a high school exit examination? Which form of scoring would provide the least useful feedback?

2. Is the scoring guide in Figure 1.3 a holistic or an analytic rubric?

3. What does rating augmentation do in terms of scale length?

4. What form of rating tool is shown below?

> *Parent functions as her/his child's teacher*
> Audiotape of parent reading or singing or telling a story to the child
> Reading log
> Parent engages with child in activities
> Parent engages child in food experience
> Parent and child learn rules of a game
> Parent plans activities appropriate for child's developmental level
> Parent teaches child social skills (such as public behavior)
> Parent writes letters of the alphabet or child's name for the child to trace

CHECKLIST 6.1

Completed	To-Do List for Developing Tools for Scoring
	Scoring Rubrics
✓	Work with an expert committee to identify the skills or features (e.g., dimensions, domains) of a performance that are important. p. 157
	Ensure that the skills or features align with the content standards established for a subject area, the goals of a program, or the KSAs identified in a professional field. pp. 157, 169
	Determine the form of scoring rubric that is appropriate (i.e., checklist, analytic rubric, or holistic rubric). pp. 157–168, 170–172
	Determine the length of the rating scale for the rubric. pp. 172–173
	Write descriptors for each score point for each of the dimensions (e.g., Organization, Content) in the rubric. pp. 173–175
	Selecting Exemplar Responses for Rater Training
	Pre-select a large sample of examinee responses that illustrate the full range of performance levels. p. 183
	Convene validation committee of experts to review the preselected sample of examinee responses and assign scores. pp. 183–184
	Use the materials scored by the validation committee to develop training materials: benchmarks, practice sets, qualifying sets, and monitoring sets. pp. 181–182, 184
	Additional Rating Tools
	Write an annotation for each exemplar to provide a justification for the score. pp. 184–184
	Develop a list of "look-fors" (i.e., indicators) that provide raters with evidence about the examinee's proficiency as reflected in the response. p. 185
	Develop a portfolio log that documents the types of artifacts included in the portfolio and indicates the dimensions for which the artifacts provide evidence. pp. 185–186
	Develop and share with raters a list of decision rules about assigning scores to nontypical responses and a list of codes for nonscorable responses. pp. 186–187

CHAPTER 7

Training Raters and Staff

INTRODUCTION

One of the most frequent criticisms of performance assessments is the assumed unreliability in the scoring of the tasks. However, with the scoring tools described in Chapter 6 and the training described in this chapter, raters can score complex performances with consistency.

TRAINING RATERS
TO EVALUATE PERFORMANCE ASSESSMENTS

The training of raters and staff is essential to obtaining reliable results. This training calibrates raters so they apply the same standards to their scoring of examinee responses (Lenel, 1990c). Experience has shown that similarity of background is insufficient to predict who will be willing and able to apply a scoring system. English teachers, for instance, have relevant background given their responsibility for teaching students to write, but their ingrained personal standards, practiced for years as they grade papers, can make it difficult for them to apply a state's scoring rubrics. Furthermore, homogeneity can only be justified if the defining attributes are relevant to raters' performance of responsibilities. Individuals with diverse careers, sharing only the 4-year degree, have been successfully trained to score both constructed and extended responses in statewide assessments. Training actually begins with the interview process, by providing applicants with enough information about the job that they can decide their suitability.

Selecting Raters and Trainers

Qualified raters are essential to achieving and maintaining a high degree of consistency and reliability in the scoring of examinee's responses. Training is important, but having good trainees to begin with is essential. In the case of writing assessment, the process typically requires that each applicant successfully complete a personal interview, a written essay, and tasks similar to the performance(s) to be scored (Penny, 2003). Such prescreening reduces the number of raters who fail to qualify after training. The initial hiring process identifies applicants who, in spite of their credentials, are not suited to the rating task.

Meaningful selection is integral to scoring. Careful selection criteria are necessary, but so far no test has been devised that can identify with certainty that an applicant has the critical attributes. The ideal rater demonstrates the ability to attend to relevant criteria, work in a structured environment, follow directions, and recognize and monitor errors in his or her own judgment. Those who assess products should be capable of ignoring surface appearance (messy handwriting, faint photocopying, video equipment failure, or all the bells and whistles that support the well-heeled, technologically advanced examinee). Raters must be able to work long hours, maintain motivation and accuracy, and set aside their own biases (Penny, 2003). Raters must also have a commitment to the intensive work schedule.

Qualifications considered important for participants involved in the scoring include an understanding of the domain being assessed and an understanding of the characteristics of the examinees who are being tested (AERA, APA, & NCME, 1999). Relevant examinee characteristics include the typical range of skill levels, familiarity with the response modes, and primary language. The SAT essays, for example, are scored by high school and college faculty who are instructors in courses that require substantial writing (Kobrin & Kimmel, 2006). Qualifications for raters for the NAEP assessment included at least a bachelor's degree in the subject area being assessed, teaching experience at the elementary or secondary level (preferred), and fluency in Spanish for the scoring of booklets answered in that language (National Center for Educational Statistics [NCES], 2000). Consistent with the recommendation of Bond and colleagues (1996), many state departments of education emphasize the need for ethnic and racial diversity among professional raters.

Experienced raters are rehired in subsequent years based on accuracy and productivity in earlier scoring projects. They provide scoring contractors with a core group of veteran raters whose expertise has been demonstrated while working on a range of performance assessments.

Training staff are chosen from a pool of veteran raters on the basis of demonstrated expertise, including strong organizational abilities, skill in training strategies, and skill at building and maintaining a professional group dynamic necessary to ensure accurate and reliable scoring. The expert staff, especially trainers, should possess all the attributes needed to be a rater, have been successful raters, and have good communication and management skills. Writing skills and background about how adults learn are needed in order for trainers to design and prepare training materials. The staff need to include individuals who are skilled at analyzing rater monitoring reports and designing retraining activities. Someone on the staff must assume responsibility for scheduling and work flow and coordinate the preparation of responses to be scored (either on paper or scanned). Given the size of a scoring center or research project, the roles of site manager, trainer, data manager, and instructional design may be shared.

Estimating the Number of Raters

Historical productivity data on the average amount of time to complete a single rating and the resolution rate can be used to calculate the number of raters needed. Experienced raters will be more productive than novice raters, so the total can be adjusted based on the ratio of experienced to novice raters.

Calculations illustrated in Figure 7.1 assume 6½ hours of rating time in an 8-hour workday, and double reads for all tests. We base the estimations on double reads because many scoring sessions use two raters in order to improve reliability (e.g., Kobrin & Kimmel, 2006; LaDuca et al., 1995). Lenel (1990c) also notes that when a single rater is used and the rater is the item author, such as can occur in credentialing or research, then the author can be so single-minded about the model answer that he or she will ignore plausible answers. Thus the examinee will benefit from the rater being exposed to another point of view in the initial readings.

In terms of reading rates, reviewing a response holistically may require from 30 seconds to 1½ minutes, whereas analytic reviewing may consume 1 to 4 minutes (Quellmalz, 1986). In contrast National Board teacher certification assessments often take hours, not minutes, to rate.

In order to determine the number of raters to hire for a project, it is necessary to factor in attrition at several points in the process: imme-

Step 1. Finding the Total Ratings to Be Completed

Number of performances		Number of times each performance is scored	Total ratings
100,000	×	2 ratings	200,000
100,000	×	2.10 ratings (2 ratings plus resolution rate of 10%)	210,000

Step 2. Total Time to Complete All Ratings

Minutes to complete single rating	Total ratings to be completed	Total rater time	
		Minutes	Hours
	Double Ratings		
2	200,000	400,000	6,666.67
5	200,000	1,000,000	16,666.67
15	200,000	3,000,000	50,000.00
	10% Resolution Rate		
2	210,000	420,000	7,000.00
5	210,000	1,050,000	17,500.00
15	210,000	3,150,000	52,500.00

Step 3. Daily Rater Productivity

Reading rates in minutes	Individual rater ratings per hour		Daily ratings completed per rater
2	30	× 6.5 hour Work Day	195
5	12		78
15	4		26

Step 4. Rating Days

Total ratings	÷	Individual rater daily rate	Number of rating days		Number of raters		Total scoring project days
200,000	÷	195	= 1,025.64	÷	50	=	20.51
					100	=	10.26
					150	=	6.84
200,000	÷	78	= 2,564.10	÷	50	=	51.28
					100	=	25.64
					150	=	17.09
200,000	÷	26	= 7,692.31	÷	50	=	153.85
					100	=	76.92
					150	=	51.28

FIGURE 7.1. Determining the number of raters needed for a scoring project.

diately following the interview, the time delay between notification of hiring and the first day of training, as a consequence of failure to meet scoring standards, and inability to maintain accuracy and productivity criteria during scoring. Our experience suggests that for every 100 raters needed to complete a project, 120–130 must be brought in for the initial interview.

Training

A general framework for training involves a review of the performance task, the scoring guide, and the benchmark performances (Claggett, 1999; Lane & Stone, 2006; Lenel, 1990c; Mullis, 1984; Quellmalz, 1986; Welch, 2006). The raters then read and score a sample of practice responses that were prescored by a validation committee. The prescored responses serve as a standard against which the rater's scores can be compared. Next raters discuss the scores they assigned to the sample responses and learn the scores assigned by the validation committee. Subsequently the raters score a new set of responses. As training nears an end the trainer monitors the accuracy of raters through the use of a qualifying set of responses. Training continues until a rater meets a preset criterion, such as 60% to 80% agreement with the expert scores of the validation committee (Moon & Hughes, 2002; Persky et al., 2003; Penny, 2003). Figure 7.2 provides key components in the training of raters to score complex extended-response performances. The components will be described in the following sections of the chapter.

Rater Training Models

Training models vary on two characteristics—who does the training and where. The content of the training, the "what," is the same. As shown in Table 7.1, the traditional model resembles the classroom, with the trainer functioning as a teacher and the raters acting as the students. Consistency is built into the system through the training materials and through the trainer-training process, which requires trainers to participate in the discussion of scores on benchmarks, practice, and qualifying materials. In writing assessment circles, this is referred to as developing a community of consensus (White, 1994). Rater questions and comments introduce variability into the training process, requiring trainers to correct any misinformation. This model is useful for small-scale scoring of performance tasks associated with program evaluations and research studies because the cost of an online system for training and rating can be

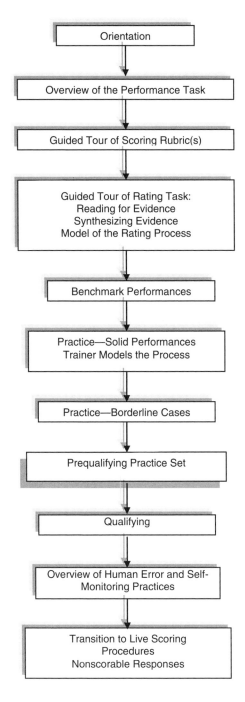

FIGURE 7.2. Stages of training raters to score complex, extended-response performances.

TABLE 7.1. Models for Training Raters

Characteristics of the model	Strengths	Limitations	Suggested uses
		The Traditional Classroom	
Group setting Trainer as a teacher Rater as a student *Format*: Pencil and Paper	• Long history of successful use • Group dynamic leads to building a community of consensus • Adaptable to sites of various sizes • Trainer has many sources of information about raters' strengths and weaknesses, not just scores on practice and quality sets • Trainer can adapt based on group needs	• Requires up-front training time for staff • Can result in inconsistent delivery of criteria if trainers differ across sites • Requires skilled trainers to manage problematic personalities • Raters move at group pace—some will need more time, others less • Raters can become confused if any inattentive or inaccurate peers do a lot of talking	• In a low-technology site, with limited or no access to programmers, tech support staff, and/or non-computer-savvy rater population • In a site with skilled trainers • In a temporary scoring site such as for a program evaluation or research study • In a site with teacher staff development as one of the project goals
		The Electronic Classroom: Online Delivery of Training	
Software package as a trainer Rater as a student *Format*: Electronic image of performances; scoring rubrics and benchmarks may also be provided in hard copy for frequent reference	• Raters receive the *same* information, as consistent delivery is built in • Raters can move at their own pace • Training parallels the online scoring process • Multiple sites can work concurrently • Individual rater data are stored and available for trainer review • Rater monitoring can be easily concealed and delivered on an individual, as-needed basis	• Requires development or purchase of well-designed software • Requires equipment and technology support • Software can limit flexibility of what can be designed for different clients • Instant messaging to ask questions can discourage inquiry • Instant messaging to reply to rater questions can require more time than face-to-face contact • Requires applicants to be familiar and comfortable with computers	• In scoring site with expert training staff and expert technical support staff • In a scoring site with access to a computer savvy rater population • In a scoring site that has a contractual relationship with one of the "electronic rating delivery systems" and with clients who are willing to limit their scoring and monitoring expectations to the preexisting software

prohibitive for short-term projects. The classroom model is also widely used by scoring contractors with skilled, experienced trainers.

The online model (e.g., Kobrin & Kimmel, 2006; Yap et al., 2005), or the electronic classroom, puts the teaching function in the hands of the online designer and the rater. In this model, raters assume most of the responsibility for training themselves. This model is used in scoring sites but also can be used in remote settings, with raters working at their own pace in their own homes or offices. Via computer, expert staff monitor rater accuracy to qualifying sets of responses and answer individual rater questions or these questions are answered by e-mail (Yap, et al., 2005). The expense of developing a Web-based training and rating system that will be used across several years makes this model most feasible for long-term projects and large-scale assessments.

What a Rater Needs to Know

Rater training, whatever the nature of the performance, must prepare the raters to evaluate the examinees' responses both accurately and efficiently. Wolcott (1998) recommends that all training systems include procedures and materials to familiarize raters with the process, the criteria, and the current performance task. In this section we present six aspects of scoring that a rater should know:

1. The purpose of the assessment
2. The evaluative criteria
3. Content background knowledge
4. The scoring process
5. Self-monitoring
6. How to work in the scoring setting (see Table 7.2)

The Purpose of the Assessment

While the assessment purpose is certainly the shortest, most straightforward part of the training process, it is the natural starting point because it enables the rater to grasp the importance of what may become a routine. Whether the purpose is to identify students who need additional instruction before moving to the next grade, to assign scores that become part of a total battery of tests that are considered by college admission officers, or to certify teachers who will receive substantial financial rewards,

TABLE 7.2. What a Rater Needs to Know

Knowledge or skill	What	Why	How acquired
Purpose of the assessment	• The broader context of the assessment program and how the results will be used	• Establish professionalism	• Opening overview—trainer or training software
Evaluative criteria	• Scoring rubrics • What features of a performance are evaluated • The differences between the performance levels • Supplemental • Decision rules • Nonscorable responses	• Internalization of uniform standards so scores assigned are consistent	• Lecture/discussion • Modeling • Think-aloud protocols using anchors • Practice
Content background knowledge	• Subject matter prior knowledge necessary to accurately evaluate performance • Subject matter expertise can be broad; knowledge to score task can be specific and detailed	• Provides consistent review of relevant knowledge and typical examinee errors, increasing consistent scoring	• Hiring of content experts • Content background teachers • Subject matter experts/ practitioners • Availability of experts and resources
Scoring process	• The process, sequence, and scoring materials used to assign scores	• Helps ensure all performances receive a thoughtful, thorough review	• Graphic display of the steps and sequence • Practice • Raters imitate trainers think-aloud modeling
Self-monitoring	• Typical types of rater error • Rater feedback conferences and/or reports	• Makes rater responsible for accuracy and productivity	• Mini-lessons • Memorable names of types of bias
Working in a scoring setting	• Logistics • Rules and regulations • Security procedures • How to use scoring programs on computer • Group dynamics	• Shifts raters accustomed to working at home to group setting	• Introduce in interview • Establish in orientation • Model throughout training process

the stakes are high. Understanding the purpose of the assessment helps raters accept the demands for professionalism and security. For example, in the training of optometrists for scoring a licensure examination, the purpose of the examination and the role of the examiners required clarification (Gross, 1993). Examiners (i.e., practicing optometrists) were told their role was to observe and record, and they should not consider themselves as scoring or passing or failing a candidate. This practice is common, so that raters do not feel overwhelmed with making pass/fail decisions and instead focus on applying the standards.

The Evaluative Criteria

The evaluative criteria typically are conveyed in scoring rubrics that indicate the features of a performance to consider and the performance expectations for the task. The performances are described along a qualitative range from "failure to meet standards," to "approaching the standard," to "meeting the standard," and "exceeding the standard."

The rubrics can only be fully understood when paired with benchmark performances that illustrate each of the score points along a continuum of standards. The benchmarks enable the rater to grasp the differences between such skills as "incomplete" and "full" mastery.

Once raters have grasped the basics of the rubrics, in some performance assessments they may require training in what is known as "decision rules" and nonscorable responses. Some assessments require a particular genre or audience, such as expository writing, and raters need to know what to do with responses that are purely narrative or address a different audience than the one assigned in a writing prompt. In other cases, essays may be evaluated solely for writing skills or separately for writing skills and content knowledge. In such cases, raters require training in what to do with content that is incorrect. Raters may be given a list of codes (see Table 6.2), to assign to responses that are off task or off topic, written in a language other than English, or too short to score. Nonscorable responses are typically verified by expert staff to ensure the accuracy of such decisions.

Content Background Knowledge

Many performance assessments require subject matter expertise that is either built into the initial hiring requirements (Kobrin & Kimmel, 2006; NCES, 2000) or acquired during training. If the client requires the expertise as a hiring requirement, it can be evaluated in the interview process and fine-tuned during training. However, credentials alone do not guarantee expertise. Social studies teachers might be experts in American history, but if the task requires knowledge of the Renaissance, the teachers will need task-specific training. Science teachers might be experts in biology or physics but lack knowledge of the periodic table in chemistry. Furthermore, they might be accustomed to teaching a select group of students (whether special education or advanced placement), and will need to broaden their framework to include the full range of examinee responses.

Training raters involves reviewing the task and supporting documents to identify key points and to determine what examinees should include in their responses. The raters would then review the rubric, benchmarks, and annotations. Subsequently they practice scoring responses, learn the correct score, and discuss the attributes of the performance that are congruent with the correct score.

The Scoring Process

Raters should be trained to approach the scoring process in a systematic fashion. Techniques to make the scoring process more systematic include (1) following a scoring path to frame the review process, (2) asking wedge questions to focus the score judgment, and (3) augmenting ratings after identifying a score family.

The Scoring Path. As trainers model the scoring of benchmark performances, raters learn the sources of information for making scoring decisions and the principal steps in decision making. As shown in Figure 7.3, the rater initially looks at the performance in its entirety, withholding judgment. Next, the rater carefully reads for evidence of strengths and weaknesses, making mental notes if the performance is relatively brief or taking notes if the performance is extensive and consists of multiple sources of data. At this point the rater makes an initial score decision. The final step is a mental justification of the score.

The skill of "reading for evidence" is essential for consistent scoring of complex performances, and it is a procedure that is rarely taught. The process has been used in research related to the assessment of the National Board of Professional Teaching Standards (NBPTS) (Bond et al., 2000; West, Gordon, Colby, & Wang, 2005) and other research projects (Gordon, 1999). It is described more fully in a later section of this chapter, using a short text to illustrate the seven types of evidence and how they are considered in making scoring decisions.

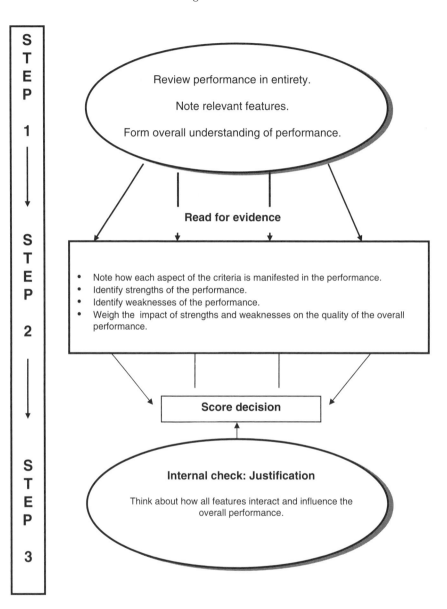

FIGURE 7.3. The scoring path and reading for evidence.

Wedge Questions. The thought of arriving at an initial decision on a 4- or 6-point scale might prove a bit intimidating for some raters. A process for focusing the rating process is provided by Geoff Hewitt (1995). In determining a score, raters first answer a "wedge question." The answer to the question focuses the rater's attention on a portion of the rubric scale (in Hewitt's procedure, the upper or lower half). For example, for a 4-point analytic rubric, the raters could be given the following directions: "For each dimension ask yourself, 'Is this aspect of the examinee's response most similar to the *rubric descriptors* for the two highest ratings or the two lowest ratings?'" If in this initial decision the rater decides the proficiency of the performance is best described by the top half of the rubric, then she asks, "Is this aspect of the examinee's response most similar to the rubric descriptor for the *high rating* or the *highest rating?*" In contrast, if the rater decides the proficiency level is best described by the bottom half of the rubric, then she asks, "Is this aspect of the student's response most similar to the *lowest rating* or the *next to lowest rating?*"

This process directs the rater to focus on the relevant rubric score-point descriptions, rather than attempting to review all of them. In our own scoring projects, we find use of wedge questions helpful for novice raters and in the use of 6-point scales. Its use is more limited with 4-point systems when a high percentage of responses are between scores at midpoint (i.e., between the 2 and the 3), rather than between the lower half and upper half.

Augmentation. Gaining more notice in the areas of credentialing examinations and educational assessment is the use of score augmentation in the rating of performance tasks. Augmentation allows raters to add a plus (+) or minus (–) designation to a rating to indicate whether an examinee's response reflected a performance level slightly higher or slightly lower than the typical response at that level (Bond, 1998; Educational Testing Service [ETS], 1999; Johnson, Penny, Schneider, et al., 2003; NBPTS, 2001; Penny, 2006; Penny et al., 2000a, 2000b; Schneider, Johnson, & Porchea, 2004). Raters are instructed first to decide on the score family (e.g., 2–, 2, 2+) for the examinee's performance level. When an examinee's response reflects a performance slightly higher than the typical response in that score family, raters are instructed to accompany the score with a plus (+). If the student response reflects a performance slightly lower than the typical response in the score family, then raters are directed to accompany the score with a minus (–). Across studies, augmentation is associated with slight increases in reliability

(Johnson, Penny, Schneider, et al., 2003; Penny et al., 2000a, 2000b; Schneider et al., 2004).

Self-Monitoring

Raters also should be taught to monitor themselves and to know that their ratings will be carefully monitored. They need to know to take regular and frequent breaks in order to remain alert and accurate. They need to review benchmarks or complete recalibration activities to prevent drift. If the nature of the responses being scored will elicit bias, then it is imperative that raters be given a vocabulary and procedure for identifying and these influences. The issue of bias will be discussed in a later section. Because self-monitoring increases the training time and becomes an issue only over the rating of numerous responses, we recommend that this aspect of training be delivered only to those raters who qualify to be hired.

Working in a Scoring Setting

While this last aspect of rater training may seem unnecessary, there are raters who have learned to score accurately but not to work in a highly structured and often group setting. The content of this part of training varies with the context. Raters working in an online scoring center will need to learn how to communicate clearly and completely through an electronic message system instead of in direct conversation with a person. Raters in both the classroom and online contexts will need to learn the expectations about work hours, productivity requirements, and how to work without interfering with other raters.

DESIGNING THE TRAINING SESSIONS

The training materials themselves and how they are sequenced move adult learners (i.e., the raters) from dependence to independence and from diverse individuals to a community of consensus. Furthermore, training moves raters from abstract descriptions of KSAs and content standards as described in the scoring rubrics, to concrete applications (the benchmarks), allowing raters to apply the rubrics and bring their personal standards in line with the required standards. It is the "doing," rather than the "seeing and hearing," that prepares raters to score large numbers of complex performance assessments. In Figure 7.4 we show

Seeing and hearing (low participation)	Continuum of participation			Doing (high participation)
Read task, scoring rubrics, and benchmark papers.	Hear explanation of scoring rubric. See overheads of anchors.	Listen to explanation of the evidence in a benchmark paper as the trainer "locates" it and comments about what it means in relation to the scoring rubric. This activity is repeated for all score points.	Practice locating, evaluating, and synthesizing the evidence, following the trainer's model.	Work in small groups with trainers, doing think-alouds that demonstrate locating, marking, recording, and synthesizing the evidence and justifying the score assigned, using the language of the rubric.
Low retention	Level of retention			High retention

FIGURE 7.4. A continuum of training participation and retention of scoring strategies.

a continuum of training activities that move from seeing and hearing to doing. We offer this continuum as a heuristic in planning training experiences. Note that as one moves from the left to the right in the continuum, training becomes more participatory. The continuum reminds us that raters might retain little of what they read, hear, or see; however, they are likely to remember much of (1) what they say and write, or (2) what they say as they perform tasks related to the scoring process. In short, they learn to rate by rating.

READING FOR EVIDENCE

Whatever the type of performance raters are required to score, they must learn how to do it and what information to use to make scoring decisions. We refer to this process as "reading for evidence" (Gordon, 1999). It is described in detail in Figure 7.5, using a short text about kudzu. (This activity would be modeled for raters using actual examinee performances, not the kudzu passage.) Learning to read for evidence is especially important when the performance is lengthy and/or there are several different sources of data. Assume for the moment that you are directed to evaluate the quality of the writing and information in the passage about kudzu in the left column of Figure 7.5. A scoring rubric indicates what aspects of the performance a rater should attend to; it does not, however, provide a broader conceptual base—what the evidence is and how it matters. Evidence is defined as any data in the performance that enable the rater to evaluate the quality of the performance with respect to the performance standards. The evidence can take a variety of forms. Evidence concerns not merely quantity, but quality, not merely "how much," but "how well done."

The more complex the examinee's task, the more varied the examinee responses and the greater the number and variety of the data for making scoring decisions, the more necessary it is to train raters to read for evidence. In many straightforward constructed-response tasks, the evidence has been preidentified and included in the scoring guides or sentence length exemplars. In such assessments, reading for evidence is greatly simplified and bias is rarely a concern. When the possible correct answers are limited, the reading for evidence task is essentially limited to "matching" rather than interpreting.

Seven classes of evidence common across content areas and types of performances are described in Figure 7.6. They are illustrated in the kudzu activity. In terms of evaluating the quality of the writing and

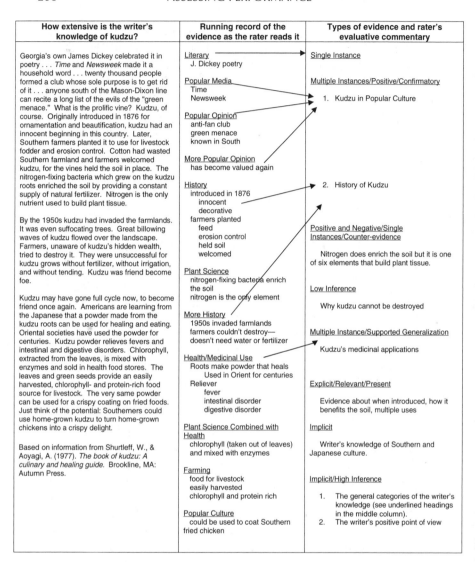

How extensive is the writer's knowledge of kudzu?	Running record of the evidence as the rater reads it	Types of evidence and rater's evaluative commentary
Georgia's own James Dickey celebrated it in poetry . . . *Time* and *Newsweek* made it a household word . . . twenty thousand people formed a club whose sole purpose is to get rid of it . . . anyone south of the Mason-Dixon line can recite a long list of the evils of the "green menace." What is the prolific vine? Kudzu, of course. Originally introduced in 1876 for ornamentation and beautification, kudzu had an innocent beginning in this country. Later, Southern farmers planted it to use for livestock fodder and erosion control. Cotton had wasted Southern farmland and farmers welcomed kudzu, for the vines held the soil in place. The nitrogen-fixing bacteria which grew on the kudzu roots enriched the soil by providing a constant supply of natural fertilizer. Nitrogen is the only nutrient used to build plant tissue.	Literary J. Dickey poetry Popular Media Time Newsweek Popular Opinion anti-fan club green menace known in South More Popular Opinion has become valued again History introduced in 1876 innocent decorative farmers planted feed erosion control held soil welcomed	Single Instance Multiple Instances/Positive/Confirmatory 1. Kudzu in Popular Culture 2. History of Kudzu Positive and Negative/Single Instances/Counter-evidence Nitrogen does enrich the soil but it is one of six elements that build plant tissue.
By the 1950s kudzu had invaded the farmlands. It was even suffocating trees. Great billowing waves of kudzu flowed over the landscape. Farmers, unaware of kudzu's hidden wealth, tried to destroy it. They were unsuccessful for kudzu grows without fertilizer, without irrigation, and without tending. Kudzu was friend become foe.	Plant Science nitrogen-fixing bacteria enrich the soil nitrogen is the only element More History 1950s invaded farmlands farmers couldn't destroy— doesn't need water or fertilizer	Low Inference Why kudzu cannot be destroyed Multiple Instance/Supported Generalization
Kudzu may have gone full cycle now, to become friend once again. Americans are learning from the Japanese that a powder made from the kudzu roots can be used for healing and eating. Oriental societies have used the powder for centuries. Kudzu powder relieves fevers and intestinal and digestive disorders. Chlorophyll, extracted from the leaves, is mixed with enzymes and sold in health food stores. The leaves and green seeds provide an easily harvested, chlorophyll- and protein-rich food source for livestock. The very same powder can be used for a crispy coating on fried foods. Just think of the potential: Southerners could use home-grown kudzu to turn home-grown chickens into a crispy delight.	Health/Medicinal Use Roots make powder that heals Used in Orient for centuries Reliever fever intestinal disorder digestive disorder Plant Science Combined with Health chlorophyll (taken out of leaves) and mixed with enzymes Farming food for livestock easily harvested chlorophyll and protein rich Popular Culture could be used to coat Southern fried chicken	Kudzu's medicinal applications Explicit/Relevant/Present Evidence about when introduced, how it benefits the soil, multiple uses Implicit Writer's knowledge of Southern and Japanese culture. Implicit/High Inference 1. The general categories of the writer's knowledge (see underlined headings in the middle column). 2. The writer's positive point of view
Based on information from Shurtleff, W., & Aoyagi, A. (1977). *The book of kudzu: A culinary and healing guide.* Brookline, MA: Autumn Press.		

FIGURE 7.5. A textual representation of how a rater thinks about and evaluates evidence.

Positive Evidence	Evidence of the examinee's knowledge, skill, or ability. Includes single instance and confirmatory evidence. A single instance provides evidence that the examinee has the knowledge but that the knowledge may be limited in scope or depth. Confirmatory evidence provides additional information (through different examples, application of the same concept or rule in different settings) that suggests deeper knowledge than a single instance. Caveat—repetition is not confirmation. The presence of positive evidence alone does not determine the score. The rater must determine whether the evidence is fundamental and essential, minor and trivial, or exceptional with respect to the examinee's task and the content being tested.
Negative Evidence	Evidence that is incorrect itself or that contradicts the positive evidence. Includes erroneous single instance, counterevidence, and the absence of evidence. Caveat—repetition of an error is not a mortal sin even though it may drive you crazy. The presence of negative evidence alone is not sufficient to determine a score. The rater must determine whether the evidence is fundamental and essential, minor or trivial, or exceptional, with respect to the examinee's task and the knowledge and skills being assessed.
Explicit Evidence/ Low Inference	Evidence that requires no interpretation or synthesis to determine the accuracy and/or inaccuracy of individual information or the overall depth of knowledge. When the evidence is explicit it is relatively easy to identify. The rater's task is low inference.
Implicit Evidence/ High Inference	Evidence that requires interpretation and/or synthesis. Implicit evidence is not announced and therefore more difficult to locate than explicit evidence. Both, however, are solid evidence of knowledge or lack of knowledge. Implicit evidence requires the rater to answer "What does this tell me?" and "How confident am I?" The rater's task is high inference.
Single Instance or Multiple Instances	"Multiple instances" refers to repetition of the same data and/or comparable information.

(continued)

FIGURE 7.6. Seven classes of evidence for reviewing performances.

Confirmatory or Counterevidence	Evidence that either confirms (is consistent or congruent with other evidence) or that contradicts or conflicts with other evidence in the performance. Confirmatory evidence allows the rater to be more certain of the judgment as it provides more data about the quality of the performance. Counterevidence, on the other hand, shows that the examinee does not have consistent control of the skill or knowledge. The rater is, as a consequence, less certain of what the examinee knows and can do.
Relevant or Irrelevant Evidence	The rater's task is to attend to evidence that is relevant to the standards and rubrics. Evidence irrelevant to the specific task, body of knowledge, or skill may take many forms, including interesting or distracting information. It can be difficult to ignore simply because it is present in the performance. Such evidence must be "mentally bracketed" and not evaluated. It must be treated as if it simply does not exist. Caveat—glib writers use irrelevant content to appear more knowledgeable than they are, whereas weak writers are unaware of the irrelevancies.
Present or Absent Evidence	Assumptions and evaluations cannot be made based on what is not there about what the examinee "would have done" or is "potentially able to do." Caveat—the evidence may be implicit, not absent.
Supported or Unsupported Generalization	A generalization is a broad statement that in and of itself sounds good; however, it "tells" rather than "shows." Generalizations are often lifted from the test material. Unsupported generalizations provide limited evidence. Supported generalizations (details, examples, explanations, applications) provide confirming evidence and evidence about the depth of knowledge. This is usually one of the easiest forms of evidence to identify. Raters must be careful, however, not to be seduced into believing the examinee "knows" just because he/she says so.

FIGURE 7.6. *(continued)*

information in the kudzu passage, the rater initially makes a running record of the evidence as he or she reads the passage. In this instance, evidence is provided by the writer's references to kudzu in literary writings, popular opinion, and history (see the middle column in Figure 7.5). Then the rater notes the types of evidence related to kudzu. For example, in the right-hand column the rater notes that the writer provided a single instance of the role of kudzu in the literature (James Dickey's poetry). The rater notes (1) positive evidence of the writer's knowledge about the topic, (2) multiple instances in which the writer relates kudzu to popular opinion, and (3) confirming evidence consistent with other information. The rater would continue this process for the entire response. In this manner, the reading for evidence provides a systematic review of complex examinee performances.

RATER BIAS AND SCORE VARIABILITY

Another issue to address in training relates to rater bias. An awareness of this issue has been with us since at least the time of the Sung dynasty (960–1279 C.E.) (Franke, 1968; Kracke, 1953; Nitko, 1983). During this period, when scoring candidates' responses in the Chinese civil service examination, the candidate's name was covered so the examiners did not know whose paper was being scored. To prevent recognition of handwriting, all papers were reproduced by copyists, and examiners only saw the copies.

Today rater training addresses sources of rater bias and the monitoring process uses safeguards to avoid rater bias affecting scores. For example, in a study related to scoring bias, raters were trained to score constructed-response, content-based items (e.g., science, social studies) (Schafer, Gagne, & Lissitz, 2005). The focus of the study was whether the scores that raters' assigned would be influenced by writing style—a form of bias since scores should reflect the correctness of an examinee's content knowledge, not writing style. Preparation of the raters for scoring included training with rubrics and exemplars. During operational scoring, table leaders conducted read-behinds of items already scored by the raters. In addition, raters scored sets of items prescored by a validation committee to assure the raters still met qualifying standards (i.e., 70% accurate) for scoring. In terms of bias, scores for the content-based items were not appreciably influenced by examinees' writing style, indicating that this form of potential bias can be controlled for in scoring.

Another important safeguard against rater error is the use of multiple ratings. Again, as far back as the Sung dynasty, two examiners read each examination paper (Kracke, 1953; Nitko, 1983). Since writing is the performance assessment with the longest history, it is used to explain how raters can respond to features of essays that are extraneous to the evaluative criteria in the rubrics. Research in the study of writing has identified many factors that contribute to rater disagreement and thus irrelevant score variability. Various sources of rater bias are shown in Table 7.3.

To raise awareness of bias, you can provide Table 7.3 as a reference for raters to keep with their rubrics and benchmark responses. Also, during training examples of responses that typically elicit such forms of bias can be included in raters' practice sets. The cartoons in Figure 7.7 show another method for making raters aware of bias. Through the use of humor, raters learn about leniency, severity, and central tendency. These cartoons provide raters with a vocabulary and awareness to monitor their rating behaviors. We cannot ask raters to stop being human; we can expect them to be fully aware and fair. These cartoons address a conflict between a rater's individual standards and those of the assessment system and interference in the application of the scoring criteria from a positive or negative response to the performance.

TRAINING MATERIALS AND PROCEDURES AND SCORE VARIABILITY

If rubrics are unclear, raters are insufficiently trained, and qualifying standards for raters are lenient (e.g., 60% exact agreement), then scoring will be inconsistent. Raters must be appropriately equipped to do the job. Scoring contractors are increasingly asked to meet rapid turnaround times, and training may be shortened to increase scoring time. Also, clients must provide scoring contractors sufficient lead time, which includes time to receive and process the tests, to develop training materials that the client has checked and approved, and to prepare expert training staff by having them participate in the development of training activities and materials. If the rubrics are untested, the benchmarks and other training papers inconsistently rated, or the training abbreviated, then raters will be ill equipped to do their jobs. Adherence to the characteristics of rubrics and benchmarks described earlier in this chapter will contribute to the development of a scoring system that will avoid undesirable score variability and provide quality scores.

TABLE 7.3. Types of Rater Bias

Types of Bias	Tendency for a rater to . . .
Appearance	Score based on the looks of the response
Central tendency	Assign scores primarily around the scale midpoint
Clashing standards	Score lower because his or her personal grading standards conflict with standards expressed in the rubric
Clashing values	Score lower when the values expressed in the response conflict with those of the rater
Fatigue	Allow scores to be affected by being tired
Halo effect	Score higher because some positive aspect of a performance positively influences a rater's judgment
Handwriting	Allow handwriting to influence his or her scores
Item-to-item carryover	Score higher a response because an examinee's performance on the preceding item was exemplary
Language	Score according to language usage when other dimensions are the focus of the rating
Length	Score lengthy responses higher
Leniency/severity	Score too easily or harshly
Personality clash	Lower a score because he or she hates a particular topic
Repetition factor	Lower a score because she or he has read about a topic or viewed a response repeatedly
Self-scoring	Read more into the response than is there
Skimming	Scan the document and not read the whole response
Sudden death	Score lower due to some aspect of the performance that provokes a negative rater response
Sympathy score	Allow the content to appeal to his or her emotions or allow a sparse performance to elicit his or her desire to reward effort
Test-to-test carryover	Score lower a response that meets the pre-stated expectations, but the response appears somewhat lackluster as compared to exemplary responses that preceded it
Trait	Focus on one aspect (i.e., trait), such as conventions, and give too much weight to this trait in arriving at a score

Note. Summarized from Breland and Jones (1984); Chase (1986); Daly and Dickson-Markman (1982); Hopkins (1998); Lumley (2002); Markham (1976); Penny (2003); Spandel (2001); Stewart and Grobe (1979); Weigle (1998).

The Severe Rater

The Just-Right Rater

The Lenient Rater

The Central Tendency Rater

FIGURE 7.7. Examples of humorous images used to train raters about bias.

TRAINING SCRIPTS

A sample training script is shown in Figure 7.8. If trainers use such a script, then the chance of error due to different trainers emphasizing different information is reduced. Note that the training activities follow the generalized stages of training outlined in Figure 7.2. The level of detail in the script is intended for the novice rater, that is, it explains why the trainer is doing and saying certain things. Also, the script is based on complex, constructed responses, in this case a high school essay exam that is analytically scored for both content knowledge (science or social studies) and written composition. The script can be adapted for use as you prepare to train raters to score essays, portfolios, or other performance tasks.

MONITORING OF TRAINING

Training is a great leveler and a powerful vehicle for building a community of consensus. Training (and retraining), however, can inadvertently be sources of variability and error. Trainers influence what raters learn to expect. Different trainers explaining the same assigned scale value can lead raters to lower or raise their expectations. One trainer might reiterate the relevant features of the score point 2, while the other might indirectly shift standards by saying, "It's just barely a 2. I can see how you might give a 1." As discussed in the standardization section of Chapter 5, efforts should be taken to ensure standardization in training, possibly by assembling all trainers in a centralized location and by using common scripts and materials across trainers and sites.

The standardization of training is supported by monitoring. Thus knowing what occurs during training is important. Monitoring by the client includes approval of all training staff and training materials developed by the scoring agency. It is also important to observe directly any training delivered via the classroom model to ensure adherence to the standardized training materials and procedures. Monitoring might occur through site visits to observe training or to interview recent trainees, through videotapes of training sessions, and through electronic transmittal of training and qualifying files. The client may want the scoring contractor to send electronic files in real time to "observe" training and qualifying rather than be on site.

(Text continues on page 219)

SEQUENCE OF TRAINING ACTIVITIES	TRAINER NOTES AND STRATEGIES
I. Orientation	
GOAL: Create an environment in which effective training and scoring can occur. A. Trainers introduce themselves. B. Raters introduce themselves. C. Overview of the training process— what types of activities and the time frame (3–4 days). D. House rules and daily details, such as 1. Sign-in, sign-out procedure 2. Start on time, end on time 3. Breaks and lunch hours 4. Closest restrooms 5. No food or drink at scoring tables 6. Getting comfortable, creating working space 7. Need for quiet during rating 8. State procedure for identifying silent reading time, read for discussion, including questions E. Sign and return confidentiality forms. F. State goal of training: Rate the students' papers accurately and efficiently. G. Form initial groups at tables for training: 1. 3–4 per group 2. Setup groups to include novice and experienced raters and a mix of subject-matter experts H. Distribute training manuals.	All trainers participate in the initial activities, "Orientation" and "Introduction to Rating," to establish their roles as experts, leaders, and equals. Ask raters to identify subjects taught, current school, and/or previous experience with scoring. *Points to emphasize:* • Rating is different from grading and evaluating student learning using your own standards. • We want you to succeed. • Different people learn in different ways and at different rates. Don't be discouraged if you experience difficultly with this learning process. • Training is continuous throughout the scoring process. Establish the expectation that you will be moving people from group to group as a learning strategy. If you have to move people to keep them on task, the move is expected rather than punitive.
II. Introduction to the Rating Process	
GOAL: All raters share a common understanding of the "big picture." A. Shifting from personal standards to the rubric. Raters are asked to write their names. When everyone is finished, they are asked to do it again—with the opposite hand. They are then asked to describe the two different experiences of the same "performance task."	Activity minimizes threat of learning new process and having to pass a test. It also sets the stage for intellectual and emotional shifts that raters will have to make to internalize the rubric. Discussion should elicit the differences: • Slower—requires conscious thought and effort • Awkward and uncomfortable • Criticism directed at self • Comparison to others in the group

(continued)

FIGURE 7.8. Example of a training script.

SEQUENCE OF TRAINING ACTIVITIES	TRAINER NOTES AND STRATEGIES

B. Review training sequence, qualifying process, and the starting point.
C. Presentation of the examinee test materials. Note these key points:
  1. Examinee responses are draft documents; consider time and resource limits.
  2. Purpose of documents is contained in test to stimulate recall of prior knowledge. Raters must distinguish between original ideas and copying of documents.
D. Present an overview of the scoring rubric and rating process.
  1. Rubric is analytic; performance in one feature shouldn't influence score in another. Score each feature holistically, based on criteria in rubric and benchmarks.
  2. Each score point represents a range of competence.
  3. An individual response won't match a score point exactly. Rubrics acquire meaning through benchmarks and training materials.
  4. Reading to rate is different from classroom testing. Distinguish between errors and flaws. Learn to recognize correct but limited responses.
  5. Limit note-taking as you score; students won't see your comments. Your job is to rate, not "improve" the writer.
  6. Teachers CAN score accurately outside their discipline.
	Let raters know what to expect as soon as you can—what will happen during training in order to prepare them, what will happen during scoring.
	
	Points to emphasize:
	• Training is developmental. Learning to score requires explanation, practice, feedback, and more practice.
	• Provide instruction on the use of all materials.
	• Don't assume they are self-explanatory. Explain all parts of any form or guide you use.
	• Use appropriate terms clearly and consistently throughout the process ("rubric," "domain," "exact agreement," "adjacent scores.") Avoid jargon and any unnecessary terms.

III. Reading for Evidence	
A. Purpose: To base score on the relevant data in the examinee's response. B. Definition and types of evidence.	Use types of evidence handout and kudzu mini-lesson to illustrate process and concepts of reading for evidence.

(continued)

FIGURE 7.8. *(continued)*

SEQUENCE OF TRAINING ACTIVITIES	TRAINER NOTES AND STRATEGIES

C. Significance of evidence:
  1. Determined by the particular feature and rubric
  2. Concept of balancing the evidence
  3. Synthesis questions
	Reading for evidence activity is repeated using the benchmarks.
	
	Points to emphasize:
	• Read forward and think back.
	• Evidence is rubric and domain driven.
	• Read for the positive. Be aware that this requires a shift from <u>reading to instruct</u> ("Let me find what's wrong so I can help the child fix it") to <u>reading to rate.</u>

IV. Subject-Matter Content Training	

GOAL: All raters understand the knowledge and skills addressed in the examinee's task, can access the information they need and use it to evaluate the accuracy and thoroughness of students' responses.
 	
A. Raters read the task and supporting documents provided to cue prior knowledge.
B. Focus on the task; identify key points:
  1. What should the student include in his/her response?
  2. What are formal requirements of the task?
  3. What factual information do the documents give?
C. Raters read prepared training materials.
D. Direct instruction by trainer.
E. Raters study and practice using new information.
F. Identify additional content resources (textbooks, Internet) in the room.
	Encourage note-taking directly on content background training materials and rubrics.
	
	Remember to incorporate the full continuum of participation: say, show, write, illustrate, etc. (see Figure 7.4). Most important, let raters do what they will have to do when actually rating.
	
	Discuss "What does a high school examinee's response look like? What can an examinee accomplish in the allotted testing time?"
	
	During direct instruction, the second trainer listens, monitors responses of raters, asks clarifying questions, and keeps track of time. When one trainer is on stage the other one should not be preparing!
	
	Practice strategies:
	• Whole-group question and answer.
	• Language arts teachers practice explaining new content to science/ social studies teachers.
	• Trainer gives open-note quiz on information.
	• Raters look for information in a selected student response (use benchmark paper for this activity); discuss in small groups at tables.
	• Raters outline their own responses to task.

(continued)

FIGURE 7.8. *(continued)*

SEQUENCE OF TRAINING ACTIVITIES	TRAINER NOTES AND STRATEGIES
V. Content Rubrics	

GOAL: All raters become competent users of the science or social studies rubric.
 A. Analytic scoring in multiple domains.
 B. Go over rubric format and organization.
 C. Learn and practice one domain at a time.
 1. Raters read the domain
 2. Trainer points out details, tips about that domain
 3. Read all benchmarks and annotations for the domain
 4. Discuss, emphasizing what distinguishes adjacent score points
 5. Score the domain on 1–2 practice papers; after each domain has been scored
   a. Check individual scores by score cards
   b. Announce correct score
   c. Have one or two people who got it right explain their thinking
   d. Supplement the rationale provided by raters to cover complete, correct justification for the score
   e. Answer questions
 6. Continue scoring practice papers on this domain. When most scorers are getting correct or adjacent scores, move on to next domain
 D. Repeat process until all domains have been practiced individually.
 E. Introduce the Scoring Path.
 F. Score approximately five practice papers for all three domains; check and discuss scores after each paper.
	Points to emphasize:
	 • Notice global statements and components of the domain in box at the top of each page. Use that box to remind yourself of the big picture as you score.
	 • Make task specific notes on the rubric.
	 • The rubric isn't complete without the anchor papers.
	
	 Tips:
	 • Rotate one experienced scorer from each group to a new group.
	 • Don't let criticisms of rubric or process eat into training time.
	 • Remember to repeat advance organizers ("Now we are doing *X* so you will learn *Y*"). Keep the big picture in mind.
	
	 For benchmarks at each score point, model the decision-making process with think-aloud protocols; demonstrate how to find and evaluate different types of evidence.
	
	 When appropriate, give explicit instructions on weighting descriptors or indicators within a domain.
	
	 After discussion of each anchor and practice paper, recapitulate evidence that justifies the score.
	
	 Use the Scoring Path overhead to model the process of scoring each one of the content domains. (See Figure 7.3.)
	
	 Instruct raters on types/sources of scoring errors. (See Table 7.3.)
	 • Clashing standards
	 • Halo effect
	 • Comparing performances to each other rather than to the rubric and benchmarks
	 • Turning a holistic judgment into a piecemeal analytic judgment
	 • Hypercorrection

(continued)

FIGURE 7.8. *(continued)*

SEQUENCE OF TRAINING ACTIVITIES	TRAINER NOTES AND STRATEGIES
	Points to emphasize: • Don't change your written score after the correct score is announced. • The rater's goal is to match expert scores, not change them.
VI. Language Arts Training	
GOAL: All raters become competent users of the analytic language arts rubrics.	Content training activities are repeated, with language arts rubrics, benchmarks, and content.
VII. Prequalifying Practice Sets and Qualifying Sets	
GOAL: All raters become qualified as quickly as possible. A. Review sources for accurate scoring. B. Rate the remaining practice papers for all features; include any papers that have been partially rated. C. Have raters review their own scores, identify and note tendencies. D. Complete a practice set that is similar to the qualifying rounds (and actual scoring). All papers are completed before scores are provided. E. Provide criteria for qualifying. F. Explain procedure for rating student papers so that raters who pass the criterion test may begin immediately. G. Raters score the 10-paper qualifying round. H. Answer sheets are entered and qualifying reports produced.	*Tip:* The order for assigning domain scores is optional. Language arts teachers may be more comfortable scoring responses for language arts first, then follow with science or social studies. *Point to emphasize:* • Some people will be successful on the first qualifying tests; others will need additional practice and support. For a rater who does not qualify, identify together what will be monitored for the next day and record the plan. If this rater is less accurate in one of the domains or a portion of the score scale, agree that this will be watched and feedback provided. Use one or more qualifying papers on which there was a discrepancy to determine the problem. Focus on one feature at a time. Ask the rater, "What were you paying attention to on this feature?"
VIII. Qualifying Feedback	
A. Provide feedback individually. 1. If rater passed, a. Look over scores together. b. Ask him/her to identify strengths. c. Ask him/her to identify areas that need strengthening.	Ask rater to explain a score by pointing out specific evidence in the paper. Emphasize using anchors and rubrics as sources for accurate scoring. Model accurate scoring of a feature.

(continued)

FIGURE 7.8. *(continued)*

SEQUENCE OF TRAINING ACTIVITIES	TRAINER NOTES AND STRATEGIES

d. Direct rater to take a packet from the front of the box and begin rating student papers.
 2. If rater failed,
   a. Look over scores together.
   b. Ask him/her to point out strengths; add those you see.
   c. Ask him/her to point out areas that need further practice or training; add those you see.
   d. Identify focus and method for relearning, and make a plan with the rater.
B. Provide appropriate additional coaching and practice.
 1. Monitor practice; check to be sure there is genuine practice before administering second test.
 2. Have rater model the think-aloud reading for evidence/comparing evidence to scoring rubrics/assigning a score/justifying the score.
 3. Let the rater tell you when he/she is ready for retest.
C. Give second 10-paper qualifying to raters who failed to meet the standard in the first round.
	Provide additional papers and ask rater to use annotation form to record evidence for decision. Be sure to discuss these notes with him/her, when finished.
	
	If problems persist, try to determine and respond to the specific obstacle to accurate scoring:
	1. Insufficient understanding of the content
	2. Difficulty using rubric
	3. Using classroom rather than rubric standards
	4. Attitude toward student
	5. Attitude/beliefs about assessment itself
	6. "Pet peeves"
	7. Frustrations directed at trainers
	8. Outside or personal distractions
	
	Tips: Restate the goal; keep track of time; don't argue or become a personal counselor.

FIGURE 7.8. *(continued)*

DISMISSING TRAINEES

After all of the training, some rater trainees will not meet the accuracy in scoring that is required. While it may sound harsh to dismiss trainees who do not demonstrate a solid understanding of the rating task, borderline qualifiers consume staff time in the form of monitoring and feedback. Furthermore, if they have to be dismissed during the scoring session all their scores have to be deleted and all their work redone. And though the staff has direct contact with the rater-trainees, the most important people are the examinees. The emphasis in this section of the scoring chapter is thus on maintaining accuracy.

Testing agencies, research projects, and program evaluations might dismiss raters who do not achieve adequate agreement; however, school systems or licensing boards may not be able to exempt a rater trainee from scoring (Quellmalz, 1986). If a rater trainee cannot be dismissed, such as might be the case of a lawyer who serves on the licensure board, then the staff may continue training to improve the accuracy of the trainee's scores. A fail-safe solution is to use corrective procedures. Such procedures include the use of two raters' scores instead of only one. The use of two raters allows staff to monitor during operational scoring to identify any pair of ratings that differ markedly from the other ratings for a particular response. The response can be scored by an expert rater when scores differ markedly, especially when a discrepancy occurs at the pass–fail score.

THE ROLE OF EXPERT TRAINING STAFF

The most straightforward way to describe the role of expert training staff is that they are the most accurate of raters and they are skilled teachers. Trainers typically begin as raters and move up through the ranks to become validity raters (those whose ratings are used to monitor the accuracy of other raters), trainers, and project management. The skills and talents of experts are summarized in Figure 7.9.

In terms of rating, Hieronymus and colleagues (1987) indicated that the expert raters should have experience in the scoring of constructed-response items, advanced training in the subject area being scored, familiarity with a wide range of student capabilities, the respect of his or her colleagues, and the ability to communicate clearly (p. 5). Additional criteria for classification as an expert rater include higher levels of accuracy and consistency in the assignment of scores than other raters (Claggett, 1999; Diederich, 1974; Myers, 1980; Taylor, 1998; Wolcott, 1998; Wolfe, 1997).

Training of Expert Staff

Rating accuracy is a necessary but incomplete qualification for trainers who are expected to deliver training via the classroom model. The cognitive coaching model developed by Arthur Costa (1991) provides helpful advice for experts on how to ask raters questions that will enable the trainers to elicit the information needed to identify what raters do not know and need to know. Effective questions share five characteristics:

1. How to select, construct, and sequence training materials, including
   - benchmarks
   - practice
   - qualifying
   - monitoring

2. Teaching and supervising adults
   - Constructing content training for experts and nonexperts
   - People management
   - Listening and feedback
   - Effective questioning

3. Monitoring rater data sources and how to use them to identify and correct rating errors
   - seeded responses
   - need for individual retraining
   - need for group retraining

4. Security procedures

5. Logistics (to meet accuracy and productivity goals)

6. Record keeping

7. Everything raters have to know
   - The purpose of assessment
   - The evaluative criteria
   - Content background
   - The scoring process
   - Self-monitoring tools
   - How to work in the scoring setting

FIGURE 7.9. Skills required of expert staff.

1. They are nonjudgmental. That is, they avoid expressing negative presuppositions. The language is neutral and focuses on the work, not the rater.

2. They are focused on evidence. They point the rater toward rubrics, benchmarks, and evidence in the performance. They encourage the rater to respond in terms of the evidence instead of value judgments and personal preferences.

3. They are probing. The questions are intended to get the rater to generate detailed, concrete information. They ask the rater to elaborate, compare, and/or analyze.

4. They are followed by silence to give the rater time to think and respond. They encourage self-directed reflection.

5. They are carefully constructed. They ask specifics about what, where, and how—not why. Their interest is to get the rater thinking.

These questions can be employed in group settings or individual conferences.

Once rater training is completed, the focus shifts from education to scoring and maintaining rater accuracy. In the next chapter, we describe the components of operational scoring.

FURTHER READING

Wolcott, W., with Legg, S. (1998). *An overview of writing assessment: Theory, research, and practice.* Urbana, IL: National Council of Teachers of English.

Presents a chapter on rater training in the area of writing assessment. Other topics in the text include portfolio assessment and forms of scoring (e.g., holistic, analytic, and primary trait).

Chapter Questions

1. Consider an augmented 4-point rubric. Identify the score families.

2. What does the training script contribute to standardization?

3. During rater training for a writing assessment, an English professor had trouble achieving congruence with the training papers (Penny, 2003). In one instance the professor assigned a 2 to a paper that was assigned a 3 by the validation committee. The professor considered the paper vapid and inadequate. Subsequently, he withdrew from training.

   a. What form of rater bias could have influenced the professor's scores?

   b. Describe how this form of bias could influence the scores given by this rater.

CHECKLIST 7.1

Completed	To-Do List for Training Raters and Staff
	Recruiting Raters
✓	Develop screening procedures, such as the potential rater completing a task (e.g., essay) similar to the one that examinees completed. p. 191
	Determine preexisting rater qualifications for hiring, such as a degree in the area being assessed. pp. 191–192
	Estimate the number of raters required to score the tasks. pp. 192–194
	Training Raters
	Describe the broader purpose of the assessment program. pp. 197–199
	Introduce rater trainees to the performance task, the rubric, and the annotated benchmarks. pp. 198–199
	Develop content knowledge that raters must have for scoring by reviewing the task and identifying the attributes that examinees should include in their responses. pp. 198–200
	Guide rater trainees through the scoring path and reading for evidence. pp. 200–201
	Train raters to ask wedge questions to focus their review of the relevant performance levels in the rubric. p. 202
	Train raters to augment scores by identifying a score family (e.g. 3–, 3, 3+) for the response and deciding whether the performance is slightly lower than typical for that level (assign 3–), slightly higher than the typical response (assign 3+), or a typical response (assign a 3). pp. 202–203
	Lead rater trainees in practice scoring, modeling the process for them. pp. 198, 203–209
	Administer qualifying sets to determine if rater trainees attain the required qualification score. p. 194
	Provide additional training on bias and self-monitoring for those who qualify as raters. pp. 198, 203, 209–212
	Provide guidelines on working in a scoring setting. pp. 198, 203
	Dismiss rater trainees who do not attain the required qualification score. p. 220

(continued)

CHECKLIST 7.1. *(continued)*

Completed	To-Do List for Training Raters and Staff
	Expert Staff
	Reduce errors due to different trainers providing different information by providing the trainers with a training script and monitoring the sessions. pp. 213–219
	Develop expert staff for long-term scoring projects and assessment centers. pp. 220–221

CHAPTER 8

Scoring and Monitoring

INTRODUCTION

To this point, you have developed scoring rubrics, selected benchmark performances to illustrate each score level in the rubric, and trained the raters. The more rigor built into the training process, combined with a final phase of training that closely parallels "live" scoring, the smoother the transition to "live" or operational scoring will be. During training, raters become dependent upon immediate feedback to make adjustments in their scoring behaviors. Effective monitoring during scoring simply provides a less frequent but still sufficient form of feedback.

In this chapter, we present various methods to provide raters with feedback about their scoring. We include a discussion about monitoring rater statistics, their agreement levels with other raters, and the agreement of raters' scoring with peers and expert judges. Subsequently, we describe methods for resolving score discrepancies when raters disagree. First, however, we briefly discuss the logistics of running a scoring center.

FACILITY AND LOGISTICS

Scoring and monitoring can occur using the classroom model, led by training experts; the classroom model with scoring completed online; or remote scoring (Kobrin & Kimmel, 2006; NCES, 2000; Yap et al., 2005). The greater the number of activities conducted on-site, the more attention must be paid to personal needs. A scoring center must be quiet, provide adequate lighting to minimize eye strain, and be furnished with sufficient table space and chairs comfortable for extended periods of sitting (Hieronymous et al., 1987). In the instance of high-stakes assessment, security procedures such as photo identification badges, a locked rating area, and a sign-in/sign-out procedure help to ensure that no tests are removed from the scoring site.

Raters need a room for meals and breaks and a place for storing personal items. If the break room is established as the only area for food and drinks, accidents that damage examinee responses or computer equipment are easily avoided (Hieronymous et al., 1987).

By addressing expectations and procedures in the interview process and implementing them from the beginning of training, they are unlikely to become an issue once scoring has begun. Temporary work such as rating attracts a wide variety of applicants, some of whom will be working in a highly structured work environment for the first time.

MONITORING THE QUALITY OF RATINGS

The requirement that the raters hired for operational scoring will have high agreement levels with scores assigned by a validation committee is a first step in ensuring the quality of scores. However, procedures also must be in place to ensure that these raters maintain their skills over tasks and time. Slippage, also referred to as rater drift, from the established scoring standards occurs as a natural result of the scoring process (Baker, Aschbacher, Niemi, & Sato, 1992; Becker & Pomplun, 2006; Quellmalz, 1986). Procedures for detecting error and drift are important to establish, increasing in importance as the stakes attached to test results contribute to promotion, graduation, licensure, or certification decisions.

Many of these procedures rely on the reliability or consistency in the decisions that raters render. Multiple judgments on the same item by raters using the same scoring system are one safeguard. Such multiple ratings provide the data for determining rater reliability (LaDuca et al., 1995). Frequent rotation of raters who work in teams provides another form of monitoring. With rotation, interrater comparisons and read-behinds from different team leaders increase, resulting in the quick identification of raters who are outliers. Since all raters, including team leaders, are to use the same scoring criteria, a rater who does not "agree" with a number of other raters and expert staff will be obvious in the data.

To maintain reliable and valid scoring, several monitoring methods are employed. These methods include administering recalibration sets, performing read-behinds, reviewing rater statistics, assessing rater agreement, and conducting validity checks.

Recalibration Sets

Raters are influenced by the performances they score; this is a simple reality of performance assessment. Thus when scoring occurs over several days, as is the case in licensure tests, typical practice is the recalibration of raters (Lenel, 1990c; Weigle, 2002). Recalibration sets are pre-scored examinee responses that are used in a refresher practice session before drift occurs and serve to remind raters of the uniform standards.

If the scoring contractor has the luxury of presenting raters with randomized or mixed papers, raters will be less likely to be influenced by the order of the papers they read. If, however, the contractor is working with a "first papers in, first reports out" delivery model, raters may develop a response set based on the homogeneity of papers from the same classroom or school system. For example, a response set can be a rater scoring a set of essays from a classroom in which little writing was taught. After reading numerous poorly written essays, the rater might assign low scores to papers that are of a higher performance level. Thus the writer has developed a response set in her scoring based on the homogeneity of the essays. In large-scale testing, recalibration sets are administered at the beginning of each shift, or even twice a day, to bring raters back to the full range of responses.

A limitation of the use of recalibration sets is that raters can alter their behavior to satisfy the scoring criteria, appearing more accurate than they actually are. In his essay on his experiences as a rater, Penny (2003) reports such an altering of behavior when he received sets of pre-scored validity papers to rate. Whether raters alter their behavior or not, recalibration sets remind the raters of the uniform standards and full range of the scale. These sets can also be constructed to address immediate needs, such as an apparent loss of the high end of the scale.

Read-Behinds and Read-Aheads

On a daily basis, trainers and other members of the expert staff review the scores that raters assigned to examinee responses. In this process, referred to as read-behinds and read-aheads in the scoring of written products, expert staff serve as the second reader of a random sample of the papers scored by their team members (National Center for Educational Statistics [NCES], 2000). In addition, expert staff sometimes read behind raters and trainers on other teams who are scoring on the same task. The scoring director or someone assigned the "scoring monitor" function looks at the reports of "paired scores" to determine rater error or to find any trend differences between teams. Trainers conduct read-behinds across teams because, in their conversations and musings about examinee responses, team members influence one another and an entire team may drift high or low.

Read-aheads can vary in terms of when they are completed. Training and expert staff might be able to provide first reads and ratings so that when raters complete the second reads, the team leader has immediate access to comparative data. It is especially useful to employ this procedure immediately after training, when raters are first making the change to rating a large number of products in a single shift.

Review of Rater Statistics

As a rating session progresses, a rater usually generates enough scores to calculate various statistics to examine the resulting score quality. Useful statistics include rater means and standard deviations and score frequencies.

Rater Means and Standard Deviations

If means are calculated for each rater and for the group, then a rater's mean that is higher than the group's mean may indicate leniency. In addition, a rater's mean that is lower than the group's mean may indicate rater severity (Coffman, 1971a; Lenel, 1990c). Raters whose scores differ from experts' and other raters' scores should be examined for leniency or severity, and possibly receive feedback and additional training.

The standard deviation represents the spread of scores around a mean. For example, a 6-point task with a mean of 3 and a standard deviation of 1 will have about 68% of the scores between 2 and 4, and 95% of the scores will be between 1 and 5. Thus the scores cover most of the range of the rubric. If the standard deviation were only half a point (i.e., 0.5), then about 68% of the scores are between 2.5 and 3.5, and 95% of the scores will be between 2 and 4. Hence, few scores are very high or very low, perhaps indicating the raters stayed in the middle of the rubric in assigning scores (Coffman, 1971a; Lenel, 1990c). Thus item means and standard deviations can provide useful information about raters' use of the scoring scale.

Score Frequencies

The frequencies for each rater allow the team leader to monitor the productivity of each rater (Weigle, 2002). In addition, a frequency distribution report indicates whether a rater is using all score points. In Table 8.1, note that Rater 1 concentrated 71.5% of his scores on the high end of the scale (i.e., ratings of 2 and 3). Rater 4, in contrast, assigned 64.5% of her scores on the low end of the score scale (i.e., ratings of 0 or 1). Reviewing benchmarks for all four levels might be a productive strategy to use with these raters.

Score frequencies also allow a review of whether a rater demonstrates a central tendency bias or restriction of range bias (Engelhard, 1994). Central tendency is detected by examining the percentage of a rater's scores around the scale midpoint, whereas restriction of range is detected when reviewing distribution of a rater's score along a continuum of examinee competence. In Table 8.2, a central tendency bias could account for the raters' assignment of most scores in the 3–5 range.

If raters' scores are cross-tabulated, as shown in Table 8.3, the percentage of discrepant ratings can be seen (Weigle, 2002). In Table 8.3, agreement is defined as exact or adjacent. The shaded areas show agreement and the areas not shaded provide information about the number of discrepant scores and the score range where disagreement occurs. In the example, 35 (17.5%) of the essay ratings did not agree. The greatest occurrence of disagreement was for the essays receiving a 0 by Rater 1 and a score of 2 or 3 by Rater 2, perhaps indicating a need for the trainer to review the essays receiving discrepant scores with the raters.

TABLE 8.1. Frequency of Ratings for an Essay Prompt

Scores	Rater 1		Rater 2		Rater 3		Rater 4	
	n	%	n	%	n	%	n	%
0	30	15.0	57	28.5	43	21.5	73	36.5
1	27	13.5	61	30.5	56	28.0	56	28.0
2	73	36.5	59	29.5	66	33.0	38	19.0
3	70	35.0	23	11.5	35	17.5	33	16.5

Note. From Johnson, Penny, Fisher, and Kuhs (2003). Copyright 2003 by Taylor & Francis Group, LLC. Adapted by permission.

TABLE 8.2. Frequencies of Raters' Scores across a Writing Achievement Continuum

	Rater 1		Rater 2	
Score levels	n	%	n	%
1	0	0	0	0
2	2	2	1	1
3	29	24	30	25
4	48	40	48	40
5	35	29	36	30
6	6	5	5	4

Note. From Johnson, Penny, and Gordon (2001). Copyright 2001 by Sage Publications, Inc. Reprinted by permission.

Review of Rater Agreement

Myriad methods exist for examining interrater agreement. Three common methods include examining percent agreement, Spearman's rank-order correlation (also referred to as Spearman's rho), and an index of dependability from generalizability theory. In this section we focus on percent agreement and Spearman's rank correlation. We save for the last chapter the discussion of the use of generalizability theory to estimate interrater reliability. Presentation of interrater reliability with the broader issue of score reliability allows a more cohesive treatment of generalizability theory in estimating reliability.

TABLE 8.3. Cross-Tabulation of Raters' Scores

	Rater 2				
Rater 1	0	1	2	3	Total
0	28 14%	1 0.5%	1 0.5%	0 0%	30 15%
1	12 6%	10 5%	4 2%	1 0.5%	27 13.5%
2	13 6.5%	34 17%	25 12.5%	1 0.5%	73 36.5%
3	4 2%	16 8%	29 14.5%	21 10.5%	70 35%
Total	57 28.5%	61 30.5%	59 29.5%	23 11.5%	

Note. From Johnson, Penny, Fisher, and Kuhs (2003). Copyright 2003 by Taylor & Francis Group, LLC. Reprinted by permission.

Percent Agreement

Percent agreement between a pair of raters provides a measure of rater consistency. Often in scoring, a rater is paired with another rater for a set of tasks (e.g., essays) and then paired with a different rater for the next set of tasks. Such rotation of raters allows the comparison of a rater's scores with different peers and the examination of agreement with other raters. The idea of varying the pairing of raters is important because a low percent agreement for a pair of raters only informs you that a problem exists; it does not tell you which rater is problematic. If a rater is paired with different raters, then analysis of percent agreement across pairings will help identify a problematic rater.

A limitation of this type of report is that, when produced quickly, it lacks correction for ratings of responses that are difficult to score and are part of rescoring and the resolution report. Thus a very productive rater or an expert reader assigned to score problematic papers or monitor problem raters can falsely appear to be less accurate than they are in reality.

In addition, sole reliance on percent agreement for gauging rater agreement can be problematic because the limited range of the scales in some rubrics can inflate estimates of interrater agreement. The number of ratings available to raters in a given rubric can lead to a degree of agreement between the raters, and that agreement is, in part, an artifact of the rubric, not the training of the raters. As an example, consider a flat distribution of expected ratings arising from a 4-point rubric. That is, 25% of the ratings are 1's, 25% are 2's, 25% are 3's, and 25% are 4's. Moreover, consider that the raters are independently assigning ratings in a *random* manner, not according to the quality of the performances. The exact agreement of two such raters would be 25%. The exact and adjacent agreement of two such raters for this 4-point rubric would be 75% due to chance alone!

Of course, such a situation in which raters randomly assign scores is not tenable because raters are trained to apply a rubric and its anchors in a systematic fashion. Scores are determined through the independent evaluation of the performance by the raters, but in the evaluation, the raters apply the same process of comparing the performance against a rubric and exemplars. Thus, the anticipation is that a pair of raters will reach the same decision regarding a given example, which is what typically happens in a performance assessment.

However, consider the previous untenable example of uncorrelated raters, but now, with expected ratings that follow a normal-like (i.e., centrally mounded and symmetrical) distribution, not a flat distribution. In addition, consider that the center of the distribution is centered on the midpoint of the rubric.

To examine the expected percent agreement between the scores when the correlation of the ratings varies from 0 to 1, we conducted a brief Monte Carlo simulation involving 500 simulated papers and two raters under the condition of a normal-like distribution centered on the rating rubric, either 4 or 6 points.

Table 8.4 presents the agreement that arises in such a situation. The first column indicates the spurious agreement between the ratings under the condition of no correlation between the ratings. Note that uncorrelated ratings achieve 73% exact and adjacent agreement using the 4-point rubric. In addition, expert raters often must demonstrate exact and adjacent agreement with validation exemplars at 90%. Using a 4-point rubric, the correlation between such ratings would be between .5 and .6, suggesting shared variability between the ratings of approximately 25–36%. The pattern for the 6-point rubric is similar to that of the 4-point rubric. Thus when relying on agreement levels in monitoring operational scoring, it might appear that rater consistency is high; however, the resulting interrater reliability coefficients might be lower than desired. For this reason, it appears prudent also to calculate rater agreement and interrater reliability during scoring. Percent agreement may best serve in keeping a running tally during scoring to make sure raters are maintaining consistency.

Spearman's Rank-Order Correlation

Spearman's rank-order correlation coefficient provides an interrater reliability estimate that takes into account chance agreement (Hayes & Hatch, 1999), as well as accounting for changes in the ranks of the scores. This index, however, does not take into account whether a rater effect (e.g., rater leniency or severity) contributes to mean differences in scores (Shavelson & Webb, 1991). This index is also limited to the estimation of interrater reliability based on rater pairs. As described earlier in the discussion of percent agreement, by varying rater pairs across sets of tasks, the Spearman rank-order correlation can be calculated for the set of tasks that raters score in common, and then the reliability estimates compared to see whether correlations are systematically low when one rater is part of a pairing.

In calculating the Spearman rank-order correlation, we recommend that you use a statistical package, such as SPSS or SAS. We make this

TABLE 8.4. The Relation between Agreement Levels and Correlation Estimates of Interrater Reliability

Rubric scale	Agreement	Correlation between raters										
		.00	.10	.20	.30	.40	.50	.60	.70	.80	.90	.95
		Percent agreement between ratings using a 4- and 6-point rubric										
4	Exact	28	30	33	35	37	40	45	50	57	68	78
	Exact and adjacent	73	77	80	83	85	89	92	95	98	100	100
6	Exact	26	28	30	32	34	35	40	46	52	64	75
	Exact and adjacent	69	74	77	79	82	87	90	94	98	100	100

233

recommendation because the formula for calculating Spearman's rank-order correlation that is found in most measurement texts results in a spuriously inflated correlation when several examinees receive the same ratings (i.e., their ratings are tied). Given that rubrics often use 4-point or 6-point scales, many examinees receive the same rating (i.e., tied rankings). A procedure to correct for the ties is available for the rank-order correlation; however, the required equations used in the correction are numerous (Sheskin, 2004, pp. 1065–1069) and not amenable to hand calculations.

Fortunately, programs such as SPSS incorporate the corrections in their calculation of the Spearman rank-order correlation. Holistic scores from a rating session of portfolios are shown in Figure 8.1. Notice the number of tied ratings for Rater 1: seven ratings of 4, eleven ratings of 3, and eleven ratings of 2. Thus the Spearman correlation coefficient would be inflated if the tie corrections were not used. To obtain the Spearman rank-order correlation in SPSS, as shown in Figure 8.1, you select Analyze, Correlate, and Bivariate. After selecting Bivariate, a pop-up window presents the options of Spearman, Pearson, and Kendall's tau-b. Select Spearman, then click OK. An output window pops up and shows that in our example the Spearman correlation is 0.68.

If the scores from two raters are combined for reporting, then the pooling of the ratings is analogous to lengthening a test (Thorndike,

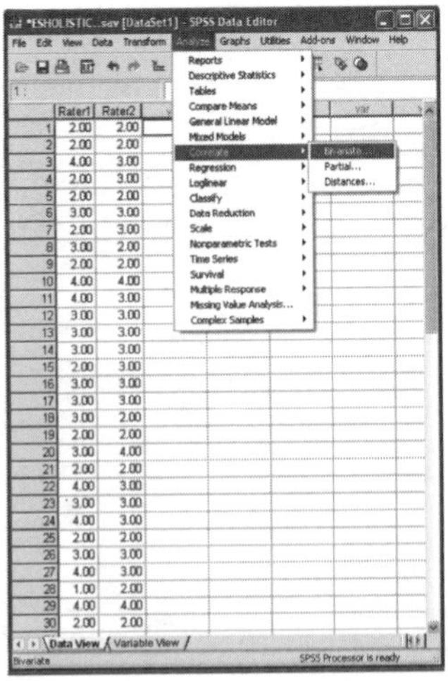

FIGURE 8.1. Use of SPSS to calculate Spearman's rank-order correlation. SPSS screen shot reprinted with permission from SPSS.

Cunningham, Thorndike, & Hagen, 1991). Thus the application of the Spearman–Brown prophecy formula to the Spearman correlation is appropriate. For two raters, the formula is

$$\frac{2 \times r}{1 + r}$$

where r is the Spearman rank-order correlation between the two raters' scores. For the portfolio ratings in Figure 8.1, the result is

$$\frac{2 \times .69}{1 + .69} = \frac{1.38}{1.69} = 0.82$$

Thus interrater reliability for the holistic scoring is .82. This procedure assumes the raters are equally qualified. The addition of less qualified raters can reduce the reliability of the reported scores.

Validity Checks

Validity checks are conducted using prescored, individual validity responses or "seeded performances" that are indistinguishable from other examinee responses (Wolcott, 1998). The seeded performances are "fed" to each rater on a regular basis. Ideally, a group of experts has selected these examinee performances and scores have been determined in the expert group review process (Johnson, Penny, Fisher, et al., 2003; Yap et al., 2005). Agreement with expert judgment as reflected in seed performances introduces the validity of rater scores that is absent from measures of interrater agreement. Some seeded performances are currently produced examinee responses; others are drawn from the archives of previous test administrations.

As soon as an individual rater scores some of the seeded performances, the team leader or supervisor compares each rater's scores with the "true" scores assigned by the validation committee. At the end of the shift, the scoring director closely checks the cumulative validity report agreement percentages for any rater with exact and/or adjacent agreement percentages that fall below a predetermined threshold (e.g., 80%). Thresholds can be built into the monitoring software so that problem raters are easily identified on often lengthy reports. In such instances when a rater has drifted significantly, that individual's work on live responses would be quickly reviewed by the scoring director or team leader. Should retraining be judged necessary, the team leader may conference with the rater to try to determine the source of the problem, and then take appropriate steps to bring the rater's scores into alignment. Conversations in online scoring centers are conducted through a message board or e-mail, and the rater can be "locked out" of scoring until retraining and requalifying are complete (Yap et al., 2005).

The standard for raters' agreement with the seeded responses is often somewhat less than the standard for initial qualifying. The differing standard occurs because responses selected from operational tasks are not as clear-cut examples of given score categories as the training and qualifying materials prepared ahead of time with feedback from the complete pool of experts.

One of the strengths of scoring performances that are delivered via computer instead of paper, such as in the Internet-based tests of the South Carolina Arts Assessment Program (Yap et al., 2005), is that the seeded validity performances can be delivered at variable rates. If scoring is conducted at multiple sites, a random sample from the same large collection of seeded performances can be scored at each of the different sites to determine consistency across sites.

MONITORING PROCEDURES

Monitoring should be administered at different times of the day and week and throughout the duration of a scoring project. Tracking performance over time will allow for identification of slippage that occurs in the transition from training materials to current products and from the rater drift that occurs from the interaction of the rater with so many examinee responses that the scale is redefined with raised or lowered expectations.

The relatively quick checks must be completed at least daily to detect individual or site drift early. The occurrence of drift may be incremental; it should be detected while it is small enough for intervention to be immediate and effective. Benchmarks from previous administrations serve as an anchor to the past (indicating a change in scoring standards or consistency over time). Checks produced from current examinee responses allow for the possibility that the quality and types of examinee responses have and will change since the pilot or field test and familiarity or instruction or test prep improves. Anchors assembled across sites will be essential for determining whether examinees from diverse locations are evaluated equitably irrespective of the assessment site.

Checks used to monitor rater accuracy should be administered more frequently in the early stages of the scoring project to determine whether the raters have made the transition from training to current products. Also, checks should be administered more frequently to raters who (1) have been identified as problematic on the basis of the rating reports of current products and (2) are more productive and thus influencing more candidates' scores.

Checks should be assembled to sample those decisions that the raters have to make most often and those that contribute most to the pass–fail decision. As much as possible, they should be clear-cut, on-point score values, if this reflects the products themselves. The number of sets needed will vary with the size of the scoring site. More checks will be needed for "pencil and paper" to prevent their recognition through changes in appearance because of repeated handling or through conversations raters have with one another.

Sample Reports
to Illustrate Rater Accuracy Data

Sample rater reports for analytic and holistic writing assessments illustrate the rater report process. For the sake of illustration, for the analytic rubric, scores from 1 to 4 are assigned in the domains of Focus, Organization, Style, and Conventions (see Figures 8.2 and 8.3). Training and monitoring reports used in both these scoring programs are described, with an emphasis on the information that is shared directly with each rater. Generally, the format of and information contained in training and monitoring reports is the same so that training prepares each rater to monitor his or her accuracy and, under the direction of a staff member, to self-correct.

The rater agreement report (see Figure 8.2), which becomes a rater validity report during scoring, is based on the comparison of the rater's scores with cases that have been prescored by a validity committee. For each of the four domains, two types of information are provided: the percent of agreement with the true scores and, when there is disagreement, the direction of disagreement. The rater has scored 20 papers with the following levels of agreement: 75% for Focus, 100% for Organization, 75% for Style, and 100% for Conventions.

In terms of agreement with the true scores, percentages are provided for exact, adjacent (1 point either higher or lower than the true score), and discrepant ratings. The percentage of the rater's scores that were

	% Agreement			% Disagreement		
Domain	Exact	Adjacent	Discrepant	Count	% High	% Low
Focus	75	25	0	5	0	100
Organization	100	0	0	0	0	0
Style	75	25	0	5	0	100
Conventions	100	0	0	0	0	0

Number of papers: 20

    % Total Exact Agreement   87.5
    % Total Adjacent Agreement   12.5
    % Total Discrepant   0

FIGURE 8.2. Rater agreement report.

adjacent were 25% for Focus and 25% for Style. The rater had no scores that were discrepant.

The rate of disagreement is based on the number of papers listed in the "count" column and the percentage of instances in which the rater's scores were higher or lower than the true scores are included in the "high" and "low" columns, respectively. In this example, for the adjacent scores for the Focus and Style criteria the rater's scores were lower than the scores provided by the validity committee.

The bottom section of the report, with total percentages, summarizes the rater's accuracy across the four domains. Overall exact agreement was 87.5% and adjacent agreement was 12.5%.

The same report can be produced during scoring with prescored, seeded validity papers serving as the known cases. Because these papers are mixed with actual operational student responses, raters know that a portion of the papers rated daily included "seeded" papers, but not which ones.

The matrix report shown in Figure 8.3 allows the supervisor to look at rater accuracy by score point. The diagonal of the matrix (underlined and bolded numbers) shows the number of times on the 20 papers that the rater and true scores intersected, that is, that the rater assigned the true score. Adding the number of scores assigned indicates the total number of papers at each score point. For instance, in the Focus criterion at the 1 score level the number is 5 + 3 = 8.

The data to the right of each underlined diagonal number show how many times the rater assigned scores higher than the true score and how

RATER DOMAIN MATRICES

Focus

Rater scores	1	2	3	4	% Exact	% Adj.	% Disc.
True scores							
1	**5**	0	0	0	100	0	0
2	3	**4**	0	0	57	43	0
3	0	0	**5**	0	100	0	0
4	0	0	2	**1**	33	67	0
Rater	8	4	7	1			

Organization

Rater scores	1	2	3	4	% Exact	% Adj.	% Disc.
True scores							
1	**6**	0	0	0	100	0	0
2	0	**6**	0	0	100	0	0
3	0	0	**5**	0	100	0	0
4	0	0	0	**3**	100	0	0
Rater	6	6	5	3			

Style

Rater scores	1	2	3	4	% Exact	% Adj.	% Disc.
True scores							
1	**6**	0	0	0	100	0	0
2	2	**1**	0	0	33	67	0
3	0	0	**7**	0	100	0	0
4	0	0	3	**1**	25	75	0
Rater	8	1	10	1			

Conventions

Rater scores	1	2	3	4	% Exact	% Adj.	% Disc.
True scores							
1	**3**	0	0	0	100	0	0
2	0	**4**	0	0	100	0	0
3	0	0	**7**	0	100	0	0
4	0	0	0	**6**	100	0	0
Rater	3	4	7	6			

FIGURE 8.3. Rater matrix report.

much higher the scores were. The data to the left of the diagonal number show how many scores were low and by how many points. For example, in the Focus domain, the 1 scores that the rater assigned were correct, four of the 2 scores were correct, but three times the rater assigned a 1 instead of a 2. All five of the 3 scores were correct. Once the rater assigned a 4 that was correct, but two other times the rater assigned a 3 rather than a 4.

The rater has a severity bias in that he tends to assign lower scores than warranted. Also, the rater, having assigned a score of 1 eight times, is comfortable with harsh judgments and might be unlikely to assign top scores. Any meaning attached to the trends in this report must be kept in context (i.e., what the supervisor knows from other current reports and the rater's history). What this report does suggest is that the rater does not assign 4's in Focus and Style.

To evaluate the quality of ratings, we recommend looking at how a rater (1) uses the scale in comparison to expected score distributions (when known), (2) assigns scores in comparison to the range of scores being assigned by the experts, and (3) changes in any of the indicators over time to show that retraining has improved scoring behaviors.

Baseline data are established by looking at the scoring distributions of expert raters. The baseline data can be used to quickly identify outliers and initiate other monitoring procedures such as full packet read-behinds or read-aheads. Notice in Figure 8.4 that Rater B assigned 16% of the responses a score of 1, whereas the experts only assigned a rating of 1 to 6% of the responses. The figures in the sample do

RATER VALIDITY REPORT
UNIFORM SCORE REPORT

Rater	Expert Baseline %			
	Score 1	Score 2	Score 3	Score 4
	6%	33%	42%	17%
A	3%	30%	51%	13%
B	16%	29%	41%	12%
C	5%	34%	41%	18%

FIGURE 8.4. Rater validity report.

vnot total 100%, reflecting that 2–3% of the ratings were nonscorable responses.

Monitoring a rater's scoring provides a safeguard against inappropriate ratings. However, even with the best of training and monitoring, rating errors will occur. One technique for reducing the effect of such errors on examinees' scores is to combine the judgments of more than one rater to form reported scores. The combination of multiple scores is more apt to reflect the true rating than any single rating. A typical approach is to use the average of two ratings, supplemented by a third rating from an expert judge when the original scores differ by more than a scale point. This resolution process, or rescore process as it is often called, is also a form of monitoring and can be a source of feedback to the original raters. A number of resolution methods and the research about them are described below.

SCORE RESOLUTION MODELS

Additional information that is useful for monitoring during scoring is the resolution requirements for a rater (Weigle, 2002). Maintaining a count for the number of a rater's scores that require adjudication provides information about productivity, especially if this information is accompanied by a count of the discrepancies that were resolved in the rater's favor. Is this section we describe methods for resolving score discrepancies.

The resolution of discrepant scores traces back to early Sung China (960–1279 C.E.). Two examiners read the written civil service examinations independently. Then a third examiner received the grades and, if necessary, resolved them (Kracke, 1953). This method has elements common to the resolution methods described in this section.

Rater Mean

As shown in Table 8.5, the rater mean method of resolution simply uses the average of the two original ratings to produce the operational score; the model is generally applied in the first stage of scoring when raters assign adjacent scores (Johnson, Penny, & Johnson, 2000). Resolution for adjacent scores is necessary when rating agreement is other than exact because testing programs commonly report only one score to the public, and high-stakes decisions are typically based on comparison of a single score to a cut score.

TABLE 8.5. Major Models of Score Resolution

Resolution methods	When applied	Qualifications of adjudicator	Description
Rater mean	Raters assign adjacent scores.	No adjudicator.	Combines (i.e., averages or sums) the two original ratings to produce the operational score.
Parity	Raters assign nonadjacent scores.	Adjudicator might be an expert or another rater with a similar level of expertise as the original raters.	Solicits the score of a third rater; i.e., adjudicator. Combines the three scores, i.e., the two original raters' scores and the adjudicator's score.
Tertium quid	Raters assign nonadjacent scores.	Adjudicator might be an expert or another rater with a similar level of expertise as the original raters.	Solicits the score of an adjudicator. Combines the adjudicator's score with the closest score of the original raters. Discards discrepant rating.
Expert	Raters assign nonadjacent scores.	Adjudicator is someone with substantially more experience and accuracy in scoring than the original raters.	Solicits the score of an expert adjudicator. Adjudicator's score replaces both original scores.
Discussion	Raters assign nonadjacent scores.	No adjudicator.	Requires that the two original raters rescore the response that received discrepant ratings. Raters mutually review the scoring guide, compare the response to benchmark performances, review the features of the response that support the initial ratings, consider any evidence that challenges the original judgments, and seek consensus on a final score.

Parity

The parity method incorporates the judgment of a third rater during adjudication. The third rater might be either an expert or another rater with a similar level of expertise as the original raters. The hallmark of the parity model is that all three ratings produced in the scoring process are considered equally viable and are combined through averaging or summing to form an operational score (Johnson, Penny, & Johnson, 2000; Wolcott, 1998). The score provided by the third rater can serve to moderate the extreme judgment of one or both of the original raters.

Tertium Quid

The tertium quid model of score resolution also incorporates the judgment of a third rater during adjudication. The name of the model derives from the medieval practice in which a deadlock in a debate is resolved by eliciting a decision from a third party in favor of one of the disputants (Cherry & Myer, 1993. Several variations of tertium quid appear in the literature (Johnson, Penny, & Johnson, 2000). In one form, a third rater (i.e., adjudicator) conducts a blind review of the response and the adjudicator's score is matched with the closest original rating. The matched scores are then summed or averaged, and the discrepant rating is eliminated. When the third score is midway between the two original scores, some studies report averaging the original scores, doubling the third score, or combining the third score with the higher, not just the closer, of the two original scores (Johnson, Penny, & Johnson, 2000; Hieronymus et al., 1987; LeMahieu et al., 1995; Livingston, 1998).

In two additional variations of the tertium quid model, the adjudicator does not complete a blind review, but instead examines the original scores in making a final determination of the operational score. In one procedure, the third rater selects one of the two original scores to be retained and that score is doubled (Cherry & Meyer, 1993. In the other variation, the third rater reviews the response and moves one of the previously awarded scores up or down (Myers, 1980).

The level of expertise of the third rater in the tertium quid model of score resolution also varies. In some applications of tertium quid, the expertise of the third rater is comparable to that of the original raters (Hogan & Mishler, 1980; Livingston, 1998). In other instances, an expert rater provides the third reading and then the expert's score is matched with the closest original rating (Diederich, 1974; Hieronymus et al., 1987; LeMahieu et al., 1995; Wolcott, 1998).

Underlying the variations in tertium quid is that the adjudicator's score can determine which of the original ratings will be retained. Although the judgment of the third rater plays a substantial role in awarding the final score, the influence of the adjudicator's rating on the operational score is moderated by the judgments of the original raters.

Expert Judgment

A requisite condition in the expert judgment model of score resolution is that the adjudicator is someone with substantially more expertise in the scoring of performance assessments. What differentiates this model from tertium quid is that the expert's score replaces both original ratings and subsequently becomes the reported score (Johnson, Penny, & Johnson, 2000; Lane & Stone, 2006; Patsula, Clauser, Clyman, & Fan, 1998; Penny, 2003). In other words, the expert's score does not moderate either or both of the original scores; it replaces them. The elimination of both the original scores in the expert model implies that the judgment of the expert provides a more accurate estimate of the examinee's proficiency than do the combined judgments of the original raters. In some scoring facilities, the expert functions as a team leader for a group of raters. If the score of the team leader determines which of the original scores is to be used to form the operational score, then the reported score becomes a function of the team where it was scored.

Another form of the expert judgment model has been described in the scoring guides of the National Board for Professional Teaching Standards (NBPTS) (2001). The NBPTS's certification process gauges whether a teacher meets professional standards using school-site portfolio entries and assessment center exercises. Portfolio entries and exercises that receive discrepant ratings are scored a third time by the trainer of the raters (NBPTS, 2001, p. 12). The operational score is formed by doubling the trainer's score, adding the original ratings, and then dividing by 4. The weighting of the score of the trainer (i.e., expert) indicates the trainer's score is of greater value than the original ratings; however, retention of both original ratings moderates the trainer's score.

Discussion by Original Raters

Discussion is described in the literature as a method for (1) scoring portfolios (Moss, Schutz, & Collins, 1997) and (2) resolving discrepant ratings when raters score independently (e.g., Baker & Wigfield, 1999; Clauser, Clyman, & Swanson, 1999; Cronbach, Linn, Brennan, & Haertel, 1997; Johnson, Willeke, Bergman, & Steiner, 1996; Lenel, 1990c; Welch & Martinovich-Barhite, 1997). When used as the primary scoring method, discussion requires raters to form initial assertions about the performance level reflected in the portfolio content, mutually review the evidence, provide additional evidence for one another, challenge assertions by searching for counter examples, review multiple sources of information, and reach a final consensus on a performance level (Moss et al., 1997).

When used as a score resolution method, discussion often requires that the two original raters rescore the examinee response that received discrepant ratings. The raters mutually review the language in the scoring guide, compare the response to benchmark performances, review the features of the performance that support the initial ratings, consider any evidence that challenges the original judgments, and seek consensus on a final score (Johnson, Penny, Gordon, Shumate, & Fisher, 2005).

Discussion appears useful in small research studies and program evaluations. For large-scale testing, however, the practice might prove unwieldy due to the time required for the discussion, the logistics of scheduling a common time for raters to meet, and the space required for raters to meet without disturbing others.

EFFICACY OF RESOLUTION METHODS

Prior studies of resolution have indicated that interpretations of examinees' performance are likely to vary according to the resolution method. For example, correlational analyses indicated that decisions based on examinee rank order, such as entry into a program using relative performance, are likely to vary somewhat (Johnson, Penny, Fisher, et al., 2003; Johnson, Penny, & Gordon, 2001). In addition, the choice of the discrepancy resolution method might affect the magnitude of the resultant score that is reported to the public (Johnson et al., 2001). Interpretations of examinees' proficiency levels in terms of absolute performance, such as pass/fail decisions, also appear to vary when different score resolution, methods are applied (Johnson, Penny, Fisher, et al., 2003; Johnson, Penny, & Gordon, 2000; Johnson et al., 2001).

Given that interpretations about proficiency vary across resolution methods, reliability and validity investigations were needed to provide guidance about which method(s) might produce more appropriate decisions about examinees. Findings include that interrater reliability appears slightly higher for the parity method (Johnson, Penny, Fisher, et al., 2003; Johnson, Penny, & Gordon, 2000; Johnson et al., 2001) and low validity coefficients were associated most frequently with the tertium quid method (Johnson, Penny, Fisher, et al., 2003).

Two studies (Johnson, Penny, & Gordon, 2000; Johnson et al., 2001) show that experts do not completely agree in their assessments of student performances and that the inclusion of expert judgment into the scoring process introduced error variance into scores. However, the decision of the adjudicator (i.e., the expert) was critical in determining the final score when the tertium quid method was applied.

When raters disagree systematically (e.g., leniency or severity), the impact of adjudication on passing rates was substantial in one study

(Johnson, Penny, Fisher, et al., 2003). The impact of the adjudicator's decision was the most substantial when a rater on a team was severe or lenient. If discrepancies between raters were random (i.e., the raters' means were essentially equal), then resolution had little overall impact on the passing rate. The influence of the adjudicators' score in lowering or raising the pass–fail rates demonstrates the need to examine the appropriateness of decisions based on resolution methods dependent on adjudicators' decision.

In a study of scores resolved through discussion, the operational scores formed by applying the rater mean method and the discussion method correlated similarly with the expert-criterion scores (Johnson et al., 2005). However, in no instance did averaging the original scores produce higher correlations with the expert-criterion scores than the discussion scores. In addition, the descriptive analyses revealed smaller mean differences between discussion scores and the expert-criterion scores than between the averaged scores and the expert-criterion scores; these differences, however, were generally not statistically significant.

At this point we would suggest avoiding the expert and tertium quid methods unless the third rater is an expert whose scores correlate highly with the validation scores in qualifying and seed papers. Given equally qualified raters, the parity method appears appropriate for use in low-stakes program evaluations or research studies. For high-stakes assessments, it is unlikely that combining all three scores will be acceptable to policymakers. Imagine trying to justify an examinee's final score being based on scores of 2, 4, and 5 (Gordon, 2000). Including the rating of 2 will raise questions. In the case of high-stakes assessment, it appears reasonable to employ an expert third rater who has superior agreement levels with the validity committee scores.

Your determination of the manner of resolution will affect your staffing requirements. The discussion method will require more of the raters' time, necessitating hiring additional raters. Use of the expert method of resolution will require developing expert staff members who can adjudicate. Attracting and retaining such raters will likely require additional financial resources.

Monitoring operational scoring can reduce error in raters' judgments. Examining the quality of scores from a performance assessment extends into issues of task difficulty and a task's relationship with other test items, estimates of score reliability, and collection of evidence about the accuracy of decisions based on these scores. These topics are addressed in Chapters 9 and 10.

FURTHER READINGS

Weigle, S. (2002). *Assessing writing.* New York: Cambridge University Press.

Reviews methods of examining rater consistency in the context of a writing assessment.

Wolcott, W., with Legg, S. (1998). *An overview of writing assessment: Theory, research, and practice.* Urbana, IL: National Council of Teachers of English.

Presents brief discussion of the monitoring of raters' scoring.

Chapter Questions

1. According to Table 8.4, if two raters achieve 90% agreement (i.e., exact and adjacent) for a 6-point rubric, the actual correlation between the raters could be at what level?

2. For the Style domain in Figure 8.3, how many ratings of 2 did the rater assign?

   a. How many ratings of 2 were assigned by the validity committee?

   b. For the score level of 2 in the Style domain, did the rater typically assign higher scores or lower scores than the validity committee?

3. In Figure 8.4, which rater appeared more lenient than did the validity committee?

   a. How might this leniency influence the validity of the reported scores?

4. Using a 6-point rubric, list the ratings that are in adjacent agreement.

CHECKLIST 8.1

Completed	To-Do List for Scoring and Monitoring
	Facility and Logistics
✓	Create a scoring site that supports raters in the conduct of their duties. Attend to noise level, lighting, comfortable furniture, an area for breaks, and so forth. pp. 225–226
	Establish security procedures to ensure (1) confidentiality of examinee information and (2) protection of examination materials for high stakes tests. p. 226
	Explain expectations and procedures in the initial interview with rater trainees and implement during training. p. 226
	Monitoring the Accuracy of Ratings
	Administer recalibration sets on a frequent basis. p. 227
	Conduct reviews (i.e., read-behinds or read-aheads) of a sample of the responses each rater has scored. pp. 227–228
	Review each rater's statistics (e.g., mean, standard deviation, score frequencies) as scoring progresses. pp. 228–230
	Review each rater's agreement (e.g., percent agreement, correlation) with other raters. pp. 230–235
	Conduct validity checks by mixing responses that were prescored by the rangefinding committee in with "live" responses. pp. 235–236
	Develop reports to summarize rater data. pp. 236–241
	Establish methods for resolving scores when raters assign discrepant ratings. pp. 241–246

Forming Scores
and Item-Level Analyses

INTRODUCTION

In Chapter 7, we described training procedures that are implemented to reduce rater error in scoring. Included in Chapter 8 were methods for gauging rater consistency and accuracy. In this chapter, we describe methods for forming operational scores, examining task difficulty, estimating score reliability, and investigating validity. We revisit the Oral Clinical Examination (OCE; see Table 1.1) to illustrate these procedures, so we open with a brief review of the examination.

THE ORAL CLINICAL EXAMINATION

The OCE is used by the American Board of Pediatric Dentistry (ABPD) as part of the assessment given to candidates seeking diplomate designation (i.e., Board-certified pediatric dentist; Penny, 2006). The examination is a structured compendium of eight carefully selected cases presented in two parts. Two examiners use a 4-point analytic rubric composed of three domains to assess the responses of candidates to each case. The domains assessed are (1) Data Gathering/Diagnosis, (2) Management/Treatment Planning, and (3) Treatment Variations/Complications. The first two scores (i.e., 1 and 2) of the 4-point rubric indicate the two levels of inadequate response, whereas the upper two scores (i.e., 3 and 4) indicate the two levels of an adequate response. Anchors defining these scores use previously scored candidate responses as exemplars.[1] The anchors are used in extensive training of the examiners.

Examiners are permitted to augment their ratings by the addition of a plus or minus to indicate when a candidate's response appears above or below the anchor for a given rating. The examiners do not use augmentation when the candidate's response was equivalent to the anchor. The operational definition of the plus or minus is the addition or subtraction of one-third of a point to the initial integer rating. To this end, a "3–" (3 − .333 = 2.667) becomes the lowest passing rating that can be assigned to a candidate, whereas a "2+" (2 + .333 = 2.333) becomes the highest failing rating that an examiner can assign.

Although 2.5 is considered the effective passing score during rater training, an ABPD committee of expert examiners reviews the videotapes of candidate performances to determine whether the examiners were lenient or severe in their evaluations of the candidates. In the event that the review committee determines that the examiners were lenient or severe, the committee can recommend to the Board that it raise or lower the passing standard by some fraction of the standard error of the measure (SEM) associated with the final reported scores. Specifically, this SEM is computed from the reliability of the final reported scores using the following formula:

$$SEM = S_x \sqrt{1 - r_x}$$

where S_x and r_x are the standard deviation and reliability (e.g., internal consistency) of the reported scores, respectively. For example, if the standard deviation and reliability were 0.3 and 0.94, respectively, the SEM would be 0.3*sqrt(1 − .94), or approximately 0.07. Thus the committee might recommend to the Board that they raise or lower the passing standard by some unit of 0.07.

We present the OCE slightly differently than as it is seen by candidates. The OCE has two parts, and we have described one of those parts; the second part is identical in form, although the context of the tasks is different. The reported score is the average of the results from those two parts. For providing an example in this chapter, we elected to maintain the simplicity of studying a single part as though it were the entire exam. The reason the ABPD uses the second part is to enhance the accuracy of the reported scores and to provide greater content and context coverage.

FORMING OPERATIONAL SCORES

A first step in any analysis is the formation of operational scores. In forming these scores, issues to consider include augmentation and resolution; treatment of zero; weighting; composite scores and diagnostic feedback; multiple-hurdle and compensatory models; and norm- and criterion-referenced score interpretation.

Augmentation and Resolution

The procedures associated with augmentation and score resolution were described in Chapters 7 and 8, respectively. We briefly address the effect of each procedure in forming the operational score. In the use of augmentation, the result of a rater choosing to augment a rating is the increase or decrease of the rating by 0.33, or about one-third of a point, where the value of one-third results in the distance between all rating points being numerically equal. Raters do not actually calculate the values and record them. Rather, a rater indicates a plus or minus augmentation. The ratings and augmentation designation are entered in a database, and then the final rating is calculated in a computer-based scoring routine. We do not recommend hand calculation by raters because of the opportunity to make a calculation error that might adversely affect an examinee.

In terms of score resolution, we again recommend that the formation of the final score be completed after data are entered into database. The decision rule for resolving the discrepant scores should be programmed into the scoring routine and the appropriate ratings combined to calculate a final score. For example, if you are using the expert version of tertium quid (see Table 8.5), then in formulating the final score the scoring program will combine the expert rater's score with the closest score of the original raters and ignore the discrepant rating.

Treatment of Zero

On occasion, a presentation is not scorable. For example, a student might refuse to write an essay and instead turn in a blank page or draw a picture. The student might write the essay in an unexpected language (e.g., using Spanish when the assessment requires English). Alternatively, an examinee in a credentialing examination might disregard the topic as presented, choosing instead to write on another topic. In addition, an examinee might cheat by copying the essay of another examinee, either completely or in part.

Such performances (e.g., writing samples, lab reports) do not fit the rubric, even at the lower end of the scale, and generally receive special marks (see Table 6.2) to indicate the nonscorable nature of the work. How such special cases are handled in the computation of operational scores depends on the policy of the assessment agency.

The use of zero to indicate nonscorable samples is common. One way to view the nonscorable response derives from the scoring of multiple-choice items. Generally, for each multiple-choice item an examinee selects one of the options (e.g., A, B, C, or D) and she receives credit if the correct option is selected. At times, however, the examinee does not select any of the options, and at times the examinee might mark two or more options. The result in either case is the examinee receives a 0 for the item because she did not demonstrate her knowledge. Similarly, in the case of a constructed-response item with a nonscorable response, if an examinee fails to demonstrate his proficiency for the item, then a score of 0 is awarded. In the case of an examination that combines multiple-choice items, constructed response, and extended response, the award of a 0 for a performance task is similar to marking incorrect those multiple-choice items that the examinee does not answer.

An alternative view is that in assigning a zero to a nonscorable task, the length of the scoring rubric is extended by a single point in a manner that is often somewhat different from the other rubric points that provide a continuum of developmental stages. For example, the College Board uses a 6-point rubric to evaluate the writing samples that are a part of the SAT, and the anchors used to illustrate the six possible scores represent stages of mastery in written expression. However, the College Board also uses a score of 0 to indicate that an essay was not written on the assigned topic, regardless of the quality of written expression demonstrated in the off-topic sample (Kobrin & Kimmel, 2006). Doing such precludes students from preparing essays beforehand, an activity that would challenge the standardization and subsequent validity of the assessment. In this example, when a 0 is assigned to an essay, it is also used in the computation of the reported score.

Implicit and Explicit Weighting

Weighting of items on a checklist, domains within a task, or composites within an overall test is common. Weighting occurs implicitly when combining tasks that have different scale lengths. In other instances, the items on a checklist might be weighted to reflect the importance of the skills reflected in the items. Both forms of rating are discussed below.

Scales of Different Length (Implicit Weighting)

When scores from multiple assessments are combined to form a single reported score, the scales used in those assessments influence the reported score. For example, consider combining a score that can range from 0 to 100 with a score that can range from 0 to 6. Using addition (e.g., unit-weighted composite), the reported score, which has a possible total score of 106, will exhibit primarily the characteristics of the score with the larger range. In such an instance, the score with the smaller range becomes "the drop in the bucket," that is, the information from the score with the smaller range can be lost in the overall reported score.

To preclude the loss of information that can occur when a composite score is created, the original scores can be transformed to a common metric (e.g., normal deviates or *z*-scores). Following such a transformation, the contribution of information to the reported score by the original scores is equal for all original scores. Case (2005) describes the use of *z*-scores to combine scores from essays used in state law licensure examinations with the scores from the Multistate Bar Examination, a national examination that uses multiple-choice items.

Explicit Weighting

Occasionally a reported score is computed from multiple scores, of which some are considered more important than others. Gulliksen (1987) discusses how the weights used in a composite can be obtained. In some instances, such as in licensure, these weights are the result of expert discussion and statistical consensus building. In other cases, these weights are derived empirically from the statistical characteristics (e.g., reliability, standard error, factor analysis) of an examination.

The Clinical Skills Examination, one of three components in the examination of the National Board of Examiners in Optometry, provides an example of the use of weights (Gross, 1993). In the Clinical Skills Examination, examinees perform 18 clinical skills using actual patients, each skill having 9 to 42 items that are scored. These skills are completed in five clinical examination stations with two to six clinical skills performed at each station and 41 to 73 items per station for a total of 279 items. Each skill is divided into component items and each item on a checklist is scored as Yes if the procedure is completed satisfactorily and No if performed incorrectly. Examiners record their judgment (i.e., yes or no) on a scannable behavioral checklist.

Criticality weights have been determined for each item of the Clinical Skills Examination. A nine-person examination committee determined by consensus the criticality of each item. Based on the committee recommendations, each of the items is weighted on a scale of 1–10. After weighting, the total number of points is 798, with a score of 650 required for passing the examination.

The Georgia High School Writing Test provides an example from education. In determining a student's writing score, Georgia weights the domain of Ideas 40% and the domains of Organization, Style, and Conventions 20% (Georgia Department of Education, 2007). Scores are calculated as shown in Table 9.1.

The use of a composite to produce a reported score potentially influences the reliability (e.g., KR-20, test–retest) of the reported score. Gulliksen (1987, Ch. 20) discussed in detail the effect that the use of weighting in the computation of reported scores can have on the reliability of reported scores. However, a complete discussion of the effect that weighting has on the reported scores is beyond the scope of this text. To summarize briefly, the reliability of a composite (i.e., reported score) is a complex function of (1) the number of measures used in the composite, (2) the weighting of those measures, and (3) the intracorrelations among those measures. Gulliksen (1987) summarizes those effects as follows:

> Whenever a single total score is to be derived from a number of separate scores, the weighting problem cannot be avoided. However, if *many* different scores with reasonably *high* correlations are being combined, the result-

TABLE 9.1. Writing Domains and Weightings Used in the Calculation of Operational Scores in the Georgia Writing Assessment

Domain	Weight	Domain weight
Ideas	2 × each rater's raw score	40%
Organization	1 × each rater's raw score	20%
Style	1 × each rater's raw score	20%
Conventions	1 × each rater's raw score	20%

ing composite will be fairly similar for a large variety of weights. If, however, relatively *few* items are to be combined, there is a *low* correlation among these items, the standard deviation[2] of the weights being considered is fairly *large*, and the correlation between the two sets of weights is *low*, the two resulting composites will be low. (p. 355)

Composite Scores and Diagnostic Feedback

The use of a single reported score is an efficient manner for determining if a performance on an examination with several parts is sufficient to constitute a passing score. However, these single scores do not often provide sufficient information regarding deficiencies and strengths of those examinees who fail and who need additional preparation before retesting.

The *Standards* (AERA, APA, & NCME, 1999) require that reliable diagnostic feedback be available to those who take examinations. That feedback can often take the form of the original scores that were used in the computation of the diagnostic score, but often that feedback can be presented in a more nuclear manner if the original scores themselves are composites. Such "layers" of scores are often useful to guide those who seek additional preparation before retesting in that the additional preparation can be focused directly on the areas where deficiencies were observed.

For example, the ABPD offers diagnostic feedback to those candidates who fail the OCE. Recall that a pair of ABPD examiners provides ratings on a scale of 1 to 4 on each of the following three domains: (1) Data Gathering/Diagnosis, (2) Management/Treatment Planning, and (3) Treatment Variations/Complications.

The average rating awarded by the examiners on each domain is presented to candidates who fail in order to provide those candidates with insight into the domains where additional preparation is needed. In addition, the ABPD provides this domain-specific diagnostic information for particular types of cases (e.g., trauma, disease) to assist failing candidates in focusing their preparation further.

---

[2]The phrase "standard deviation of the weights" can lead to some confusion. Remember that if the weights are not equal to one another, then there is a distribution of those weights, and that distribution has a standard deviation. To this end, what Gulliksen is saying is that if the weights vary greatly, then the correlation of composites created by using two such sets of weights will not be as high as it would be if the dispersion (standard deviation) of the weights were smaller.

Multiple-Hurdle Model

Due to the resources required in assessing with performance tasks, some credentialing bodies require examinees to pass initial examinations that use multiple-choice formats and then follow with performance tasks. For example, candidates may not take the OCE without having first passed the Qualifying Examination. The Qualifying Examination is a pair of 200-item examinations usually given in a single day in the morning and afternoon. However, the ABPD does permit candidates to "bank" a pass on one part (i.e., morning or afternoon) of the exam and then repeat the other part that was failed at a later administration. If the candidate fails the other part on the second attempt, that candidate must then begin the entire Qualifying Examination over.

Because the Qualifying Examination and the OCE are administered and evaluated independently, and because passing the Qualifying Examination is a requirement to be eligible for the OCE, we refer to this form of examination usage as "multiple hurdle." Just as a hurdler in a race must clear the hurdles consecutively, the candidates must pass the two examinations one after the other.

Compensatory Model

An example of a compensatory model is the SAT writing assessment. The writing section of the SAT consists of two assessments. The first part uses multiple-choice items; the second, a student-written essay (Kobrin & Kimmel, 2006). The scores for the multiple-choice writing section range from 20 to 80 points. Two readers use a 6-point rubric to score the essay. The scores from the two readers are added to create an essay score on the range from 2 to 12 points. Essays that are off topic or illegible receive a score of 0.

The essay score is combined with the score from the multiple-choice section to create a scaled score on the range 200 to 800 points. The relative magnitudes of the multiple-choice scaled score and the essay score produces a weighting of approximately 75% for the multiple-choice and 25% for the essay (Kobrin & Kimmel, 2006).

Because a strong performance on one part of the writing assessment can compensate for poor performance on the essay, the scoring model represented is compensatory. However, because of the unequal weighting of the two sections in the creation of the final score, the ability of a strong performance on the essay to compensate for a weak performance on the multiple-choice section is reduced.

Norm-Referenced versus Criterion-Referenced Score Interpretation

If the examination score of an individual is evaluated in the context of the scores of others on the exam, then the scoring is considered norm referenced. Such scoring is useful in situations where the ranking of individuals is considered more important than the determination of an individual's standing on a trait. An example is provided by the SAT writing section, which many universities use as one source of information to rank applicants for admission to undergraduate programs.

The appropriate norm group used with norm-referenced examinations depends on the individual taking the examination as well as the intended use of the examination. For example, The TerraNova, The Second Edition (CTB McGraw-Hill, 2002), a norm-referenced examination with selected- and constructed-response items, is used to assess student achievement at particular grade levels. The use of this examination to assess the learning of a fifth-grade student would include normative information based on the results of other similar students.

If an individual's examination score is evaluated using an external standard, such as a cut score, then the scoring is considered criterion referenced. Criterion-referenced scores are generally intended to measure how well an individual has learned a specific body of knowledge and skills. Criterion-referenced tests produce scores that describe an individual's performance compared with specified standards, which are usually defined in a process that is external to the examination's development. In education, an example is the aforementioned National Assessment of Educational Progress, which describes student performance on subject-area examinations, such as reading, writing, science, and mathematics (e.g., Grigg et al., 2003). Student scores on an examination are compared to cut scores and the student's achievement level identified as being at a basic, proficient, or advanced level.

The examinations used for certification and licensure are generally, if not completely, criterion referenced as a matter of public protection. Physicians must demonstrate sufficient learning before they are licensed to practice. If no candidates score sufficiently well to meet the external criterion (i.e., pass score) established to define acceptable knowledge for competent practice, then none of those candidates receives certification or licensure. Hence the licensing or certification body achieves its mission to protect the public. Examples of criterion-referenced examinations are numerous and include the United States Medical Licensing Examination (USMLE) used to license physicians, National Council Licensure Examination (NCLEX) used to license nurses, and the National Home Inspector Examination (NHIE) used to license home inspectors.[3]

DEFINING A PASSING STANDARD
FOR USE WITH PERFORMANCE ASSESSMENT

We have spent a lot of time describing how to go about creating, administering, scoring, and interpreting a performance assessment, and the question has surely arisen in your thinking as to how we decide what makes a passing score. For many people working in assessment, how we go about setting a passing standard is in many ways the most important step in developing the assessment. This is by no means an effort to minimize the other steps taken in building a performance assessment. Frankly, all the steps are equally important, and a shortcut taken at one point can jeopardize the rest of the work. The problem is that often the passing score of an examination will come under legal scrutiny first, especially if a well-connected examinee takes the examination and fails by a small margin.

We plan to cover the main points of passing standard studies for performance assessment to provide a framework from which you may continue. However, bear in mind that the methodology of passing standard studies represents a broad field of study all by itself, and an in-depth review of those procedures is beyond the scope of this book. To accommodate the need for further study of the methodology of passing standard studies,[4] we suggest additional sources in Further Readings at the end of this chapter.

In the following sections, we first describe a classical method for setting a passing standard when using an examination that contains all multiple-choice items. We do so because examinations often use both multiple-choice items and performance tasks. Thus we start with multiple choice, move to performance assessment, and conclude with estab-

---

[3]Licensure of home inspectors is done by individual states, and some of those states use NHIE pass–fail status as a part of the licensure process. The Examining Board of Professional Home Inspectors, which owns the NHIE, does not certify or license home inspectors.

[4]Often authors use "performance standard" instead of "passing standard." By performance standard, authors refer to the level of performance required to pass an exam or to achieve a certain level of designation (e.g., basic, proficient, advanced). We intentionally chose not to use "performance standard" because of the potential confusion that name would probably create in the context of this similarly named book.

lishing a passing standard based on multiple-choice and performance tasks.

Setting a Passing Standard for a Multiple-Choice Examination

When you were in school you took many tests, and the teacher of the class generally established the passing score for the examination. In American classrooms, 70% correct is a very common passing score. (In Australia, that figure is often 60% correct.) For the examinations used in certification and licensure, the *Standards* require that the passing score be established using criterion-referenced methodology (AERA, APA, & NCME, 1999). For examinations designed to determine whether an examinee has achieved minimum competence, that criterion is often the collected opinion of many experts in the given field. However, it is generally not sufficient simply to ask the experts what the passing percentage should be and then use the average. Instead, we use a process designed to reduce, although not eradicate, the subjectivity of their opinions. The following paragraphs present a brief description of this process.

Angoff (1971, p. 515) wrote a footnote[5] in which he described a process by which experts could estimate the probability that a minimally qualified examinee would answer a question correctly. The average of those probabilities for all the items on the examination across all the experts would then represent that panel of experts' estimate of what the passing score should be. You should note at this point that there is no one "Angoff procedure"; rather, there are many variations on Angoff's theme, and when someone tells you they used the Angoff procedure to determine a passing standard, you should ask a few follow-up questions for clarification.

What we present now is one manner in which a modified Angoff procedure is used to determine a passing standard for a certification examination, say the Certified Naysayer Examination[6] (CNE). The CNE is a 150-item examination based on a role delineation that was completed 2 years ago. The Certification Board of Professional Naysayers (CBPN) has assembled a panel of 12 highly qualified experts to participate in the standard-setting study.

---

[5]It is unlikely that any footnote in this text will be cited in the subsequent literature as often as Angoff's footnote has been cited.

[6]This examination and the associated certifying body are fictitious.

The panel gathers in a meeting room in a hotel in downtown Chicago to begin its deliberations at 8:00 A.M. The first activity is a round of personal introductions. Some of the panelists are old friends whereas others are new. Following the introductions the meeting facilitator, usually a psychometrician with experience in conducting standard-setting studies, presents the group with a brief outline of the day's activities. After questions and answers, the facilitator passes out nondisclosure agreements (NDAs) to the panelists. (Most certification and licensure examinations are considered secure, and the certifying bodies usually protect themselves from exam compromise by the use of NDAs at meetings where exam content is made available.)

After the NDAs are discussed, signed, and collected, the panelists each receive a copy of the exam. Their instructions are to take the exam without discussion. When they are finished with the exam, they receive the answer key so they can grade their work. Although the panelists are not required to share their grades, many do so as they discuss their experience with the exam. (Generally, no record of panelist scores is made after the meeting, and the tests and answers are usually destroyed.)

The purpose of having the panelists take the exam is to give them some insight into what the examinees experience when they take the examination for certification. Although the panelists are usually not held to the same degree of security as the examinees, it is generally beneficial for the seasoned professionals to better understand the process of taking an examination. Moreover, no one panelist is usually able to answer all the questions correctly because the content of the question represented an area of practice with which the panelist is not familiar. There are other reasons for seasoned professionals to miss questions developed for minimally competent examinees, but that discussion is not germane to this review of a modified Angoff study.

When the panelists have finished reviewing the exam, they are led in a discussion of the characteristics of the minimally qualified examinee. How much education and training is expected? Is on-the-job training and experience expected? If so, how much? What other expectations does the certifying body have of the examinees? Generally, no time limit is placed on this discussion because it is critical to the validity of the entire study that the panelists have a clear understanding of the preparation of the minimally qualified examinees.

When the meeting facilitator is confident that the panelists share a deep understanding of the qualifications of the minimally qualified examinee, the data-gathering portion of the meeting begins. The facilitator asks each panelist to estimate the number of minimally qualified examinees (out of 100) who would answer each item correctly. Often the facilitator asks the panelists to use only multiples of 5 or 10 with these estimates; these estimates are already sufficiently subjective, and it is unlikely that estimates with more digits (e.g., 63.975) offer additional precision or consistency. In addition, the facilitator points out that there is a minimum number, usually about 25 for four-option multiple-choice items, whereas the maximum number could be 100, but is more likely 90.

Before the facilitator releases the panelists to review the items, additional consensus-building activities occur. The facilitator might ask the panelists to rate the first five or so items, and then the panelists discuss their reasons for their ratings. Panelists who exhibit large differences are asked to discuss the sources of these differences. If the source is a misunderstanding of the qualifications of examinees at the minimally competent level, additional discussion will be necessary to bridge the gap between the panelists. The facilitator might also select additional items that appear problematic for some reason (e.g., questionable wording, regional differences in practice) for additional review and discussion by the panel. However, at some point the panelists are released to review the examination items with or without additional discussion. At this point the panelists are reminded that they do not need to agree on every rating, and that the amount of additional discussion is their decision. Often panel members will discuss their ratings for every exam item. Occasionally they work in silence until they are finished.

The ratings are collected from the panelists at the end of the study. Occasionally examinees' scores from a previous administration of the examination are available and these data enable the panelists to see the consequence (pass–fail rate) of their ratings. Based on the consequence data, some panelists choose to revisit some of their ratings in light of the likely pass—fail rate. However, at some point the panelists are finished. The ratings are then examined statistically, and some ratings (or panelists) might be removed from the study if certain statistical criteria for quality are not met (e.g., set responding, extreme outliers). In the end, the average rating from a panelist is the percent correct passing score from that panelist. The average of the panelists' averages is the suggested percent passing score for the examination, and the certifying body then meets to review the results of the study and to make the final decision regarding the passing score. (The final decision might be to use the average from the study, or to adjust the passing score by some amount statistically determined, usually a multiple of the *SEM*. The *SEM* is usually computed from the panelists averages, but the value can be the *SEM* of the examination.)

Setting the Passing Standard
When Scoring Rubric Anchors Indicate Development

Many performance assessments use a scoring rubric for which the anchors of the rubric points describe levels of development. For example, the performance component of the National Interpreters Certification (NIC) uses a scoring rubric with five possible scores where each score represents an incremental step toward mastery. Moreover, the NIC scoring rubric is applied analytically to several criteria, and the anchor descriptions change to match the dimension being assessed.

The development of a passing standard for an assessment using this type of scoring rubric can be conceptualized as an extension of the Angoff-type procedure. For this study the panelists identify the score that they would expect the minimally competent examinee to receive for each dimension assessed; this procedure is similar to the extended Angoff procedure described by Hambleton and Plake (1995). For each panelist, these estimated expected scores are then used to compute the expected reported score for the minimally competent examinee. The expected reported score from each panelist is then averaged to determine the expected reported score from the panel for the minimally competent examinee.

If consequence data are available, panelists might choose to revisit some of their expected scores. In addition, panelists might discuss their decisions to build consensus around their expectations of minimal competence. In the end, the results from the passing standard study are reported to the certifying body, which then makes a formal decision regarding the passing score.

Note that this procedure could be made more like an Angoff-style study by asking the panelists to estimate the percent of minimally competent examinees who would receive each of the possible ratings (e.g., 10% receive a 1, 30% receive a 2, 40% receive a 3, 10% receive a 4, 10% receive a 5) for each dimension. The sum of the percents (expressed as a fraction) times the rating (e.g., $.1 \times 1 + .3 \times 2 + .4 \times 3 + .1 \times 4 + .1 \times 5$) gives the expected score, 2.8 in this example, for the given dimension. These expected scores can then be used to create the expected reported score for the minimally competent examinee.

Setting the Passing Standard
When Scoring Rubric Anchors Indicate Quality

The scoring rubric for some performance assessments have the passing point embedded. The OCE and the ethical decision-making portion of the NIC both use scoring rubrics with embedded passing scores. In both instances, the scoring rubric contains four score points. The first and second points are given to examinees found to have inadequate skills. The third and fourth points are awarded to examinees found to have adequate skills. In both examples, the midpoint of the rating scale, 2.5, is the passing score.

In Table 9.2, the scoring categories with overarching descriptions are given for the OCE. Organizations using such rubrics generally go to great lengths to create exemplars for each level. In particular, these organizations want the distinction between the 2 and the 3 to be as clear as possible. These exemplars are then used in the training materials for raters.

Setting the Passing Standard Using Examinee Work Samples

Examinee work samples are used in the analytic judgment method developed by Plake and Hambleton (1999/2000, 2001). In this form of standard setting, panelists review a set of examinee responses for each performance task. The set of responses cover the full range of examinee performances; however, panelists are not aware of the scores on the examinees' responses. Panelists use a classification scale to rate the

TABLE 9.2. Scoring Rubric for the Oral Clinical Examination

Rating	Description
4	Demonstrates full and in-depth understanding of the application of the skill within the context of the case.
3	Demonstrates use of the skill appropriately within the context of the case.
2	Demonstrates less than full understanding of the application of the skill to the case.
1	Demonstrates wrong or inappropriate understanding of the application of the skill to the case.

Note. Reproduced with permission from the American Board of Pediatric Dentistry (2007).

responses in terms of passing standards. An example of a classification scale used in education is below basic, basic, proficient, and advanced. Within each category, the performance could then be rated low, middle, or high.[7] For example, an examinee could be rated low basic, middle basic, or high basic. In a credentialing examination the classification levels can be low competent and high incompetent (O'Neill, Buckendahl, Plake, & Taylor, 2007).

After panelists rate the examinees' responses they discuss responses for which there is a wide range of ratings. Subsequently, panelists independently assign ratings for all the examinees' responses. This process is completed for each performance task. The passing standard is based on the scores on the examinees' responses and the panelists' ratings. One method for arriving at a passing standard involves calculating the average score for the responses associated with borderline scores. For example, using a basic standard, all of the responses rated as high below basic and low basic are used to calculate the average score and this average becomes the passing standard for the basic performance level. Averages are similarly calculated for other performance levels to establish the standard for each level. Then a total assessment passing standard can be attained by summing across the standard established for each task.

Establishing the Passing Standard for Examinations with Multiple-Choice and Performance Tasks

Establishing a passing standard using multiple-choice items and performance tasks can be achieved by summing across the passing standard established for each item and task. The total score, then, would be the passing standard representing a compensatory model. Some agencies, however, require examinees' to pass each component of an examination, which constitutes a multiple-hurdle model. For example, high school exit examinations often require students to pass a reading test, mathematics test, and writing test. In this instance, a passing standard is established for each examination. O'Neill and colleagues (2007) describe a hybrid (e.g., compensatory) model that establishes a passing score for the overall examination, but for the various examination components allows examinees to earn minimum values that are slightly lower than the overall passing score.

---

[7]This example is a form of rating augmentation.

ITEM-LEVEL ANALYSES

Item-level analyses provide statistical information about the functioning of an item or task. Four statistics relevant to the review of performance tasks are (1) task mean and standard deviation, (2) item difficulty, and (3) item discrimination.

Task Mean and Standard Deviation

The task mean is simply the sum of all the examinees' ratings on the task divided by the number of examinees. A high mean can indicate an easy item and a low mean might indicate a difficult item.

Table 9.3 presents simulated data for 30 candidates from an administration of the OCE. Two examiners score each candidate. Each candidate is presented with four cases, and each case response is judged on three domains. Hence the column heading "C1a" represents Case 1, Domain A scores.

To score these data, we first compute the mean of an examiner's ratings for each case and candidate. Excel uses the word "average" to name the function that computes the mean. There is no "mean" function in Excel per se. The use of Excel is common in these applications, and a thorough description is beyond the scope of this text. However, those who use Excel should be careful when missing data are present because the manner in which Excel handles missing data in computations (e.g., providing the mean of nonmissing cells) can run counter to the intent of the analyst and the needs of the testing agency.

Recall that the examiners for the OCE use augmentation to adjust the ratings up or down by one-third. For example, Examiner 1 awarded a 3– (i.e., 2.67) to Candidate 1's response for Case 1 in Domain A. The operational use of the minus is to subtract one-third from the 3.

The mean of an examiner's case ratings awarded to a candidate is the examiner's score for the candidate. The mean of the two examiner scores is the reported score for the candidate. These data are presented in Table 9.4.

We can compute the mean of the reported scores for these 30 candidates using the "AVERAGE" function in Excel. Applying this function to these data produces a mean score of 3.05. Similarly, the standard deviation of the reported scores for these five candidates can be computed in Excel using the "STDEVP"[8] function. The value resulting from

---

[8]Excel uses STDEV to compute a sample standard deviation and STDEVP to estimate the population standard deviation.

TABLE 9.3. Simulated Data from Scores on the Oral Clinical Examination

Examiner	Candidate	C1a	C1b	C1c	C2a	C2b	C2c	C3a	C3b	C3c	C4a	C4b	C4c
1	1	2.67	3.00	3.00	3.33	2.00	1.67	2.00	3.00	2.00	2.67	1.67	1.67
2	1	3.00	4.00	3.00	4.00	3.00	1.67	2.33	2.33	2.67	4.00	2.67	2.67
1	2	4.00	4.00	3.67	4.00	3.00	3.00	4.00	4.00	4.00	4.00	3.00	3.00
2	2	2.33	3.00	2.33	3.33	3.00	3.00	2.00	3.33	3.33	2.67	3.33	2.33
1	3	2.33	2.33	3.33	3.00	3.33	3.67	3.33	3.33	2.33	1.67	3.00	2.67
2	3	3.00	2.33	3.00	3.00	2.67	2.67	3.00	3.33	3.00	2.67	3.00	3.00
1	4	3.67	3.67	3.33	3.33	3.00	3.33	3.67	3.00	3.00	3.67	3.67	4.00
2	4	3.33	2.67	2.67	3.00	2.33	2.33	3.00	2.67	3.33	3.33	3.00	3.33
1	5	4.00	4.00	3.00	3.00	3.00	2.00	3.00	2.67	2.67	3.33	3.67	3.00
2	5	4.00	4.00	4.00	3.00	3.33	3.67	4.00	4.00	3.33	3.33	4.00	3.67
1	6	3.67	4.00	3.67	3.67	3.33	3.67	4.00	4.00	4.33	3.67	4.00	4.00
2	6	3.33	3.67	3.67	4.00	4.00	4.00	4.00	4.00	4.00	4.00	4.00	4.00
1	7	3.33	3.00	3.33	3.67	3.33	3.33	2.33	2.33	1.67	2.33	2.33	2.33
2	7	2.67	3.33	3.33	3.33	3.00	3.00	2.67	2.67	3.00	4.00	2.33	3.00
1	8	3.00	4.00	4.00	4.00	4.00	4.33	3.00	3.67	4.33	3.67	3.00	3.67
2	8	2.33	3.33	3.33	3.33	3.67	4.00	2.33	2.67	4.00	2.67	2.67	2.67
1	9	2.67	2.67	2.33	2.67	3.00	2.33	2.33	2.67	2.67	3.33	2.33	2.33
2	9	2.67	2.33	1.67	2.33	2.67	2.33	2.67	2.67	2.67	3.00	2.67	2.67
1	10	3.00	3.00	3.00	4.00	3.00	2.33	3.00	3.00	3.00	3.00	2.33	3.00
2	10	3.00	2.67	3.00	2.33	2.67	3.00	3.00	3.00	3.00	2.67	2.33	2.67
1	11	4.00	3.00	4.33	4.00	3.33	2.67	3.00	3.33	3.33	4.00	4.00	4.00
2	11	3.33	3.67	3.33	3.00	2.33	2.33	3.00	3.00	3.00	3.33	3.33	3.33
1	12	3.67	4.00	4.00	4.00	4.00	4.33	4.00	4.00	4.33	4.33	4.33	4.33
2	12	4.00	3.33	3.33	3.33	3.33	3.33	3.33	3.33	4.00	4.00	4.00	3.00
1	13	2.33	2.67	2.33	3.00	3.00	3.00	3.00	2.33	3.00	3.00	4.00	3.00
2	13	1.67	2.67	2.33	3.33	3.00	2.67	3.00	3.00	2.67	2.00	2.67	2.33
1	14	3.67	3.33	2.67	3.33	3.33	2.33	3.33	3.00	3.00	2.67	2.00	2.00
2	14	3.33	3.33	3.00	2.67	4.00	2.67	2.33	3.33	3.33	3.33	2.67	3.00
1	15	2.33	2.33	2.67	2.33	2.33	1.67	3.00	2.67	2.00	2.67	3.33	2.67

		C1	C2	C3	C4	C5	C6	C7	C8	C9	C10	C11	C12	C13
15	2	2.67	2.33	2.67	1.67	2.67	2.33	1.00	1.33	1.33	2.33	2.33	2.33	2.33
16	1	3.00	2.33	2.67	3.33	3.33	3.00	3.33	2.67	4.00	3.33	3.33	3.33	3.33
16	2	2.67	2.00	4.00	3.33	3.33	4.00	4.00	4.00	4.00	4.00	4.33	4.00	4.00
17	1	2.33	2.00	2.33	4.00	3.00	3.33	2.00	1.67	2.67	2.67	1.67	3.00	3.00
17	2	2.00	1.67	2.33	2.33	2.67	3.00	2.67	2.67	2.67	3.33	3.00	3.33	3.33
18	1	3.67	3.33	3.67	3.33	3.33	3.33	4.00	2.33	3.00	4.33	4.00	3.33	3.33
18	2	3.33	3.00	3.33	4.00	3.67	4.00	3.00	3.00	4.00	2.67	2.67	3.67	3.67
19	1	3.33	3.00	2.33	2.33	3.00	3.33	2.33	2.67	3.33	4.33	4.00	3.67	3.67
19	2	2.33	2.33	2.33	2.67	2.33	3.00	2.33	2.33	3.00	3.00	3.00	3.00	3.00
20	1	4.00	2.33	4.00	4.00	2.33	3.67	2.67	4.00	4.00	3.33	3.00	3.00	3.67
20	2	2.67	2.67	4.00	2.67	2.67	3.33	3.00	3.00	3.33	4.00	3.33	3.33	3.33
21	1	4.00	4.00	3.00	2.67	4.00	4.00	3.33	3.33	4.00	4.33	4.00	4.00	4.00
21	2	4.00	4.00	4.33	4.00	4.00	4.00	4.00	3.33	3.67	2.67	4.00	4.00	3.67
22	1	2.33	3.00	2.33	3.00	2.33	2.67	2.33	2.67	2.00	4.00	2.33	2.33	3.00
22	2	3.00	4.00	2.33	4.00	4.00	3.67	4.33	4.33	4.33	3.33	3.67	3.67	4.00
23	1	2.67	2.67	3.00	3.00	2.67	2.67	2.33	3.00	3.00	3.00	3.33	3.33	3.67
23	2	2.33	2.33	3.00	2.00	2.00	2.00	2.67	2.33	2.00	2.00	3.00	3.00	3.00
24	1	3.00	3.00	2.67	4.00	3.33	2.67	3.00	3.00	3.00	3.33	3.00	3.00	3.00
24	2	2.00	2.33	3.33	2.00	2.00	2.67	3.00	3.33	3.33	2.67	2.67	3.00	3.00
25	1	2.33	2.33	2.67	3.00	3.00	2.33	2.33	2.33	2.33	2.67	2.67	3.00	3.00
25	2	2.67	2.67	4.00	3.00	2.67	2.67	2.00	2.67	2.67	2.67	2.67	3.33	3.33
26	1	1.67	1.67	3.00	2.00	2.67	2.33	2.33	2.33	3.33	3.00	1.33	3.00	3.00
26	2	3.33	3.67	3.33	3.67	4.00	3.33	4.00	3.67	4.00	3.33	3.33	3.67	4.00
27	1	3.33	3.33	4.00	3.00	2.67	3.33	2.67	2.67	2.67	3.67	3.33	4.00	3.67
27	2	3.67	3.33	3.67	3.67	3.00	3.33	3.00	3.33	3.67	4.00	3.33	3.67	3.00
28	1	4.00	4.00	2.67	3.33	4.00	4.00	4.00	4.00	4.00	3.00	4.00	3.00	3.00
28	2	3.33	3.00	2.67	3.33	3.67	3.33	3.67	3.67	4.33	2.67	3.33	3.00	1.67
29	1	2.67	2.33	3.33	2.67	2.33	2.67	2.67	2.33	2.67	2.00	2.00	1.67	2.67
29	2	2.67	2.33	2.67	3.00	3.00	2.33	2.33	2.67	2.67	2.33	2.00	2.67	2.33
30	1	2.33	2.33	1.33	2.33	2.33	2.33	2.33	1.67	1.00	3.00	2.67	2.33	3.00
30	2	2.33	1.67	1.00	2.00	2.67	3.00	2.33	2.00	1.67	3.00	3.00	3.00	2.67

TABLE 9.4. Means of Examiner Scores by Case

Examiner	Candidate	Examiner scores by case				Averages of case scores				Reported score
		ECase1	ECase2	ECase3	ECase4	Case1	Case2	Case3	Case4	
1	1	2.89	2.33	2.33	2.00	3.11	2.61	2.39	2.56	2.67
2	1	3.33	2.89	2.44	3.11					
1	2	3.89	3.33	4.00	3.33	3.22	3.22	3.45	3.06	3.24
2	2	2.55	3.11	2.89	2.78					
1	3	2.66	3.33	3.00	2.45	2.72	3.06	3.06	2.67	2.88
2	3	2.78	2.78	3.11	2.89					
1	4	3.56	3.22	3.22	3.78	3.23	2.89	3.17	3.50	3.19
2	4	2.89	2.55	3.11	3.22					
1	5	3.67	2.67	2.78	3.11	3.84	3.00	3.28	3.34	3.36
2	5	4.00	3.33	3.78	3.56					
1	6	3.78	3.56	4.11	3.89	3.67	3.78	4.06	3.95	3.86
2	6	3.56	4.00	4.00	4.00					
1	7	3.22	3.44	2.11	2.33	3.28	3.28	2.45	2.72	2.93
2	7	3.33	3.11	2.78	3.11					
1	8	3.56	4.22	3.67	3.45	3.39	3.95	3.34	3.06	3.43
2	8	3.22	3.67	3.00	2.67					
1	9	2.44	2.67	2.56	2.66	2.33	2.56	2.62	2.72	2.56
2	9	2.22	2.44	2.67	2.78					
1	10	3.00	3.11	2.89	2.78	2.95	2.89	2.95	2.67	2.86
2	10	2.89	2.67	3.00	2.56					
1	11	4.11	3.33	3.22	4.00	3.78	2.94	3.11	3.67	3.37
2	11	3.44	2.55	3.00	3.33					
1	12	4.00	4.11	4.11	4.33	3.89	3.72	3.83	4.00	3.86
2	12	3.78	3.33	3.55	3.67					
1	13	2.78	3.00	2.67	2.89	2.50	3.00	2.84	2.50	2.71
2	13	2.22	3.00	3.00	2.11					
1	14	3.22	3.00	3.22	2.45	3.22	3.06	3.11	2.84	3.06
2	14	3.22	3.11	3.00	3.22					

1	15	2.44	2.11	2.56	2.78	2.39	1.67	2.39	2.67	2.28
2	15	2.33	1.22	2.22	2.56					
1	16	3.33	3.33	3.22	2.67	3.72	3.67	3.39	2.78	3.39
2	16	4.11	4.00	3.55	2.89					
1	17	2.45	2.11	3.44	2.22	2.84	2.39	3.06	2.11	2.60
2	17	3.22	2.67	2.67	2.00					
1	18	3.89	3.11	3.33	3.44	3.45	3.22	3.61	3.39	3.42
2	18	3.00	3.33	3.89	3.33					
1	19	4.00	2.78	2.89	3.22	3.50	2.67	2.78	2.78	2.93
2	19	3.00	2.55	2.67	2.33					
1	20	3.00	3.56	3.33	2.89	3.17	3.34	3.11	2.73	3.08
2	20	3.33	3.11	2.89	2.56					
1	21	4.11	3.55	3.56	4.00	4.11	3.61	3.78	4.00	3.88
2	21	4.11	3.67	4.00	4.00					
1	22	2.56	2.33	2.67	2.78	3.01	3.33	3.28	3.28	3.22
2	22	3.45	4.33	3.89	3.78					
1	23	3.22	2.78	2.45	2.56	3.11	2.56	2.23	2.45	2.58
2	23	3.00	2.33	2.00	2.33					
1	24	2.67	3.00	3.33	3.00	2.84	3.11	2.78	2.72	2.86
2	24	3.00	3.22	2.22	2.44					
1	25	2.89	2.33	2.78	2.44	2.84	2.39	2.78	2.67	2.67
2	25	2.78	2.45	2.78	2.89					
1	26	2.00	2.66	2.33	2.00	2.61	3.28	3.00	2.84	2.93
2	26	3.22	3.89	3.67	3.67					
1	27	3.33	2.67	3.00	3.22	3.45	3.00	3.17	3.33	3.24
2	27	3.56	3.33	3.33	3.44					
1	28	4.00	4.00	3.89	4.00	3.67	3.95	3.67	3.67	3.74
2	28	3.33	3.89	3.44	3.33					
1	29	2.56	2.56	2.56	2.56	2.45	2.56	2.67	2.56	2.56
2	29	2.33	2.56	2.78	2.56					
1	30	2.22	1.67	2.33	2.00	2.56	1.84	2.45	1.84	2.17
2	30	2.89	2.00	2.56	1.67					

Note. Reproduced with permission from the American Board of Pediatric Dentistry (2007).

this computation is approximately 0.45. Thus the reported scores were distributed about the mean with standard deviation of approximately one-half scale point.

Task Difficulty Index (p-Value)

With the multiple-choice format and checklists, item difficulty is defined as the proportion of examinees who answer an item correctly (Fortune & Cromack, 1995). To that end, the name can be misleading. The values of item difficulty range from 0 to 1, where low values indicate items that were difficult for examinees. Items with high values of difficulty were found easy by examinees.

An analogous statistic to use for constructed- and extended-response items is described by Huynh, Meyer, and Barton (2000), who state, "The p-value is the ratio of the item mean to the item maximum possible score" (p. 30). For example, for a task that uses a rubric with a rating scale of 1 to 4, if six examinees receive scores of 1.0, 2.0, 2.0, 3.0, 2.0, and 2.0, then the mean is 2.0 and the p-value is .50 (i.e., 2.0/4.0) and the task is moderately difficult. In the Huynh and colleagues (2000) technical report, the mean p-values for the English language arts and mathematics open-ended and extended-response items across fifth to eighth grade ranged from .26 to .65.

We can compute the difficulty of the cases in the OCE by computing the mean of each and dividing those respective means by 4, which is the maximum score possible. This process is analogous to computing classical item difficulty for dichotomous items (e.g., multiple-choice, true–false). Table 9.5 shows the mean scores for the candidates on each case as awarded by the examiners. In this example, Case 1 presented the 30 candidates with the least difficulty; Case 4, the greatest. However, the observed differences in case difficulty are small.

Shifts in an item's difficulty from one administration indicate that the examinees found the item different in difficulty from one adminis-

TABLE 9.5. Difficulty of Cases as Reflected in Means and p-Values

	Case 1	Case 2	Case 3	Case 4	Reported score
Mean	3.16	3.02	3.06	2.97	3.05
Difficulty	0.79	0.75	0.76	0.74	0.76

tration to another. This change could be the result of different degrees of preparation by examinees in the groups of candidates. In the case of the item being easier, it could also be the result of item overexposure or perhaps even test compromise, where candidates have the opportunity to learn particular items, not examination content in general.

Acceptable values of item difficulty are generally between .30 and .90, and intermediate values (e.g., .50) contribute the greatest variability to examination scores. Items that are very difficult or very easy generally do not contribute much information regarding the pass–fail status of the typical examinee.

Discrimination Index

Item discrimination, typically reported as the point-biserial correlation of item score (i.e., 0, 1) with the total test score, is conceptualized as ranging from −1 to +1. If examinees who do well on the examination answer the item correctly, whereas, examinees who do poorly on the examination answer the item incorrectly, the item discrimination is positive and approaches +1. As the test scores of the examinees who answered the item correctly become mixed (i.e., some have high test scores, whereas others have low total test scores), and a similar mixture of examinees answered incorrectly, then the item discrimination becomes smaller. A negative value of item discrimination is often an indication that the item is keyed incorrectly.

To calculate a discrimination statistic for constructed-response and extended-response tasks, Huynh and colleagues (2000) used an item–criterion correlation, with the criterion being the total raw score on both the multiple-choice and the open-ended items. When the score points of an item were large (e.g., 15 or 30 points), the extended-response item was not included in the criterion. This was implemented to prevent the large number of score points from inflating the correlation index. The Pearson correlation was used to estimate the point-biserial index. In the report by Huynh and colleagues, the mean correlations for the English language arts and mathematics open-ended and extended-response items across fifth to eighth grade ranged from .50 to .76. These values offer some guidance in considering acceptable values for discrimination indices for performance tasks.

Table 9.6 demonstrates the computation of discrimination for the case scores for the OCE. With a discrimination index of 0.86, Case 1 is highly discriminating between low-performing examinees and high-performing examinees. To calculate the discrimination index we used

TABLE 9.6. Discrimination Index: Correlation between Case Means and Reported Scores

Candidate	Case 1	Reported score
1	3.11	2.67
2	3.22	3.24
3	2.72	2.88
4	3.23	3.19
5	3.84	3.36
6	3.67	3.86
7	3.28	2.93
8	3.39	3.43
9	2.33	2.56
10	2.95	2.86
11	3.78	3.37
12	3.89	3.86
13	2.50	2.71
14	3.22	3.06
15	2.39	2.28
16	3.72	3.39
17	2.84	2.60
18	3.45	3.42
19	3.50	2.93
20	3.17	3.08
21	4.11	3.88
22	3.01	3.22
23	3.11	2.58
24	2.84	2.86
25	2.84	2.67
26	2.61	2.93
27	3.45	3.24
28	3.67	3.74
29	2.45	2.56
30	2.56	2.17
Discrimination	0.86	

the correlation (CORREL) function in Excel. In particular, the value estimated is the Pearson correlation between a given column of domain scores and the column of reported scores. Strictly speaking, the Spearman correlation would be more appropriate for this computation. However, as the sample grows from the given 30 candidates to a larger number and the observed distribution of scores become more centrally mounded and symmetrical, the values produced by the Spearman computation converge on the values of the Pearson computation. Hence, in most reasonable applications, the Pearson computation is sufficient to estimate discrimination.

Item-level analyses allow us to examine the quality of items and tasks associated with an assessment. In the next chapter, we examine test-level analyses, which provide statistical information about the functioning of the test as a whole.

FURTHER READINGS

Cizek, G. (Ed.). (2001). *Setting performance standards: Concepts, methods, and perspectives.* Mahwah, NJ: Erlbaum.

Reviews a broad set of methodologies that can be used to set passing scores. Includes the body of work method, the bookmark procedure, the analytic judgment method, the integrated judgment procedure, and a cluster analysis procedure.

Cizek, G., Bunch, M., & Koons, H. (2004). An NCME module on setting performance standards: Contemporary methods. *Educational Measurement: Issues and Practice, 23*(4), 31–50.

Discusses contemporary methods to establish passing standards (or passing scores) for examinations that use multiple-choice and/or performance tasks. Includes bookmarking, Angoff variations, and holistic methods. The article can be downloaded at *www.ncme.org/pubs/items.cfml.*

Chapter Questions

1. Suppose that an end-of-course assessment in art included (1) a 100-item multiple-choice examination, (2) a portfolio of six paintings, and (3) an essay for which the prompt is to critique a painting.

   a. Create a plan to combine the scores on each of the three components to provide a single reported score (compensatory model). Demonstrate how this composite would produce reported scores.

   b. If you assign weights to the scores on the components, how would you determine that the weights you select are valid? Demonstrate how these weights influence the reported scores that you gave in the previous question.

   c. Create a plan to determine the passing point of the reported score using a compensatory model.

d. Create a plan to determine the passing points of the reported scores using a multiple-hurdle model.

e. Explain the benefits and detriments of using (1) a compensatory model and (2) a multiple hurdle model for reporting scores to

- Students who took the exam
- Students considering going to a given school
- Institutions where the students studied
- Faculty who taught the students
- Admissions personnel at schools who consider admitting the students who took the exam for further study

f. Create a plan to control the retake policy for the exam using both the compensatory and multiple-hurdle models. Explain why each element of the policy is necessary.

CHECKLIST 9.1

Completed	To-Do List for Analysis of Task Scores
	Forming Operational Scores
✓	Create a computer scoring program to apply augmentation and resolution rules to ratings. p. 251
	Determine whether a score of zero should be included in calculations of operational scores or treated as missing. pp. 251–252
	Determine if implicit weights of scales with different lengths are appropriate. pp. 252–253
	Determine whether explicit weights are required for some task items and, if so, include such weights in the scoring program. pp. 253–255
	Decide the domains or subscores that will provide diagnostic feedback to the examinees. p. 255
	Decide whether examinees will be required to successfully pass initial examinations before attempting the performance assessment (multiple-hurdle model) or whether examinees will complete all components of the assessment regardless of scores on any given assessment (compensatory model). p. 256
	Determine whether a passing standard (i.e., cut score for passing) is required for the assessment. pp. 258–264
	Item-Level Analyses
	Review task means and standard deviations to determine task difficulty and range, respectively. pp. 265–270
	Calculate task p-value (task mean ÷ scale length) to put all tasks on the same percentage scale. pp. 270–271
	Calculate task discrimination index to examine the correlation between the task score and total test score. pp. 271–272

CHAPTER 10

Test-Level Analyses

INTRODUCTION

You have designed an assessment, constructed items and tasks, administered the examination as a field test, developed scoring tools, trained raters, and monitored the scoring of the performance tasks. Item-level statistics have informed you about the functioning of items and tasks. Now test-level analyses will provide statistical information about the functioning of the test as a whole. Key qualities of performance tasks to review at the test level include reliability and validity.

INDICES OF RELIABILITY

The review of reliability allows test developers to examine the stability of scores associated with an assessment. Various conditions introduce error variance to scores. As shown in Table 10.1, common forms of error variance include items, raters, and occasions. In this section, we describe statistical indices used to estimate the reliability of performance assessments and examinations that use both performance tasks and multiple-choice items.

Cronbach's Alpha

One classical form of reliability estimate is the alpha coefficient. A Cronbach (1951) introduced the alpha coefficient as an index of equivalence, or internal consistency. The formula is

TABLE 10.1. Types of Reliability Estimates

Reliability types	Form of error variance	Data format	Item types
Cronbach's alpha	Item/task or rater	Dichotomous (0, 1) and polytomous (e.g., one to four rubric scales)	Multiple choice, checklists, or constructed response
Küder–Richarson 20	Item/task	Dichotomous only	Multiple choice, checklists, or constructed response
Split-half	Item/task	Dichotomous and/or polytomous	Multiple choice, checklists, constructed response, extended-response
Parallel forms	Item/task	Dichotomous and/or polytomous	Multiple choice, checklists, constructed response, extended-response
Test–retest	Occasion	Dichotomous and/or polytomous	Multiple choice, checklists, constructed response, extended-response
Generalizability	Rater, task, occasion, etc.	Dichotomous and/or polytomous	Multiple choice, checklists, constructed response, extended-response

Note. Of these forms of reliability, Cronbach's alpha and generalizability theory are the two indices most relevant in terms of performance assessment.

$$\alpha = \frac{k}{k-1}\left(1 - \frac{\sum \sigma_i^2}{\sigma_w^2}\right)$$

where k is the number of test items, σ_i^2 is the variance of item i, and σ_w^2 is the variance for the test. Typically used to estimate error attributable to items, Cronbach's alpha is considered a measure of internal consistency. However, coefficient alpha also has been used to estimate inter-rater reliability by treating raters as items (e.g., Abedi, 1996). The items do not have to be scored as right/wrong (e.g., 0, 1) to be used with this measure (see Table 10.1); thus alpha can be used to examine reliability when scores include polytomous ratings (e.g., 1-4 or 1-6) from rubrics.

Computing Cronbach's Alpha Using the Oral Clinical Examination Data

To compute Cronbach's alpha using the Oral Clinical Examination (OCE) data, we created a worksheet in Excel and imported those data into SPSS. The format of those data appear in Table 10.2.

The code generated by the statistical package SPSS to compute Cronbach's alpha is as follows:

```
RELIABILITY
  /VARIABLES=case1 case2 case3 case4
  /FORMAT=NOLABELS
  /SCALE(ALPHA)=ALL/MODEL=ALPHA
  /SUMMARY=TOTAL .
```

TABLE 10.2. Data for Calculation of Cronbach's Alpha

Candidate	Case 1	Case 2	Case 3	Case 4
1	3.11	2.61	2.39	2.56
2	3.22	3.22	3.45	3.06
3	2.72	3.06	3.06	2.67
4	3.23	2.89	3.17	3.50
5	3.84	3.00	3.28	3.34
6	3.67	3.78	4.06	3.95
7	3.28	3.28	2.45	2.72
8	3.39	3.95	3.34	3.06
9	2.33	2.56	2.62	2.72
10	2.95	2.89	2.95	2.67
11	3.78	2.94	3.11	3.67
12	3.89	3.72	3.83	4.00
13	2.50	3.00	2.84	2.50
14	3.22	3.06	3.11	2.84
15	2.39	1.67	2.39	2.67
16	3.72	3.67	3.39	2.78
17	2.84	2.39	3.06	2.11
18	3.45	3.22	3.61	3.39
19	3.50	2.67	2.78	2.78
20	3.17	3.34	3.11	2.73
21	4.11	3.61	3.78	4.00
22	3.01	3.33	3.28	3.28
23	3.11	2.56	2.23	2.45
24	2.84	3.11	2.78	2.72
25	2.84	2.39	2.78	2.67
26	2.61	3.28	3.00	2.84
27	3.45	3.00	3.17	3.33
28	3.67	3.95	3.67	3.67
29	2.45	2.56	2.67	2.56
30	2.56	1.84	2.45	1.84

The text in Figure 10.1 presents the output from SPSS for this analysis. The calculations using the variance associated with items and the variance for the test are shown below:

$$\alpha = \frac{k}{k-1}\left(1 - \frac{\sum \sigma_i^2}{\sigma_w^2}\right) = \frac{4}{4-1}\left(1 - \frac{.231 + .299 + .208 + .282}{3.21}\right) = .9097$$

There are two decisions to be made when reviewing this output. First, is the value of alpha sufficient? In this example, that value appears at the bottom of the output, and the value for these data is .9098. Cronbach's alpha is a measure of internal consistency, and in this example we are satisfied with the consistency of these measures.

The second decision involves the value of alpha if each set of the case scores is removed and alpha is recomputed for the remaining three cases. If a large change occurs in the value of alpha with the removal of one case, then the removed case is somehow different from the remain-

```
****** Method 1 (space saver) will be used for this analysis ******

  R E L I A B I L I T Y   A N A L Y S I S   -   S C A L E   (A L P H A)


Item-total Statistics

                Scale        Scale       Corrected
                Mean         Variance    Item-          Alpha
                if Item      if Item     Total          if Item
                Deleted      Deleted     Correlation    Deleted

CASE1           9.0480       2.016       .766           .893
CASE2           9.1913       1.855       .761           .897
CASE3           9.1493       1.994       .847           .868
CASE4           9.2403       1.825       .823           .873


Reliability Coefficients

N of Cases =      30.0              N of Items =   4

Alpha =      .909
```

FIGURE 10.1. SPSS output for calculation of Cronbach's alpha.

ing cases, and that difference would likely motivate further examination. In this example, a review of the column labeled *Alpha if Item Deleted* shows no substantial changes were seen in the values of alpha.

Küder–Richardson Formula 20

In the instance where all item scores are dichotomous, such as check-lists, short constructed-response items, and multiple-choice items, item variance is written as $\Sigma p_i q_i$, and the above equation for coefficient alpha becomes the well-known Küder–Richardson Formula 20 (KR-20; Küder & Richardson, 1937):

$$r_w = \frac{k}{k-1}\left(1 - \frac{\sum p_i q_i}{\sigma_w^2}\right)$$

KR-20 is interpreted the same as Cronbach's alpha. Both indices represent the average value achieved by conducting all possible split-half measures of reliability on the examination.

Split Halves

In 1910, Spearman and Brown simultaneously published articles in the *British Journal of Psychology* that outlined a method for splitting the items from a single administration of a test into two halves in order to investigate reliability. Spearman (1910) subsequently described the method of splitting the test into two halves composed of odd items and even items that has become associated with the estimation of split-half reliability.

Splitting a test into even and odd items is not the only method for creating two halves of an examination. For example, Cronbach (1943, 1949) describes the parallel split method, which is analogous to the use of parallel forms to estimate reliability. In this method, you split items on one test to make two forms similar in content, difficulty, and range of difficulty. Cronbach also indicates that you should pair items with same format, such as multiple choice with multiple choice and true–false with another true–false. In the context of performance assessment, then, a constructed-response item would be paired with constructed-response item and an extended-response item would be paired with another extended-response item. Of course such pairing requires a test to contain reasonably parallel sets of items, and it might be unreasonable for a test to contain two extended-response items with similar content and difficulty.

Spearman (1910) offered the equation shown below for estimation of the increase of the reliability coefficient that was based on the division of measurements into two forms:

$$r_w = \frac{pr_{ab}}{1+(p-1)r_{ab}}$$

where r_{ab} is the reliability coefficient based on the halves of the test, p is the number of times the test is lengthened or shortened, and r_w is the estimated reliability coefficient for the whole test.

For a split-half test, the corrected reliability estimate is based on the full-length test, which is twice as long, resulting in the well-known formula:

$$r_2 = \frac{2r_1}{1+r_1}$$

where r_1 is the reliability estimate based on the split halves and r_2 is the estimate of the full-length test. Recall that in Chapter 8 we discussed that this formula is also appropriate for adjusting the interrater reliability estimate when the operational score is the sum of two raters' scores.

Test–Retest

We can estimate test–retest reliability by computing the Pearson correlation between test scores after we administer the same test to the same sample on two different occasions. This methodology assumes that there is no substantial change in the construct measured between the two occasions, the most important assumption being that the first administration did not cause changes in the apparent preparation of the examinees.

The time allowed between the measures is also important. If we measure the same construct twice, the correlation between the two observations will depend, in part, on how much time elapses between the two measurements. The shorter the time between the measures, the higher the correlation is likely to be because there is less opportunity for extraneous factors (e.g., unexpected learning) to influence the scores.

The test–retest method of estimating reliability also assumes the examinees have little recall of the actual test content. Such an assumption might be tenable for a 60-item, multiple-choice test. However, examinees are more likely to remember the items in a test with a limited number of constructed- or extended-response items, raising questions about the use of test–retest estimates of reliability for performance tasks.

Parallel Forms

Reliability estimates based on parallel forms, also referred to as alternate form and equivalent form, offer a method for avoiding the recall of items when using performance tasks. In parallel forms reliability, we first create two equivalent forms of the test that measure the same construct in the same way. One way to do this is to create a large set of items that address the same construct and then randomly select the questions for two forms. Next we administer both forms to the same group of people, and the Pearson correlation between the two sets of scores is the estimate of parallel form reliability. If the administration of the alternate forms allows a brief lapse of time, then the reliability estimate also incorporates the measurement error that a test–retest reliability study would estimate. One practical problem with the parallel form approach is the development of many items that measure the same construct.

The use of parallel forms is similar to split-half reliability in that the questions on the test come from the same pool. The primary difference is that parallel forms are constructed such that the two forms can be used independently and yet still be considered equivalent measures. Split halves, in contrast, are not meant to be used independently.

Parallel forms are useful when one is concerned about the threat to internal validity of the experiment posed by repeated testing using the same form. If we use Form A as a pretest and Form B as a posttest, we reduce that problem. Moreover, if we randomly assign individuals to receive Form A or B on the pretest, and then we switch the form assignments on the posttest, the crossed design permits us to empirically assess the effect of using the exams in a given order.

Generalizability Theory

Within the framework of generalizability theory, an investigation of reliability involves two studies: generalizability (G) and decision (D). In the G-study, the researcher identifies possible sources of error variance, referred to as facets (e.g., raters, tasks, occasions), and designs a study for estimating the variance associated with persons (objects of measurement) and the error variance associated with each of the facets. More specifically, generalizability theory uses ANOVA to partition score variability into a main effect for persons, a main effect for each facet, and the combination of the previous components. An observed score is represented with a linear model that incorporates the facets that introduce error into the measurement. The use of generalizability theory to examine interrater reliability provides an example of a one-facet generalizability study.

Generalizability Theory and Interrater Reliability

In an evaluation that uses portfolios as a data collection method, the raters who score the portfolios are likely to be one facet of interest since their judgments about the level of proficiency reflected in the portfolio content will contribute one source of measurement error. In a study where all facets are crossed—all raters score all portfolios—the model for an observed score (X_{pr}) for a portfolio scored by one rater is:

$$X_{pr} = \mu + \nu_p + \nu_r + \nu_{pr}$$

where μ is the grand mean across population and facets, and represents the effects for this study (i.e., person, raters, and a person-by-rater interaction) (Brennan, 1992).

The variance of the scores over persons and raters is:

$$\sigma^2(X_{pr}) = \sigma^2_p + \sigma^2_r + \sigma^2_{pr,e}$$

Variance components associated with the facets—raters, in this case—are estimates of error variance and are used in the D-study to investigate how the facets of an assessment can be altered to improve reliability. The D-study is analogous to the use of the Spearman–Brown prophecy formula in classical test theory to determine the reliability of test scores when increasing (or decreasing) items on a test. In a D-study the conditions of a facet are similarly manipulated to estimate the reliability of scores for various designs. To return to our previous example, in a portfolio assessment the researcher might use the variance components associated with a rater facet in the G-study to determine in a D-study how many raters are required to reduce error variance associated with rater judgments to achieve an acceptable level of interrater reliability.

Fixed Versus Random Facets. In preparation for the estimation of reliability in a D-study, you must decide whether each facet is random or fixed. The decision to consider a facet as fixed or random affects the magnitude of the reliability coefficient because random facets contribute error variance to score reliability whereas fixed facets do not. The choice between approaches, however, should not be based on which design results in the higher correlation coefficient; rather, the design of the analysis should be based on conceptual grounds (Shavelson & Webb, 1991). The authors state that a facet can be considered random "if the size of the sample is much smaller than the size of the universe, and the sample is either drawn randomly or is considered to be exchangeable with any other sample of the same size drawn from the universe" (p. 11). For example, if in the scoring of portfolios a researcher considers it reasonable to substitute other raters for the current sample of raters, then the rater facet is random since different raters may assign different scores, thus contributing to error variance.

In contrast, a facet is fixed if the conditions of the facet are limited, or if the investigator does not consider the conditions of the facet interchangeable with similar conditions of the facet. An example of a fixed facet might be the evaluative criteria used in the assessment of student writing. Evaluative criteria, such as Ideas, Organization, Voice, Word Choice, Sentence Fluency, and Conventions (Spandel, 2001), might constitute the universe of literary elements of interest in the assessment of student writing. Whereas the writing prompts and the raters may be considered samples from a larger universe of facet conditions, the same evaluative criteria (e.g., Ideas, Organization) would be applied in future replications of the writing assessment. In summary, random and fixed facets can be distinguished by determining whether the conditions of the facets are likely to change (random) or remain the same (fixed) in replications of the assessment.

Relative or Absolute Decisions. In the design of a D-study the investigator must also decide whether scores will be interpreted for relative or absolute decisions. In relative decisions, the ranking of individual or group scores is the focus of the evaluation or research study. For example, in a program evaluation, when determining which projects with positive ratings in site reviews are to receive continued funding, if ratings are interpreted via relative standing (i.e., ranking) of programs, then the generalizability coefficient is appropriate for estimating reliability.

The G-coefficient is calculated by dividing person variance by the variance attributable to persons and the variance attributable to interactions between persons and facets. Thus, as shown below, in a G-study with raters as a facet, the generalizability coefficient would decrease if subjects' relative standing, as measured by the person-by-rater interaction, changed across raters:

$$\rho^2 = \frac{\sigma^2(p)}{\sigma^2(p)+\sigma^2(pr)}$$

The generalizability coefficient is analogous to Pearson's and Spearman's correlations in that it measures changes in rank order, but not changes in mean performance.

If a participant's absolute performance is of interest, then the phi coefficient, also referred to as an index of dependability (Brennan & Kane, 1977), is the appropriate estimate of reliability. The phi coefficient estimates reliability when changes in participant proficiency levels or examinee performance on a criterion-referenced test are of interest. The phi coefficient incorporates into the denominator all error variance attributable to main effects *and* interactions. To return to the example of investigation of the interrater reliability of a performance task where raters comprise the only facet, the phi coefficient will be:

$$\Phi = \frac{\sigma^2(p)}{\sigma^2(p)+\sigma^2(r)+\sigma^2(pr)}$$

Examination of the formula demonstrates that the phi and generalizability coefficients will be the same if there is no main effect due to a facet, such as a rater facet. As compared with the generalizability coefficient, the phi coefficient will be a lower estimate of reliability because it takes into account any variance attributable to a main effect, such as raters or other facets of interest. If the reliability of examinee cut scores or changes in proficiency levels are of interest, then evaluators will want to determine that there is no effect due to rater leniency or severity. That is,

TABLE 10.3. GENOVA Estimates of Variance Components for Holistic Scores

Effect	df	SS mean scores	SS for score effects	Mean squares	Estimated variance components
Person (P)	36	546.00000	26.86486	0.74625	0.2927928
Rater (R)	1	519.35135	0.21622	0.21622	0.0015015
PR	36	552.00000	5.78378	0.16066	0.1606607

the index of dependability will provide a reliability estimate that takes into account shifts in rater means and allows retraining of raters who are overly severe or lenient in scoring.

To illustrate the application of G-theory in calculating interrater reliability, we examine the holistic ratings from the scoring of a set of portfolios. The analysis was completed using GENOVA,[1] a program developed by Crick and Brennan (1984). The code used in GENOVA for analyzing rater reliability when using holistic scores is shown in Figure 10.2. A few specifics about the GENOVA code will help your review.

EFFECT cards are used to specify the facets for GENOVA. In Figure 10.2, the object of measurement is specified as * P 37 0. The * specifies that this facet is the object of measurement in the analysis. The P indicates the letter to be used to label this facet. The 37 indicates that the portfolios for 37 participants are included in the analysis. The 0 stipulates that P is a random effect. Notice the spaces between the *, P, 37, and 0.

The + R 2 0 specifies the rater facet and indicates that two raters scored each portfolio. The 0 specifies that an infinite universe was available from which raters could have been sampled (i.e., rater is a random effect).

Notice that the card labels (e.g., STUDY, COMMENT, EFFECT) occupy columns 1–12 and the commands begin in column 13. The STUDY card at the top of the program allows the GENOVA user to title the analysis and document program output. The COMMENT card also allows the user to write comments about the analysis. GENOVA only prints the comments; it does not process the comments. In Figure 10.2, the OPTIONS card indicates that the information for all records are to be printed. The FORMAT card specifies the data structure. Each record has two values (i.e., a portfolio score from each of two raters). Each value takes two spaces, and the values do not have decimals.

The PROCESS card indicates that the cards for this study have been read and data can be processed. Data immediately follow the PROCESS card.

At the end of the analysis, in the D-study (noted as DSTUDY in the GENOVA code) we request generalizability estimates based on using up to eight raters. The DSTUDY card indicates a set of cards for the D-study

---

[1]GENOVA is available at *www.education.uiowa.edu/casma/GenovaPrograms.htm.* Documentation about the code used in GENOVA is available in the publication *Manual for GENOVA: A Generalized Analysis of Variance System* (Crick & Brennan, 1984). This publication is also on the website.

```
STUDY        DATA SET 1 - RANDOM MODEL - P X  R DESIGN - RUN 1
COMMENT      # RECORDS = 37
COMMENT      # VALUES PER RECORD = 2
COMMENT
OPTIONS      RECORDS ALL
EFFECT       * P 37 0
EFFECT       + R 2 0
FORMAT       (2F2.0)
PROCESS
 2 2
 3 3
 3 3
 3 3
 3 3
 3 2
 1 2
 1 2
 3 3
 2 2
 2 2
 2 2
 3 3
 4 3
 3 3
 3 2
 2 1
 3 3
 4 4
 3 2
 2 2
 3 3
 3 4
 3 3
 3 3
 3 3
 3 2
 2 3
 3 3
 3 3
 2 2
 3 3
 3 3
 3 2
 3 3
 2 1
 3 3
COMMENT   HOLISTIC SCORES DSTUDY EVEN START
DSTUDY       RATERS 1 2 3 4 5 6 7 8    HOLISTIC
DEFFECT      $ P
DEFFECT      R 1 2 3 4 5 6 7 8
ENDDSTUDY
FINISH
```

FIGURE 10.2. Code for conducting a generalizability analysis with GENOVA.

287

follow. The DEFFECT cards describe the object of measurement ($ P) and facets (R) and sample size (e.g., 1–8 raters in the rater facet). The ENDDSTUDY card terminates the D-study cards. The FINISH card indicates execution of GENOVA. The ENDSTUDY card should be the last card in the GENOVA code.

The variance estimates from the GENOVA output are shown in Table 10.3. The variance component for persons is 0.293, for raters is 0.002, and for persons by raters is 0.161. Notice that raters contribute little variance to portfolio scores.

Using the ratio of person variance (P) to person and error variance (rater and person by rater), the phi coefficient for the holistic scores is calculated by:

$$\Phi = \frac{.2927928}{.2927928 + .0015015 + .1606607} = .64356$$

The phi coefficient of .64 estimates the reliability of holistic scores based on judgments of one rater; however, the evaluators in this study averaged the scores from two raters. The D-study section of the GENOVA output provides estimates of reliability for multiple raters; the reliability estimate for scores based on two raters is .78 (see Figure 10.3). In the case of one facet (i.e., rater), application of the Spearman–Brown prophecy formula also allows estimation of the reliability of scores based on two raters' judgments, producing the same estimate as the D-study.

If relative performance were the focus of decisions made with the holistic scores, a G-coefficient (ρ^2) would be calculated using the person variance and the error variance associated with the interaction between person and raters in the denominator. The error variance associated with the rater facet would be omitted from the denominator because a shift in means due to rater leniency or stringency is not of concern when decisions are based on relative performance. Indicating little error in scores due to a rater effect, the G-coefficient for relative decisions is .65 for scores based on a single rater and remains .78 for scores based on the judgments of two raters (see the column labeled GEN. COEF. in Figure 10.3).

It is also worth noting that as the number of raters increase from one to three, the phi coefficients increase from .64, to .78, then to .84. However, after three raters, the coefficients increase only .02 or so for each additional rater, indicating that little would be gained by scoring with more than three raters.

```
SUMMARY OF D STUDY RESULTS FOR SET OF CONTROL CARDS NO. 001

                                                 V A R I A N C E S
              SAMPLE SIZES       -------------------------------------------------------------------------
D STUDY                                     EXPECTED   LOWER    UPPER
DESIGN  INDEX=  $P    R          UNIVERSE   OBSERVED   CASE     CASE                GEN.
NO      UNIV.=  INF.  INF.       SCORE      SCORE      DELTA    DELTA      MEAN     COEF.    PHI
----------------------------     -------------------------------------------------------------------------
001-001         37    1          .29279     .45345     .16066   .16216    .01376   .64570   .64356
001-002         37    2          .29279     .37312     .08033   .08108    .01084   .78471   .78313
001-003         37    3          .29279     .34635     .05355   .05405    .00986   .84538   .84416
001-004         37    4          .29279     .33296     .04017   .04054    .00937   .87937   .87838
001-005         37    5          .29279     .32492     .03213   .03243    .00908   .90111   .90028
001-006         37    6          .29279     .31957     .02678   .02703    .00889   .91621   .91549
001-007         37    7          .29279     .31574     .02295   .02317    .00875   .92731   .92668
001-008         37    8          .29279     .31288     .02008   .02027    .00864   .93581   .93525
```

FIGURE 10.3. G-coefficients and phi coefficients from GENOVA output for a D-Study.

Generalizability Theory and Score Reliability

In the prior section, we examined the use of generalizability theory to estimate interrater reliability. In the case of interrater reliability, only one facet, the rater facet, is included in the estimation of a generalizability coefficient or index of dependability. When additional facets, such as a task facet (i.e., each case in the Oral Clinical Examination can be treated as a task), are included in generalizability analyses, then the reliability estimate is typically referred to as score reliability. Of interest in generalizability analyses are facets related to raters, tasks, and occasions because research indicates that an examinee's performance is likely to vary to some degree from one rater to another, one task to another, and one occasion to another (e.g., Brennan & Johnson, 1995; Dunbar et al., 1991; Gao et al., 1994; Linn & Burton, 1994; Shavelson et al., 1993; Webb et al., 2000).

In a two-facet generalizability study, if all facets are crossed (i.e., all raters score all tasks), the model for an observed score (X_{prt}) for a task scored by one rater is:

$$X_{prt} = \mu + v_p + v_r + v_t + v_{pr} + v_{pt} + v_{rt} + v_{prt}$$

where μ is the grand mean across population and facets, and v represents the effects for this study (i.e., person, raters, tasks, and interactions) (Brennan, 1992).

The variance of the scores over persons, raters, and tasks is:

$$\sigma^2(X_{prt}) = \sigma^2_p + \sigma^2_r + \sigma^2_t + \sigma^2_{pr} + \sigma^2_{pt} + \sigma^2_{rt} + \sigma^2_{prt,e}$$

In conducting the generalizability analyses for the Oral Clinical Examination (OCE), the facets of raters and tasks are treated as random. According to Shavelson and Webb (1991), tasks may be considered random if (1) the size of the sample is smaller than the size of the universe and (2) the sample is considered interchangeable with any other similar-sized samples from the universe (p. 11). To determine whether a facet should be treated as random, Shavelson and Webb (1991) suggest asking the following question: "Am I willing to *exchange* the conditions in the sample for any other same-size set of conditions from the universe?" (p. 11). An affirmative response indicates the facet is random. In the OCE, the raters and the tasks represent a sample of the conditions that are interchangeable for a similar group of raters or a similar set of tasks. Thus we treated these two facets as random in the generalizability analyses.

In the analyses, the domains for the tasks were treated as a fixed facet. In the domains facet, the domains are (1) Data Gathering/Diagnosis, (2) Management/Treatment Planning, and (3) Treatment Variations/Complications. These same domains are used to score each administration of the OCE and are not considered interchangeable with other performance domains. A facet may be treated as fixed when, in the words of Shavelson and Webb (1991), "the entire universe of conditions is small and all conditions are included in the measurement design" (p. 65). Analysis of a fixed facet may occur by averaging over the conditions of the facet, in this instance the domains, or conducting an analysis for each condition (Shavelson & Webb, 1991). In the following analyses, we averaged across the three domains within a case. Thus examinees' scores are shown at the case level in Figure 10.4.

For the equation, the index of dependability, or ϕ (phi), as described by Brennan and Kane (1977) is given by the following equation:

$$\phi = \frac{\sigma_p^2}{\sigma_p^2 + \left(\dfrac{\sigma_r^2}{n_r} + \dfrac{\sigma_t^2}{n_t} + \dfrac{\sigma_{pr}^2}{n_r} + \dfrac{\sigma_{pt}^2}{n_t} + \dfrac{\sigma_{rt}^2}{n_r n_t} + \dfrac{\sigma_{prt}^2}{n_r n_t} \right)}$$

where σ_p^2 is the variance estimate for persons, σ_r^2 is the variance estimate for raters, σ_t^2 is the variance estimate for tasks, σ_{pr}^2 is the variance estimate for the person by rater interaction, σ_{pt}^2 is the variance estimate for the person by task interaction, σ_{rt}^2 is the variance estimate for the rater by task interaction, $\sigma_{prt,e}^2$ is the variance estimate for error, n_r is the number of raters, and n_t is the number of tasks.

Shavelson and Webb (1991) state that "if the generalizability coefficient is viewed more broadly as the universe-score variance divided by the sum of the universe score variance plus the error variance, then the phi coefficient can be seen as a generalizability coefficient for absolute decisions" (pp. 93–94). Examples of absolute decisions are the pass–fail decisions that result in the graduation of a student, the licensure of a physician, and the certification of a nursing specialist.

Computing Score Reliability for the Oral Clinical Examination. To compute an estimate of score reliability for the OCE, we used the simulated data from the 30 candidates that we have been exploring in this chapter. However, some rearrangement of those data was necessary for use with GENOVA. As shown in Figure 10.4, for each candidate we created a line of data for the examiners' ratings of each case where Case 1, Case 2, Case 3, and Case 4 from the first examiner appeared as the first four values with the four case ratings from the second examiner appearing as the last four ratings on the same line, creating one line of eight values for each candidate. Figure 10.4 displays the GENOVA code that processes these data.

Contrast the code with the code in Figure 10.2. Note that one difference is associated with the FORMAT card in which the 8F5.2 describes the layout of the data to be processed. In this dataset, there are eight values for each record. Each value takes five spaces, and each value has two decimals. A space appears before each value to make the data easier for us to read. (GENOVA does not require the spaces to be able to read the data accurately; *we* need the spaces to be able to make sure what we process is what we intended.)

Other differences of note are that * P is associated with scores from 30 candidates and that one of the EFFECT cards stipulates a task effect: + T 4 0. A DEFFECT card now identifies a task effect with five levels.

GENOVA produces 23 pages of output for an analysis such as this one. The discussion of most of that output is beyond the scope of this book; however, the value we need to report the score reliability observed in this dataset appears on the next-to-last page, which we have copied to Figure 10.5. Based on two raters and eight tasks, score reliability from this part of the OCE as observed in this simulated dataset is .66259.

EVALUATION OF RELIABILITY ESTIMATES

How does one know if reliability is at an acceptable level? Several sources provide guidance in the interpretation and evaluation of reliability estimates. Some authors indicate that research studies and low-stakes assessments require a minimal reliability of 0.70, whereas applied settings with high-stakes tests require a minimal reliability of 0.90 (Herman, Aschbacher, & Winters, 1992; Nunnally, 1978). However, Phillips (2000) reported that Texas courts found a graduation test sufficiently reliable with total score reliabilities above .85.

In addition, evaluation of a reliability estimate requires consideration of whether interpretation of scores will focus on individual scores or the group mean. For example, Thorndike (2005) demonstrated that

```
STUDY         Domain A - RANDOM MODEL - P X R X T DESIGN
COMMENT
COMMENT       # RECORDS = 30
COMMENT       # VALUES PER RECORD = 8
COMMENT
OPTIONS       RECORDS ALL    CORRELATION
EFFECT        * P 30 0
EFFECT        + R 2 0
EFFECT        + T 4 0
FORMAT        (8F5.2)
PROCESS
 2.89 2.33 2.33 2.00 3.33 2.89 2.44 3.11
 3.89 3.33 4.00 3.33 2.55 3.11 2.89 2.78
 2.66 3.33 3.00 2.45 2.78 2.78 3.11 2.89
 3.56 3.22 3.22 3.78 2.89 2.55 3.11 3.22
 3.67 2.67 2.78 3.11 4.00 3.33 3.78 3.56
 3.78 3.56 4.11 3.89 3.56 4.00 4.00 4.00
 3.22 3.44 2.11 2.33 3.33 3.11 2.78 3.11
 3.56 4.22 3.67 3.45 3.22 3.67 3.00 2.67
 2.44 2.67 2.56 2.66 2.22 2.44 2.67 2.78
 3.00 3.11 2.89 2.78 2.89 2.67 3.00 2.56
 4.11 3.33 3.22 4.00 3.44 2.55 3.00 3.33
 4.00 4.11 4.11 4.33 3.78 3.33 3.55 3.67
 2.78 3.00 2.67 2.89 2.22 3.00 3.00 2.11
 3.22 3.00 3.22 2.45 3.22 3.11 3.00 3.22
 2.44 2.11 2.56 2.78 2.33 1.22 2.22 2.56
 3.33 3.33 3.22 2.67 4.11 4.00 3.55 2.89
 2.45 2.11 3.44 2.22 3.22 2.67 2.67 2.00
 3.89 3.11 3.33 3.44 3.00 3.33 3.89 3.33
 4.00 2.78 2.89 3.22 3.00 2.55 2.67 2.33
 3.00 3.56 3.33 2.89 3.33 3.11 2.89 2.56
 4.11 3.55 3.56 4.00 4.11 3.67 4.00 4.00
 2.56 2.33 2.67 2.78 3.45 4.33 3.89 3.78
 3.22 2.78 2.45 2.56 3.00 2.33 2.00 2.33
 2.67 3.00 3.33 3.00 3.22 2.22 2.44
 2.89 2.33 2.78 2.44 2.78 2.45 2.78 2.89
 2.00 2.66 2.33 2.00 3.22 3.89 3.67 3.67
 3.33 2.67 3.00 3.22 3.56 3.33 3.33 3.44
 4.00 4.00 3.89 4.00 3.33 3.89 3.44 3.33
 2.56 2.56 2.56 2.56 2.33 2.56 2.78 2.56
 2.22 1.67 2.33 2.00 2.89 2.00 2.56 1.67
COMMENT   BEGINNING OF DSTUDY
DSTUDY        RATERS  1 2
DEFFECT       $ P
DEFFECT       R 1 2
DEFFECT       T 1 2 3 4 8
ENDDSTUDY
FINISH
```

FIGURE 10.4. Code for a GENOVA analysis for raters and tasks.

293

SUMMARY OF D STUDY RESULTS FOR SET OF CONTROL CARDS NO. 001

V A R I A N C E S

D STUDY DESIGN NO	INDEX= $P UNIV.= INF.	R INF.	T INF.	UNIVERSE SCORE	EXPECTED OBSERVED SCORE	LOWER CASE DELTA	UPPER CASE DELTA	CASE MEAN	GEN. COEF.	PHI
	SAMPLE SIZES									
001-001	30	1	1	0.13173	0.35860	0.22687	0.23103	0.01612	0.36735	0.36313
001-002	30	2	2	0.13173	0.22639	0.09466	0.09674	0.00963	0.58187	0.57657
001-003	30	2	3	0.13173	0.21390	0.08217	0.08356	0.00852	0.61584	0.61187
001-004	30	2	4	0.13173	0.20766	0.07593	0.07697	0.00796	0.63436	0.63120
001-005	30	2	8	0.13173	0.19829	0.06656	0.06708	0.00713	0.66433	0.66259

FIGURE 10.5. GENOVA output that shows generalizability estimates for two levels for raters and five levels for tasks.

a reliability of .70 for individual scores produced stable mean scores for groups composed of 25 members. Hill (2002) demonstrated that a reliability estimate of 0.80 for individual student scores translates to a reliability estimate of 0.87 when based on a group mean composed of 25 members. When the number of observations increases from 25 to 50, Hill (2002) indicated that the reliability for group means increases from 0.87 to 0.93.

STANDARD ERROR OF MEASURE

Reliability estimates can be used to calculate a standard error of the measure (*SEM*) for an assessment. The *SEM* is an estimate of how close an observed score approximates the true score. As noted earlier, the formula to estimate the *SEM* is:

$$SEM = S\sqrt{1-r}$$

where S is the standard deviation of the test scores and r is the reliability (e.g., internal consistency, split halves) of the test.

For example, if Elliot has a score on 75 on a test with an *SD* of 15 and a reliability estimate of .96, the *SEM* of Elliot's score is 3. Because we know, Elliot's score of 75 is only an estimate of his true score, we can estimate the range in which we are 95% confident we have captured Elliot's true score by computing the 95% confidence interval (*CI*)around Elliot's score, or:

$$95\%CI = 75 \pm 2 \times 3$$

which suggests that Elliot's true score is bounded by the interval 69 to 81 with 95% confidence.

AN EXAMPLE OF ESTIMATING RELIABILITY

Of interest in the use of performance tasks is estimating the reliability of an examination with a mix of item formats. Huynh and colleagues (2000) reported that Cronbach's alpha is appropriate to estimate reliability when multiple-choice and constructed-response items are scored with dichotomous scales or scales of 0–2, 0–3, or 0–4. In estimating the reliability of a state-level achievement test, Huynh and colleagues noted that the maximum scores of the extended-response items was 15 for grades 3 through 6 and 30 for grades 6 through 8. With such a range of possible scores, the extended-response items result in scores with large variance. Huynh and colleagues indicated the use of alpha alone would be inappropriate because the large variance associated with the total score would result in underestimation of reliability estimates.

Because items in an assessment can vary considerably in their score range, Huynh and colleagues (2000) combined Cronbach's alpha and the Spearman–Brown formula as described by Lord and Novick (1968). They first computed Cronbach's alpha for the multiple-choice and constructed-response portions of the test. Subsequently, the Spearman–Brown formula was used to adjust the alpha coefficient to the final reliability estimate for the entire test. The adjustment was based on the test lengthening factor $k = m/n$, where m is the maximum possible score (MPS) for the entire test (i.e., multiple choice, constructed response, and extended response) and n is the MPS for the combined multiple-choice and constructed-response portions.

VALIDITY

The *Standards* indicate that validity is a unitary concept of "the degree to which all the accumulated evidence supports the intended interpretation of test scores for the proposed purpose" (AERA, APA, & NCME, 1999, p. 11). Thus the investigation of the validity of interpretations about examinee performance proceeds with the collection of forms of validity evidence. Those forms of evidence include construct, content-related, convergent and discriminant, criterion-related (concurrent and predictive), and consequential.

Construct

Tests are used as measures of constructs (e.g., algebra readiness, science achievement). As described in the *Standards*, the term *construct* refers to "a concept or characteristic that a test is designed to measure" (AERA, APA, & NCME, 1999, p. 5). The *Standards* provide the following definition of construct validity:

> A term used to indicate that the test scores are to be interpreted as indicating the test taker's standing on the psychological construct measured by

the test. A construct is a theoretical variable inferred from multiple sources of evidence. (AERA, APA, & NCME, 1999, p. 174)

Supporting the construct validity of an assessment is a validity argument, which is "An explicit scientific justification of the degree to which accumulated evidence and theory support the proposed interpretation(s) of test scores (p. 184).

Table 10.4 presents evidence of construct validity for the South Carolina Arts Assessment Program (SCAAP) Visual Arts examination. Recall that the performance assessment is accompanied with 45 multiple-choice items. In Table 10.4, the means of the multiple-choice examinations are presented for each performance task score, and we see that as the task score increases, so do the mean scores for the multiple-choice section of the SCAAP examination. This analysis provides initial evidence to support the assessments are measuring a common construct.

Forms of evidence to be considered in validating interpretations of scores from performance assessment are described in the following sections.

Content-Related Validity Evidence

Content-related validity evidence describes the degree to which the content of the examination questions represents the content of the subject they are intended to assess. For example, the items of an examination to certify the knowledge of an individual as a home inspector are reviewed by a committee of expert home inspectors to ensure that the

TABLE 10.4. Construct Validity Evidence for the SCAAP Visual Arts Examination

| Performance task score | Drawing task | | Writing about drawing task | |
	N	Multiple-choice raw score (mean)	N	Multiple-choice raw score (mean)
0	55	23.28	1,128	25.11
1	371	23.04	309	27.62
2	801	25.86	166	28.72
3	402	29.03	45	30.78
4	131	32.30	40	31.10
Total	1,688	26.22	1,688	26.22

items selected to be on the examination are appropriate for the intended use. In writing assessment, expert committee members determine the match between writing prompts and objectives (i.e., content standards) (Quellmalz, 1986). For the National Assessment of Educational Progress (NAEP) writing assessment, components are reviewed by teachers, teacher educators, state officials, and measurement specialists for "curricular relevance, developmental appropriateness, fairness, and adherence to the framework and test specifications" (Persky et al., 2003, p. 5). The NAEP science assessment is similarly reviewed (O'Sullivan et al., 2003).

Crocker (1997) provides guidance on the conduct of the review of items. She identified the following steps for inclusion in a content review of performance assessment exercises:

1. Defining the content domain,

2. Identifying criteria for evaluating the exercises,

3. Structuring the review task for the expert judges,

4. Developing forms for judges to use in recording their response,

5. Specifying qualifications of judges and recruiting them,

6. Determining the minimum number of judges needed,

7. Assessing reliability of judges' ratings, and

8. Summarizing and reporting the judges' ratings in an interpretable and constructive format for feedback to test developers or users. (p. 84)

Convergent Validity Evidence

To study convergent validity, we examine whether two measures that we expect to be related are actually related in an empirically demonstrable manner (see Table 10.5). For example, the developers of the Even Start portfolio used two measures to correlate with portfolio scores in a validation study (Johnson, Fisher, et al., 2003). For one measure, Even Start staff members considered the levels of literacy demonstrated by the participants with whom they worked and then rank-ordered the participants according to family literacy levels. This activity was completed before the portfolios were scored.

A second measure of family literacy was a checklist that had been previously developed by the Even Start staff and the program evaluators. Staff used the Family Literacy Checklist (FLC) to document development of family literacy in four general areas: Creating a Learning Environment, Meeting Physical Needs, Providing a Nurturing Environment, and Providing Guidance (Johnson, Fisher, et al., 2003). The Creating a Learning Environment section of the checklist is shown in Table 10.6. The staff members completed the checklist toward the end of the program year, prior to the portfolio scoring session.

Investigation of the validity of the portfolio assessment used the analytic composite scores and the holistic rubric scores. The validity study revealed correlations in the expected positive direction with the two criterion-related measures used in this study. Moderate correlations were found between the FLC scores and the holistic scores ($r = .52$) and the analytic composite scores ($r = .54$). It should be noted that the team created the FLC for assessing an array of family literacy skills associated with the Even Start program, thereby offering some support that the portfolio assessment and the FLC measure a common construct of family literacy. The significant correlation between the independent judgment of the family educator and the raters' holistic scores ($r = .50$) and analytic composite scores ($r = .59$) provided additional convergent validity evidence.

Discriminant Validity Evidence

To study discriminant validity, we collect evidence about whether two measures we do *not* expect to be related are actually not related in an empirically demonstrable manner. For example, the GRE Analytic Writing measure correlates .02 with the Quantitative measure of the GRE and .55 with its Verbal measure (Educational Testing Service [ETS], 2004), thus providing initial evidence that the Analytic Writing measure provides information about a different construct than the quantitative measure.

Criterion-Related Validity Evidence

Criterion-related validity evidence expresses the association between a score on the examination and a defined outcome. For example, a sufficient score on a driving exam is associated with a sufficiently qualified (and safe) driver. A sufficient score on a placement examination is associated with success in a given class. In these two examples, criterion-related validity predicts later behavior or success. However, criterion-related validity can also be defined in the sense of concurrent validity.

TABLE 10.5. Types of Validity Evidence for Performance Assessments

Validity evidence	Purpose of the evidence	Form of evidence	Example	Rationale
Construct	Build a validity argument for the interpretation of scores as indicating an examinee's standing on the concept or characteristic measured by the assessment.	Validity argument of the degree to which evidence and theory support score interpretations.	Cognitive studies examine the kinds of writing tasks and degrees of skills that differentiate novice and expert writers (Quellmalz, 1986).	Expert/novice studies provide a basis for selection of dimensions to rate essays (Quellmalz, 1986).
Content	Review the process for specifying the test content, the relevance of the content domain to score interpretations, and the degree to which the content of an assessment represents the content domain.	Committee of experts completes the review and documents the review process and outcomes.	An expert committee of arts teachers and leaders reviewed the content of the SCAAP to ascertain the linkage between the items and the state content standards.	The items were developed by arts teachers based on a table of specifications. The teachers identified the standard and Bloom's cognitive level when entering the items in an item bank. The expert committee reviewed items for appropriate classification.
Convergent	Demonstrate that two measures that are expected to be related are actually related in an empirically demonstrable manner.	Correlation between performance task and another measure of the same construct.	Essay scores on a bar examination should correlate moderately positively with scores on the multiple-choice Multistate Bar Examination.	Both the essays and multiple-choice items are addressing KSAs important in the practice of law and should correlate. The essay assessment will require skills, such as organizing an argument, not required in the multiple-choice items, so the correlation should be moderate, not high.

300

Discriminant	Demonstrate that two measures that are *not* expected to be related are actually not related.	Correlation between performance task and a measure of a different construct.	Scores on mathematics performance tasks should correlate weakly with scores on reading and writing performance tasks.	Mathematics performance tasks might be verbally loaded because of the language to establish a context and the requirement to write a justification for an answer. However, the correlation between language arts skills and mathematics scores should be lower than, for example, the correlation between scores from a mathematics performance assessment and scores from a multiple-choice mathematics test.
Concurrent	Demonstrate the relation between an assessment and an alternative measure of the same construct.	Correlation between the scores on the measure and an alternative measure.	Even Start portfolio scores and scores on the Home Screening Questionnaire (HSQ).	The Even Start family literacy portfolio should correlate with the HSQ, an instrument that assesses home factors contributing to the social, emotional, and cognitive development of a child.
Predictive	Indicate the degree to which scores from an assessment can accurately predict scores on a criterion later.	Correlate scores from an assessment with scores obtained at a later date from a criterion measure.	SAT writing scores used to predict first-year college performance.	Students scoring higher on the SAT written examination should perform better in the first year of college than those students scoring lower on the SAT, especially in classes requiring writing.

TABLE 10.6. Section from the Family Literacy Checklist

Providing a nurturing environment	Regularly	Occasionally	Not often
Displays verbal or physical affection to child	——	——	——
Provides positive encouragement to child	——	——	——
Supports child's independence	——	——	——
Responds positively to child's needs	——	——	——
Communicates acceptance of child	——	——	——

Concurrent Validity Evidence

Concurrent validity evidence provides information about the association between an assessment and an alternative examination of the same construct (AERA, APA, & NCME, 1999). An example of evidence used in a concurrent validity study is the correlation between the Even Start portfolio scores and scores from the Home Screening Questionnaire (HSQ) (Coons, Gay, Fandal, Ker, & Frankenburg, 1981). According to Coons and colleagues, the HSQ assesses home factors contributing to the social, emotional, and cognitive development of a child. Surprisingly, the correlations between the score for the Even Start portfolio and HSQ were not significantly different from 0.0.

Predictive Validity Evidence

Predictive validity evidence provides information about whether a score on an examination predicts future performance. For example, Norris and colleagues (2006) assessed the predictive validity of SAT writing scores. They correlated scores from the writing assessment with first-year college grade point averages (GPA) and GPA in English composition courses. The correlation between SAT essay scores and first-year college GPA was 0.20 when corrected for range restriction. The correlation between the essay scores and English composition GPA was 0.18 when corrected for range restriction. In addition, the SAT writing scores (i.e., multiple-choice items and essay score) resulted in an increment of 0.01 to the predictive validity attained by using SAT verbal and math scores and high school GPA to predict first-year college GPA.

Consequential Validity Evidence

Consequential validity is a source of some controversy in the testing community. Some in testing argue that consequential validity refers to the social consequences arising from the use of a particular examination for a particular purpose. For example, the use of a standardized examination in the selection of students for medical school admissions has some demonstrable social consequence if the examination is found to favor one group over another.

Others argue that social consequences arising from test use are not a reasonable consideration in the process of establishing the validity of an exam. For example, Messick (1993b) writes, "it is not that adverse social consequences of test use render the use invalid but, rather, that adverse social consequences should not be attributable to any source of test invalidity such as construct-irrelevant variance" (p. 88).

The development of performance assessments along the lines described in *Assessing Performance* should reduce extraneous factors that might influence examinee scores. To reduce error in assessing performance, assessment practitioners develop test specifications to frame the test development process; develop tasks and submit them to a review process by experts; field-test these tasks and examine their quality; finalize tasks and administer them under standardized conditions; prepare raters to apply rubrics and benchmarks to score the tasks; and examine the reliability and validity of the final test. In each step of the process, the assessment practitioners work closely with expert committees or program staff to guide the task development. The implementation and documentation of these strategies contribute to producing assessments that can support accurate decisions in education, licensure, certification, research, and program evaluation.

FURTHER READINGS

Brennan, R. (1992). An NCME instructional module on generalizability theory. *Educational Measurement: Issues and Practice, 11*(4), 27–34.

Summarizes the issues to be addressed in the conduct of a generalizability study. The article can be downloaded at *www.ncme.org/pubs/items/21.pdf.*

Messick, S. (1996). Validity of performance assessments. In G. Phillips (Ed.), *Technical issues in large-scale performance assessment* (pp. 1–18). Washington, DC: National Center for Education Statistics.

Reviews validity issues relevant to performance assessment. The entire book can be downloaded at *nces.ed.gov/pubsearch/pubsinfo. asp?pubid=96802*.

Shavelson, R., & Webb, N. (1991). *Generalizability theory: A primer.* Newbury Park, CA: Sage.

Describes the issues in a generalizability study and provide examples. If paired with the Brennan article, provides the reader with a grasp of generalizability theory and the methods for estimating G-coefficients.

Chapter Questions

1. As noted earlier, some universities use the writing section of the SAT to make decisions about applicants' admission.

   a. Are these decisions likely to be relative or absolute?

   b. Which generalizability coefficient would be appropriate to estimate?

2. List the types of validity evidence that would be collected for investigating the use of a writing assessment as a requirement for high school graduation.

   a. Describe the interpretation of each form of validity evidence.

3. List the forms of reliability that would likely be used to evaluate an end-of-course biology assessment.

   a. Describe the interpretation of each form of reliability.

4. As described in Chapter 1, some states supplement the multiple-choice Multistate Bar Examination with the Multistate Performance Test. How does the addition of the essay influence the

   a. Reliability of the examination?

   b. Validity of the examination?

   c. Expense of the examination?

   d. Marketability of the examination?

5. If the NAEP visual arts assessment did not include a task in which the students draw a picture, describe how such an omission would influence the

   a. Reliability of the examination?

   b. Validity of the examination?

   c. Expense of the examination?

   d. Marketability of the examination?

6. Assume that an end-of-course assessment in the visual arts included a 100-item multiple-choice examination, a portfolio of six paintings, and an essay for which the prompt is to critique a painting.

   a. Explain why or why not you would expect the reported scores to correlate with the average of teacher-assigned course grades.

   b. Explain why or why not you would expect a given pair of component scores to correlate.

   c. Which component of this examination would you expect the faculty to say had the best predictive validity? Explain your reasoning for your choice.

   d. Suppose you determine that the scores on the three components correlate highly for the students in your program.

      • Which component provides the most cost-effective assessment?

      • What would be likely consequences that you would expect if you reduced the assessment to this single component?

   e. Suppose you determine that the scores on the three components have low correlations. What would such a finding tell you about the assessment?

CHECKLIST 10.1

Completed	To-Do List for Test-Level Analyses
	Test-Level Analyses
✓	Estimate test score reliability using appropriate indices (e.g., alpha, KR20, generalizability index). pp. 276–296
	Study the validity of score interpretation. pp. 296–303

Glossary

Accommodations. Adaptations to test administration and/or format to make an examination accessible to an examinee who, due to a disability, is unable to complete the examination under standard conditions. Often these accommodations include extended time and large print.

Adjacent agreement. Scores that are within 1 point of each other.

Adjudication. The process by which the disagreement in scores assigned by two raters is resolved.

Alternate forms. Different forms of the same exam that measure the same construct in the same manner. These multiple forms are developed with the same specifications, but with different items that measure the same content, and the forms are considered interchangeable.

Analytic rubric. A scoring guide that separates the critical aspects of a performance into dimensions for scoring. Each dimension receives a separate score, which may then be summed for a total score.

Annotation. A written rationale for the score assigned to a response by a validation committee.

Artifacts. Portfolio entries (e.g., videotapes of performances, reflective essays) that provide evidence of an examinee's proficiency level.

Benchmarks. Examples of examinees' responses to performances tasks. These examples are used to represent the level of quality at a given point (e.g., a rating of 3) on a scoring rubric along the entire performance continuum.

Calibration. In performance assessment, the training and monitoring of raters to develop and maintain consistency in scoring.

Candidate. Examinee taking an examination for certification or licensure.

Certification. A pedigree extended by a nongovernmental agency after an examinee has demonstrated a certain set of skills and knowledge.

Clinical examination. A form of performance assessment in which a candidate for licensure or certification completes work samples critical to the execution of responsibilities in his or her profession.

Cognitive process skills. Mental activities, such as analysis, evaluation, synthesis.

Commentaries. *See* Annotation.

Comments. *See* Annotation.

Compensatory scoring. A scoring model in which a low score in one area of an assessment can be compensated for by a high score in another area.

Composite score. A formula-based score that combines two or more sets of scores. Weights on scores can also be included in the computation of the composite.

Computer-based delivery. Delivery of a computerized examination over a network or some other form of information distribution.

Computer-based test (CBT). *See* Computer-based delivery.

Construct. A theoretical variable (i.e., concept or characteristic) that an examination seeks to measure (e.g., reading achievement, nursing skill).

Construct-irrelevant variance. The variance of a test score that is the result of something other than the construct the examination is intended to measure (e.g., score variance associated with raters).

Construct representativeness. Construct underrepresentation. A threat to validity in which the assessment fails to include important dimensions.

Construct validity. *See* Validity.

Constructed response. An item format used on examinations where the examinee creates a short response, rather than selects a response as in multiple choice.

Content standards. The important concepts, skills, and strategies in a subject area (e.g., history, science, mathematics, reading). Such standards define the content of an examination.

Content validity. Evidence of the degree to which an examination contains appropriate content.

Convergent validity. Evidence that two measures that are expected to be related are actually related in an empirically demonstrable manner.

Credentialing boards. Legal entities charged with the oversight of a licensure or certification program.

Criteria. A set of qualities (e.g., accuracy, organization, tonality) by which an examinee's performance is rated.

Criterion-related validity. Evidence that scores on a test are related to scores on another measure that is based on a similar construct.

Criterion-referenced score interpretation. Test scores that indicate the standing of the examinee in terms of status (e.g., pass–fail, basic/proficient/ advanced) as defined by a committee of subject matter experts.

Cut score. The minimum score needed to pass an examination. *See also* Passing standard.

Dimensions. *See* Criteria.

Discrimination index. The correlation between an item score and the total test. The correlation assesses the ability of an item or task to distinguish between high and low scorers on the examination.

Discriminant validity. Evidence that two measures that are *not* expected to be related are actually not related (e.g., writing scores and task scores on mathematics items that require examinees to justify their solutions).

Discussion. The process of score resolution by which raters whose scores do not agree discuss the reasons for their discrepant ratings and reach a consensus.

Domain. *See* Criteria.

Equivalent forms. *See* Alternate forms.

Evidence. Any data in a performance that enable the rater to evaluate the quality of the examinee's proficiency with respect to the performance standards.

Exact agreement. Ratings that are the same.

Examination. A set of question or prompts used to measure knowledge, skill, or ability.

Examinee. The person taking a test.

Examiner. The person who administers an examination. *See also* Test examiner.

Exemplars. *See* Benchmarks.

Expert judgment. The process of rater disagreement resolution by which the scores of the original raters are replaced by the score from a single rater with greater experience and scoring accuracy.

Expert rater. A person trained to apply a scoring rubric to estimate the degree of proficiency displayed in a performance sample and who can do so with greater agreement with validation samples. This rater often serves as a team leader or trainer for a group of raters.

Extended response. Tasks requiring examinees to answer in more than a single sentence or paragraph. Essays are one form of extended response.

Holistic rubric. A scoring guide that combines criteria to describe an overall performance. Raters use such a rubric to assign a single score to identify the quality of a performance.

Internet-based delivery. Delivery of a computerized examination over the Internet, often to a secure location.

Internet-based test (IBT). *See* Internet-based delivery.

Interrater reliability. A measure of the degree to which a pair of raters is producing the same score for the same performance.

Intranet. A private network of computers.

Item. A sentence, question, or paragraph that elicits a response from an examinee.

Judge. *See* Rater.

Kernels. A list of possible subjects or topics that are familiar to examinees and appropriate for developing prompts for tasks.

Knowledge, skills, abilities (KSA). Attributes of examinees that credentialing examinations are used to measure.

Licensure. Privilege to practice in a profession that the government grants to an individual.

Linear composite. A composite score produced using a linear algebraic expression. The total correct of an examination is a linear composite score because it is the sum of all the item scores.

Look-fors. A list of items or artifacts that raters should review (i.e., look for) in scoring a performance.

Moderation. *See* Adjudication.

Monitor. *See* Proctor.

Monitoring sets. Sets of task responses that are prescored by a validation committee and are used to determine that raters have not drifted from the standards set by the committee. During operational scoring, raters score monitoring sets and these scores are compared with the ratings of the validation committee.

Multiple hurdle. Examination process in which an examinee must pass one examination to be eligible for the subsequent examination.

Norm-referenced score interpretation. The meaning of scores derived from the examinee's ranking as compared with a group of people who have taken the exam before (e.g., your score placed you at the 88th percentile, meaning you scored as well or better than 88% of the examinees who took this examination).

Open ended. A task that allows multiple correct answers (e.g., narrative writing, art portfolio).

Open response. A task in which the response must address specific content (e.g., diagnosis of an illness).

Operational score. The final score as reported to examinees.

Parallel forms. *See* Alternate forms.

Parity model. The process by which rater disagreement is resolved by averaging the scores from the disagreeing raters with the score from a third rater.

Passing standard. The minimum score needed to pass an examination.

Performance. The execution of a series of acts to alter the environment in specified ways (e.g., a law candidate reviewing documents to write a proposal for a settlement or a teacher preparing a portfolio with reflections about her instruction).

Performance assessment. A system that includes (1) a purpose for the assessment, (2) tasks or prompts that elicit the performance, (3) a response demand that focuses the examinee's performance, and (4) systematic methods for rating performances.

Performance levels. In performance assessment, the levels of quality that represent the scale points of a rating rubric.

Performance standard. *See* Passing standard.

Polytomous scales. Scoring guides with more than two rating levels (e.g., 1, 2, 3, 4).

Practice sets. Prescored sets of responses through which raters, or judges, practice and learn the application of a scoring rubric.

Proctor. The person who assists the test examiners in distributing materials and monitoring the room for possible inappropriate examinee behaviors.

Proficiency levels. *See* Performance levels.

Prompt. The instructions that establish the problem or scenario for a task and elicit a response from an examinee.

Qualifying sets. Prescored responses with which raters are tested to determine if they meet the criteria to score tasks.

Rangefinding. Process by which an expert committee reviews large numbers of examinee responses to select exemplars of each score point in the full range of examinee performances.

Rater. A person trained to apply a scoring rubric to estimate the degree of proficiency displayed in a performance sample.

Rater agreement. A measure of the consistency of a pair of raters.

Rater mean. The resolution process by which rater disagreement is resolved by averaging the scores from the two original raters.

Rating. A scale point on a scoring rubric.

Read-behind/read-ahead. A procedure in which trainers and expert staff serve as a second reader of a sample of responses scored by a rater to monitor the quality of the rater's scores. Read-ahead differs from read-behind in that the staff read a sample of responses prior to the rater scoring them.

Reader. *See* Rater.

Recalibration sets. *See* Monitoring sets.

Reliability. The degree to which examinees' scores on an assessment are consistent across repetitions of the assessment (i.e., a measure of the "repeatibility" of exam scores).

Reported score. *See* Operational score.

Resolution. The process by which the disparate scores of a pair of raters are combined to form a single score.

Rubric. A scoring guide with a scale accompanied by descriptive anchors that define the possible scores for examinee performance.

Score. The rating of the examinee on an item, a group of items, or the entire examination.

Scoring criteria. *See* Criteria.

Scoring guides. A class of instruments (e.g., checklists, analytic rubrics, holistic rubrics) that specify criteria for rating examinee responses. *See also* Rubric.

Seeded papers. *See* Seeded responses.

Seeded responses. Prescored examples of examinee responses that are mixed in with live responses to monitor a rater's agreement with validation scores during operational scoring.

Selected response. A test item format that offers answer options (i.e., responses) from which the examinee chooses (i.e., selects).

Server. A computer that provides information to another computer.

Simulation. A form of performance assessment that mimics the actual conditions under which the task would naturally be performed (e.g., flight simulation).

Split-halves reliability. The correlation between the scores produced by splitting a test into two halves.

Standardized patient. A person trained to portray a patient scenario, or an actual patient using his or her own history and physical exam findings, for the assessment of the examining skills of a health care provider.

Standard setting. A judgmental process by which qualified persons make reasoned judgments about the level of performance required to pass an exam or to achieve a certain level of designation (e.g., basic, proficient, advanced).

Station. The area at which the examinee performs the task required in the assessment.

Subject-matter expert (SME). A person who is an authority in the subject matter that an examination will assess.

Table leader. *See* Expert rater.

Table of specifications. A chart that lists the test content and specifies the number or percentage of test items that cover each content area.

Task. In role delineation in the credentialing field, a statement of an activity carried out by a trained professional in the course of performing the activities of the profession. The task statement has several components (e.g., the activity, the object of the activity, how the activity is accomplished, and why the activity is performed). In education, a subject-matter exercise for which students must create a response.

Team leader. *See* Expert rater.

Tertium quid. The process by which rater disagreement is resolved by matching the score of a third rater with the closer of the two original raters.

Test administrator. The person who manages the staff, arranges schedules and rooms, and oversees the distribution of materials.

Test examiner. The person who distributes the examinations and reads the test instructions to the examinees.

Test framework. A section of the test design that describes the construct or domain that is the focus of the assessment.

Test plan. *See* Test specifications.

Test specifications. A description of the test characteristics and its components.

Testing agency. A company that provides test development, delivery, and diagnostic analyses.

Test–retest reliability. A measure of score consistency for a test that is administered on different occasions.

Trainer. *See* Expert rater.

Training sets. Prescored responses (e.g., essays, science experiments) used to train raters to apply the scoring criteria.

Transparency. Clarity of a task in terms of what the examinee is to do and how the performance will be evaluated.

Unit-weighted composite. A linear composite in which all the components have a unit (1) coefficient.

Validation committee. The committee that decides the levels of quality or proficiency that define each scale point of a rating rubric. This committee assigns scores to sets of examinee responses that will be used in training and monitoring raters.

Validation samples. Exemplar performances used in the training of raters to anchor the scale points of the scoring rubric.

Validity. The extent to which evidence supports test score interpretation for a given purpose.

Validity criterion. A set of exemplar performances used to establish the anchors for a rubric.

Weighted composite. A linear composite in which the coefficients of the components can be different from one another.

Written rationale. *See* Annotation.

References

Abedi, J. (1996). Interrater/test reliability system (ITRS). *Multivariate Behavioral Research, 31*(4), 409–417.

Abedi, J. (2003, July). *Linguistic modification of test items.* Paper presented at the National Center for Research on Evaluation, Standards, and Student Testing (CRESST) conference, Los Angeles, CA.

American Board for Certification in Orthotics and Prosthetics. (n.d.). *About ABC.* Retrieved February 11, 2006, from *www.abcop.org/About.asp*

American Board of Pediatric Dentistry (ABPD). (2007). *Oral clinical examination handbook.* Retrieved February 18, 2007, from *www.abpd.org/ pamphlets/oral_handbook.pdfvv*

American Educational Research Association (AERA), American Psychological Association (APA), & National Council on Measurement in Education (NCME). (1999). *Standards for educational and psychological testing.* Washington, DC: AERA.

Americans with Disabilities Act (ADA). (1990). Public Law No. 101-336, Section 201. Retrieved December 18, 2006, from *ada.gov/pubs/ada. txt*

Anderson, L. W., Krathwohl, D. R., Airasian, P. W., Cruikshank, K. A., Mayer, R. E., Pintrich, P. R., Raths, J., & Wittrock, M. C. (2001). *A taxonomy for learning, teaching, and assessing: A revision of Bloom's taxonomy of educational objectives* (abr. ed.). Upper Saddle River, NJ: Pearson Education, Inc.

Angoff, W. (1971). Norms, scales, and equivalent scores. In R. Thorndike (Ed.), *Educational measurement* (2nd ed., pp. 508–600). Washington, DC: American Council on Education.

Arter, J. (1992). *How to evaluate the quality of a performance assessment.* Portland, OR: Northwest Regional Educational Laboratory.

Arter, J., & McTighe, J. (2001). *Scoring rubrics in the classroom.* Thousand Oaks, CA: Corwin Press.

315

Bachman, L. (2002). Alternative interpretations of alternative assessments: Some validity issues in educational performance assessments. *Educational Measurement: Issues and Practice, 21*(3), 5–18.

Baker, E. (1997). Model-based performance assessment. *Theory into Practice, 36*(4), 247–254.

Baker, E., Aschbacher, P., Niemi, D., & Sato, E. (1992). *CRESST performance assessment models: Assessing content area explanations.* Los Angeles: University of California, Graduate School of Education, National Center for the Study of Evaluation, Standards, and Student Testing (CRESST).

Baker, L., & Wigfield, A. (1999). Dimensions of children's motivation for reading and their relations to reading activity and reading achievement. *Reading Research Quarterly, 34*(4), 452–477.

Baron, J. B. (1991). Strategies for the development of effective performance exercises. *Applied Measurement in Education, 4*(4), 305–318.

Becker, D., & Pomplun, M. (2006). Technical reporting and documentation. In S. Downing & T. Haladyna (Eds.), *Handbook of test development* (pp. 711–723). Mahwah, NJ: Erlbaum.

Bloom, B. S. (Ed.). (1956). *Taxonomy of educational objectives: Handbook 1. Cognitive domain.* New York: David McKay.

Boissonnade, P. (1927). *Life and work in medieval Europe* (E. Power, Trans.). New York: Knopf.

Bond, L. (1998). Culturally responsive pedagogy and the assessment of accomplished teaching. *Journal of Negro Education, 67*(3), 242–254.

Bond, L., Moss, P., & Carr, P. (1996). Fairness in large-scale performance assessment. In G. Phillips (Ed.), *Technical issues in large scale performance assessment* (pp. 117–140). Washington, DC: National Center for Education Statistics.

Bond, L., Smith, T., Baker, W., & Hattie, J. (2000). *The certification system of the National Board for Professional Teaching Standards: A construct and consequential validity study.* Greensboro: University of North Carolina, Center for Educational Research and Evaluation.

Braswell, J., Lutkus, A., Grigg, W., Santapau, S., Tay-Lim, B., & Johnson, M. (2001). *The nation's report card: Mathematics 2000* (NCES 2001–517). Washington, DC: U.S. Government Printing Office.

Breland, H. (1983). *The direct assessment of writing skill: A measurement review* (Technical Report No. 83-6). Princeton, NJ: College Entrance Examination Board.

Breland, H., & Jones, R. (1984). Perceptions of writing skills. *Written Communication, 1*(1), 101–109.

Brennan, R. (1992). An NCME instructional module on generalizability theory. *Educational Measurement: Issues and Practice, 11*(4), 27–34.

Brennan, R., & Johnson, E. (1995). Generalizability of performance assessments. *Educational Measurement: Issues and Practices, 14*(4), 9–12, 27.

Brennan, R., & Kane, M. (1977). An index of dependability for mastery tests. *Journal of Educational Measurement, 14,* 277–289.

Brown, W. (1910). Some experimental results in the correlation of mental abilities. *British Journal of Psychology, 3,* 296–322.

California State Board of Education. (2005). English-language arts content standards for California public schools kindergarten through grade twelve. Retrieved September 7, 2006, from www.cde.ca.gov/re/pn/fd/documents/elacontentstnds.pdf

Camara, W. (2003). *Scoring the essay on the SAT writing section* (Research Summary No. 10). New York: The College Board. Retrieved February 4, 2007, from *www.collegeboard.com/research/pdf/031367researchsummary_26516.pdf*

Case, S. (2005). Demystifying scaling to the MBE: How'd you do that? *The Bar Examiner, 74*(2), 45–46.

Ceprano, M., & Garan, E. (1998). Emerging voices in a university pen-pal project: Layers of discovery in action research. *Reading Research and Instruction, 38*(1), 31–56.

Chambers, K., Boulet, J., & Gary, N. (2000). The management of patient encounter time in a high-stakes assessment using standardized patients. *Medical Education, 34*(10), 813–817.

Chase, C. (1986). Essay test scoring: Interaction of relevant variables. *Journal of Educational Measurement, 23,* 33–41.

Cherry, R., & Meyer, P. (1993). Reliability issues in holistic assessment. In M. Williamson & B. Huot (Eds.), *Validating holistic scoring for writing assessment: Theoretical and empirical foundations* (pp. 109–141). Cresskill, NJ: Hampton Press.

Cizek, G. (2001a). Cheating to the test. *Education Next.* Retrieved January 28, 2007, from *www.hoover.org/publications/ednext/3390971.html*

Cizek, G. (Ed.). (2001b). *Setting performance standards: Concepts, methods, and perspectives.* Mahwah, NJ: Erlbaum.

Cizek, G., Bunch, M., & Koons, H. (2004). An NCME module on setting performance standards: Contemporary methods. *Educational Measurement: Issues and Practice, 23*(4), 31–50.

Claggett, F. (1999). Integrating reading and writing in large-scale assessment. In C. Cooper & L. Odell (Eds.), *Evaluating writing: The role of teachers' knowledge about text, learning, and culture* (pp. 344–365). Urbana, IL: National Council of Teachers of English.

Clauser, B. (2000). Recurrent issues and recent advances in scoring performance assessments. *Applied Psychological Measurement, 24*(4), 310–324.

Clauser, B., Clyman, S., & Swanson, D. (1999). Components of rater error in a complex performance assessment. *Journal of Educational Measurement, 36*(1), 29–45.

Clauser, B., Ripkey, D., Fletcher, B., King, A., Klass, D., & Orr, N. (1993). A comparison of pass/fail classifications made with scores from the NBME standardized-patient examination and Part II examination. *Academic Medicine, 68*(10), S7–S9.

Clemans, W. (1971). Test administration. In R. Thorndike (Ed.), *Educational measurement* (2nd ed., pp. 188–201). Washington, DC: American Council on Education.

Coffman, W. (1971a). Essay examinations. In R. Thorndike (Ed.), *Educational measurement* (2nd ed., pp. 271–302). Washington, DC: American Council on Education.

Coffman, W. (1971b). On the reliability of ratings of essay examinations in English. *Research in the Teaching of English, 5*, 24–36.

Cohen, A., & Wollack, J. (2006). Test administration, security, scoring, and reporting. In R. Brennan (Ed.), Educational measurement (4th ed., pp. 355–386). Westport, CT: American Council on Education and Praeger.

Coons, C., Gay, E., Fandal, A., Ker, C. & Frankenburg, W. (1981). *The Home Screening Questionnaire reference manual.* Denver: J.F.K. Child Development Center.

Costa, A. L. (Ed.). (1991). *Developing minds: Programs for teaching thinking.* Alexandria, VA: Association for Supervision and Curriculum Development.

Council of Chief State School Officers. (2002). *Annual survey of student assessment programs, 2000/2001.* Washington, DC: CCSSO Publications.

Creighton, S. (2006). *Examining alternative scoring rubrics on a statewide test: The impact of different scoring methods on science and social studies performance assessments.* Unpublished doctoral dissertation, University of South Carolina, Columbia.

Crick, J. E., & Brennan, R. L. (1984). *Manual for GENOVA: A generalized analysis of variance system.* Iowa City, IA: American College Testing Program.

Crocker, L. (1997). Assessing content representativeness of performance assessment exercises. *Applied Measurement in Education, 10*(1), 83–95.

Crocker, L., & Algina, J. (1986). *Introduction to classical and modern test theory.* Fort Worth, TX: Holt, Rinehart, & Winston.

Cronbach, L. (1943). On estimates of test reliability. *Journal of Educational Psychology, 34*, 485–494.

Cronbach, L. (1949). *Essentials of psychological testing.* New York: Harper & Brothers.

Cronbach, L. (1951). Coefficient alpha and the internal structure of tests. *Psychometrika, 16*, 297–334.

Cronbach, L., Linn, R., Brennan, R., & Haertel, E. (1997). Generalizability analysis for performance assessments of student achievement or school effectiveness. *Educational and Psychological Measurement 57*(3), 373–399.

CTB McGraw-Hill (2002). *TerraNova, the second edition: Technical bulletin 1.* Monterey, CA: CTB McGraw-Hill.

Daly, J., & Dickson-Markman, F. (1982). Contrast effects in evaluating essays. *Journal of Educational Measurement, 19*(4), 309–316.

Daro, P. (1996). Standards and portfolio assessment. In J. Baron & D. Wolf (Eds.), *Performance-based student assessment: Challenges and possibilities: Ninety-fifth yearbook of the National Society for the Study of Education* (pp. 239–260). Chicago: University of Chicago Press.

De Champlain, A., & LaDuca, A. (2007). Examining contextual effects in a practice analysis. *Educational Measurement: Issues and Practice, 26*(3), 3–10.

De Champlain, A., Macmillan, M., King, A., Klass, D., & Margolis, M. (1999). Assessing the impacts of intra-site and inter-site checklist recording discrepancies on the reliability of scores obtained in a nationally administered standardized patient examination. *Academic Medicine, 74*(10), S52–S54.

De Champlain, A., Macmillan, M., Margolis, M., Klass, D., Nungester, R., Schimpfhauser, F., et al. (1999). Modeling the effects of security breaches on students' performances on a large-scale standardized patient examination. *Academic Medicine, 74*(10), S49–S51.

Diederich, P. (1974). *Measuring growth in English.* Urbana, IL: National Council of Teachers of English.

Downing, S. (2006). Twelve steps for effective test development. In S. Downing & T. Haladyna (Eds.), *Handbook of test development* (pp. 3–25). Mahwah, NJ: Erlbaum.

Dows, M. (2005). One administrator's thoughts on—and experiences with—security of test materials. *The Bar Examiner, 74*(3), 6–9, 11–13.

Duhl, S., & Duhl, G. M. (2004). Testing applicants with disabilities. *The Bar Examiner, 73*(1), 7–32.

Dunbar, S., Koretz, D., & Hoover, H. (1991). Quality control in the development and use of performance assessments. *Applied Measurement in Education, 4*(4), 289–303.

Dwyer, C. (1993). Innovation and reform: Examples from teacher assessment. In R. Bennett & W. Ward (Eds.), *Construction versus choice in cognitive measurement* (pp. 265–289). Hillsdale, NJ: Erlbaum.

Dwyer, C. (1998). Psychometrics of Praxis III: Classroom performance assessments. *Journal of Personnel Evaluation in Education, 12*(2), 163–187.

Educational Testing Service (ETS). (1999). *Technical analysis report.* Princeton, NJ: Author.

Educational Testing Service (ETS). (2002). *How to interpret and use GRE Analytical Writing (GRE-AW) scores.* Princeton, NJ: Author.

Educational Testing Service (ETS). (2004). *The GRE Analytic Writing measure: An asset in admissions decisions.* Princeton, NJ: Author.

Education Testing Service (ETS). (2005). *GRE details: Test takers.* Retrieved January 3, 2006, from *www.ets.org*

Eisner, E. (1999). The uses and limits of performance assessment. *Phi Delta Kappan, 80*(9), 658–660.

Engelhard, G., Jr. (1994). Examining rater errors in the assessment of written composition with a many-faceted Rasch model. *Journal of Educational Measurement 31*(2), 93–112.

Federation of State Medical Boards of the United States (FMBUS) & National Board of Medical Examiners (NBME). (2004). *2005 USMLE Step 2 clinical skills (CS) content description and general information.* Retrieved May 26, 2006, from *www.usmle.org/step2/Step2CS/Step2CS2005GI/2005Step2CS.pdf*

Federation of State Medical Boards of the United States (FMBUS) & National Board of Medical Examiners (NBME). (2008). *United States Medical Licensure Examination Step 2 clinical skills (CS) content description and general information: 2008.* Retrieved January 10, 2008, from *www.usmle.org/Examinations/step2/step2ck_content.html*

Federation of State Medical Boards of the United States (FMBUS) & National Board of Medical Examiners (NBME). (2007). *Bulletin of information: 2008.* Retrieved February 4, 2008, from *http://www.usmle.org*

Federation of State Medical Boards of the United States (FMBUS) & National Board of Medical Examiners (NBME). (2005). *USMLE orientation materials: Onsite orientation for Step 2 CS.* Retrieved December 30, 2005, from *www.usmle.org/Orientation/2005/menu.htm*

Feuer, M., & Fulton, K. (1993). The many faces of performance assessment. *Phi Delta Kappan, 74*(6), 478.

Fitzpatrick, R., & Morrison, E. (1971). Performance and product evaluation. In R. Thorndike (Ed.), *Educational measurement* (pp. 237–270). Washington, DC: American Council of Education.

Florida Department of Education. (2005). *Grade level expectations for the sunshine state standards: Mathematics: 6–8.* Retrieved September 7, 2006, from *www.firn.edu/doe/curric/prek12/pdf/math6.pdf*

Fortune, J., & Cromack, T. (1995). Developing and using clinical examination. In J. Impara (Ed.), *Licensure testing: Purposes, procedures, and practices* (pp. 149–165). Lincoln, NE: Buros Institute of Mental Measurement.

Franke, W. (1968). The reform and abolition of the Chinese examination system. *Harvard East Asian Monographs, 10.*

Gao, X., Shavelson, R., & Baxter, G. (1994). Generalizability of large-scale performance assessments in science: Promises and problems. *Applied Measurement in Education, 7*(4), 323–342.

Georgia Department of Education. (2001). *Assessment and instructional guide for the Georgia high school writing test.* Atlanta: Author.

Georgia Department of Education. (2006). *Assessment and instructional guide for the Georgia High School Writing Test.* Atlanta: Author.

Georgia Department of Education. (2007). *Georgia writing assessments: Weighting of domains.* Atlanta: Author.

Gitomer, D. (1993). Performance assessment and education measurement. In R. Bennett & W. Ward (Eds.), *Construction versus choice in cognitive measurement* (pp. 241–263). Hillsdale, NJ: Erlbaum.

Godshalk, F., Swineford, F., & Coffman, W. (1966). *The measurement of writing ability.* Princeton, NJ: College Entrance Examination Board.

Gong, B., & Reidy, E. (1996). Assessment and accountability in Kentucky's school reform. In J. Baron & D. Wolf (Eds.), *Performance-based student assessment: Challenges and possibilities* (pp. 215–233). Chicago: National Society for the Study of Education.

Gonzales, P., Guzmán, J., Partelow, L., Pahlke, E., Jocelyn, L., Kastberg, D., et al. (2004). *Highlights from the trends in international mathematics and science study (TIMSS) 2003* (NCES 2005–005). Washington, DC: U.S. Government Printing Office.

Gordon, B. (1999). *Reading for evidence.* Athens: University of Georgia, Georgia Center for Assessment.

Gordon, B. (2000, April). *A practitioner's perspective on scoring resolution methods: In defense of differences.* Paper presented at the annual meeting of the American Educational Research Association, New Orleans, LA.

Gosling, G. (1966). *Marking English compositions.* Victoria: Australian Council for Educational Research.

Greenwald, E., Persky, H., Campbell, J., & Mazzeo, J. (1999). *The NAEP 1998 writing report card for the nation and the states* (NCES 1999-462). Washington, DC: U.S. Government Printing Office.

Grigg, W., Daane, M., Jin, Y., & Campbell, J. (2003). *The nation's report card: Reading 2002* (NCES 2003-521). Washington, DC: U.S. Government Printing Office.

Gronlund, N. (2003). *Assessment of student achievement* (7th ed.). Boston: Allyn & Bacon.

Gronlund, N. (2006). *Assessment of student achievement* (8th ed.). Boston: Allyn & Bacon.

Gross, L. (1993, Winter). Assessing clinical skills in optometry: A national standardized test. *CLEAR Exam Review*, 18–23.

Gulliksen, H. (1987). *Theory of mental tests*. New York: Wiley.

Guskey, T. (1994). Introduction. In T. Guskey (Ed.), *High-stakes performance assessment: Perspectives on Kentucky's educational reform* (pp. 1–5). Thousand Oaks, CA: Corwin Press.

Haertel, E., & Linn, R. (1996). Comparability. In G. Phillips (Ed.), *Technical issues in large-scale performance assessment* (pp. 59–78). Washington, DC: National Center for Education Statistics.

Haladyna, T. (2004). *Developing and validating multiple-choice items* (3rd ed.). Mahwah, NJ: Erlbaum.

Haladyna, T., & Shindoll, R. (1989). Item shells: A method for writing effective multiple-choice test items. *Evaluation and the Health Professions, 12*, 97–104.

Hale, M. (1982). History of employment testing. In A. Wigdor & W. Garner (Eds.), *Ability testing: Uses, consequences, and controversies. Part II: Documentation section* (pp. 3–38). Washington, DC: National Academy Press.

Hambleton, R., & Plake, B. (1995). Using an extended Angoff procedure to set standards on complex performance assessments. *Applied Measurement in Education, 8*(1), 41–55.

Haney, W., Russell, M., & Bebell, D. (2004). Drawing on education: Using drawings to document schooling and support change. *Harvard Educational Review, 74*(3), 241–272.

Hayes, J., & Hatch, J. (1999). Issues in measuring reliability: Correlation versus percentage of agreement. *Written Communication, 16*(3), 354–367.

Hayes, J., Hatch, J., & Silk, C. (2000). Does holistic assessment predict writing performance?: Estimating the consistency of student performance on holistically scored writing assignments. *Written Communication, 17*(1), 3–26.

Herman, J., Aschbacher, P., &Winters, L. (1992). *A practical guide to alternative assessment*. Alexandria, VA: Association for Supervision and Curriculum Development.

Hertz, N., & Chinn, R. (2000). *Licensure examinations*. Retrieved January 10, 2008, from *www.clearhq.org/Licensure_examinations.htm*

Hewitt, G. (1995). *A portfolio primer: Teaching, collecting, and assessing student writing*. Portsmouth, NH: Heinemann.

Hieronymous, A., Hoover, H., Cantor, N., & Oberley, K. (1987). *Handbook for focused holistic scoring*. Chicago: Riverside.

Hill, R. (2002, April). *Examining the reliability of accountability systems*. Paper presented at the annual meeting of the American Educational Research Association, New Orleans, LA.

Hogan, T., & Mishler, C. (1980). Relationships between essay tests and objective tests of language skills for elementary school students. *Journal of Educational Measurement, 17,* 219–227.

Hopkins, K. (1998). *Educational and psychological measurement and evaluation* (8th ed.). Needham Heights, MA: Allyn & Bacon.

Hoskin, K. (1979). The examination, disciplinary power and rational schooling. In *History of education* (Vol. 8, pp. 135–146). London: Taylor & Francis.

Humphris, G., & Kaney S. (2000). The Objective Structured Video Exam for assessment of communication skills. *Medical Education, 34,* 939–945.

Huot, B. (1990). The literature of direct writing assessment: Major concerns and prevailing trends. *Review of Educational Research, 60*(2), 237–263.

Huynh, H., Meyer, P., & Barton, K. (2000). *Technical documentation for the 1999 Palmetto Achievement Challenge Tests of English language arts and mathematics, grades three through eight*. Columbia: University of South Carolina.

International Reading Association (IRA) & National Council of Teachers of English (NCTE). (1996). *Standards for the English language arts*. Newark, DE: International Reading Association.

International Test Commission. (2006). International guidelines on computer-based and internet-delivered testing. *International Journal of Testing, 6*(2), 143–171.

Jaeger, R., Mullis, I., Bourque, M., & Shakrani, S. (1996). Setting performance standards for performance assessments: Some fundamental issues, current practice, and technical dilemmas. In G. Phillips (Ed.), *Technical issues in large scale performance assessment* (pp. 79–115). Washington, DC: National Center for Education Statistics.

Jakwerth, P. (1999). TIMMS performance assessment results: United States. *Studies in Educational Evaluation, 25,* 277–281.

Johanson, G., & Motlomelo, S. (1998, April). *An item format continuum for classroom assessment*. Paper presented at the annual meeting of the American Educational Research Association, San Diego, CA.

Johnson, R., Fisher, S., Willeke, M., & McDaniel, F. (2003). Portfolio assessment in a collaborative program evaluation: The reliability and validity of a family literacy portfolio. *Evaluation and Program Planning, 26,* 367–377.

Johnson, R., McDaniel, F., & Willeke, M. (2000). Using portfolios in program evaluation: An investigation of interrater reliability. *American Journal of Evaluation, 21*(1), 65–80.

Johnson, R., Penny, J., Fisher, S., & Kuhs, T. (2003). Score resolution: An investigation of the reliability and validity of resolved scores. *Applied Measurement in Education, 16*(4), 299–322.

Johnson, R., Penny, J., & Gordon, B. (2000). The relation between score resolution methods and interrater reliability: An empirical study of an analytic scoring rubric. *Applied Measurement in Education, 13*(2), 121–138.

Johnson, R., Penny, J., & Gordon, B. (2001). Score resolution and the interrater reliability of holistic scores in rating essays. *Written Communication, 18*(2), 229–249.

Johnson, R., Penny, J., Gordon, B., Shumate, S., & Fisher, S. (2005). Resolving score differences in the rating of writing samples: Does discussion improve the accuracy of scores? *Language Assessment Quarterly, 2*(2), 117–146.

Johnson, R., Penny, J., & Johnson, C. (2000, April). *A conceptual framework for score resolution in the rating of performance assessments: The union of validity and reliability.* Paper presented at the annual meeting of the American Educational Research Association, New Orleans, LA.

Johnson, R., Penny, J., Schneider, C., Porchea, S., Mazzie, D., & Hoffman, D. (2003, April). *Score augmentation and the variability of the rater and task facets in generalizability studies.* Paper presented at the annual meeting of the American Educational Research Association, Chicago.

Johnson, R., Willeke, M., Bergman, T., & Steiner, D. (1996). *Collaboration to create a family literacy portfolio system to assess program impact: Year two.* Paper presented at the annual meeting of the American Evaluation Association, Atlanta, GA.

Johnson, R., Willeke, M., Bergman, T., & Steiner, D. (1997). Family literacy portfolios: Development and implementation. *Window on the World of Family Literacy, 2*(2), 10–17.

Johnson, R., Willeke, M., & Steiner, D. (1998). Stakeholder collaboration in the design and implementation of a family literacy portfolio assessment. *American Journal of Evaluation, 19*(3), 339–353.

Kane, M. (1997). Model-based practice analysis and test specifications. *Applied Measurement in Education, 10*(1), 5–18.

Khattri, N., Reeve, A., & Kane, M. (1998). *Principles and practices of performance assessment.* Mahwah, NJ: Erlbaum.

Khattri, N., & Sweet, D. (1996). Assessment reform: Promises and challenges. In M. Kane & R. Mitchell (Eds.), *Implementing performance assessment: Promises, problems, and challenges* (pp. 1–21). Mahwah, NJ: Erlbaum.

Klein, S., Stecher, B., Shavelson, R., McCaffrey, D., Ormseth, T., Bell, R., et al. (1998). Analytic versus holistic scoring of science performance tasks. *Applied Measurement in Education, 1*(2), 121–137.

Knapp, J., & Knapp, L. (1995). Practice analysis: Building the foundation for validity. In J. Impara (Ed.), *Licensure testing: Purposes, procedures, and practices* (pp. 93–116). Lincoln, NE: Buros Institute of Mental Measurement.

Kobrin, J., & Kimmel, E. (2006). *Test development and technical information on the writing section of the SAT reasoning test.* New York: College Board. Retrieved November 17, 2006, from *www.collegeboard. com/research/pdf/RN-25.pdf*

Koretz, D., Stecher, B., Klein, S., & McCaffrey, D. (1994). The Vermont portfolio assessment program: Findings and implications. *Educational Measurement: Issues and Practice, 13*(3), 5–16.

Kracke, E. (1953). *Civil service in early Sung China.* Cambridge, MA: Harvard University Press.

Küder, G., & Richardson, M. (1937). The theory of the estimation of test reliability. *Psychometrika, 2*(3), 151–160.

LaDuca, A. (1994). Validation of professional licensure examinations. *Evaluation and the Health Professions, 17,* 178–197.

LaDuca, A. (2006). Commentary: A closer look at task analysis: Reactions to Wang, Schnipke, and Witt. *Educational Measurement: Issues and Practices, 25*(2), 31–33.

LaDuca, A., Downing, S., & Henzel, T. (1995). Systematic item writing and test construction. In J. Impara (Ed.), *Licensure testing: Purposes, procedures, and practices* (pp. 117–148). Lincoln, NE: Buros Institute of Mental Measurement.

Lamb, K. (2001). How to avoid losing a test book: Interviews with the experts. *The Bar Examiner, 70*(3), 18–27.

Lane, S. (1993). The conceptual framework for the development of a mathematics performance assessment instrument. *Educational Measurement: Issues and Practices, 12*(2), 16–23.

Lane, S., Liu, M., Ankenmann, R., & Stone, C. (1996). Generalizability and validity of a mathematics performance assessment. *Journal of Educational Measurement, 33*(1), 71–92.

Lane, S., & Stone, C. (2006). Performance assessment. In R. Brennan (Ed.), *Educational measurement* (4th ed., pp. 387–431). Westport, CT: American Council on Education and Praeger.

Lau, G., & LeMahieu, P. (1997). Changing roles: Evaluator and teacher collaborating in school change. *Evaluation and Program Planning, 20*(1), 7–15.

LeMahieu, P., Gitomer, D., & Eresh, J. (1995). Portfolios in large-scale assessment: Difficult but not impossible. *Educational Measurement: Issues and Practice, 14*(3), 11–16, 25–28.

Lenel, J. (1990a). The essay examination part I: The problem of low reliability. *The Bar Examiner, 59*(1), 18–22.

Lenel, J. (1990b). The essay examination part II: Construction of the essay examination. *The Bar Examiner, 59*(2), 40–43.

Lenel, J. (1990c). The essay examination part III: Grading the essay examination. *The Bar Examiner, 59*(3), 16–23.

Linn, R., Baker, E., & Dunbar, S. (1991). Complex, performance-based assessment: Expectations and validation criteria. *Educational Researcher, 20*(8), 15–21.

Linn, R., & Burton, E. (1994). Performance-based assessment: Implications of task specificity. *Educational Measurement: Issues and Practices, 13*(1), 5–8, 15.

Livingston, S. (1998, April). *Results of the pilot test of the School Leaders' Licensure Assessment.* Paper presented at the annual meeting of the American Educational Research Association, San Diego, CA.

Longford, N. T. (1994). Reliability of essay rating and score adjustment. *Journal of Education and Behavioral Statistics, 19*(3), 171–200.

Lord, F., & Novick, M. (1968). *Statistical theories of mental test scores.* Reading, MA: Addison-Wesley.

Lumley, T. (2002). Assessment criteria in a large-scale writing test: What do they really mean to the raters? *Language Testing, 19*(3), 246–276.

Macmillan, M., De Champlain, A., & Klass, D. (1999). Using tagged items to detect threats to security in a nationally administered standardized patient examination. *Academic Medicine, 74*(10), S55–S57.

Madaus, G., & O'Dwyer, L. (1999). A short history of performance assessment. *Phi Delta Kappan, 80*(9), 688–695.

Markham, L. (1976). Influences of handwriting quality on teacher evaluation of written work. *American Educational Research Journal, 13*, 277–284.

Marzano, R. J. (2001). *Designing a new taxonomy of educational objectives.* Thousand Oaks, CA: Corwin Press.

Massachusetts Department of Education. (2001). Science and technology/engineering curriculum framework. Retrieved March 29, 2006, from www.doe.mass.edu/frameworks/scitech/2001/standards/ls6_8.html

Massachusetts Department of Education. (2005). *Principal's administration manual: Massachusettes Comprehensive Assessment System.* Retrieved January 15, 2006, from *www.doe.mass.edu/mcas/2005/admin/manual/PAM.pdf*

Mead, R., Smith, R., & Melby, K. (2003). *Technical analysis: Pennsylvania System of School Assessment 2002, Writing PSSA Grade 6 and 9.* Harrisburg: Pennsylvania Department of Education.

McColly, W., & Remstad, R. (1965). Composition rating scales for general merit: An experimental evaluation. *Journal of Educational Research 59*, 55–56.

McMillan, J. H. (2001). *Classroom assessment: Principals and practice for effective instruction* (2nd ed.). Boston: Allyn & Bacon.

Messick, S. (1993a). Trait equivalence as construct validity of score interpretation across multiple methods of measurement. In R. Bennett & W. Ward (Eds.), *Construction versus choice in cognitive measurement* (pp. 61–73). Hillsdale, NJ: Erlbaum.

Messick, S. (1993b). Validity. In R. Linn (Ed.), *Educational measurement,* (3rd ed., pp. 13–103). Washington, DC: American Council on Education.

Messick, S. (1994). The interplay of evidence and consequence in the validation of performance assessments. *Educational Researcher, 23*(2), 13–23.

Messick, S. (1996). Validity of performance assessments. In G. Phillips (Ed.), *Technical issues in large-scale performance assessment* (pp. 1–18). Washington, DC: National Center for Education Statistics.

Metfessel, N., Michael, W., & Kirsner, D. (1969). Instrumentation of Bloom's and Krathwohl's taxonomies for the writing of behavioral objectives. *Psychology in the Schools, 6,* 227–231.

Microsoft. (1993/1994). *Microsoft Word version 6.0: User's guide.* Redmond, WA: Author.

Millman, J., & Greene, J. (1993). The specification and development of tests of achievement and ability. In R. Linn (Ed.), *Educational measurement,* (3rd ed., pp. 335–366). Washington, DC: American Council on Education.

Mills, R. (1996). Statewide portfolio assessment: The Vermont experience. In J. Baron & D. Wolf (Eds.), *Performance-based student assessment: Challenges and possibilities* (pp. 192–214). Chicago: National Society for the Study of Education.

Mislevy, R., Steinberg, L., & Almond, R. (2002). Design and analysis in task-based language assessment. *Language Testing, 19*(4), 477–496.

Mislevy, R., Wilson, M., Ercikan, K., & Chudowsky, N. (2003). Psychometric principles in student assessment. In T. Kellaghan & D. Stufflebeam (Eds.), *International handbook of educational evaluation* (pp. 489–532). Boston: Kluwer Academic.

Miyazaki, I. (1976). *China's examination hell: The civil service examinations of imperial China* (C. Schirokauer, Trans.). New York: Weatherhill.

Moon, T., & Hughes, K. (2002). Training and scoring issues in large-scale writing assessments. *Educational Measurement: Issues and Practices, 21*(2), 15–19.

Morris, N. (1961). An historian's view of examinations. In S. Wiseman (Ed.), *Examinations and English education* (pp. 1–43). Manchester, UK: Manchester University Press.

Moss, P., Schutz, A., & Collins, K. (1997). *Developing coherence between assessment and reform: An integrative approach to portfolio evaluation for teacher licensure.* Paper presented at the annual meeting of the American Educational Research Association, Chicago.

MPR Associates. (1997). *Item specifications for the Voluntary National Test in 4th-grade reading.* Retrieved April 26, 2006, from *www. mprinc.com/pubs/pdf/national_test_reading.pdf*

Mullis, I. (1984). Scoring direct writing assessments: What are the alternatives? *Educational Measurement: Issues and Practices, 3*, 16–18.

Music Educators National Conference. (1994). *National standards for arts education: What every young American should know and be able to do in the arts.* Reston, VA: Author.

Myers, M. (1980). *A procedure for writing assessment and holistic scoring.* Urbana, IL: National Council of Teachers of English.

Myford, C., & Wolfe, E. (2002). When raters disagree, then what: Examining a third-rating discrepancy resolution procedure and its utility for identifying unusual patterns of ratings. *Journal of Applied Measurement, 3*(3), 300–324.

National Assessment Governing Board. (2004a). *Mathematics framework for the 2005 National Assessment of Educational Progress.* Washington, DC: Author.

National Assessment Governing Board. (2004b). *Reading framework for the 2005 National Assessment of Educational Progress.* Washington, DC: Author.

National Assessment Governing Board. (2004c). *Science framework for the 2005 National Assessment of Educational Progress.* Washington, DC: Author.

National Board for Professional Teaching Standards (NBPTS). (2001). *Early and middle childhood art: Scoring guide.* Washington, DC: Author.

National Board for Professional Teaching Standards (NBPTS). (2004a). *Adolescent and young adulthood mathematics scoring guide*: Retrieved July 28, 2005, from *www.nbpts.org/candidates/scoringguides.cfm*

National Board for Professional Teaching Standards (NBPTS). (2004b). *Early adolescent English language arts portfolio instructions.* Arlington, VA: Author.

National Board for Professional Teaching Standards (NBPTS). (2005). *Early childhood generalist scoring guide.* Arlington, VA: Author.

National Board for Professional Teaching Standards (NBPTS). (2006a). *About NBPTS*. Retrieved April 5, 2006, from *www.nbpts.org/about/index.cfm*

National Board for Professional Teaching Standards (NBPTS). (2006b). *Standards and National Board certification: Assessment development*. Retrieved April 5, 2006, from *www.nbpts.org/standards/dev.cfm#gen*

National Board for Professional Teaching Standards (NBPTS). (2007). *2007 guide to National Board certification*. San Antonio, TX: Author.

National Board for Professional Teaching Standards (NBPTS). (2008). Fees and financial support. Retrieved January 10, 2008, from *www.nbpts.org/become_a_candidate/fees_financial_support*

National Board of Medical Examiners (NBME). (2003). *Test administration handbook: A general guide of best practices for the administration of NBME subject exams*. Philadelphia: Author.

National Board of Medical Examiners (NBME). (2008). *Examination fees*. Retrieved February 4, 2008, from *www.nbme.org/programs-services/medical-students/USMLE.html*

National Center for Educational Statistics (NCES). (2000, November). How does NAEP ensure consistency in scoring? *Focus on NAEP*, 4(2), 1–4.

National Center for Education Statistics (2005). NAEP questions. Retrieved September 5, 2005, from *nces.ed.gov/nationsreportcard*

National Center for Education Statistics (NCES). (2007). What does the NAEP U.S. history assessment measure? Retrieved May 8, 2008, from *nces.ed.gov/nationsreportcard/ushistory/whatmeasure.asp*

National Conference of Bar Examiners (NCBE). (2001). *The Multistate Performance Test*. Retrieved April 22, 2006, from *www.ncbex.org/tests.htm*

National Conference of Bar Examiners (NCBE). (2004). *2004 Statistics*. Retrieved May 18, 2006, from *www.ncbex.org/stats/pdf/2004stats.pdf*

National Conference of Bar Examiners (NCBE). (2005). *The Multistate Essay Exam*. Retrieved January 3, 2006, from *www.ncbex.org/tests.htm*

National Conference of Bar Examiners (NCBE). (2006). *The Multistate Bar Examination*. Retrieved September 23, 2006, from *www.ncbex.org/multistate-tests/mbe*

National Conference of Bar Examiners (NCBE) & American Bar Association (ABA). (2005). *Bar admission requirements, 2005*. Retrieved August 29, 2005, from *www.ncbex.org/tests.htm*

National Council of State Boards of Nursing. (2004). *NCLEX-PN®: Test plan for the National Council Licensure Examination for Practical/ Vocational Nurses.* Chicago: Author.

National Council of Teachers of Mathematics (NCTM). (2000). *Principles and standards for school mathematics.* Reston, VA: Author.

National Education Goals Panel. (1996). *Profile of 1994–1995 state assessment systems and reported results.* Washington, DC: Author.

New Jersey Department of Education. (2005). *Grade Eight Proficiency Assessment (GEPA) technical report.* Trenton, NJ: Author.

Newble, D., & Jaeger, K. (1983). The affect of assessments and examinations on the learning of medical students. *Medical Education, 17,* 165–171.

Newton, T. (2005). Recent developments in high-tech cheating. *The Bar Examiner, 74*(3), 10.

Nitko, A. (1983). *Educational tests and measurement: An introduction.* New York: Harcourt Brace Jovanovich.

Norris, D., Oppler, S., Kuang, D., Day, R., & Adams, K. (2006). *The College Board SAT® writing validation study: An assessment of predictive and incremental validity* (Research Report No. 2006-2). New York: College Board.

North Carolina Department of Instruction. (1999). *Focused holistic scoring guide: The expository composition, grade 7, 1998–1999.* Raleigh, NC: Author.

Nunnally, J. (1978). *Psychometric theory* (2nd ed.). New York: McGraw-Hill.

O'Neill, T., Buckendahl, C., Plake, B., & Taylor, L. (2007). Recommending a nursing-specific standard for the IELTS examination. *Language Assessment Quarterly, 4*(4), 295–317.

O'Sullivan, C., Lauko, M., Grigg, W., Qian, J., & Zhang, J. (2003). *The Nation's Report Card: Science 2000* (NCES 2003–453). Washington, DC: U.S. Government Printing Office.

Office of Technology Assessment. (1992). *Testing in American schools: Asking the right questions* (OTA-SET-519). Washington, DC: U.S. Government Printing Office.

Patsula, L., Clauser, B., Clyman, S., & Fan, V. (1998, April). *Resolving rater discrepancies in scoring performance assessments.* Paper presented at the annual meeting of the National Council on Measurement in Education, San Diego, CA.

Penny, J. (2003). My life as a reader. *Assessing Writing, 8,* 192–215.

Penny, J. (2006). *Interrater reliability of the fall 2006 Qualifying Examination.* Technical report prepared for the American Board of Pediatric Dentists. Morrisville, NC: CASTLE Worldwide.

Penny, J., Johnson, R., & Gordon, B. (2000a). The effect of rating augmentation on inter-rater reliability: An empirical study of a holistic rubric. *Assessing Writing, 7*(2), 143–164.

Penny, J., Johnson, R., & Gordon, B. (2000b). Using rating augmentation to expand the scale of an analytic rubric. *Journal of Experimental Education, 68*(3), 269–287.

Persky, H., Daane, M., & Jin, Y. (2003). *The Nation's report card: Writing 2002* (NCES 2003-529). Washington, DC: U.S. Government Printing Office.

Persky, H., Sandene, B., & Askew, J. (1998). *The NAEP 1997 arts report card* (NCES 1999-486). Washington, DC: U.S. Government Printing Office.

Phillips, S. (2000, April). Legal corner: GI forum v. TEA. *NCME Newsletter, 8.*

Plake, B., & Hambleton, R. (1999/2000). A standard-setting method designed for complex performance assessments. *Educational Assessment, 6*(3), 197–215.

Plake, B., & Hambleton, R. (2001). The analytic judgment method for setting standards on complex performance assessment. In G. Cizek (Ed.), *Setting performance standards: Concepts, methods, and perspectives* (pp. 283-312). Mahwah, NJ: Erlbaum.

Popp, R. (1992). *Family portfolios: Documenting change in parent–child relationships.* Louisville, KY: National Center for Family Literacy.

Quellmalz, E. (1986). Writing skills assessment. In R. Berk (Ed.), *Performance assessment: Methods and applications* (pp. 492–508). Baltimore: John Hopkins University Press.

Raymond, M. (2001). Job analysis and the specification of content for licensure and certification examinations. *Applied Measurement in Education, 14*(4), 369–415.

Raymond, M. (2002). A practical guide to practice analysis for credentialing examinations. *Educational Measurement: Issues and Practice, 21*(3), 25–37.

Raymond, M. (2005). An NCME module on developing and administering practice analysis questionnaires. *Educational Measurement: Issues and Practice, 24*(2), 29–41.

Raymond, M., & Neustel, S. (2006). Determining the content of credentialing examinations. In S. Downing & T. Haladyna (Eds.), *Handbook of test development* (pp. 181–223). Mahwah, NJ: Erlbaum.

Reckase, M. (1997, March). *Statistical test specifications for performance assessments: Is this an oxymoron?* Paper presented at the annual meeting of the National Council on Measurement in Education, Chicago.

Registry of Interpreters for the Deaf. (2006). *Testing and testing process.* Retrieved January 8, 2008. from *www.rid.org/education/testing/index.cfm*

Resnick, D. (1982). History of educational testing. In A. Wigdor & W. Garner (Eds.), *Ability testing: Uses, consequences, and controversies. Part II: Documentation section* (pp. 173–194). Washington, DC: National Academy Press.

Resnick, L. B., & Resnick, D. P. (1992). Assessing the thinking curriculum: New tools for educational reform. In B. R. Gifford & M. C. O'Connor (Eds.), *Changing assessments alternative views of aptitude, achievement and instruction* (pp. 37–75). Boston: Kluwer Academic.

Roeber, E. (1996). Guidelines for the development and management of performance assessments. *Practical Assessment, Research, and Evaluation, 5*(7). Retrieved May 18, 2008 from *www.pareonline.net/getvn. asp?v=5&n=7*

Rudolph, F. (1990). *The American college and university: A history.* Athens: University of Georgia Press.

Ruiz-Primo, M., & Shavelson, R. (1996). Rhetoric and reality in science performance assessment: An update. *Journal of Research in Science Teaching, 33*(10), 1045–1063.

Ruth, L., & Murphy, S. (1988). *Designing writing tasks for the assessment of writing.* Norwood, NJ: Ablex.

Ryan, T. (2006). Performance assessment: Critics, criticism, and controversy. *International Journal of Testing, 6*(1), 97–104.

Schneider, C., Johnson, R., & Porchea, S. (2004). Factors that affect the measurement of rhythm achievement. *Visions of Research in Music Education, 5*, 6–15.

Schwartz, R., Donnelly, M., Sloan, D., Johnson, S., & Stroedel, W. (1995). The relationship between faculty ward evaluations, OSCE, and ABSITE as measures of surgical intern performance. *American Journal of Surgery, 169*, 414–417.

Schafer, W., Gagne, P., & Lissitz, R. (2005). Resistance to confounding style and content in scoring constructed-response items. *Educational Measurement: Issues and Practice, 24*(2), 22–28.

Shavelson, R., & Webb, N. (1991). *Generalizability theory: A primer.* Newbury Park, CA: Sage.

Shavelson, R. J., Baxter, G. P., & Gao, X. (1993). Sampling variability of performance assessments. *Journal of Educational Measurement, 30*(3), 215–232.

Shavelson, R., Mayberry, P., Li, W., & Webb, N. (1990). Generalizability of job performance measurements: Marine Corps rifleman. *Military Psychology, 2*(3), 129–144.

Shavelson, R., Solano-Flores, G., & Ruiz-Primo, M. (1998). Toward a science performance assessment technology. *Evaluation and Program Planning, 21*(2), 171–184.

Sheskin, D. (2004). *Handbook of parametric and nonparametric statistical procedures* (3rd ed.). Boca Raton, FL: Chapman & Hall/CRC.

Shumate, S., Surles, J., Johnson, R., & Penny, J. (2007). The effects of the number of scale points and nonnormality on the generalizability coefficient: A Monte Carlo study. *Applied Measurement in Education, 20*(4), 1–20.

Shurtleff, W., & Aoyagi, A. (1977). *The Book of Kudzu: A culinary and healing guide.* Brookline, MA: Autumn Press.

Siegel, A. (1986). Performance tests. In R. Berk (Ed.), *Performance assessment* (pp. 121–142). Baltimore: John Hopkins University Press.

Simmons, W., & Resnick, L. (1993). Assessment as the catalyst of school reform. *Educational Leadership, 50*(5), 11–15.

Sireci, S. G. (2005). Unlabeling the disabled: A perspective on flagging scores from accommodated test administrations. *The Educational Researcher, 34,* 3–12.

Smith, T., Gordon, B., Colby, S., & Wang, J. (2005). *An examination of the relationship between depth of student learning and National Board certification status.* Boone, NC: Office for Research on Teaching, Appalachian State University.

Smith, J., Smith, L., & De Lisi, R. (2001). *Natural classroom assessment: Designing seamless instruction and assessment.* Thousand Oaks, CA: Corwin Press.

Smith, W. (1993). Assessing the reliability and adequacy of using holistic scoring of essays as a college composition placement technique. In M. Williamson & B. Huot (Eds.), *Validating holistic scoring for writing assessment: Theoretical and empirical foundations* (pp. 142–205). Cresskill, NJ: Hampton Press.

Snow, R. (1993). Construct validity and constructed-response tests. In R. Bennett & W. Ward (Eds.), *Construction versus choice in cognitive measurement* (pp. 45–60). Hillsdale, NJ: Erlbaum.

Solano-Flores, G., Jovanovic, J., Shavelson, R., & Bachman, M. (1999). On the development and evaluation of a shell for generating science performance assessments. *International Journal of Science Education, 21*(3), 293–315.

South Carolina Arts Assessment Program (SCAAP). (2006). *Test administration manual for the South Carolina Arts Assessment Program: 2006.* Columbia: University of South Carolina, College of Education, South Carolina Office of Program Evaluation.

South Carolina Department of Education (SCDE). (1999). *PACT Reading/ English language arts: A blueprint for success.* Columbia, SC: Author.

South Carolina Department of Education (SCDE). (2000a). *South Carolina science curriculum standards.* Columbia, SC: Author.

South Carolina Department of Education (SCDE). (2000b). *South Carolina social studies curriculum standards.* Columbia, SC: Author.

South Carolina Department of Education (SCDE). (2000c). *Technical doc-*

umentation for the 2000 Palmetto Achievement Challenge Tests of English language arts and mathematics. Columbia, SC: Author.

South Carolina Department of Education (SCDE). (2001). *Test administrator's manual: 2001.* Columbia, SC: Author.

South Carolina Department of Education (SCDE). (2003). *South Carolina visual and performing arts curriculum standards.* Columbia, SC: Author.

South Carolina Department of Education (SCDE). (2005a). *PACT administration manual: Spring 2005.* Columbia, SC: Author.

South Carolina Department of Education (SCDE). (2005b). *South Carolina-High School Assessment Program: Fall 2005.* Columbia, SC: Author.

South Carolina Department of Education (SCDE). (2006). South Carolina end-of-course examination: Test blueprint for Algebra I and Mathematics for the Technologies II. Retrieved April 15, 2007, from *ed.sc. gov/agency/offices/assessment/programs/endofcourse/End-of-Course-ExaminationProgramEOCEP.html*

South Carolina Department of Education (SCDE). (2007) *South Carolina academic standards for English language arts.* Columbia, SC: Author.

Spandel, V. (2001). *Creating writers through 6-Trait Writing assessment and instruction* (3rd ed.). New York: Addison Wesley Longman.

Spearman, C. (1910). Correlation calculated from faulty data. *British Journal of Psychology, 3,* 271–295.

Starch, D. & Elliot, E. (1912). Reliability of grading high school work in English. *School Review, 20,* 442–457.

Starch, D., & Elliot, E. (1913). Reliability of grading high school work in mathematics. *School Review, 21,* 254–259.

Stecher, B., Klein, S., Solano-Flores, G., McCaffrey, D., Robyn, A., Shavelson, R., et al. (2000). The effects of content, format, and inquiry level on science performance assessment scores. *Applied Measurement in Education, 13*(2), 139–160.

Stewart, M., & Grobe, C. (1979). Syntactic maturity, mechanics of writing, and teachers' quality ratings. *Research in the Teaching of English, 13,* 207–215.

Stiggins, R. (1987a). Design and development of performance assessments. *Educational Measurement: Issues and Practices, 6*(3), 33–42.

Stiggins, R. (1987b). *Instructor's guide for Design and Development of Performance Assessments.* Retrieved May 18, 2008, from *www.ncme. org/pubs/items.cfm*

Stoker, H., & Impara, J. (1995). Basic psychometric issues in licensure testing. In J. Impara (Ed.), *Licensure testing: Purposes, procedures, and practices* (pp. 167–186). Lincoln, NE: Buros Institute of Mental Measurement.

Taylor, C. (1998). *An investigation of scoring methods for mathematics performance-based assessments. Educational Assessment, 5*(3), 195–224.

Thompson, R., Bosn, A., & Ruma, P. (1993). Application of assessment methods to instruction in a high school writing program. *Evaluation and Program Planning, 16,* 153–157.

Thorndike, R. (2005). *Measurement and evaluation in psychology and education* (7th ed.). Upper Saddle River, NJ: Pearson Education.

Thorndike, R. M., Cunningham, G. K., Thorndike, R. L., & Hagen, E. P. (1991). *Measurement and evaluation in psychology and education* (5th ed.). New York: Macmillan.

University of Utah Department of Pediatrics. (n.d.). *Newborn OSCE checklist.* Retrieved March 29, 2006, from *www.ped.med.utah.edu/cai/evaluation/NewbornOSCEexam.pdf*

Valencia, S., & Au, K. (1997). Portfolios across educational contexts: Issues of evaluation, teacher development, and system validity. *Educational Assessment, 4*(1), 1–35.

van der Vleuten, C., & Swanson, D. (1990). Assessment of clinical skills with standardized patients: State of the art. *Teaching and Learning in medicine, 2*(2), 58-76.

VanTassel-Baska, J., Jonson, D., & Avery, L. (2002). Using performance tasks in the identification of economically disadvantaged and minority gifted learners: Findings from Project STAR. *Gifted Child Quarterly 46*(2), 110–123.

Veal, L., & Hudson, S. (1983). Direct and indirect measures for large-scale evaluation of writing. *Research in the Teaching of English, 17,* 290–296.

Virginia Department of Education. (2001). *United States history: 1877 to the present: Curriculum framework.* Retrieved September 7, 2006, from *www.pen.k12.va.us/VDOE/Instruction/History/hist_ss_framework.html*

Virginia Department of Education. (2003). *English standards of learning curriculum framework.* Retrieved September 7, 2006, from *www.pen.k12.va.us/VDOE/Instruction/English/englishCF.html*

Walljasper, A., with Gholston, M. (1999). Drafting and grading essay questions in Oregon. *The Bar Examiner, 68*(4), 17–22.

Waltman, K., Kahn, A., & Koency, G. (1998). *Alternative approaches to scoring: The effects of using different scoring methods on the validity of scores from a performance assessment.* (CSE Technical Report 488). Los Angeles: National Center for Research on Evaluation, Standards, and Student Testing, Center for the Study of Evaluation.

Wang, N., Schnipke, D., & Witt, E. (2005). Use of knowledge, skill, and ability statements in developing licensure and certification examinations. *Educational Measurement: Issues and Practices, 24*(1), 15–22.

Wang, N., Witt, E., & Schnipke, D. (2006). Rejoinder: A further discussion of job analysis and use of KSAs in developing licensure and certification examinations: A response to LaDuca. *Educational Measurement: Issues and Practices, 25*(2), 34–37.

Webb, N. (2006). Identifying content for student achievement test. In S. Downing & T. Haladyna (Eds.), *Handbook of test development* (pp. 155–180). Mahwah, NJ: Erlbaum.

Webb, N., Schlackman, J., & Sugre, B. (2000). The dependability and interchangeability of assessment methods in science. *Applied Measurement in Education, 13*(3), 277–299.

Webber, C. (1989). The Mandarin mentality: Civil service and university admissions testing in Europe and Asia. In B. Gifford (Ed.), *Test policy and the politics of opportunity allocation: The workplace and the law* (pp. 33–57). Boston: Kluwer.

Weigle, S. (1998). Using FACETS to model rater training effects. *Language Testing, 15*(2), 263–287.

Weigle, S. (1999). Investigating rater/prompt interactions in writing assessment: Quantitative and qualitative approaches. *Assessing Writing, 6*(2), 145–178.

Weigle, S. (2002). *Assessing writing.* New York: Cambridge University Press.

Welch, C. (2006). Item and prompt development in performance testing. In S. Downing & T. Haladyna (Eds.), *Handbook of test development* (pp. 303–327). Mahwah, NJ: Erlbaum.

Welch, C., & Martinovich-Barhite, D. (1997, April). *Reliability issues and possible solutions.* Paper presented at the annual meeting of the American Educational Research Association, Chicago.

West, T., Gordon, B., Colby, S., & Wang, J. (2005). *An examination of the relationship between depth of student learning and National Board certification status.* Boone, NC: Appalachian State University, Office for Research on Teaching.

West Virginia Department of Education. (2007). *Administration manual: West Virginia online writing assessment grades 7 and 10.* Charleston: Author.

White, E. (1994). *Teaching and assessing writing: recent advances in understanding, evaluating, and improving student performance* (2nd ed). San Francisco: Jossey–Bass.

Wiggins, G. (1992). Creating tests worth taking. *Educational Leadership, 49*(8), 26–33.

Wiley, D., & Haertel, E. (1996). Extended assessment tasks: Purposes, definitions, scoring, and accuracy. In M. Kane & R. Mitchell (Eds.), *Implementing performance assessment: Promises, problems, and challenges* (pp. 61–89). Mahwah, NJ: Erlbaum.

Willard-Traub, M., Decker, E., Reed, R., & Johnston, J. (2000). The development of large-scale portfolio placement assessment at the University of Michigan: 1992–1998. *Assessing Writing, 6*(1), 41–84.

Wolcott, W., with Legg, S. (1998). *An overview of writing assessment: Theory, research, and practice.* Urbana, IL: National Council of Teachers of English.

Wolfe, E. (1997). The relationship between essay reading style and scoring proficiency in a psychometric scoring system. *Assessing Writing, 4*(1) 83–106.

Wolfe, E., & Gitomer, D. (2001). The influence of changes in assessment design on the psychometric quality of scores. *Applied Measurement in Education, 14*(1), 91–107.

Yap, C., Moore, M., & Peng, P. (2005). *Technical documentation for the South Carolina Arts Assessment Project (SCAAP) Year 3: 4th-grade music and visual arts assessments.* Columbia: University of South Carolina, Office of Program Evaluation.

Yap, C., Schneider, C., Johnson, R., Mazzie, D., & Porchea, S. (2003). *Technical documentation for the South Carolina Arts Assessment Project (SCAAP) Year 1: 4th-grade music and visual arts assessments.* Columbia: University of South Carolina, Office of Program Evaluation.

Author Index

Subject Index

345

About the Authors

Robert L. Johnson, PhD, James A. Penney, PhD, and Belita Gordon, PhD, have been involved in assessment in writing, the visual and performing arts, and licensure and certification. Their research focuses on the scoring of performance assessments and methods to improve the quality of scores associated with those assessments. Their work has been published in such journals as the *American Journal of Evaluation, Applied Measurement in Education, Assessing Writing, Language Assessment Quarterly: An International Journal, Evaluation and Program Planning*, the *Journal of Experimental Education*, the *Journal of Personnel Evaluation in Education*, the *International Journal of Engineering Education*, and *Written Communication*.